HOBBES'S BEHEMOTH

HOBBES'S BEHEMOTH

RELIGION AND DEMOCRACY

Edited by
Tomaž Mastnak

imprint-academic.com

Copyright © Imprint Academic, 2009

The moral rights of the author have been asserted
No part of this publication may be reproduced in any form
without permission, except for the quotation of brief passages
in criticism and discussion.

Published in the UK by Imprint Academic
PO Box 200, Exeter EX5 5YX, UK

Published in the USA by Imprint Academic
Philosophy Documentation Center
PO Box 7147, Charlottesville, VA 22906-7147, USA

ISBN 9 781845 401757 (cloth)
ISBN 9 781845 401764 (paperback)

A CIP catalogue record for this book is available from the
British Library and US Library of Congress

Contents

Preface vii

About the Authors ix

Tomaž Mastnak
    Introduction: The Ways of *Behemoth* 1

Noel Malcolm
    Behemoth latinus: Adam Ebert, Tacitism, and Hobbes 38

Paul Seaward
    'Chief of the ways of God':
    Form and Meaning in Hobbes's *Behemoth* 73

Johann P. Sommerville
    Behemoth, Church-State Relations,
    and Political Obligation 93

A. P. Martinich
    Presbyterians in *Behemoth* 111

Gabriella Slomp
    On Ambition, Greed, and Fear 129

Patricia Springborg
    Behemoth and Hobbes's 'science of just and unjust' 148

Geoffrey M. Vaughan
    The Audiences of *Behemoth* and the Politics of Conversation . . 170

Michael A. Soubbotnik
> De la montagne du diable à la vérité de la loi 186

Tomaž Mastnak
> Godly Democracy 210

Ingrid Creppell
> The Democratic Element in Hobbes's *Behemoth* 241

William Lund
> Neither *Behemoth* nor *Leviathan*:
> Explaining Hobbes's Illiberal Politics 269

Tom Sorell
> Schmitt, Hobbes and the Politics of Emergency 294

Robert P. Kraynak
> The Fragility of Civilization in Hobbes's
> Historical Writings. 312

Index 334

Preface

The present volume originates in the 2003 international issue of *Filozofski vestnik*, the journal of the Institute of Philosophy in the Scientific Research Centre of the Slovenian Academy of Sciences and Arts in Ljubljana. Contributions have been revised for the present edition and a substantive introduction has been added. I want to thank Matjaž Vesel, Managing Editor of *Filozofski Vestnik*, and Peter Klepec, Editor-in-Chief of *Filozofski Vestnik*, for giving me permission to reprint material from the *Behemoth* issue of *Filozofski vestnik*. I also want to thank Rado Riha, Head of the Institute of Philosophy, for his understanding and support of this project.

I thank John Dunn, Stephen Holmes, István Hont, Noel Malcolm, and Richard Tuck for their encouragement and advice at the beginning of this project. I prepared the *Behemoth* issue of *Filozofski vestnik* while a Visiting Research Fellow at the Remarque Institute of New York University. I am thankful to its Director, Tony Judt, and Jair Kessler, the Assistant Director, for their hospitality.

I prepared the present volume at the University of California, Irvine, where I am a visiting researcher. My special thanks are due to Bill Maurer, Chair of the Department of Anthropology, and David Goldberg, Director of the University of California Humanities Research Institute, who provided me with an institutional home and workspace in California.

I am grateful to my wife, Julia Elyachar, for her support through the various incarnations of this project, to my son Elijan for the behemoths and leviathans he drew for the book, and to my son Martin for his hummingbirds.

Ruth Turner has read, commented on, and edited portions of the manuscript. I am deeply grateful for her work. I would like to acknowledge the crucial role Gabriella Slomp played in the process of turning the original journal issue into a book. I would also like to thank Paolo Cristofolini and Rina Nicastro for kindly sending me a copy of Onofrio Nicastro's *Note sul Behemoth di Thomas Hobbes*, and Paul Seaward for allowing me to read the manuscript of his critical edition of *Behemoth* for the Clarendon edition of Hobbes.

Note on Citation

Throughout this volume, the following abbreviations are used:

EW

    The English Works of Thomas Hobbes, ed. Sir William Molesworth, 11 vols (London: John Bohn, 1839–45).

OL

    Opera Philosophica quae latine scripsit omnia, ed. Sir William Molesworth, 5 vols (London: John Bohn, 1839–45).

About the Authors

Ingrid Creppell is Associate Professor of Political Science at George Washington University, Washington, DC. She is the author of *Toleration and Identity: Foundations in Early Modern Thought* (New York: Routledge, 2003), co-editor of *Toleration on Trial* (Lexington Books, 2008) and articles in *Archives Européennes de Sociologie, Political Theory,* and *Res Publica*.

Robert P. Kraynak is professor of political science at Colgate University in Hamilton, New York. He is the author of *History and Modernity in the Thought of Thomas Hobbes* (Ithaca: Cornell University Press, 1990); *Christian Faith and Modern Democracy* (Notre Dame: University of Notre Dame Press, 2001); and the editor with Glenn Tinder of *In Defense of Human Dignity* (Notre Dame: University of Notre Dame Press, 2003).

William Lund is professor of political science at the University of Idaho. His research interests include the history of political thought and contemporary moral and political philosophy. He has published articles on Hobbes in *History of Political Thought, Hobbes Studies,* and *The Journal of the History of Ideas*. His work on issues in the debate between liberals and communitarians has been published in various journals, including *Social Theory and Practice, Political Research Quarterly,* and *Journal of Social Philosophy,* and as a chapter in *Autonomy and Order: A Communitarian Anthology,* ed. Edward Lehman (Lanham: Rowman & Littlefield, 2000).

Noel Malcolm is a Senior Research Fellow of All Souls College, Oxford. A member of the editorial board of the Clarendon Edition of the Works of Hobbes, he has published an edition of Hobbes's *Correspondence* in that series (2 vols, 1994), and is currently preparing both an edition of *Leviathan* (English and Latin) for it, and a biography of Hobbes. His *Aspects of Hobbes* was published by Clarendon Press in 2002. He is a Fellow of the British Academy.

A. P. Martinich, Roy Allison Vaughan Centennial Professor of Philosophy, Professor of History and Government, author of *The Two Gods of Leviathan: Thomas Hobbes on Religion and Politics* (Cambridge: Cambridge University Press, 1992), *A Hobbes Dictionary* (Oxford: Blackwell Publishers, 1995), *Thomas Hobbes* (London: Macmillan, 1997), *Hobbes: A Biography* (Cambridge: Cambridge University Press, 1999), *Hobbes* (Routledge, 2005); and editor of *Philosophy of Language*, 4 vols (Routledge, 2009).

Tomaž Mastnak is Director of Research in the Institute of Philosophy at the Scientific Research Centre of the Slovenian Academy of Sciences and Arts and is currently a Fellow at the International Center for Advanced Studies at New York University. He is the author of *Crusading Peace: Christendom, the Muslim World, and Western Political Order* (Berkeley and Los Angeles: University of California Press, 2002) and is completing a project on the history of the idea of Europe.

Paul Seaward has been Director of the History of Parliament in London since 2001. He has published work on politics in Restoration England, including *The Cavalier Parliament and the Reconstruction of the Old Regime, 1661–67* (Cambridge: Cambridge University Press, 1988), on seventeenth-century royalism and on parliament in the twentieth century. His edition of *Behemoth* for the Clarendon edition of the *Works of Thomas Hobbes* will be published in 2009. He is currently working on a biography of Edward Hyde, Earl of Clarendon, and is general editor, with Martin Dzelzainis, of an edition of Clarendon's works.

Gabriella Slomp (PhD, LSE) is Senior Lecturer in Political Theory at the University of St Andrews (Scotland). She is the author of *Thomas Hobbes and the Political Philosophy of Glory* (Houndmills: Macmillan, 2000) and of *Carl Schmitt and the Politics of Hostility, Violence and Terror* (Palgrave, 2009).

Johann P. Sommerville, professor, Department of History, University of Wisconsin, Madison. Author of *Royalists and Patriots: Politics and Ideology in England, 1603–1640* (Harlow: Longman, 1999), and of *Thomas Hobbes: Political Ideas in Historical Context* (Houndmills: Macmillan, 1992).

Tom Sorell is John Ferguson Professor of Global Ethics, University of Birmingham. Among his books is *Hobbes* (London: Routledge, 1986). He is also the editor of *The Cambridge Companion to Hobbes* (Cambridge: Cambridge University Press, 1996), of *Hobbes and History* (London: Routledge, 2000, with John Rogers), and *Leviathan After 350 Years* (Oxford: Clarendon, 2005).

About the Authors

Michael A. Soubbotnik is Maître de Conférences de Philosophie at the University Paris-Est (laboratory LISAA 4120). He is the author of *Philosophie des actes de langage: la doublure mentale et l'ordinaire des langues* (Paris: Presses Universitaires de France, 2001).

Patricia Springborg is professor in the School of Economics of the Free University of Bolzano. She is a member of the Australian Academy of Social Sciences, and has been a Visiting Fellow at research institutes in Berlin, Oxford, and Uppsala. Her publications include *The Problem of Human Needs and the Critique of Civilization* (London: Allen & Unwin, 1981), *Royal Persons* (London: Unwin Hyman,1991), *Western Republicanism and the Oriental Prince* (Cambridge: Polity, 1992), *Mary Astell* (Cambridge: Cambridge University Press, 2005), and three editions of Mary Astell's writings. She has published a number of articles on Thomas Hobbes, and a critical edition of Hobbes's *Historia ecclesiastica* (Paris: Champion, 2008).

Geoffrey M. Vaughan is assistant professor of political science at the University of Maryland, Baltimore County. His research interests include the political philosophy of Thomas Hobbes, the history and development of liberalism, and political education. Recent publications include *Behemoth Teaches Leviathan: Thomas Hobbes on Political Education* (Lanham: Lexington Books, 2002), and 'The Audience of *Leviathan* and the Audience of Hobbes's Political Philosophy', *History of Political Thought* 22 (2001).

Tomaž Mastnak

Introduction: The Ways of 'Behemoth'

In the Old Testament *Book of Job*, God spoke to Job of *behemoth* and said: 'He *is* the chief of the ways of God'.[1] Biblical exegetes and translators have reached no agreement about the meaning of this obscure verse. Hobbes's *Behemoth* is relatively obscure as well. Even Hobbes scholars have neglected *Behemoth*. When read, it has been understood (and misunderstood) in many different ways.

The present volume stems from the belief that *Behemoth* is a major work of Hobbes's. It puts *Behemoth* where it belongs: firmly within the scope of serious debates of Hobbes's thought. In this introduction, I trace the ways in which *Behemoth* has come down to us: when it was written, how it was published, and how it has been understood since it began to circulate in public — first as an unlicensed manuscript. Such an overview of past treatments will make clear, I hope, how the present volume contributes to the discussion about *Behemoth* and opens up future lines of research.

I. Fanatical pamphlet

When it was first discussed in public, Hobbes's *Behemoth* was called a 'fanatical pamhlet'. John Whitehall, a 'Barrester at Law' of the Inner Temple, published in London in 1680 his *Behemoth Arraign'd: or a Vindication of Property Against a Fanatical Pamphlet Stiled Behemoth: or, the History of the Civill Wars of England, from 1640 to 1660. Subscribed by Tho. Hobbes of Malmsbury*. The author accused Hobbes of siding with Oliver Cromwell in 1651. His *Leviathan* taught the people of England 'that their *subjection to their natural Soveraign ... was at an end*, he being then uncapable to protect them; and that they were absolved, and might submit to any one else that

---

1   Job 40: 19. I cite *The Bible: Authorized King James Version with Apocrypha*, With an Introduction and Notes by R. Carroll and S. Prickett (Oxford: Oxford University Press, 1997).

could protect them'.² In 1679, Whitehall continued, Hobbes's *Behemoth* appeared in various editions.³ '[T]here is a strange Creature risen up called *BEHEMOTH*', he wrote. Whereas 'it was the part of the *Leviathan*', because it absolved the people from subjection, 'perpetually to separate the Subjects from their King', *Behemoth* tried to '*separate* the King in his affection from his Subjects'. *Behemoth* did that because it told the king, 'with a *flattering slyness*, the *absoluteness* of his Power, the injuriousness of *Parliaments*, and that all the *Property* of the People of *England* is at his *Arbitrary* dispose, being Master of the Militia'.⁴

Whitehall also accused Hobbes of bringing up again the painful experience of the civil war. The ill that had been done, and which was 'sufficiently manifest to the world', was 'by the *goodness* and *mercy* of the King, buried in *Oblivion*. And now to rake into *old Wounds* concerning the King and his People, is certainly a thing very *unchristian*, and the hearing of it pleasant to neither'.⁵ Whitehall objected to Hobbes's 'declaiming against the Proceedings of the Parliament in 1641' only in so far as it 'reflect[ed] upon *Parliaments in general*'.⁶ But the main criticism Whitehall leveled at Hobbes was that his *Behemoth* threatened property. A threat to property was a threat to liberty:

> No man shall be *disseized*, or put out of his *Free-hold*, or *Free-customs*, or *Liberties*, except by the lawful Judgment of his Peers, or by the Law of the Land. Here's the Subject secured in his *real Estate*, of which onely can be disseizing, and also *personal Estate*: for 'tis the greatest *Franchise* or Liberty (next his *Person* secured before) a man can enjoy, not to have his Money taken from him arbitrarily, whereby he may follow his Traffick.⁷

---

2   John Whitehall, *Behemoth Arraign'd: or a Vindication of Property Against a Fanatical Pamphlet Stiled Behemoth: or, the History of the Civill Wars of England, from 1640 to 1660. Subscribed by Tho. Hobbes of Malmsbury* (London, 1680), 2–3.
3   Whitehall, *Behemoth Arraign'd*, Advertisement. Whitehall used 'that in 12º, which is of a very small Character, and printed 1679'. This seems to correspond to no. 88 in Hugh Macdonald and Mary Hargreaves, *Thomas Hobbes: A Bibliography* (London: The Bibliographical Society, 1952).
4   Whitehall, *Behemoth Arraign'd*, 3–4.
5   Whitehall, *Behemoth Arraign'd*, 5. Hobbes, in fact, conformed to the articles of the Indemnity and Oblivion Act of 1660, which did not allow giving the names of those involved in the civil war who were still alive, and even made a point of it: 'It is not necessary to name any man, seeing I have undertaken only a short narration of the follies and other faults of men during this trouble; but not (by naming the persons) to give you, or any man else, occasion to esteem them the less, now that the faults on all sides have been forgiven'. See Thomas Hobbes, *Behemoth or the Long Parliament*, ed. Ferdinand Tönnies, with an Introduction by Stephen Holmes (Chicago: The University of Chicago Press, 1990), 117. (If not otherwise indicated, I cite this edition.)
6   Whitehall, *Behemoth Arraign'd*, 4.
7   Whitehall, *Behemoth Arraign'd*, 37.

Some of those liberties were 'due by Custom', which preceded statutes. Not surprisingly, Hobbes attacked the customary law: 'But after *Behemoth* hath made a *mortal blow*, as he might well think, at *Property*, he comes like his Brother *Leviathan*, to knock down the *Common-Law*'.[8]

Insinuating that the king 'may take all our Properties', *Behemoth* would turn English people into slaves and the king into an Oriental prince: 'For that to be a *most absolute Sovereign, and to have all Power possible*, is to be like the *Mogul* or *Great Turk*, to take and destroy all put under him at his own will and pleasure'. That was a *'seditious'* doctrine, and 'dangerous to the Government'.[9] English government was precisely that 'mixt Monarchy', with which Hobbes quarrelled in *Behemoth* because he thought it necessarily undermined the supreme power, led into anarchy, and put an end to peace.[10] For its *'dangerous position'*, *Behemoth* gave 'no *reason*' and was thus 'no Statesman'.[11]

Because of its perceived lack of statemanship, *Behemoth* was for Whitehall an 'Object of Pity'. As such, he declared, 'I pass him by'.[12] At the end of his pamphlet he felt he needed to justify his having been so 'severe' with Hobbes. He was told he had been 'too *severe*' already in his critique of *Leviathan*, published a year earlier than his critique of *Behemoth*.[13] He responded to such misgivings as follows:

> let it be considered that I am *an English man*, and how severe the *Leviathan* hath been to *Religion* and the *King*: And if I seem to have been too severe in *this* against *Behemoth*, let it likewise be considered that I am *an English man*, and that *Behemoth* hath been as severe with my *Property*; which is as dear to me as my *Life*.[14]

II. Date of composition, printed editions, translations

Hobbes did not live to read Whitehall's critique, but he lived long enough to learn that his *Behemoth* appeared in an unauthorized printing. To all

---

8   Whitehall, *Behemoth Arraign'd*, 44.
9   Whitehall, *Behemoth Arraign'd*, 78–80.
10 Whitehall, *Behemoth Arraign'd*, 80–2.
11 Whitehall, *Behemoth Arraign'd*, 78, 82.
12 Whitehall, *Behemoth Arraign'd*, 82.
13 John Whitehall, *The Leviathan found out, or, The answer to Mr. Hobbes's Leviathan in that which my Lord of Clarendon hath past over* (London, 1679). In his *Behemoth Arraign'd*, 51, Whitehall cited Clarendon's critique of *Leviathan* as, also, a proper 'answer to *Behemoth*'. The most extensive discussion of Whitehall's 'indictment of Hobbes' is John Bowle, *Hobbes and His Critics: A Study in Seventeenth Century Constitutionalism* (New York: Oxford University Press, 1952), ch. 9. Bowle focused his discussion on *The Leviathan found out* and dismissed *Behemoth Arraign'd* as containing 'little that is fresh to Whitehall's argument'. Ibid., 175 n. 1. Recently, Whitehall's critique of *Behemoth* has been discussed in Jon Parkin, *Taming the Leviathan: The Reception of the Political and Religious Ideas of Thomas Hobbes in England, 1640–1700* (Cambridge: Cambridge University Press, 2007), 340–2.
14 Whitehall, *Behemoth Arraign'd*, 92.

appearance, he did not welcome the news. 'I have been told that my booke of the Civill Warr is come abroad', he wrote to his friend John Aubrey, 'and I am sorry for it, especially because I could not get his majestye to license it, not because it is ill printed or has a foolish title set to it, for I believe that any ingenious man may understand the wickednesse of that time, notwithstanding the errors of the presse'.[15] Hobbes explained more about his failed attempt to get the license in a letter to his publisher William Crooke:

> I would fain have published my Dialogue of the Civil Wars of *England*, long ago; and to that end I presented it to his Majesty: and some days after, when I thought he had read it, I humbly besought him to let me print it; but his Majesty (though he heard me gratiously, yet he) flatly refused to have it published. Therefore I brought away the Book, and gave you leave to take a Copy of it; which when you had done, I gave the Original to an honourable and learned Friend, who about a year after died. The King knows better, and is more concerned in publishing of Books than I am: Therefore I dare not venture to appear in the business, lest it should offend him. Therefore I pray you not to meddle in the business. Rather than to be thought any way to further or countenance the printing, I would be content to lose twenty times the value of what you can expect to gain by it, *&c*—I pray do not take it ill.[16]

These late letters of Hobbes indicate, first, that the book we know under the title of *Behemoth* was written 'long ago'. Hobbes most probably began working on the manuscript in 1666, when he mentioned an 'epitome' of English 'troubles' (a term often used to describe the civil war) to François du Verdus, his French correspondent and translator.[17] There is evidence that he was still working on it in 1668 and, if we rely on his autobiographical statement that he wrote it when he was about eighty years old,[18] he probably finished it in 1669.[19] We also learn from these letters that Hobbes was declined permission to publish the work and that the work then circulated in manuscript.[20] In the last year of

---

15 Hobbes to John Aubrey, 18 [/28] August 1679, in *The Correspondence of Thomas Hobbes*, ed. N. Malcolm (Oxford: Clarendon, 1997), 2. 772.
16 Hobbes to William Crooke, 19 [/29] June 1679, *The Correspondence of Thomas Hobbes*, 2. 771.
17 The letter from 20 July 1666 is lost, but Verdus, in his response to Hobbes, wrote of 'votre Epitome de vos Troubles'. Verdus to Hobbes, [3/] 13 April 1668. *The Correspondence of Thomas Hobbes*, 2. 697. See also Karl Schuhmann, *Hobbes: Une chronique* (Paris: Vrin, 1998), 198.
18 *T. Hobbes Malmesburiensis Vita*, OL 1. xx; cf. John Aubrey, *Brief Lives*, ed. A. Clark (Oxford: Clarendon, 1898), 1. 401.
19 A detailed discussion is forthcoming in Paul Seaward's 'General Introduction' to the Clarendon edition of *Behemoth*.
20 See John Aubrey [to John Locke], 11 February 1673, no. 268, in *The Correspondence of John Locke*, ed. E. S. de Beer (Oxford: Clarendon, 1976–89), 1. 376. William Crooke wrote in 1682 that Hobbes gave him the manuscript 'above twelve years since'. 'The Bookseller to the Reader', prefixed to the publication of *Behemoth* in *Tracts of Mr. Thomas Hobbs of Malmsbury, Containing*

Hobbes's life, four pirated editions were published, and another was to follow in 1680.[21] Hobbes almost certainly did not play a role in those initiatives[22] and we may accept as genuine his regrets that the book was printed. In what is probably his last letter, Hobbes thanked William Crooke for taking his 'advice in not stirring about the printing of my Book concerning the Civil Wars of *England, &c.*'.[23]

The first 'legitimate' edition of *Behemoth* appeared posthumously, printed by Crooke in 1682 in *Tracts of Mr. Thomas Hobbs of Malmsbury*. In a note to the reader, Crooke wrote the following:

> I am compell'd by the force of Truth to declare, how much both the World, and the Name of Mr. *Hobbs* have been abus'd by the several spurious Editions of the History of the Civil Wars; wherein, by various and unskilful Transcriptions, are committed above a thousand faults, and in above a hundred places whole Lines left out, as I can make appear.

Crooke went on to 'confess' that

> Mr. *Hobbs*, upon some considerations, was averse to the publishing thereof; but since it is impossible to suppress it; no Book being more commonly sold by all Booksellers, I hope I need not fear the Offence of any Man, by doing Right to the World and this Work. Which I now Publish from the Original Manuscript, done by his own Amanuensis, and given me by himself above twelve years since.[24]

Three years later, Crooke certainly did not tone down the language of advertising. His edition of Hobbes's *Behemoth* was

> printed now from his own perfect Copy, in which is many pages more than was in the former *Counterfeit Edition*; none of which Editions before this, had less than *a thousand faults* in them, whole Lines left out in *a hundred places*, which did extremely pervert the sence of the Author *Tho. Hobbs.*[25]

I. Behemoth, the History of the Causes of the Civil Wars of England, from 1640. to 1660. printed from the Author's own Copy: Never printed (but with a thousand faults) before. II. An answer to Arch-Bishop Bramhall's Book, called the Catching of the Leviathan: Never printed before. III. An Historical Narration of Heresie, and the Punishment thereof: Corrected by the true Copy. IV. Philosophical Problems, dedicated to the King in 1662, but never printed before (London, Printed for W. Crooke, 1682).

21 See Macdonald and Hargreaves, *Thomas Hobbes: A Bibliography*, nos. 86-9; Onofrio Nicastro, 'Nota al testo', in Thomas Hobbes, *Behemoth*, ed. and trans. O. Nicastro (Bari: Laterza, 1979), XLVIII-XLIX. A detailed description of these editions is forthcoming in Paul Seaward's 'Textual Introduction' to Clarendon edition of *Behemoth*.

22 Or at least wanted it to appear that he did not, as stated by Onofrio Nicastro. Nicastro, 'Introduzione', in his edition of *Behemoth*, IX.

23 Hobbes to William Crooke, 18 [/28] August 1679, *The Correspondence of Thomas Hobbes*, 2. 774.

24 'The Bookseller to the Reader', in *Tracts of Mr. Thomas Hobbs of Malmsbury*.

25 Item 23 in 'A Catalogue of BOOKS printed and sold by *William Crooke* Bookseller, at the Sign of the *Green Dragon* without *Temple-bar*, nigh the Passage into the *Temple* by *Devereux*-Court, 1685', appended to Basil Ringrose, *Bucaniers of America the second volume: containing the*

Two hundred years later, the claim that Crooke was in possession of the 'Original Manuscript' began to be questioned, but his edition was reprinted a number of times. Crooke himself also sold it 'single', as 'the perfect edition'.[26] It was printed in *The Moral and Political Works of Thomas Hobbes of Malmesbury* in 1750,[27] which was the only eighteenth-century edition, and then in Francis Maseres's collection of writings on the English civil war,[28] in Molesworth's edition of Hobbes's collected works,[29] in reprints of Molesworth's collected works,[30] and as a separate edition.[31]

In 1889, a new edition of *Behemoth*, prepared by Ferdinand Tönnies, was printed in London. One of the founders of sociology in Germany, Tönnies had also made an important contribution to the initiation of Hobbes studies. His edition of *Behemoth* is a story worth the *péripéties* on the way to the first appearances of this work of Hobbes's in print. Tönnies learned of *Behemoth* from Friedrich Paulsen, with whom Tönnies made friends after having attended, as a student, his course in philosophy at the University of Berlin. Paulsen, himself interested in the relation of Hobbes, the political theorist, to the political events of his time, encouraged Tönnies's studies of the English philosopher.[32] Those studies led Tönnies to London and Hardwick, where he discovered the manuscripts of *The Elements of Law* and of the *Short Tract*,[33] and to Oxford, where he found the manuscript of *Behemoth*, preserved at St. John's College, which he believed was the origi-

---

dangerous voyage and bold attempts of Captain Bartholomew Sharp, and others, performed upon the coasts of the South Sea, for the space of two years, &c. (London, 1685).

26 Item 24 in 'A Catalogue of BOOKS printed and sold by *William Crooke* Bookseller', cited in the previous note.
27 *The Moral and Political Works of Thomas Hobbes of Malmesbury. Never before collected together. To which is prefixed, the Author's Life* (London, 1750), 487 ff.
28 *Select Tracts relating to the Civil Wars in England, in the reign of King Charles the First; by writers who lived in the time of those wars, and were witnesses of the events which they describe* (London: R. Wilks, 1815). Ferdinand Tönnies noticed in this reprint 'a few alterations from conjecture'. 'Preface' to *Behemoth or the Long Parliament. By Thomas Hobbes of Malmesbury. Edited for the first time from the original ms. by Ferdinand Tönnies, PhD* (London: Simpkin, Marshall, and Co., 1889), ix n.1.
29 *EW* 6. 161–418.
30 The first reprint was by Scientia Verlag, Aalen, 1962; a second printing followed in 1966. Currently, volumes from this edition are printed on demand and available in electronic edition (Charlottesville, V.A.: InteLex Corporation, 1995).
31 Thomas Hobbes, *Behemoth: the history of the causes of the civil wars of England, and of the counsels and artifices by which they were carried on from the year 1640 to the year 1660. Edited by William Molesworth*, Burt Franklin research and source works series no. 38 (New York: B. Franklin, [1962]); 2nd printing in 1963.
32 Paulsen to Tönnies, 30 December 1877, in Ferdinand Tönnies and Friedrich Paulsen, *Briefwechsel, 1876–1908*, ed. O. Klose, E. G. Jacoby, and I. Fischer (Kiel: Ferdinand Hirt, 1961), 9. A good two weeks later, Tönnies was already reading *Behemoth* in *The Moral and Political Works of Thomas Hobbes*. Tönnies to Paulsen, 17 January 1878, ibid., 12.
33 Tönnies to Paulsen, 21 August 1878, *Briefwechsel*, 39.

nal manuscript.³⁴ G. Croom Robertson, whom Tönnies met during his second visit to England in 1884,³⁵ announced the edition of *The Elements* and *Behemoth* in October that year in the influential journal *Mind*, whose editor he was. Tönnies's edition of *Behemoth* was announced as 'the pure text of *Behemoth*'.³⁶

Three years later, Robertson published another note in the same journal, explaining that Tönnies's editions of the *Elements* and *Behemoth*, which had been 'announced to appear in the winter of 1884', were,

> in point of fact, almost completely printed off early in 1885. After an unexplained delay of eighteenth months on the part of the publisher, the remaining few pages ... were got into print last autumn, and nothing appeared to stand in the way of definitive publication in October. Since then it has been found impossible, by any and every means yet employed, to obtain from Mr. Thornton the least hint of his intentions regarding the volumes, or any kind of accommodation by which the results of the foreign scholar's laborious research may be allowed to see the light.³⁷

'Mr. Thornton', the prospective publisher, was the Oxford publisher James Thornton, who had recently published a reprint of Andrew Crooke's first edition of *Leviathan*.³⁸

By the end of 1885, Tönnies contemplated a new journey to London and Oxford, because Thornton had not replied to his letters. He feared that the publisher was going to defraud him.³⁹ In 1886, Robertson published his book on Hobbes. Tönnies complained to a friend that Robertson did not acknowledge in his book what he had taken from Tönnies. But, Tönnies added with some sarcasm, Robertson was nevertheless so kind as to offer his help with Thornton, and wrote to him – apparently with 'no success'.⁴⁰ In the summer of 1888, Tönnies traveled to England to deal with the still

---

34 See E. G. Jacoby, *Die moderne Gesellschaft in sozialwissenschaftlichen Denken von Ferdinand Tönnies: Eine biographische Einführung* (Stuttgart: Ferdinand Enke, 1971), 122. A detailed description and analysis of *Behemoth* manuscripts is forthcoming in Paul Seaward's 'Textual Introduction' to Clarendon edition of *Behemoth*.

35 Tönnies to Paulsen, 11 May 1884, *Briefwechsel*, 199. The meeting could not take place during his first visit because of Robertson's poor health. See Tönnies, '[Lebenserinnerungen aus dem Jahre 1935 an Kindheit, Schulzeit, Studium und erste Dozententätigkeit (1855–94)]', in vol. 23, pt. 2 of *Ferdinand Tönnies Gesamtausgabe* (Berlin: Walter de Gruyter, 1998–), 542–3.

36 Editor's note in *Mind* 9 (1884), no. 36, 618.

37 *Mind* 12 (1887), no. 47, 481 n. 1. In his memoirs, Tönnies spoke of his 1884 journey to London to see his two editions of Hobbes through print, but that the project became, due to a 'total failure of the publisher [das gänzliche Versagen des Verlegers]', a cause for many worries. Tönnies, '[Lebenserinnerungen]', 549.

38 *Leviathan, or the matter, forme, and power of a common-wealth ecclesiasticall and civill.* By **Thomas Hobbes of Malmesbury** (Oxford: James Thornton, 1881). That was a small edition of 250 copies on Dutch hand-made paper.

39 Tönnies to Paulsen, 23 November 1885, *Briefwechsel*, 220.

40 Tönnies to Paulsen, 14 July 1886, *Briefwechsel*, 225. Tönnies wrote a lengthy review of Robertson's book, in which he kept silent about Robertson's silence about his debt to Tönnies.

unresolved problem.[41] Thornton went bankrupt and Tönnies decided to buy off the printed copies from the Unwin Brothers printing house himself, he paid for the binding, and commissioned the London firm Simpkin, Marshall & Co. to sell the books. In 1889, *Behemoth* and *The Elements of Law* were finally on the market.[42] Robertson welcomed the new editions and praised the 'service here rendered by a foreign scholar to the reputation of a great English thinker'.[43]

But Tönnies's trials were not yet over. In December 1895, most of the printed copies perished in a fire in Chilworth, Surrey, where they were stored. Only about 20 copies each of *Behemoth* and the *Elements* survived which was about as many as Tönnies had in his possession.[44] At that point, he did not keep his feelings secret. 'The misfortune, linked with these books, has been big', he wrote to a friend.

> That I spent a very big amount of time and effort on this, that the printing cost me 2,000 M[arks], from which hardly as many hundreds have returned, all this does not count that much; that I, however – if I leave aside your mindfulness and a few isolated notices – have not received a whiff of thankfulness from the learned world makes it hard for me to resist bitterness in my heart. If Hobbes were an Alexandrian commentator on Aristotle, I would, with the reconstruction of those works, doubtlessly have had to become a member of the Berlin Academy.[45]

One of those 'notices' was the announcement in the *Annals of the American Academy of Political and Social Sciences* that

> DR. FERDINAND TÖNNIES, the editor of the famous works of Hobbes, *The Behemoth* and *The Elements of Law*, has made the Academy the authorized agent for the sale of these books in America, permitting them to be sold to members of the Academy at cost price. This is a rare opportunity to obtain two books which should be in the library of any person interested in political science.[46]

See *Philosophische Monatshefte* 23 (1887), 287–306. But see Tönnies, 'Hobbes-Analekten', *Archiv für Philosophie* XVII (1904), 316–17, where he did say something on the subject.

41 Tönnies to Harald Höffding, 14 October 1888, in Ferdinand Tönnies and Harald Höffding, *Briefwechsel*, ed. C. Bickel and R. Fechner (Berlin: Duncker & Humblot, 1989), 34.
42 See Jacoby, *Die moderne Gesellschaft*, 20.
43 Review of *The Elements of Law Natural and Politic. By Thomas Hobbes of Malmesbury*, and *Behemoth or the Long Parliament. By Thomas Hobbes of Malmesbury*, *Mind* 14 (1889), no. 55, 429, 433.
44 Tönnies to Höffding, 15 December 1895, *Briefwechsel*, 47; Ferdinand Tönnies, *Hobbes Leben und Lehre* (Stuttgart: Friedrich Fromman, 1896), X.
45 Tönnies to Höffding, 15 December 1895, *Briefwechsel*, 47.
46 'Notes', *Annals of the American Academy of Political and Social Sciences* 1 (1891), 512.

Introduction: The Ways of 'Behemoth'

What was left after the fire, Tönnies offered for sale himself.[47] In the mid-1920s, he still felt that the recognition for his work on Hobbes had not been forthcoming—especially not from England and America.[48] This was rectified, though much later, with the reprinting of his edition of *Behemoth*: in 1969 in London with M. M. Goldsmith's introduction,[49] and in 1990 in Chicago with Stephen Holmes's introduction.[50]

The first known translation of *Behemoth* was into Latin. It was made in 1708 by Adam Ebert, Professor at Frankfurt an der Oder University, and deposited by him in the King of Prussia's library.[51] German translation was appended to a study of Hobbes's relation to the 'political parties of the great English revolution' by Julius Lips. The translation was done by Lips and reviewed by Tönnies, who also wrote a preface as a gesture of support for the 'young scholar'.[52] Italian translation was prepared by Onofrio Nicastro and appeared at the third centenary of the first, unauthorized, English printing of *Behemoth*.[53] A French translation by Luc Borot appeared as a volume in the outstanding French edition of Hobbes's collected works.[54] Both translations are based on scrupulous original research and collation of printed editions and manuscripts. Both also have substantial introductions. Spanish and Slovenian translations, prepared on the basis of Tönnies's edition, also have a sizable introduction and postscript, respectively.[55]

---

47 Tönnies, *Hobbes Leben und Lehre*, X. In the second edition of his Hobbes book, Tönnies announced that there were only a very few copies available, which could be obtained directly from him 'as long as the stock lasts'. Ferdinand Tönnies, *Thomas Hobbes der Mann und der Denker* (Osterwieck and Leipzig: A. W. Wickfeldt, 1912), XIV.
48 Tönnies to Höffding, 2 September 1925, *Briefwechsel*, 171.
49 *Behemoth or the Long Parliament, by Thomas Hobbes of Malmesbury. Edited by Ferdinand Tönnies, Second edition, With a new Introduction by M.M. Goldsmith* (London: Frank Cass, 1969); also printed in the US (New York: Barnes and Noble, [1969]).
50 Hobbes, *Behemoth* (see n. 5).
51 See Noel Malcolm's contribution in this volume.
52 Julius Lips, *Die Stellung des Thomas Hobbes zu den politischen Parteien der großen englischen Revolution. Mit erstmaliger Übersetzung des Behemoth oder Das Lange Parlament. Mit einem Einführung von Ferdinand Tönnies* (Leipzig: E. Wiegandt, 1927; reprint Darmstadt: Wissenschaftliche Buchgesellschaft, 1970). A revised Lips's translation was published by Herfried Münkler: *Thomas Hobbes, Behemoth oder Das Lange Parlament*, trans. J. Lips, revised by H. Münkler (Frankfurt/M: Fischer, 1991). Münkler added ten pages of explanatory notes and a postscriptum, 'Thomas Hobbes' Analytik des Buurgerkrieges'.
53 See n. 21.
54 Thomas Hobbes, *Béhémoth ou Le Long Parlement*, ed. and trans. Luc Borot (Paris: Vrin, 1990).
55 Thomas Hobbes, *Behemoth: Estudio preliminar, traducción y notas de Miguel Ángel Rodilla* (Madrid: Tecnos, 1992); Thomas Hobbes, *Behemot, ali Dolgi parlament*, trans. Z. Erbežnik, postscript T. Mastnak (Ljubljana: Studia humanitatis, 2005).

III. Books and articles on *Behemoth*

What I have presented so far is a brief outline of the history of the writing and publication of *Behemoth*. That history is convoluted enough and still awaits a critical edition as its symbolic closure. The history of the reception of *Behemoth* is much more open-ended. *Behemoth* has always been overshadowed by the more famous *Leviathan*, and students of Hobbes have generally neglected it.

There is evidence that allows us to infer that, when it was first printed, *Behemoth* made quite a stir. One piece of that evidence is Crooke's statement that, at the turn of the 1670s and 80s, 'no Book [was] being more commonly sold by all Booksellers' than *Behemoth*.[56] Once he himself published it, Crooke kept advertising it for years.[57] One should also bear in mind that *Behemoth* first appeared in a time of great political agitation.[58] It seems to have been among those books 'which reflect contemporary concerns'.[59] Its pirated editions may have been put on the market as a warning against a threatening civil war.[60] For the conservatives 'who felt that they were now reliving the crisis of the 1640s, *Behemoth* could not have been more relevant'.[61] 'At that Time, when Things were fresh in Memory', one can read in the 1750 edition of Hobbes's works, *Behemoth* 'was much read and admired'.[62] But, on the other hand, the book was rarely mentioned in print[63] — I have only found references in James Tyrrell,[64] Peter

---

56 See n. 24.
57 See 'A Catalogue of BOOKS printed and sold by *William Crooke* Bookseller', attached to Ringrose, *Bucaniers of America* (see n. 25); and 'BOOKS Printed for *W. Crooke*, at the Green-Dragon without Temple-Bar. 1691', appended to John Wright, *A sermon preached at the parish church of Solihull in Warwickshire, December 21. 1690 On occasion of the death of Anne, the wife of the reverend and worshipful Henry Greswold* (London, 1691).
58 Nicastro, 'Introduzione', VII ff.; Parkin, *Taming the Leviathan*, 337.
59 See James L. Salter, 'The Books of an Early Eighteenth-Century Curate', *The Library*, ser. 5, 33 (1978), no. 1, 35. Salter published the probate inventory of a young Warwickshire curate, who died in 1705. Among the books of the curate, who matriculated from Magdalen Hall, Oxford, in 1694/95, there was the 1679 printing of *Behemoth, History of the causes of the civil wars of England*, bought for 1 s. Ibid., 42.
60 Hans-Dieter Metzger, *Thomas Hobbes und die Englische Revolution, 1640–1660* (Stuttgart: Frommann-holzboog, 1991), 311.
61 Parkin, *Taming the Leviathan*, 339.
62 'The Life of Thomas Hobbes', in *The Moral and Political Works of Thomas Hobbes*, xx.
63 It was mentioned, though, in discussions of the Privy Council on 'illegal provocative literature of all kinds' in September 1679, and in private correspondence. See Parkin, *Taming the Leviathan*, 340.
64 The reference is to Hobs's 'little Dialogue of the civil wars of *England*'. *Patriarcha non Monarcha. The Patriarch Unmonarch'd: being Observations on A late Treatise and divers other Miscellanies, Published under the Name of Sir Robert Filmer, Baronet*, etc. (London, 1681), 151; see also Parkin, *Taming the Leviathan*, 365.

Pett,⁶⁵ and Anthony Wood⁶⁶ — and Whitehall's *Behemoth Arraign'd* was to be the only book, or booklet, published on this work of Hobbes's for almost three hundred years.

It is thus understandable that the observation that *Behemoth* has been much neglected by historians in general and Hobbes scholars in particular is widespread in the relevant literature.⁶⁷ Soon after Tönnies's edition appeared, James Fitzjames Stephen wrote that the work 'ought to be far better known than it is'.⁶⁸ Eighty years later MacGillivray stated that the work had been 'unjustly neglected',⁶⁹ while Richard Ashcraft pointed out that in the 'scores of considerations of Hobbes' political theory extant, virtually no attention has been paid to his *Behemoth*'.⁷⁰ Recently, Jeffrey Collins has called *Behemoth* 'Hobbes's most neglected major work'.⁷¹ From one of Hobbes's 'minor works' in Stephen's article,⁷² *Behemoth* has thus been promoted to a 'major work'.⁷³ If such an assessment will bring about

---

65 Peter Pett, *The obligation resulting from the Oath of Supremacy to assist and defend the pre-eminence or prerogative of the dispensative power belonging to the King, his heirs and successors*, etc. (London, 1687), 22; idem, *The happy future state of England: or, a discourse by way of letter to the late Earl of Anglesey*, etc. (London, 1688), The Preface to the Reader D*, 70, 188, 200. On Pett, see Mark Goldie, 'Sir Peter Pett, Sceptical Torysm and the Science of Toleration in the 1680s', in *Persecution and Toleration: Papers read at the twenty-second summer meeting and the twenty-third winter meeting of the Ecclesiastical History Society*, ed. W.J. Sheils, *Studies in Church History*, 21 (Oxford: Basil Blackwell, 1984). Goldie, ibid., 247, characterized *The happy future state of England* as 'eirenic, Erastian and Hobbesian in outlook'.

66 Anthony à Wood, *Athenae Oxonienses: an exact history of all the writers and bishops who have had their education in the most ancient and famous University of Oxford*, etc. (London, 1692), 2. col. 481. Cf. Anthony Wood, *Athenae oxonienses: An Exact History of all the Writers and Bishops who have had their Education in the University of Oxford. To which are added the Fasti, or Annals of the said University*, ed. Ph. Bliss (London: Printed for F. C. and J. Rivington et al., 1813-20), 3. col. 1213.

67 Within this consensus, A. P. Martinich, *Thomas Hobbes* (New York: St. Martin's Press, 1997), 111, is unique in pointing out that the neglect of *Behemoth* was linked to the neglect of the second half of *Leviathan*. He credited John Pocock for having done 'much to change this situation'; so did Richard Tuck, 'The Civil Religion of Thomas Hobbes', in *Political Discourse in Early Modern Britain*, ed. N. Phillipson and Q. Skinner (Cambridge: Cambridge University Press, 1993). See J. G. A. Pocock, 'Time, History, and Eschatology in the Thought of Thomas Hobbes', in *The Diversity of History: Essays in honour of Sir Herbert Butterfield*, eds J. H. Elliott and H. G. Koenigsberger (Ithaca, New York: Cornell University Press, [1970]). Jean Terrel, *Le vocabulaire de Hobbes* (Paris: Ellipses, 2003), 61, suggests under the heading 'Royaume de ténèbres (*kingdom of darkness, regnum tenebrarum*)', that *Behemoth* is a history of a 'particularly dark' political period.

68 James Fitzjames Stephen, *Horae Sabbaticae: Reprint of Articles Contributed to 'The Saturday Review'*, Second Series (London: Macmillan, 1892), 39.

69 Royce MacGillivray, 'Thomas Hobbes's History of the English Civil War: A Study of *Behemoth*', *Journal of the History of Ideas* 31 (1970), no. 2, 179.

70 Richard Ashcraft, 'Ideology and Class in Hobbes' Political Theory', *Political Theory* 6 (1978), no. 1, 28. Cited approvingly by Robert P. Kraynak, *History and Modernity in the Thought of Thomas Hobbes* (Ithaca, New York: Cornell University Press, 1990), 32, n. 1.

71 Jeffrey R. Collins, *The Allegiance of Thomas Hobbes* (Oxford: Oxford University Press, 2007), 59.

72 Stephen, *Horae Sabbaticae*, 36.

73 W. H. Greenleaf, 'A Note on Hobbes and the Book of Job', *Anales de la Catedra 'Francisco Suarez'* 14 (1974), 17, called *Behemoth* one of 'two of Hobbes' major political works' whose titles were

more research, and perhaps even generate controversy,[74] about *Behemoth* remains to be seen.

It was only in 1977 that Onofrio Nicastro, a former professor at the University of Pisa and a 'major historian of early modern English philosophical culture',[75] published his *Note sul Behemoth*.[76] Printed in 105 copies, this publication is a rarity and has never had the circulation it deserves.[77] With notes cut down to meet 'publishing exigencies', the essay served for the introduction to Nicastro's translation of *Behemoth*. Simon Dir-Ching Kow submitted a PhD thesis to the University of Toronto's Graduate Department of Political Science on *Leviathan Against Behemoth*, in which he compared Milton and Hobbes's views on the relation between the state and religiously based conflict.[78] The thesis, to the best of my knowledge, has not been printed. Nicolas Dubos is completing a PhD thesis on profane and sacred history in the work of Thomas Hobbes, which pays considerable attention to *Behemoth*. The work is conducted under the supervision of Jean Terrel at the Université Michel de Montaigne Bordeaux III.[79] In 2002, Geoffrey Vaughan, at the time Assistant Professor in the University of Maryland's Department of Political Science, published his *Behemoth teaches Leviathan*, in which he explored Hobbes's views on political

---

taken from the *Book of Job*; but he did not say much more about *Behemoth* in this article. Much earlier, V. Beonio-Brocchieri, *Studi sulla filosofia politica di T. Hobbes* (Torino: Fratelli Bocca, 1927), 95, called *Behemoth* Hobbes's 'major historiographical work'. Kraynak, *History and Modernity*, 33, called *Behemoth* a 'work of primary importance'.

74   Geoffrey M. Vaughan, *'Behemoth' teaches 'Leviathan': Thomas Hobbes on political education* (Lanham, Md.: Lexington Books, 2002), 107, has observed that not only has scholarly commentary 'been very sparse' but that it has 'not been very controversial' either – 'which is unusual for the study of Hobbes'.

75   See also M. J. Redmond, 'Italian Studies in Early Modern English History: Two Recent Publications', *Cromohs*, 9 (2004), 4, URL: http://www.cromohs.unifi.it/9_2004/redmond_villani.html; Scott Mandelbrote, in his review of *Religione, politica e commercio di libri nella Rivoluzione inglese: Gli autori di Giles Calvert, 1645–1653* by Mario Caricchio, *The Library* 7 (2006), no. 4, 462, mentioned 'a thriving school of students of English religious and and political radicalism that developed in Italy under the wing of the late Onofrio Nicastro'. See Paolo Cristofolini, 'Ricordo di un amico', *Cromohs*, 8 (2003): 1–7, URL: http://www.cromohs.unifi.it/8_2003/cristofolini.html.

76   Onofrio Nicastro, *Note sul* Behemoth *di Thomas Hobbes* (Pisa: Felici, 1977).

77   Gian Mario Cazzaniga, 'Prefazione', in Onofrio Nicastro, *Politica e religione nel seicento inglese: Raccolta di scritti* (Pisa: Edizioni ETS, 1995), 10, called Nicastro's publications on Hobbes 'semiclandestine'. I wish to thank Prof. Paolo Cristofolini and Mrs Rina Perona Nicastro for kindly providing me with a copy. In a personal communication, Prof. Cristofolini wrote of 'questo raro lavoro di Onofrio Nicastro, il quale, per troppa modestia, non dava quasi mai diffusione ai suoi scritti (il *Behemot* da Laterza fa eccezione!)'.

78   Simon Dir-Ching Kow, '*Leviathan* Against *Behemoth*: Hobbes and Milton on Religious Conflict and the State', Graduate Department of Political Science, University of Toronto, 2001.

79   Nicolas Dubos, *Histoire profane et histoire sacrée dans l'oeuvre de Thomas Hobbes*, Université Michel de Montaigne Bordeaux III, to be completed in 2009.

education.⁸⁰ All these works, Vaughan's in particular, give substantial attention to *Behemoth*. But if we accept that *Behemoth* is not their main subject, and if we leave aside articles and book chapters, the issue of *Filozofski vestnik*, from which the present volume originates,⁸¹ has thus been next to Nicastro's *Note sul Behemoth* the only monograph on Hobbes's *Behemoth* since the appearance of Whitehall's pamphlet in 1680.

Nor have there been many articles and book chapters dedicated to *Behemoth*. The first article dealing specifically with *Behemoth* appears to have been published no earlier than 1970, written by Royce MacGillivray, historian at the University of Waterloo, Ontario.⁸² Noting in his opening paragraph that, while there were 'useful short discussions in several books', there was 'no detailed discussion of the work as a whole', MacGillivray explained that he was going to attempt 'a treatment of the main aspects of the book' as a history of the English civil war.⁸³ With minor changes, MacGillivray included the material from this article in his book on restoration historians and the civil war,⁸⁴ but does not seem to have taken up the subject again.

German political theorist Bernard Willms published two articles on *Behemoth* in the mid 1970s, in which he took issue with the language politics of contemporary student movements and brought to the fore the political relevance of that work of Hobbes's.⁸⁵ Next, chronologically, was an article by Francesco Fagiani on 'construction and dissolution of

---

80 Vaughan, *'Behemoth' teaches 'Leviathan'*. There are some other books and articles that sport *Behemoth* in their titles even though they are not dedicated to *Behemoth*. See Dietrich Braun, *Der sterbliche Gott oder Leviathan gegen Behemoth: Erwägungen zu Ort, Bedeutung und Funktion der Lehre von der Königherrschft Christi in Thomas Hobbes' 'Leviathan'* (Zurich: EVZ, 1961); Hermann Klenner, 'Leviathan und Behemoth, oder Vernunft und Aufruhr', postscript to Thomas Hobbes, *Leviathan, oder Materie, Form und Gewalt eines kirchlichen und staatlichen Gemeinwesens, Teil I und II* (Leipzig: Philipp Reclam jun., 1978); Francesco Viola, *Behemoth o Leviathan? Diritto e obbligo nel pensiero di Hobbes* (Milano: A. Giuffrè, 1979); Herbert W. Schneider, 'Thomas Hobbes from *Behemoth* to *Leviathan*', in *Hobbes's Science of Natural Justice*, eds C. Walton and P. J. Johnson (Dordrecht: M. Nijhoff, 1987). To this category belong also Carl Schmitt, 'Behemoth, Leviathan und Greif', *Deutsche Kolonial-Zeitung* 55 (1943); Angelo Bolaffi, 'Una favola sullo scontro mortale tra Leviathan e Behemoth', ch. 4 in idem, *Il crepuscolo della sovranità: Filosofia e politica nella Germania del Novecento* (Roma: Donzelli, 2002); Filippo Ruschi, 'Leviathan e Behemoth: Modelli egemonici e spazi coloniali in Carl Schmitt', *Quaderni fiorentini* 33-4 (2004/2005). The first was an extract from Schmitt's *Land und Meer* (see n. 180), and the other two were inspired by Schmitt's work.
81 *Behemoth*, [ed. T. Mastnak,] *Filozofski vestnik* 24 (2003), no. 2.
82 Beonio-Brocchieri, *Studi sulla filosofia politica di T. Hobbes*, dedicated ch. 3 of his book, 'Il pensatore giudice dei suoi tempi', to Hobbes's views in—mainly—*Behemoth*. But this is a chapter *from*, rather than *on*, *Behemoth*.
83 MacGillivray, 'Thomas Hobbes's History', 179.
84 Royce MacGillivray, *Restoration Historians and the English Civil War* (The Hague: Martinus Nijhof, 1974), 61-83.
85 Bernard Willms, 'Staatsräson und das Problem der politischen Definition: Bemerkungen zum Nominalismus in Hobbes' "Behemoth"', in *Staatsräson: Studien zur Geschichte eines politischen Begriffs*, ed. R. Schnur (Berlin: Duncker & Humblot, 1975); idem, 'Systemüberwindung und

political bodies'. In *Leviathan*, Hobbes formulated the rules of his 'moral and civil science', necessary for establishing a stable and long-lasting political structure, whereas in *Behemoth* he analyzed the causes and ways of its dissolution.[86] Robert Kraynak, professor of political science at Colgate University, proposed in his article on *Behemoth* that this much-neglected work provided the key to a clearer understanding of the central problem Hobbes grappled with in his 'political science'.[87] Since that problem lay in destabilizing effects of doctrinal warfare, which was the result of the foundation of Hobbes's contemporary societies on 'authoritative opinion', Kraynak in his article offered a historical and psychological interpretation of Hobbes's analysis of opinion.[88] In an article published at about the same time, Paulette Carrive, professor at Université de Paris I (Panthéon-Sorbonne), looked into how *Behemoth* complemented *Leviathan*.[89] Kraynak returned to the subject of his article in an important chapter in his book on history and modernity in Hobbes.[90] Thematically close was a study on political psychology in *Behemoth* by Stephen Holmes, then professor of political science and law at the University of Chicago, as was his contemporaneous introduction to the Chicago reprint of *Behemoth*.[91] From that time is also a study of dramatic conflict and the function of negative biblical images in *Behemoth* by Noam Flinker of Haifa University.[92]

In the last twelve years, there appeared a series of articles on *Behemoth* as a historiographical work. Authors include Luc Borot, professor in the

---

Bürgerkrieg: Zur politischen Bedeutung von Hobbes' Behemoth', in *Freiheit und Sachzwang: Beiträge zu Ehren Helmut Schelsky*, ed. H. Baier (Opladen: Westdeutscher Verlag, 1977).

86 Franceso Fagiani, 'Leviathan contra Behemoth: Costruzione e dissoluzione dei corpi politici', *Materiali per una storia della cultura giuridica* 11 (1981), no. 2, 248.

87 Kraynak's PhD thesis was in political sciences: 'The Politics and Science of Thomas Hobbes', Harvard University, 1977. The work was not available to me at the time of writing.

88 Robert P. Kraynak, 'Hobbes's *Behemoth* and the Argument for Absolutism', *American Political Science Review* 76 (1982).

89 Paulette Carrive, 'Béhemoth et Léviathan', in *Hobbes, Philosophie, Politique, Cahiers de Philosophie Politique et Juridique de l'Université de Caen* 3 (1983).

90 '*The Behemoth*: Doctrinal Politics and the English Civil War', ch. 2 in Kraynak, *History and Modernity*.

91 Stephen Holmes, 'Political Psychology in Hobbes's *Behemoth*', in *Thomas Hobbes and Political Theory*, ed. M. G. Dietz (Lawrence, Kansas: University Press of Kansas, 1990); idem, 'Introduction' to Chicago reprint of *Behemoth* (see n. 5). Two other contributions to Dietz's volume pay more than usual attention to *Behemoth*: Deborah Baumgold, 'Hobbes's Political Sensibility', and Mary G. Dietz, 'Hobbes's Subject as Citizen'. They point to the 'malignancy of ambition' (Baumgold, 'Hobbes's Political Sensibility', 85) and to 'citizen morality', which cannot be reduced to the 'calculation of interest and the geometry of force' (Dietz, 'Hobbes's Subject', 96), as the themes which were brought to the fore in *Behemoth*. The themes of ambition and glory are further developed in Gabriella Slomp, *Thomas Hobbes and the Political Philosophy of Glory* (New York: St. Martin's Press, 2000).

92 Noam Flinker, 'The View from the "Devil's Mountain": Dramatic Tension in Hobbes's *Behemoth*', *Hobbes Studies* 2 (1989).

Department of Anglophone Studies at the Université Paul Valéry Montpellier III, the editor and translator of the French edition of *Behemoth*;[93] Michael Szczekalla, currently Associated Lecturer at the Ernst Moritz Arnd Universität Griefswald;[94] Fritz Levy, professor of history at the University of Washington;[95] David Wootton, currently professor of history at the University of York;[96] and Nicolas Dubos, at the time Associate Professor of philosophy at the Université Michel de Montaigne Bordeaux III.[97]

IV. Patterns of interpretation

If we look at these publications and at mentions or short discussions of *Behemoth* in the extensive literature on Hobbes, we can detect some common traits, trends, and general characteristics. In a *longue durée* perspective, one can observe a shift from the appreciation of *Behemoth* as a work of political theory to its description as a history of the civil war. What carried weight for John Whitehall late in the seventeenth century were pernicious principles of Hobbes's political philosophy.[98] In the eighteenth century, Bishop Warburton said of *Behemoth* that it was 'full of paradoxes, like all his other writings', and '[m]ore philosophical, political—or any thing rather than historical; yet full of shrewd observations'.[99] Early in the nineteenth century, Francis Maseres indicated some disagreements with Hobbes's historical judgment regarding the merits of particular persons discussed in *Behemoth*. But what mattered most to him were Hobbes's views 'concerning the nature of Civil Government in General, and the

---

93 Luc Borot, 'History in Hobbes's Thought', in *The Cambridge Companion to Hobbes*, ed. T. Sorell (Cambridge: Cambridge University Press, 1996); idem, 'Hobbes's *Behemoth*', in *Hobbes and History*, eds G. A. J. Rogers and T. Sorell (London: Routledge, 2000). The latter is a translation of a portion of Borot's introduction to Hobbes, *Béhémoth ou Le Long Parlement*.

94 Michael Szczekalla, 'Leviathan und Behemoth—Natur und Geschichte bei Hobbes' *Saeculum* 49 (1998).

95 Fritz Levy, 'The Background of Hobbes's *Behemoth*', in *The Historical Imagination in Early Modern Britain: History, Rhetoric, and Fiction, 1500–1800*, eds D. M. Kelley and D. H. Sacks (Cambridge: Cambridge University Press and Woodrow Wilson Center, 1997).

96 David Wootton, 'Thomas Hobbes's Machiavellian Moments', in Kelley and Sacks, *The Historical Imagination in Early Modern Britain*; reprinted in *Literature Criticism from 1400 to 1800*, vol. 142, ed. T. Schoenberg (Detroit: Gale Group, 2008).

97 Nicolas Dubos, 'Lectures de *Béhémoth*', in *Hobbes: nouvelles lectures*, eds J. Berthier and J. Terrel, *Lumière*, no. 10, 2007.

98 For an interesting appraisal, see Nicastro, *Note*, 12, and 'Introduzione', XLVI–XLVII, that while Whitehall's critique was uncouth, it nevertheless addressed the key issue, which was to cost James II his throne.

99 Cited in William Thomas Lowndes, *The bibliographer's manual of English literature, containing an account of rare, curious, and useful books published in or relating to Great Britain and Ireland, from the invention of printing* (London: William Pickering, 1834), 2. 938.

Monarchical Government of England in particular'.[100] He cared so much about those 'erroneous Opinions' that he appended his own remarks to the reprint of *Behemoth*.[101]

In Tönnies, we may sense a climate change. In his 1889 edition, he recommended *Behemoth* as of 'high interest to the historical student as well as to the philosopher and politician'.[102] For some of his contemporaries, *Behemoth* was simply a history. Robertson, for example, who in his pioneering work on Hobbes mentioned *Behemoth* only once, praised the 'extremely spirited style', in which Hobbes's account of the 'social and religious conditions that led to the Revolution' was written.[103] Leslie Stephen, too, praised Hobbes's style but was more reserved about the merits of his historical explanations: 'He too often, like many better historians, finds it enough to explain events by the wickedness of the other side. That agreeable theory is an excuse for not attempting to discover the causes of discontent'.[104] Whereas Hobbes's style has almost unanimously been praised,[105] his history has met with less approval. The point here, however, is not approval but the characterization of *Behemoth* as a historiographical work. This characterization may well be at odds with Hobbes's own understanding of his work,[106] yet it has become so standard in Hobbes studies that I think it is superfluous to document it. No less an authority than Quentin Skinner holds *Behemoth* to be a work of Hobbes as a 'historian'.[107]

If *Behemoth* is seen as historiography, two questions emerge: What kind of history did Hobbes write, and how reliable a source was his history?

---

100 Maseres, 'Preface' to *Select Tracts*, 1. lxxix.
101 Maseres, 'Remarks on Some Passages in the foregoing Tract of Mr. Thomas Hobbes, of Malmesbury, entitled Behemoth ... Which seem to be grounded on erroneous Opinions concerning Civil Government, and the Constitution of the Monarchy of England', *Select Tracts*, 2. 657–71.
102 Tönnies, 'Preface', x.
103 George Croom Robertson, *Hobbes* (Edinburgh: William Blackwood, 1910), 198.
104 Leslie Stephen, *Hobbes* (New York: Macmillan, 1904), 29.
105 An exception is G. P. Gooch, *Hobbes: Annual Lecture on a Master Mind, Henriette Hertz Trust of the British Academy, 1939* (London: Humphrey Milford, s.a.), 38, who considered *Behemoth* written in a 'scolding vein'. Generally, see also G. A. J. Rogers, 'Introduction' to *Perspectives on Thomas Hobbes*, eds G. A. J. Rogers and A. Ryan (Oxford: Clarendon, 1988), 6: 'There is, however, one aspect of Hobbes on which there has always been agreement. He was a master of English prose'.
106 We have seen (n. 15) that Hobbes, upon learning about a pirated edition of the book we today know as *Behemoth*, complained about 'a foolish title set to it'. The title of the first three editions was *History of the Civil Wars of England. From the Year 1640, to 1660*. See Macdonald and Hargreaves, *Thomas Hobbes: A Bibliography*, nos. 86–7a. It is plausible that Hobbes complained precisely about naming his book 'History'.
107 Quentin Skinner, *Reason and Rhetoric in the Philosophy of Hobbes* (Cambridge: Cambridge University Press, 1996), 241. For Richard Tuck, *Philosophy and Government, 1572–1651* (Cambridge: Cambridge University Press, 1993), 343, a history of the civil war is *Behemoth's* 'ostensible theme'.

Introduction: The Ways of 'Behemoth' 17

We have already met with some scepsis regarding the value of Hobbes's historical account. Yet that account has been used as a historical source. But most often when that happens, one can hardly overlook the paradox that, as a 'history of the English civil war', *Behemoth* is not used as a source for the history of the English civil war. Rather, it is seen as providing material for the study of larger, and occasionally smaller, issues. One such larger issue, which some time ago had commanded considerable attention, was the emergence of 'bourgeois society'. C. B. Macpherson found *Behemoth* an important source for supporting his thesis on the rise of what he famously called 'possessive individualism'. From Hobbes's remarks in *Behemoth* it was clear that he was 'not so blind as to miss the fact that there was a class division in England ... He saw, too, that the growth of the market relation had undermined the old values, and that the new men of mercantile wealth had enough cohesion to foment civil war'. However, because he insisted on the necessity of 'a self-perpetuating sovereign body', his conclusions were 'inapplicable to the possessive market society, and unacceptable to the proponents of market society in seventeenth-century England'.[108]

Linked with such attributions of the English civil war to 'the new strength of market morality and of market-made wealth' was the attention given to the role of merchants and large commercial centers, such as London, in the social transformation.[109] Often cited in this connection was Hobbes's comment that 'the city of London and other great towns of trade, having in admiration the great prosperity of the Low Countries after they had revolted from their monarch, the King of Spain, were inclined to think that the like change of government here, would to them

---

108 C. B. Macpherson, *The Political Theory of Possessive Individualism: Hobbes to Locke* (Oxford: Oxford University Press, 1962), 94; see also 64–6. Some such insights go back to Marx and Engels, who identified Hobbes and the 'first English revolution' as the moment of the emergence of the theory, which subsumed all social relations to the 'One abstract money- and haggling relation'. They, however, referred only to *Leviathan*. See especially *Die deutsche Ideologie*, Karl Marx and Friedrich Engels, *Werke* (Berlin: Dietz, 1961–74), 3. 394–7. For a critique of Macpherson's thesis, see Keith Thomas, 'The Social Origins of Hobbes's Political Thought', in *Hobbes Studies*, ed. K. C. Brown (Cambridge, Mass.: Harvard University Press, 1965), who made good use of *Behemoth*. See also William Letwin, 'The Economic Foundations of Hobbes's Politics', in *Hobbes and Rousseau: A Collection of Critical Essays*, eds M. Cranston and R .S. Peters (Garden City, New York: Doubleday, 1972). For a recent endorsement of Macpherson's interpretation, see George Yerby, *People and Parliament: Representative Rights and the English Revolution* (Houndmills: Palgrave Macmillan, 2008), 55 ff., Appendix 1. In Yerby's judgment, *Behemoth* 'is a very perceptive assessment of the dominant socio-economic trends of the age, and the contribution that they made to the struggle for sovereignty between crown and parliament'. Ibid., 265.

109 Macpherson, *The Political Theory*, 65: Hobbes 'treated the war as an attempt to destroy the old constitution and replace it with one more favourable to the new market interests'.

produce the like prosperity'.[110] Penelope Corfield, for example, corroborated Hobbes's comment. 'The Parliamentarians in 1642 were not republicans', she wrote. 'But they shared a growing feeling that the unpredictability of Stuart kings was bad for business confidence and for trade'.[111] A recent study has argued, without recourse to Hobbes (yet not without implications for our judgment of Hobbes), that London's wealth was the single most important element in Parliament's victory.[112]

Another larger issue was constitutionalism or, more specifically, the history of English constitutionalism. George Peabody Gooch, in a lecture to the British Academy the year that World War II began, understood the subject of *Behemoth*, written in Hobbes's 'vigorous old age', to have been 'the constitutional struggle'. As a liberal Member of Parliament earlier in his life, Gooch was not sympathetic to Hobbes's presentation of that struggle. He found it 'superficial and unimaginative'. Hobbes's 'measureless contempt' for 'continual changes of régime' was as alien to him as Hobbes's attitude toward the 'principle of representation on which our liberties have been built'. That principle left the old 'impenitent absolutist', Hobbes, 'cold'.[113] More recently, Deborah Baumgold and Quentin Skinner, among others, have read *Behemoth* as an analysis of the 'constitutional struggle between Parliament and king' and considered it of interest for the study of arguments about English constitutional history.[114] In his most recent work, Skinner underlines, in unexpectedly strong words, the 'ferocity' and 'violence' of Hobbes's polemics in *Behemoth* against the

---

110 *Behemoth*, 3–4. Christopher Hill, *A Nation of Change and Novelty: Radical Politics, Religion and Literature in Seventeenth-Century England* (London: Routledge, 1990), 48–9, pointed out that Hobbes's comment was accurate. Christopher Hill, *Intellectual Origins of the English Revolution Revisited* (Oxford: Clarendon, 1997), 306, reminded his readers of another relevant comment Hobbes made in *Behemoth*: that the Presbyterians 'did never in their sermons, or but lightly, inveigh against the lucrative vices of men of trade or handicraft'. See *Behemoth*, 25.

111 Penelope Corfield, 'Economic Issues and Ideologies', in *The Origins of the English Civil War*, ed. C. Russell (London: Macmillan, 1973), 218. See also Roger Howell, 'Neutralism, Conservatism and Political Alignment in the English Revolution: The Case of Towns, 1642-9', in *Reactions to the English Civil War, 1642– 1649*, ed. J. Morrill (New York: St. Martin's Press, 1983), 67, 77; Stephen Porter, 'Introduction', in *London and the Civil War*, ed. by S. Porter (Houndmills: Macmillan, 1996), 1.

112 Benn Coates, *The Impact of the English Civil War on the Economy of London, 1642–50* (Aldershot: Ashgate, 2004).

113 Gooch, *Hobbes*, 35–8.

114 Deborah Baumgold, *Hobbes's Political Theory* (Cambridge: Cambridge University Press, 1988), 71; Quentin Skinner, 'History and Ideology in the English Revolution', *The Historical Journal* 8 (1965), no. 2, 156, 159, 170; idem, *Reason and Rhetoric*, 431 ff; *Visions of Politics*, vol. 3: *Hobbes and Civil Science* (Cambridge: Cambridge University Press, 2002), 13; idem, 'Classical Liberty and the Coming of the English Civil War', in vol. 2 of *Republicanism: A Shared European Heritage*, eds M. van Geldern and Q. Skinner (Cambridge: Cambridge University Press, 2002), 15 ff.; idem, *Hobbes and Republican Liberty* (Cambridge: Cambridge University Press, 2008), 139 ff.

republican idea of liberty and its proponents.[115] Thematically belonging to this context is Susan Moller Okin's study of *A Dialogue between a Philosopher and a Student of the Common Laws of England* and of *Behemoth*, in which she argues that, in these late works, Hobbes's attitude toward parliament shifted. Of crucial importance was the clear distinction, in these works, between the monarch as a 'politic' and a 'natural person',[116] which implied that, in these different capacities, he was owed different types of obligations.[117]

As a history by an eyewitness,[118] however, *Behemoth* has for some time now been valued not so much as a history of the events seen than as a work relevant for the history of seeing those events and for understanding Hobbes himself. For J. F. Stephen, *Behemoth*'s importance lay mainly in providing a window into mentalities of those times: 'it is the only contemporary account which shows us what sceptical men of the world thought of the great contest and of its party cries'.[119] Tönnies and L. Stephen narrowed the lens even more. For Tönnies, *Behemoth* was very revealing of Hobbes's mentality.[120] L. Stephen commented that *Behemoth* was of interest because it threw 'some light upon Hobbes's sympathies when the war was actually raging'.[121] This particular line of inquiry has recently been carried out in some detail by Jeffrey Collins, analyzing *Behemoth* as providing 'retrospective evidence' for Hobbes's positive attitude toward the Independents and Cromwell.[122] Some fifteen years earlier, Hans-Dieter Metzger argued that *Behemoth* was a testimony to Hobbes's political antipathies, especially to the decades long animosity between

---

115 Skinner, *Hobbes and Republican Liberty*, 179.
116 See *Behemoth*, 51.
117 Susdan Moller Okin, '"The Soveraign and His Counsellours": Hobbes's Reevaluation of Parliament', *Political Theory* 10 (1982), no. 1, especially 50-64.
118 This quality was pointed out by Meseres, *Select Tracts*, 1. lxxviii.
119 J. F. Stephen, *Horae Sabbaticae*, 39.
120 '*Behemoth*, ce livre qui est tellement significatif de le mentalité du philosophe'. Ferdinand Tönnies, 'Contribution à l'histoire de la pensée de Hobbes', in vol. 22 of *Ferdinand Tönnies Gesamtausgabe*, 451. In the German original: the book, 'das für die Denkungsart des Philosophen so bedeutsam ist'. Ibid., 544. This text, the preface to seven unpublished letters of Hobbes, lay unpublished for thirty years, to be eventually printed in *Archives de philosophie* 12 (1936), just in time for Tönnies to authorize the French translation before his death.
121 L. Stephen, *Hobbes*, 29.
122 Collins, *The Allegiance of Thomas Hobbes*, especially 151 ff. Johann Sommerville, 'Hobbes and Independency', in *Nouve prospettive critiche sul* Leviatano *di Hobbes nel 350o anniversario di pubblicazione/New Critical Perspectives on Hobbes's* Leviathan *upon the 350th Anniversary of its Publication*, eds L. Foisneau and G. Wright (Milano: FrancoAngeli, 2004), 170-1, cited *Behemoth* to prove the opposite. George E. G. Catlin, *Thomas Hobbes as Philosopher, Publicist and Man of Letters* (Oxford: Basil Blackwell, 1922), 16-17, maintained that *Behemoth* was written *in order to* 'bind up the "Leviathan" theory of sovereignty ... with the cause of loyalist legitimism', that is, to demonstrate Hobbes's 'perfervid loyalty'.

Hobbes and Edward Hyde.[123] Richard Tuck and, in greater detail, Philip Milton discussed *Behemoth* in the context of their research of Hobbes's views on heresy (and of his fears that he could be burned as a heretic).[124] In general, this take on *Behemoth* has best been described by MacGillivray, when he wrote that the book may be seen as telling us 'more about Hobbes than about the Civil War'.[125]

These considerations have not yet answered the question of what kind of history did Hobbes write. Tönnies, who called *Behemoth* 'the most remarkable work' written by the octogenarian philosopher, was among the first to offer an explanation. Hobbes's history, he said, was thickly interspersed with reflections and was perhaps the first rationalistic interpretation of contemporary history of the type, which was to become popular with Voltaire.[126] MacGillivray pointed to the importance of the dialogue form, in which *Behemoth* was written, which he regarded as 'a very uncommon form for a history at any period'.[127] But what distinguished this work of Hobbes's even more from contemporaneous histo-

---

123 Metzger, *Thomas Hobbes und die Englische Revolution, 1640–1660*, 92.
124 Richard Tuck, *Hobbes* (Oxford: Oxford University Press, 1989, 34–6; idem, *Philosophy and Government*, 341–4; Philip Milton, 'Hobbes, Heresy and Lord Arlington', *History of Political Thought* 14 (1993), no. 4. See also J. A. I. Champion, '*An Historical Narration Concerning Heresie*: Thomas Hobbes, Thomas Barlow, and the Restoration debate over "heresy"', in *Heresy, Literature, And Politics in Early Modern English Culture*, eds D. Loewenstein and J. Marshall (Cambridge: Cambridge University Press, 2006), 227–8; Parkin, *Taming the Leviathan*, 240.
125 MacGillivray, 'Thomas Hobbes's History', 179.
126 Ferdinand Tönnies, *Thomas Hobbes Leben und Lehre*, 3rd ed. (Stuttgart: Frommann, 1925), 61. For a more descriptive formulation of the same thought see Tönnies, 'Herbert Spencers soziologisches Werk', originally included in his *Soziologische Studien und Kritiken, Erste Sammlung* (1924), now in vol. 15 of *Ferdinand Tönnies Gesamtausgabe*, 137, where Tönnies wrote that the 'cunning lawgivers, founders of religion, and shavelings play already in *Hobbes* (especially in "Leviathan" and "Behemoth") the same role, which *Voltaire* was later to elevate to have European currency in the educated circles'. A similar view was held by Brokdorff, when he wrote that in his historical work, in *Behemoth*, Hobbes 'appears as the typical man of the Enlightenment'. Baron Cay von Brokdorff, *Hobbes als Philosoph, Pädagoge und Soziologe, Erster Band*, 2nd edn (Kiel: Lipsius and Tischer, 1929), 120.
127 MacGillivray, 'Thomas Hobbes's History', 180. The recognition of the importance of the dialogue form was expressed already in Leopold von Ranke, *Englische Geschichte*, ed. W. Andreas (Wiesbaden: Emil Vollmer, 1957), 2. 515, who in his excellent brief appreciation of Hobbes called *Behemoth* a 'historical dialogue'. Noel Malcolm, *Aspects of Hobbes* (Oxford: Oxford University Press, 2002), 24, called *Behemoth* 'dialogue-history'. Miriam M. Reik, *The Golden Lands of Thomas Hobbes* (Detroit: Wayne State University Press, 1977), 191–3, reflected on the advantages of *Behemoth*'s dialogue form for reaching—and instructing—a wider audience. For Vaughan, the dialogue form was of central importance, since it was the vehicle for achieving the purpose of the work, which, as Vaughan has argued, was political education. Vaughan, *'Behemoth' teaches 'Leviathan'*, especially 114 ff. On civic education, see also Dietz, 'Hobbes's Subject', 100: '*Behemoth*'s contribution, in addition to its astute analysis of the causes of civil strife, is to bring this case for civic education in public duty to the forefront of English political life'. One of the best discussions of *Behemoth* as 'the masterpiece of Hobbesian dialogue' is Luc Borot, 'Hobbes, Rhetoric, and the Art of the Dialogue', in *Printed Voices: The Renaissance Culture of Dialogue*, ed. D. Heitsch and J.-F. Vallée (Toronto: University of Toronto Press, 2004), 181–4.

ries of the civil war, was 'the sheer quantity of ideas that Hobbes brings to it'.[128] Such appraisal is undoubtedly compatible with Levy's recent characterization of *Behemoth* as a Baconian 'ruminated history'.[129] Bacon used that term to describe 'politique discourse and obseruation' on a 'a scattered History' of actions 'thought worthy of memorie'. As such, this type of history belonged, more than anywhere else, 'amongst Bookes of policies'.[130] Since Machiavelli was the master of such *'discourse vpon Histories or Examples'*,[131] Wootton's designation of *Behemoth* as 'a study in Machiavellian politics' seems convincing.[132] (As a curiosity I want to note that John Cleveland called 'Old *Machiavel*' 'great *Behemoth*'s younger Brother'.[133])

Behemoth thus emerges as a political treatise. It has often emerged as such in a very specific sense, when it was understood as the result of the application of Hobbes's political theories on historical material. Both James Fitzjames Stephen and Leslie Stephen were of that view. The latter wrote that 'Hobbes's political theory was fully formed before the outbreak of the war. He watched the events with interest, but of course knew beforehand that they would only conform his theory'.[134] The understanding of the formation of Hobbes's political theory has since changed, but what has not changed as much is the view that *Behemoth* came after the theory had been formed. Richard Peters opined that, under the Restoration, 'Hobbes made few more contributions to knowledge though he never desisted from writing'. *Behemoth* exemplified that as 'a history of the period 1640-60 interpreted in the light of Hobbes's main tenets about society'.[135] Goldsmith, in his preface to the much-cited reprint of Tönnies's edition of *Behemoth*, was of the same opinion. In *Behemoth*, he wrote, Hobbes explained the rebellion, which 'did not require a new

---

128 MacGillivray, 'Thomas Hobbes's History', 180. Martine Watson Brownley, 'Sir Richard Baker's "Chronicle" and Later Seventeenth-Century English Historiography', *The Huntington Library Quarterly* 52 (1989), no. 4, 490, cites *Behemoth* as an example of the trend in English historiography in the second half of the seventeenth century, in which '[p]ast actions began to function simply as excuses for political discourse'.
129 Levy, 'The Background of Hobbes's *Behemoth*', 248-50; see also Borot, 'Introduction' to *Béhémoth*, 15; Vaughan, *Behemoth teaches Leviathan*, 94, 114 ff.
130 See Bacon, *The Advancement of Learning*, ed. M. Kiernan, vol. 4 of *The Oxford Francis Bacon* (Oxford: Clarendon, 2000), 70.
131 Bacon, *The Advancement of Learning*, 162.
132 Wootton, 'Thomas Hobbes's Machiavellian Moments', 228. For Machiavellian traits in *Behemoth*, see also Nigel Smith, *Literature and Revolution in England, 1640– 1660* (New Haven: Yale University Press, 1994), 352.
133 'The Publick Faith', in *The Works of Mr. John Cleveland: containing his poems, orations, epistles, collected into one volume, with the life of the author* (London, 1687), 201.
134 L. Stephen, *Hobbes*, 29; see J. F. Stephen, *Horae Sabbaticae*, 39.
135 Richard Peters, *Hobbes* (Harmondsworth: Penguin, 1956), 42, see also 64.

theory; it only required that Hobbes use his old one to explain the phenomena'.[136]

Behemoth has been read not only as an application of Hobbes's political philosophy on history but as a test or an explanation of his political philosophy as well. Ralph Richardson, for example, said that Hobbes was 'first and foremost a philosopher', who 'turned to history largely to find a tool with which to test his own science of politics'.[137] Pierre Naville, for his part, wrote that, in *Behemoth*, Hobbes looked backward to explain 'the principles which he had so masterfully defined in *Leviathan*'.[138] Comparisons of *Behemoth* with Hobbes's other writings also have some such explanatory value, in the eyes of Hobbes's interpreters. Tom Sorell, for example, said that there is a 'close match' between what Hobbes wrote on the break-up of states in chapters on the causes of sedition in *The Elements of Law*, *De Cive*, and *Leviathan*, and at the beginning of *Behemoth*.[139] The most thorough comparison of how *Behemoth* and *Leviathan* (in particular) explain the causes of the weakening and dissolution of the state was made by Paulette Carrive.[140] From a different perspective, John Watkins compared these two works and their treatment of the civil war. Having pointed out that *Leviathan* was, in Hobbes's own words, 'occasioned by the disorders of the present time', Watkins noted that '*Behemoth* was also concerned with these disorders'. The difference between the two works was that, 'whereas *Leviathan* is prescriptive, *Behemoth* is descriptive'.[141]

It would be difficult to carry a comparison like this much further. Often, *Behemoth* seems to be at disadvantage when compared to *Leviathan*. 'To approach "Behemoth" with expectations nourished by "Leviathan" will

---

136 M. M. Goldsmith, 'Introduction' to Frank Cass reprint of *Behemoth*, xiv. In his *Hobbes's Science of Politics* (New York: Columbia University Press, 1966), 232–41, Goldsmith gives a more nuanced picture. Ultimately, Hobbes explained the phenomena of history by reducing them to the categories of his own theory (ibid., 241), but that was true of all his works dealing with history. *Behemoth* stands out as his 'most elaborate explanation of Civil War'. (Ibid., 235.)

137 R. C. Richardson, *The Debate on the English Revolution* (London: Methuen, 1977), 21. Martinich, *Thomas Hobbes*, 115, gave some credence to the explanation that *Behemoth* was written 'to provide a case study that confirmed the political theory expressed in *The Elements of Law*, *De Cive* and *Leviathan*'. This comes close to reading *Behemoth* as a 'demonstration of the truth of Hobbism'. Michael G. Finlayson, *Historians, Puritanism, and the English Revolution: The Religious Factor in English Politics before and after the Interregnum* (Toronto: University of Toronto Press, 1983), 49.

138 Pierre Naville, *Thomas Hobbes* (Paris: Plon, 1988), 27.

139 Tom Sorell, *Hobbes* (London: Routledge & Kegan Paul, 1986), 127. But in the opening of this book Sorell wrote that, in *Behemoth*, Hobbes used his theory of the rights of sovereigns, formulated in earlier writings, to 'relate the "causes, pretensions, order, and artifice" of the events of 1640 to 1660', and characterized *Behemoth* as one of Hobbes's writings 'in which the principles of politics provided the main subtext'. Ibid., 1.

140 Carrive, 'Béhemoth et Léviathan', 14 ff.

141 J. W. N. Watkins, *Hobbes's System of Ideas: A Study in the Political Significance of Philosophical Theories* (London: Hutchinson University Library, 1965), 14–15.

bring disappointment', wrote Willms.¹⁴² 'Readers of *Behemoth* who are looking for further evidence to support the claims made in *Leviathan* will be disappointed', argued Vaughan.¹⁴³ The systematic form of *Leviathan*, even its sheer size and, of course, the frontispiece, have no counterpart in *Behemoth*. '*Leviathan* is Hobbes's philosophy in systematic form; *Behemoth* is his philosophy in pedagogic form', wrote Vaughan, in whose view the two books have a different purpose and cannot, strictly speaking, be compared.

Both works, however, engaged key political and political-philosophical issues. Watkins, characterizing the 'descriptive' *Behemoth*, noted that in *Behemoth* Hobbes gave a causal explanation of the 'disorders'¹⁴⁴ and showed that the English civil war was a result of divided authority, whereas divided authority was a product of ideological disputes.¹⁴⁵ Hobbes himself of course did not speak of 'ideological disputes'. He spoke of the power of opinion. '[T]he power of the mighty', he famously wrote in *Behemoth*, 'hath no foundation but in the opinion and belief of the people'.¹⁴⁶ As such, opinions were central to his analysis of the causes of the English civil war. The 'seed' of the war was 'certain opinions in divinity and politics', and what effectively led to the outbreak of war was the seduction of the people by ministers of the church and religious sectarians, and by 'democratical' orators, who succeeded to 'draw the people to their opinions'.¹⁴⁷ That some historians were sceptical of Hobbes's approach¹⁴⁸ is perhaps less surprising than the time it took for political theorists to pick up this issue.

---

142 Bernard Willms, *Die Antwort des Leviathan: Thomas Hobbes' politische Theorie* (Neuwied: Luchterhand, 1970), 32.
143 Vaughan, *'Behemoth' teaches 'Leviathan'*, 100.
144 In her discussion of the status of history in Hobbes's work, Carrive, 'Béhemoth et Léviathan', 12-13, underlined the importance of the causal explanation: it promoted history to the world of science, to the service of the 'science of just and unjust' (for which history as the record or relation of events did not qualify). See also Goldsmith, *Hobbes's Science of Politics*, 235 ff. But see J. G. A. Pocock, 'Thomas May and the Narrative of Civil War', in *Writing and Political Engagement in Seventeenth-Century England*, eds D. Hirst and R. Strier (Cambridge: Cambridge University Press, 1999), 114, that representing 'the true causes, originall and growth of them', of the civil war was already Thomas May's ambition in his *The History of the Parliament of England*.
145 Watkins, *Hobbes's System of Ideas*, 16.
146 *Behemoth*, 16.
147 *Behemoth*, [v], 23.
148 E.g., B. H. G. Wormald, *Clarendon: Politics, History and Religion 1640-1660* (Cambridge: Cambridge University Press, 1989), 223, writing that whereas Clarendon may have underestimated 'the part played by theoretical ideas in the course of English events, Hobbes must be charged with having exaggerated it. Hobbes had all the doctrinaire's respect for the ideas of other people. He rated highly what he regarded as erroneous notions as a cause of disruptions'. Wormald referred to *Behemoth*, 112, 114.

Tönnies in his *Critique of Public Opinion* cited Hobbes more than once and in particular pointed to the importance of Hobbes's dictum that 'the world is governed by opinion', but curiously enough did not refer to *Behemoth*.[149] Helmut Schelsky thus played a pioneering role in developing, or exploiting, this subject. In his dissertation, written 1938-40, in which he attempted an intellectual synthesis of his experiences from university seminars and as a Nazi student activist,[150] he identified Hobbes's view of the foundation of the power of the mighty in the opinion of the people as a crucial statement of Hobbes's political theory and, correspondingly, appreciated the importance of *Behemoth*. In his endeavor to elaborate a more activist interpretation of Hobbes than Carl Schmitt's, he drew the consequences of that insight. The right to leadership (*Führungsrecht*) of the consciousness and beliefs of the citizens, he argued, belonged to the unrenouncable rights and tasks of the sovereign. If the power is founded in the opinion of the subjects, then the power over the consciousness belongs to the power of the sovereign.[151] Schelsky's thesis was not published until 1981, in a small printing, and has never exercised much influence. A rare and clear case of such influence is Bernard Willms, who published one of his articles on *Behemoth* in the *Festchrift* to Schelsky.[152] Kraynak's studies of the importance of opinion and of doctrinal politics, however, which put *Behemoth* at the center of the study of Hobbes's political theory, appear to have been developed independently of Schelsky's early work.[153] A narrower understanding of the opinion, on which rests the 'power of the mighty', has been suggested by Samantha Frost: that opinion is the 'reputation or opinion' of the power of the sovereign 'in the general populace'.[154]

The remedy against the evils of divided sovereignty was obvious, and Hobbes never did tire of offering it. *Behemoth* was thus, 'each step on the

---

149 Tönnies, *Kritik der öffentlichen Meinung, 1922*, eds A. Deichsel, R. Fechner and R. Wassner, vol. 14 of *Ferdinand Tönnies Gesamtausgabe*, 128; cf. Tönnies, '[Formen der Öffentlichen Meinung]', in vol. 23, pt. 2 of *Ferdinand Tönnies Gesamtausgabe*, 203. Hobbes's citation is from *The Elements of Law* I. xi. 6. See Thomas Hobbes, *Human Nature and De Corpore Politico*, ed. J. C. A. Gaskin (Oxford: Oxford University Press, 1994), 72.
150 I am summarizing Schelsky's own retrospective decription from 1980. Helmut Schelsky, *Thomas Hobbes: Eine politische Lehre* (Berlin: Duncker & Humblot, 1981), 11.
151 Schelsky, *Thomas Hobbes*, 327, 426-7.
152 Willms, 'Systemüberwindung und Bürgerkrieg' (see n. 85).
153 Kraynak, 'Hobbes's *Behemoth*'; idem, *History and Modernity*, ch. 2. See also William R. Lund, 'Hobbes on Opinion, Private Judgement and Civil War', *History of Political Thought* 13 (1992), no. 1; Todd Butler, *Imagination and Politics in Seventeenth-Century England* (Aldershot: Ashgate, 2008), 170.
154 Samantha Frost, *Lessons from a Materialist Thinker: Hobbesian Reflections on Ethics and Politics* (Stanford: Stanford University Press, 2008), 157.

way, a plaidoyer for the absolute and undivided sovereignty'.[155] Since sovereignty has often been seen as the central question of Hobbes's political philosophy and since that question is the pivotal question of the discussion in *Behemoth*,[156] *Behemoth* qualifies as a work of political philosophy. Moreover, as Luc Borot has argued, *Behemoth* 'takes further the philosophical case for treating the sovereign as the only author of law and as the only legal authority'.[157]

In the historical struggles of the English civil war, the question of undivided sovereignty was, surely, for an Erastian like Hobbes, the question of the role and place of religion in civil life; that is, the question of ecclesiastical government and its relation to the civil government. Hobbes concern was to affirm and reaffirm the principle of the civil sovereign's authority over religious matters, the principle that 'the King is the head of the Church', so that by consequence obeying God meant obeying the 'King's laws and public edicts'.[158] Thus, as Shapin and Scheffer pointed out, in Hobbes's 'particular historical analysis of the Civil War just concluded', no one among those most responsible for the calamities had been 'more reprehensible than those ecclesiastics who claimed delegated power from God that bypassed the civil authority and those, whether ordained or not, who claimed private inspiration directly from the Deity'.[159] Hobbes's 'deep concern in *Behemoth* ... with the power of religion to yield political power' is indeed hard to miss.[160]

Among Hobbes's contemporaries, Anthony Wood, for example, wrote that *Behemoth*—which in his view contained 'many faults'—carried 'several things against religion, antient learning, Universities, &c.'.[161] (And

---

155 Carrive, 'Béhemoth et Léviathan', 31. Among the readers of Hobbes who were of this opinion was John Dewey, 'The Motivation of Hobbes's Political Philosophy', in *Thomas Hobbes in His Time*, eds R. Ross, H. W. Schneider and Th. Waldman (Minneapolis: University of Minnesota Press, 1974), 12.
156 J. F. Stephen, *Horae Sabbaticae*, 42, saw the whole book turning around the question of sovereignty.
157 Borot, 'History in Hobbes's Thought', 318.
158 *Behemoth*, 53, 58. Francis Campbell Hood, *The Divine Politics of Thomas Hobbes: An Interpretation of Leviathan* (Oxford: Clarendon Press, 1964), 22, referred to *Behemoth*, 58, as a summary of Hobbes's 'Christian political thought', written at about the same time as the other summary, in the last chapter of the Latin edition of *Leviathan*.
159 Steven Shapin and Simon Schaffer, *Leviathan and the Air-Pump: Hobbes, Boyle, and the Experimental Life* (Princeton, N. J.: Princeton University Press, 1985), 97, cf. 311, 325. For Hobbes's systematic rejection of 'private inspiration', see Kinch Hoekstra, 'Disarming the Prophets: Thomas Hobbes and Predictive Power', in *Nouve prospettive critiche sul* Leviatano, with a number of references to *Behemoth*.
160 Butler, *Imagination and Politics*, 169. See also Arnold A. Rogow, *Thomas Hobbes: Radical in the Service of Reaction* (New York: Norton, 1986), 211: Behemoth was 'in large part given over to religion and the usurpation by the popes and bishops of powers rightfully belonging to monarchs and other civil sovereigns'.
161 Anthony à Wood, *Athenae Oxonienses*, 2. col. 481; see also Bliss ed., 3. col. 1213.

Hobbes's chief criticism of universities was that they were seminaries of clericalism.) Among our contemporaries, Holmes spoke of the 'all-importance of religion in Hobbes's theory', which is in no other work of Hobbes 'displayed more clearly' than in *Behemoth*.[162] Collins, working on recovering 'the full political implications of *Behemoth*', maintains that it is 'essential' to understand *Behemoth* as 'at once a history of the civil war and a treatise on the nature of religious power'. The work gives both evidence on how the civil war heightened 'Hobbes's ecclesiological concerns' and 'establishes Hobbes's belief that the English Civil War was fundamentally a religious war fought in defence of Erastianism'. *Behemoth* was both an 'indictment of clerical dualism and a defence of the religious power of the temporal state'.[163]

V. Myth and politics: a cautionary tale

As Hobbes's 'mature understanding of political breakdown and the reestablishment of authority',[164] *Behemoth* is an eminently political work. But politics, for Hobbes, could not be reduced to rational communicative action. In *Behemoth*, Hobbes was preoccupied with 'the sources of human irrationality'as a shaping force of politics.[165] Another not exclusively rational dimension of the work, on which its later readers dwelt, is linked to the title. The title under which this work of Hobbes's has been circulating from the fourth unauthorized edition onward,[166] if not earlier, brings in—or provides an excuse to the interpreters for bringing in—the mythical dimension of politics. Nothing that Hobbes himself might have said about that title is preserved. Quite likely he had not said a thing. It is even possible that *Behemoth* was not the title he chose.[167]

Robertson, in his review of Tönnies's edition, wrote that 'most important gain of all', which he linked to the new edition, was that 'we now

---

162 Holmes, 'Introduction' to *Behemoth*, xlix.
163 Collins, *The Allegiance of Thomas Hobbes*, 82. See also A. P. Martinich, *Hobbes* (New York: Routledge, 2005), 22: Hobbes wrote *Behemoth* 'to press his political views that religion should be controlled by the sovereign and that the power and authority of the sovereign ought to be absolute'. See also Daniele Francesconi, 'The Languages of Historical Causation in David Hume's History of England', *Cromohs*, 6 (2001) URL: http://www.cromohs.unifi.it/6_2001/francesconi.html, 8: 'Hobbes recognised that the civil war had to be explained through the long-term problem of the conflict between ecclesiastical power and stately institutions, as well as the middle-term question of the growth of presbyterianism'.
164 Holmes, 'Political Psychology', 120.
165 Holmes, 'Political Psychology', 122; see also his 'Introduction' to *Behemoth*.
166 *Behemoth; or an Epitome of the Civil Wars of England, From 1640, to 1660.* By Thomas Hobs of Malmsbury (London, 1679). See Macdonald and Hargreaves, *Thomas Hobbes: A Bibliography*, no. 88.
167 For a brief discussion, see Vaughan, *'Behemoth' teaches 'Leviathan'*, 109–10. Jean Terrel, *Hobbes: vies d'un philosophe* (Rennes: Presses universitaires de Rennes, 2008), 177 n. 32, is an exception in stating unequivocally that Hobbes did not give this title to his work.

Introduction: The Ways of 'Behemoth'

learn the true title of the work with its special significance'. Robertson first referred to the title of Crooke's 1682 printing: 'Followed by the old sub-title, "The History of the Causes of the Civil Wars of England from 1640 to 1600", the name *Behemoth* seemed nothing more than a verbal fancy after the name *Leviathan*'. With Tönnies's discovery and printing of the St. John's College manuscript of *Behemoth*, believed to be the original, it was now possible to see that, as *Leviathan*

> was taken from the Book of Job to pictorially mark 'The Matter, Form and Power of a Commonwealth Ecclesiastical and Civil', so Hobbes went back to the same source for the name of the other monster to figure 'The Long Parliament' that had reared itself for so many years against the lawful government of this country.[168]

Robertson linked the name behemoth to a political phenomenon. That was not unprecedented but was still a novelty. John Whitehall, for example, did not take the title seriously. Behemoth, for him, was a figure 'for a Westminster-Stage'.[169] But Maseres, in the beginning of the century at the end of which Robertson published his review of *Behemoth*, connected the figure of behemoth to rebellion. He wrote that Hobbes gave his work

> the odd name of *Behemoth*, which signifies in Hebrew language an Elephant, seeming to think that the civil dissentions of such a numerous and powerful people, as the English nation, might be justly compared to the wild and formidable motions of that enormous animal when provoked.[170]

I am more inclined to link this image of a raging elephant to the British colonial imagination of the time than to the Hebrew or to biblical exegesis. In Hebrew, *behemôt* is intensive (feminine) plural of *behemâ* — 'beast', 'ox'; collective: 'beasts', 'cattle' — but in Job 40:15-24, the grammatical forms pertaining to behemoth are all masculine singular. Thus, the 'figure suggested is a singular being of awesome dimensions'.[171] And in biblical exegesis, the times when interpreters, eager to identify the biblical monster with an animal, used to suggest the elephant, were over when Bochart in 1663 published his *Hierozoicon* and argued that behemoth was the hippopotamus.[172]

James Fitzjames Stephen proved that a more accurate usage of Hebrew could still produce a captivating image. He wrote that the 'strange title was probably meant to show that, as the commonwealth is Levia-

---

168 Review of *The Elements of Law* and *Behemoth*, Mind 14 (1889), 433.
169 Whitehall, *Behemoth Arraign'd*, 3.
170 Maseres, 'Preface' to *Select Tracts*, 1. lxxviii.
171 B. F. Batto, 'Behemoth', in *Dictionary of Deities and Demons in the Bible (DDD)*, eds K. van der Toorn, B. Becking and P. W. van der Horst (Leiden: E. J. Brill, 1995), col. 315.
172 Samuel Bochart, *Hierozoicon, sive, bipertitum opus De animalibus Sacræ Scripturæ* (Londini, 1663), 2. col. 754.

than—the most wonderful work of God—so a rebellious assemblage is an aggregation of monsters'.[173] Tönnies, for his part, suggested that the title *Behemoth* 'explains the book as the counterpart to Leviathan: the state is one monster, the revolution the other'.[174] At the close of the nineteenth century, we thus get articulated the opposition between *Leviathan* and *Behemoth* (with which, as it is well known, Hobbes himself had toyed, but in a quite different sense),[175] in which *Leviathan* stands for commonwealth, the state or the legitimate sovereign, and *Behemoth* for civil discord, rebellion, or revolution.[176]

Such characterization of these two works can also be interpreted in a way which represents *Behemoth* as complementing *Leviathan*.[177] Most of the interpretations of *Behemoth-Leviathan* relation, however, insist on the opposition between the two monsters. Neither view has, strictly speaking, much to do with Hobbes. Hobbes's explicit references to the sources of his leviathan image—there are no references with regard to behemoth—are to the *Book of Job*, where behemoth and leviathan are related to God and to man, but do not stand in any direct relation to each other. Interpreting their textual proximity as complementary, is unwarranted, and as antagonistic, far-fetched. Hobbes's '*Behemoth against Leviathan*' suggestion to Bramhall might indicate that Hobbes was acquainted with other

---

173 J. F. Stephen, *Horae Sabbaticae*, 39. Nicastro, *Note*, 6, suggested that Stephen alluded to the plural of the Hebrew name behemoth. Borot, 'Introduction', 21, also saw the possibility of rapprochement between the Hebrew plural and the contemporary fear of the people as the many-headed monster. Braun, *Der sterbliche Gott*, 196 n. 14, wrote that Hobbes doubtlessly thought of behemoth as 'the mythical pluralistic counter-power to his total state'.
174 Tönnies, *Thomas Hobbes*, 61. (This passage is the same in all three editions of this work.)
175 Hobbes replied to Bishop Bramhall, who had intimated that 'two of our own Church' were 'answering' *Leviathan*, that they should not 'so mispend their time; but if they will needs do it, I can give them a fit Title for their Book, *Behemoth against Leviathan*'. What Hobbes objected to, here, was Bramhall's calling *Leviathan* '*Monstrum horrendum, informe, Ingens, qui lumen ademptum*'. Those words, Hobbes retorted, did not apply to *Leviathan*. Even if he allowed Bramhall 'the word *Monstrum*', none of the epithets would stick. The suggestion to use that title was made under the same condition. Hobbes, *The Questions Concerning Liberty, Necessity, And Chance. Clearly Stated and Debated Between Dr. Bramhall Bishop of Derry, And Thomas Hobbes of Malmesbury* (London, 1656), 20; see *EW* 5. 27. John Laird, *Hobbes* (London: E. Benn, [1934]; reprint New York: Russell & Russell, 1968), 36, was among the few who have questioned the fitness of the suggested title: 'One would naturally think that the Long Parliament was supposed to be a detestable monster, Hobbes's artificial man benign giant; but in Job xl.19, Behemoth was said to be "the chief of the ways of God."'
176 Schneider, 'Thomas Hobbes from *Behemoth* to *Leviathan*', 219, wrote that, in 1640, Hobbes was 'alarmed by the chaos in Great Britain [sic]', and that it was this 'war of all against all', to which he 'later gave the monstrous title of *Behemoth*'. Elsewhere, Schneider wrote that *Leviathan* and *Behemoth*, as titles of Hobbes's books, 'serve to give a religious tone to the subject matter'. Herbert W. Schneider, 'The Piety of Hobbes', in *Thomas Hobbes in His Time*, 85.
177 e.g., Herfried Münkler, *Thomas Hobbes* (Frankfirt/M.: Campus, 1993), 24–5, 58.

ancient literary sources, in which leviathan and behemoth appear. That is quite plausible but to date remains speculation.[178]

The speculation about the opposition between leviathan and behemoth took a vicious turn in Carl Schmitt. In his *Leviathan*, Schmitt construed a Jewish 'political myth' of the combat between leviathan and behemoth, which became a source of contamination of the study of Hobbes.[179] In his later work, Schmitt linked behemoth and leviathan to his construct of the universal historical opposition between the land and the sea.[180] Schmitt characterized Hobbes's *Behemoth* as 'a historical description of the Presbyterian and Puritan revolution of 1640-1660', and explained the title as follows: 'Behemoth is here, according to the title that is given no further explanation in the text of the book, a symbol for the anarchy, brought about by religious fanaticism and sectarianism, that during the Puritan revolution destroyed the English commonwealth'. Leviathan and behemoth related to each other as the state and revolution, and 'according to the formulation of an outstanding English Hobbes expert, C. E. Vaugham [*sic*], leviathan is "the only corrective" of behemoth. The state absolutism is, accordingly, the suppressor of a chaos that, in the core, that is, in individuals, is irrepressible'.[181]

Schmitt misread Vaughan, for whom leviathan as the 'corrective' of behemoth was a hypothetical argument of an imagined defender of Hobbes, which as an interpretation of Hobbes he deemed 'worth nothing'.[182] But Schmitt's account was nevertheless taken over by a number of Hobbes interpreters, from the respectfully polemical Schelsky to Willms (and beyond).[183] Willms was an Assistant Professor to Schelsky, was close to Carl Schmitt, and was politically active on the extreme right of German

---

178 The combat between leviathan and behemoth is a theme in Rabbinical Judaism. The most comprehensive discussion is K. William Whitney, *Two Strange Beasts: Leviathan and Behemoth in Second Temple and Early Rabbinic Judaism*, Harvard Semitic Monographs, 63 (Winona Lake, Indiana: Eisenbraus, 2006). Hobbes's contemporary antagonist John Wallis was more consistent with Hobbes's references to the *Book of Job* (where the monsters do not fight each other) than many a later day Hobbes interpreter. In one of his polemics against Hobbes, Wallis called Hobbes Leviathan and Hobbes's then supporter Stubbe, Behemoth. 'I have done now with Behemoth, and Leviathan too'. John Wallis, *Hobbiani Puncti Dispvnctio. Or The Vdoing of Mr Hobs's Points; In Answer to M. Hobs's Stigmai. Id est, Stigmata Hobbii* (London, 1657), 30; cf. Metzger, *Thomas Hobbes und die Englische Revolution*, 205-5; and Malcolm's note in *The Correspondence of Thomas Hobbes*, 2. 899 ff, especially 900.
179 Carl Schmitt, *Der Leviathan in der Staatslehre des Thomas Hobbes: Sinn und Fehlschlag eines politischen Symbols* (Hamburg: Hanseatische Verlagsanstalt, 1938), especially 11, 16-18. For a more detailed discussion, see Tomaž Mastnak, 'Schmitt's Behemoth', *Critical Review of Social and Political Philosophy* 13 (2010), no. 2.
180 Carl Schmitt, *Land und Meer: Eine weltgeschichtliche Betrachtung* (Leipzig: Philipp Reclam jun., 1942), 9-10. See also Bolaffi, *Il crepuscolo*, ch. 4; Ruschi, 'Leviathan e Behemoth'.
181 Schmitt, *Der Leviathan*, 33-4.
182 C. E. Vaughan, *Studies in the History of Political Philosophy before and after Rousseau, Volume I: From Hobbes to Hume* (Manchester: Manchester University Press, 1939), 53-4.
183 Schelsky, *Thomas Hobbes*, 8, 427 ff.

politics. His essays on *Behemoth* attacked head on contemporary leftist activism.[184] One can thus trace continuity in intellectually conservative and politically right-wing interpretations of *Behemoth*. However, on a conceptually more or less identical basis, Franz Neumann twisted and turned Schmittian interpretation in the politically opposite direction.

That direction had actually had a respectable tradition in Germany, which Schmitt, Ritterbusch and the like interrupted. On the biographical level, Julius Lips, *Behemoth*'s translator into German, was in 1933 the only 'Aryan' ethnologist in Germany who refused to bow to the Nazis and soon had to flee the country.[185] Tönnies was a 'Kathedersozialist', whom the Nazis stripped of his professorship in 1933, three years before his death. As an old man, he was seen waving his walking stick at the Nazis. On the theoretical level, Karl Korsch looked to Hobbes's *Behemoth* for inspiration and help with analyzing the events and developments of the 1920s and 1930s, marked by the 'reversal of revolutionary transformation' of European society. In attempting to solve that 'bewildering problem', Korsch and his addressees on the radical left 'may expect with Hobbes (when in his *Behemoth* he traced the course of the English revolution and counter-revolution of 1640–1660) that we too, looking back from the Devil's Mountain upon the historical development of the last twenty years, shall have "a prospect of all kinds of injustice, and all kinds of folly, that the world could afford, and how they were produced by their dams hypocrisy and self-conceit, where of then one is double iniquity and the other double folly"'. On Hobbes's model, they were to get '"full insight" into the actions which then took place and into "their causes, pretensions, justice, order, artifice and event"'.[186]

In 1942, Neumann published his *Behemoth*.[187] The book was in many ways a response to Schmitt's *Leviathan*. In the 'Note on the Name Behemoth', prefacing the 'Preface', Neumann first gave a terse summary of the background and meaning of the mythical figures leviathan and behe-

---

184 Willms, 'Staatsräson'; idem, 'Systemüberwindung und Bürgerkrieg'.
185 See 'Preface' to Julius Ernst Lips, *The Savage Hits Back*, with an introduction by B. Malinowski, trans. V. Benson (New Hyde Park, N.Y.: University Books [1966]). Judging by Eva Lips, *Zwischen Lehrstuhl und Indianerzelt: Aus dem Leben und Werk von Julius Lips* (Berlin: Rütten & Loening, 1965), Hobbes studies were not Lips's main preoccupation. His book on Hobbes is mentioned ibid., 25–6.
186 Karl Korsch, 'State and Counter-Revolution', *The Modern Quarterly* 11 (1939), no. 2, 67. The citations within citations are from Hobbes, *Behemoth*, 1 (with a few inexactitudes). There are some differences between the English and German version of the text. See also Korsch, 'Staat und Konterrevolution', in Karl Korsch, *Politische Texte*, eds E. Gerlach and J. Seifert (Frankfurt/M: Europäische Verlagsanstalt, 1974), 180–94.
187 Franz Neumann, *Behemoth: The Structure and Practice of National Socialism* (Toronto, New York: Oxford University Press 1942); in the same year, the book was published in London by V. Gollancz. An expanded 2nd edn was published by Oxford University Press in 1944. I cite reprint of the 2nd edn (New York: Harper & Row, 1966).

moth, which tacitly refuted Schmitt's tendentious constructs on the same subject. Then Neumann turned to Hobbes, noting that it was Hobbes who had made 'both the leviathan and the behemoth popular'. In his *Leviathan*, Neumann continued, Hobbes had analyzed the state, which he characterized as 'a political system of coercion in which vestiges of law and of individual rights are still preserved'. In *Behemoth*, Hobbes depicted 'a non-state, a chaos, a situation of lawlessness, disorder and anarchy'.[188] Then came the decisive turn: since National Socialism was a social formation in which the ruling groups controlled the rest of the population 'directly, without the mediation of that rational though coercive apparatus hitherto known as the state', that is, since National Socialism was not a state but, rather, 'a non-state, a chaos, a rule of lawlessness and anarchy, which has "swallowed" the rights and dignity of man', Neumann called it behemoth.[189]

Neumann's *Behemoth* was an immensely popular book. As such, it has spread wide the name behemoth—not in that metaphorical sense in which the word is often used to designate anything from big American cars to big countries, but in a pointedly political sense and with reference to Hobbes. Important here is that, while Neumann's book has not directly contributed to the study of Hobbes, it unequivocally posited Hobbes, and in particular his *Behemoth*, as of direct relevance for the study of our contemporary political phenomena, especially those that are not 'amenable to rational ... analysis'.[190] *Behemoth* was thus definitively established as a cautionary tale, which it had always, at least dimly, been held to be. This is how it is still read today: as a 'cautionary tale of civil disintegration and of the power of opinion, of the combustible nature of error conjoined with ambition and fear',[191] or as 'the history of the ultimate dissolution'.[192]

---

188 Neumann, *Behemoth*, xii.
189 Neumann, *Behemoth*, xii, 459–70.
190 Duncan Kelly, 'Rethinking Franz Neumann's Route to *Behemoth*', *History of Political Thought* 23 (2002), no. 3, 490, points this out as the 'fundamental problem' with which Neumann grappled. That is why it is 'perhaps unsurprising' that Neumann (directly quoting Hobbes's *Behemoth*) 'should have chosen to call his text, with its attendant theological and apocalyptic connotations, *Behemoth*'.
191 Conal Condren, *Thomas Hobbes* (New York: Twayne Publishers, 2000), 99. Finlayson, *Historians*, 51, also described *Behemoth* as a 'cautionary tale'.
192 Dubos, 'Lectures de *Béhémoth*', 149. In the context of the English civil war, that dissolution was the 'dissolution of government'. Pocock has credited Thomas May with taking that phrase 'from parliamentary resolutions' and helping to establish it 'as a key term in the seventeenth-century political argument and analysis'. J. G. A. Pocock, 'Medieval Kings at the Court of Charles I: Thomas May's Verse Histories', in *Perspectives on Early Modern and Modern Intellectual History: Essays in Honor of Nancy S. Struever*, eds J. Marino and M. W. Schlitt (Rochester, New York: University of Rochester Press, 2000), 442; see also idem, 'Thomas May and the Narrative of Civil War', 131. Hobbes himself wrote of the 'Dissolution of a Common-wealth' or 'civitatis dissolutio' in his systematic political treatises, and made the

VI. The present volume

The contributions in this volume do not belong to a particular school of thought; their authors are not committed to a specific common methodology nor do they share a political cause. Judging by their contributions, however, they all consider Hobbes's *Behemoth* to be a work worth studying. Their decision to contribute to this volume can be understood as stating that there is still much that can and needs to be said about this particular work of Hobbes's, and that there is much as well that this work can tell us about Hobbes's other writings and his life, about his views of and attitudes to contemporary events and developments and, perhaps, about his political allegiance(s). The history of the reception of *Behemoth* is an element in the history of Western political thought, which can throw light on that history. Our own reception of *Behemoth* is both an element in our conversation with, and shaping of, the past and also an element in how the past is informing our efforts to make sense of the world we live in.

Some of the contributors to this volume have written on *Behemoth* before; it is interesting to see how their present contributions relate to what they said before. But all of the contributors relate in one way or another to what has already been said about Hobbes and his *Behemoth* — to the history of the debates, or lack of debates, which I have outlined. As such, I believe, this volume takes these debates further. In this final portion of the introduction, I want to briefly present the chapters to follow.

Noel Malcolm has discovered a previously unknown Latin translation of *Behemoth*, the work of German scholar Adam Ebert, who taught law at the University of Frankfurt an der Oder. Completed in 1708, the translation was deposited in the King of Prussia's library and has never been published. Ebert was interested in 'reason of state' and in Tacitist theory of political action and was, as such, fascinated with Cromwell. Testifying to that fascination was the title he gave to his translation of Hobbes: *De Rebus gestis Olivarij Cromwellj Protectoris sive Historia Bellorum Civilium Angliae ab Anno 1640 usq[ue] ad Annum 1660*, that is, *On the Deeds of the Protector Oliver Cromwell*, which presented *Behemoth* as a celebration of Cromwell's political skills. Ebert was a late representative of the Tacitist tradition, and his reading of Hobbes responded to some elements genuinely present in Hobbes's political thought. In Malcolm's understanding,

---

dissolution of the state the subject of *Behemoth*. See also Onofrio Nicastro, 'Le vocabulaire de la dissolution de l'État', in *Hobbes et son vocabulaire: Études de lexicographie philosophiqu*e, ed. Y.Ch. Zarka (Paris: Vrin, 1992). For Laurie M. Johnson, *Thucydides, Hobbes, and the Interpretation of Realism* (DeKalb: Northern Illinois University Press, 1993), 11, Hobbes's account of the English civil wars in *Behemoth* depicts 'all the evils of the natural condition of mankind'.

however, Hobbes went beyond Tacitism to reach a very different view of politics and government.

Paul Seaward asks a very basic question: What is the point of *Behemoth*? That is a difficult question because *Behemoth*, as Seaward writes, is perhaps the oddest and most obscure of Hobbes's major works. The oddity and the lack of clarity can partly be explained by *Behemoth*'s difficult publishing history and by its ambiguous title. Part of the explanation lies in the form in which the work is written. The dialogue form is ill suited for narrating historical events. In addition to that, the narrative, for which Hobbes borrowed heavily from his sources—Heath's *Chronicle* and Husbands's collection of civil war documents—is interspersed with ironic commentary, often directly in reaction to the sources themselves, and intertwined with summaries of the views Hobbes expounded in other works (particularly in the *Leviathan*). A careful reading shows that some of the most significant parts of *Behemoth* constitute a shrewd and provocative assault on the central claims of the Restoration Church of England to a close alliance with the monarchy of Charles II, coupled with a recommendation that the universities, controlled by the clergy, should be radically reformed. Hobbes, it appears, wanted to demonstrate that the Anglican clergy were essentially as untrustworthy as all other clergy, Roman or Presbyterian.

Two other contributors, Aloysius Martinich and Johann Sommerville, take a close look at how Hobbes in *Behemoth* dealt with organized religion and its role in the civil war. They both start with Hobbes's blaming of the English civil war, in the opening pages of *Behemoth*, on ambitious clerics and their seditious teachings, especially Presbyterians. Sommerville focuses on what Hobbes said against Catholic and Presbyterian theories of church-state relations. He does so through taking issue with those interpreters, who had argued that Hobbes supported the Independents and that traces of that support are still visible in *Behemoth*, where Hobbes treats Independency and Oliver Cromwell with notable mildness. Sommerville holds this interpretation unsustainable. *Behemoth* sides strongly with the royalist cause in the wars, condemning those who fought against the king as traitors. In both *Leviathan* and in *Behemoth*, Hobbes displays little sympathy with the Independents or the Rump parliament. In both books he maintains many distinctively royalist views on politics and church-state relations, though he breaks with most royalists by attacking divine right episcopacy.

Martinich's question is whether Hobbes's accusations of Presbyterians were accurate. In order to answer the question, he tries to identify whom Hobbes is talking about when he uses the term 'Presbyterian' for a minister. The religious Presbyterians emerged after fighting had broken out between royalist and parliamentary forces and after the opening of the Westminster Assembly of Divines in 1643. In the early 1640s, Martinich emphasizes, there was no substantial English Presbyterianism. He argues that Hobbes applied the term to puritan ministers, notably some closely connected with members of Parliament. The puritans opposed the Laudian church and the concept of *jure divino* episcopacy but many would have accepted a form of episcopacy. Sermons by puritan ministers, often co-ordinated with MPs, contributed to the political instability of 1640 and after. However, Hobbes's use of 'Presbyterian' to refer to puritans of the early 1640s was misleading, and not innocent. Hobbes projected onto them the militant attitudes of the mid 1640s, and coupled them with political opponents of the king. But, notwithstanding his inaccuracies and exaggerations, Hobbes was right to identify actions by disgruntled clergy as one of the causes of the civil war.

A group of chapters engages with issues of Hobbesian political philosophy in *Behemoth* and with *Behemoth* in the broader context of Hobbes's political philosophy. Gabriella Slomp enters the debate on whether, and to what extent, Hobbes's account of human motivation in *Leviathan* provides an insight into the narrative of *Behemoth*. She specifically examines the role that the three passions that Hobbes singled out in Chapter 13 of *Leviathan* as leading to conflict — that is, desire of gain, fear for safety, and ambition — play in his own account of the Civil War. She argues, first, that although Hobbes resorts to two of the greatest motivational forces described in *Leviathan*, 'ambition' and 'greed', to explain the sources and dynamics of the English civil war, in *Behemoth* he adds the crucial proviso that these passions alone, without widespread ignorance about the meaning and value of civil obedience, would have found 'no hands'. Her second point is that, in the transition from *Leviathan* to *Behemoth*, we witness a major change regarding the third greatest human motivation, fear. In his late work, Hobbes renounces the idea that fear is the passion to be 'reckoned upon'.

Patricia Springborg makes a contribution to the debate on Hobbes's 'science of *just* and *unjust*'. She advances a set of arguments. First, that we must take seriously Hobbes's claim in *Behemoth* that 'the science of *just* and *unjust*' is a demonstrable science, accessible to those of even the meanest capacity. Second, that *Leviathan* is the work in which this science, intended as a serious project in civic education, is set out. Third, that Hobbes is prepared to accept, like Plato and Aristotle, 'giving to each his own' as a preliminary definition of justice, from which, however, he draws some very un-Aristotelian conclusions. Fourth, that though in Hobbes's theory '*just* and *unjust*' are equivalent to 'lawful and unlawful', this is far from being a simple statement of legal positivism, but rather the conclusion of a practical syllogism. Fifth, that the impediments to this demonstrable science of justice being universally accepted are twofold. Hobbes explained them in terms of religion and the role of preachers and educators produced by the universities, on the one hand, and by the activity of 'democratical gentlemen' and classical republicans dominating parliament, on the other. Sixth, that Hobbes's account of the transition from *jus* to *lex*, specified in terms of a transition from the state of nature to that of civil society, although Epicurean in origin, is much closer to a conventional civil law position.

The question of civic education is taken up by Geoffrey Vaughan. He approaches that question through clarifying the function of *Behemoth*'s dialogue form. He argues that it is crucial to understand that, casting *Behemoth* as a dialogue, Hobbes is addressing two audiences. There is the immediate audience within the dialogue, that is, the younger interlocutor. He is the audience of the history of the English civil war as it is presented to him; he is the audience of the narrative. But there is also the audience of the dialogue as a whole, the audience of the meta-narrative. Once we understand this twofold structure we can begin to see that *Behemoth* is Hobbes's example of how to educate people in their duties through the use of history. Thus, *Behemoth* is not Hobbes's history of the war, nor is it an attempt to understand the war through the prism of Hobbesian theory. Instead, it is an education for the reader in how to make his or her interlocutors into good subjects.

Michael Soubbotnik, too, opens his contribution with a reflection on the dialogue that takes place in Hobbes's *Behemoth*. The two interlocutors, placed on the Devil's Mountain, do not get involved in a dialogue that leads to conversion. Instead, in their unequal experience and knowledge, they are driven by the shared desire to understand the spectacle of twenty years of ferocious discord and its causes, that prospect 'of all kinds of injustice, and of all kinds of folly', that opens from the Devil's Mountain. Their dialogue is a historical and political inquiry, which is driven by the passion of curiosity. That passion is the opposite of cupidity, which had led the proponents of vacuous opinions to sedition and civil war. Hobbes's analysis in *Behemoth*, staged by his two obedient and critical *personae dramatis*, challenges a whole society's discursive system in the name of political truth. That political truth is founded in the pragmatics of civil laws, which are both commands and true ethical statements.

Democracy is the focal point of another set of chapters. In my own contribution I argue that the question of democracy is a central, if neglected, question in *Behemoth*. Hobbes's coupling of religious malcontents and parliamentarian opposition to the king might be questioned on grounds of historical accuracy, but his argument that both religious and secular forces opposed to the king during the English civil war were striving to establish democracy, is clear and needs to be taken seriously as a theoretical argument. Hobbes did not work with a definition of democracy but rather, in the course of his argument, produced a number of equivalences and oppositions that determine the reader's understanding of democracy as an explosive mixture of Greco-Roman political sentiments and ideas, and religious lust for domination. Whereas in his earlier works, Hobbes discussed democracy mainly as a form of government, in *Behemoth* democracy, inseparable from religion, becomes a force destructive of government, a godly practice of anti-governmentality.

Ingrid Creppell examines *Behemoth* as an extended description of and reaction to the dynamism, both positive and negative, of new conditions of democracy. She sees Hobbes as responding not just to disorder *per se*, but to disorder resulting from a democratizing world and the demands of mobilized populations. On one level, Hobbes attacks democracy as a realm of elite competition that destroys a public good. On another level, however, he recognizes the necessity of constructing political principles as responsive to a politicized people and accepts the relevance of the people's judgment. Correspondingly, in his history of the English civil war, Hobbes emphasizes the ideological contention over ideas as a primary political force. That recognition has important implications for how the king must persuade the people to obey him and for how Hobbes's own positive political philosophy might be made a source of motivation for people.

William Lund argues, perhaps with a hint of irony, that Hobbes's *Behemoth* provides a vivid illustration of the historical consequences of ignoring his earlier philosophical critiques of efforts to limit or divide public authority. Hobbes's history of the English civil war is a warning against extreme claims for exempting individuals or groups from general laws. But Lund finds Hobbes's prescriptions ultimately unacceptable because they are insufficiently liberal. He argues that, while Hobbes points toward liberalism by undermining the teleological justifications of classical republican and natural law politics, he goes on to deny core liberal ideals. Hobbes's rejection of commitments to individual dignity, the acceptance of diversity, and democracy reflect his meta-ethical voluntarism, his extreme determinism, and his portrait of citizens as pure subjects. Lund's conclusion is that Hobbes ends up defending an opaque and absolute sovereign authority, which must be rejected in confronting our present circumstances.

A clear reference to our current circumstances is made in Tom Sorell's contribution. Sorell refers to an influential contemporary debate on sovereignty revolving around Carl Schmitt's pronouncements on emergency, and to the emergency proclaimed in the United States in the aftermath of attacks on 11 September 2001. Sorell considers how Schmitt's theory applies to that emergency. This consideration is of interest for our understanding of Hobbes because Schmitt reads Hobbes as a philosopher who thinks that politics is a response to emergency, and adapts what he takes to be Hobbesian ideas to give a politics of emergency of his own, one that was supposed to have particular relevance to the upheavals of the Weimar Republic. Sorell answers the question, which he initially poses with a reference to *Behemoth*, to what extent do Hobbes's political ideas lend themselves to a general theory of civil emergency, indirectly. He claims that Schmitt's theory, when applied, has considerable shortcomings. But, he concludes, those shortcomings are not always inherited from Hobbes.

Robert Kraynak brings in a civilizational dimension. In his understanding, Hobbes's political science rests on the historical claim that civilization is inherently fragile and prone to degenerate into civil war. Since that claim is not systematically proven in Hobbes's political treatises, it must be reconstructed from his extensive set of historical writings, including *Behemoth*. Through a careful examination of these writings, Kraynak shows that Hobbes has a coherent theory of history, which traces the evolution of man from barbarism to civilization and identifies the weakness of civilization as its tendency to produce doctrinal warfare. Having laid out this historical critique, Kraynak argues that Hobbes is an optimist in believing that the doctrinal wars of civilization can be overcome by a process of enlightenment that would end man's irrational behavior and establish 'immortal peace'. In conclusion, Kraynak indicates that a more pessimistic view of history and human nature than Hobbes's might be more accurate.

Noel Malcolm

'Behemoth latinus'
Adam Ebert, Tacitism, and Hobbes

In the Staatsbibliothek, Berlin, there is a little-noticed manuscript entitled

> Thomas Hobbes De Rebus gestis Olivarij Cromvellj Protectoris sive Historia Bellorum Civilium Angliae ab Anno 1640 usq[ue] ad Annum 1660. Linguâ Anglicâ in Latinam Francofurti ad Oderam translata A[nn]o 1708.
>
> (Thomas Hobbes, On the Actions of the Protector Oliver Cromwell, or, The History of the Civil Wars of England, from the year 1640 to the year 1660. Translated from the English language into Latin at Frankfurt an der Oder, in the year 1708.)

The translation is preceded by a flowery dedication to King Friedrich I of Prussia by the translator, who signs it (in his own hand, as opposed to the scribal hands of the manuscript itself) 'Devotissimus subditus Adamus Ebertus' ('your most devoted subject Adam Ebert'); a note at the end of the translation records that it was completed by Ebert on 28 June 1708.[1] This is clearly the original manuscript which Ebert gave to the king; it is a fair copy (in two scribal hands), on folio paper, handsomely bound. And, so far as one can tell, the manuscript has remained ever since in the Royal Library and the Staatsbibliothek, its modern successor.[2]

As this translation of *Behemoth* was never published, and does not seem to have been cited by any subsequent author in print, its importance must appear to be extremely slight. The translator, Adam Ebert, is easily identifiable as the scholar of that name who was a law professor at the University of Frankfurt an der Oder for many years until his death in 1735; Ebert

---

[1] Staatsbibliothek, Berlin [hereafter: 'SBB'] MS Lat. 2o 129, fos. 1r (title), 2v–6r (dedication), 279v (final note). I am very grateful to the staff of the Manuscripts Department of the Staatsbibliothek for their help during my visits there.
[2] On fo. 1r there is an early stamp in red ink: 'Ex Biblioth. Regia Berolinensi' ('from the Royal Library, Berlin').

receives brief mentions in biographical dictionaries, but remains a very little-known figure, whose reputation as an academic and littérateur has faded almost to extinction.[3] It would seem, then, that this strangely titled translation of Hobbes's work is little more than a curiosity: the product of an obscure individual's intellectual whim (and, no doubt, personal desire for royal favour), it appears to have been the object of a more or less private transaction, passing from the translator's hands to those of the king's librarian.

However, while this *Behemoth* translation may have had little or no importance—in the sense of influence on the thinking of others—it does have some significance: it can tell us some small but significant things about how Hobbes could be interpreted and appreciated in the intellectual world of late seventeenth-century and early eighteenth-century Germany. The presentation of the manuscript to the Royal Library also deserves further consideration, for this was not simply a way of consigning it either to the purely personal use of the king, or to oblivion; rather, it was a carefully calibrated form of quasi-publication. And as for the translator, Adam Ebert, the story of his life also merits more detailed investigation—not least because of the hitherto unknown fact that he had previously made the acquaintance of Hobbes in England.

II

First, however, the translation itself. Ebert was evidently working not from a manuscript but from a printed edition of the text: his title page reproduces the quotations (one from Lucretius, four from Horace) found on the title pages of most of the 1679 editions. He also reproduced the erratic page-numbering of the original; this shows that he was working from a copy of one of the 1679 duodecimo editions.[4] Ebert was an attentive reader of the text, and in three places he noted that the assignment of material to the speakers 'A' and 'B' had gone awry in the original: two of these he corrected, but one was marked with a marginal note which stated 'Here again there is a confusion of the letters representing the speakers,

---

3   See, for example, R. von Liliencron *et al.*, eds., *Allgemeine deutsche Biographie*, 56 vols (Leipzig, 1875–1912), v. 585.

4   The pagination (286 pp., with some major anomalies, including the omission of 169–214) matches that of items 87 (the self-styled 'Second Edition' of 1679) and 87a (a different issue of 87, also dated 1679) in H. Macdonald and M. Hargreaves, *Thomas Hobbes: A Bibliography* (London: The Bibliographical Society, 1952), pp. 65–66. Item 88 (also duodecimo, and also dated 1679) has a different pagination, extending to 214, not 286. Item 89 (dated 1680), which has the same pagination as item 87 and appears to be another issue of it, can be excluded: it lacks three of the quotations from Horace given on the title pages of 87 and 87a, which are reproduced by Ebert.

but it has been allowed to remain, for fear that there may be a hidden secret.'[5] Another sign of the care he took is the substantial index added to the manuscript.[6] Also added are occasional marginal notes, drawing the reader's attention to key points in the argument: for example, 'Religion is a virtue' (against 'A's' statement that 'I have placed religion amongst the virtues'), or 'Hobbes does not recognize passive obedience' (against 'A's' declaration that 'Every law is a command *to do* or *to forbear*: neither of these is fulfilled by suffering').[7] Several of these marginalia reflect the special interest in Cromwell expressed in Ebert's title: thus we have 'Why Cromwell refrained from taking the title "King"'; 'Cromwell's origins'; 'Cromwell the victor here' (against the account of the Battle of Marston Moor); 'Cromwell's first trick' (with an additional note, in Ebert's hand: 'Cromwell holds Parliament in his pocket'); 'How Cromwell arranges the murder of the King'; and 'An example of Cromwell's cunning'.[8] Here and there, important passages — for example, Hobbes's comment on the Battle of Naseby and its effects on the king's fortunes ('for by the loss of one great battle, he lost all he had formerly gotten, and at length his life') — are also given special emphasis by single or double underlinings, in red ink.[9]

Some of the other marginalia reproduce phrases from the English: 'by Way of Bargain', 'but bought them off', 'a Posture of defence', and (in Ebert's hand) 'by way of adventure', and 'Vice admiral'. These seem to indicate some uncertainty about the translations of those phrases offered in the text, which do vary in adequacy but are in no case seriously wrong.[10] From time to time, English words are also given alongside their

---

5   SBB, MS Lat. 2o 129, fo. 79v ('Hic iterum confusio Literarum colloquentium, sed tolerata metu latentis arcani'). The passage is on page 56 of T. Hobbes, *Behemoth, Or, The Long Parliament*, ed. F. Tönnies (London: Simpkin, Marshall, and Co., 1889) [hereafter: 'Tönnies edn'], beginning 'Why then were they not in all points for the King's power ... ', where it is correctly assigned to 'B'; in the 1679 edition used by Ebert (76), the preceding speech by 'A' has been merged with the one before it, by 'B', so that 'B' has two speeches in succession. The other two passages are SBB MS Lat. 2o 129, fos. 20v (Tönnies edn, 8, beginning 'But for those that die excommunicate in the Church of England ... ', correctly assigned there to 'B'; in the 1679 edition (10–11) 'A's' reply to 'B's' question is merged with the question, so that 'B' has two speeches in succession), and 162v (Tönnies edn, p. 126, beginning 'That is to say, by making poor people ... ', correctly assigned there to 'A'; in the 1679 edition, 1302 (sig. I5v) it is assigned to 'B').

6   SBB, MS Lat. 2o 129, fos. 280–5.

7   Ibid., fos. 68v, 73v (Tönnies edn, 46, 50).

8   SBB, MS Lat. 2o 129, fos. 140r ('Cur Cromvellus Regis titulo abstinuerit'), 156v ('Cromvelli primordia'), 167r ('Cromvellus hic victor'), 179r ('Primum Cromvelli artificium'; 'Cromwellus Parliamentum in sacculo tenet'), 199v ('Quomodo Cromvellus Regis caedem machinatur'), 214v ('Exemplum Calliditatis Cromvellianae') (Tönnies edn, 109, 122, 129, 138, 151, 160–1).

9   SBB, MS Lat. 2o 129, fo. 170r ('eventu quippe unius proelii sinistri cuncta perdentis tandemq[ue] et vitam') (Tönnies edn, 131–2).

10   SBB, MS Lat. 2o 129, fos. 52v ('per modum pacti'), 96r ('sed pretio eadem redemit', which fails to convey the sense of buying off), 104v ('*Statum Defensionis*', which fails to convey the sense of

translations in the text: for example, 'ex milite *provinciali* (*Train band*)', '*Rectum* (Righteousness) praescribi crebrò in Ecclesiâ audivi', and 'Civibus et istis Equitibus, qui *Knights* appellantur'.[11] Generally, Ebert's grasp of the English is good; there are some puzzling errors which may arise merely from hasty mis-reading (such as the translation of 'by some law' as '*solenni Lege*', 'by a solemn law'), and some small omissions which may have been the fault of the copyist, not the translator, but these are few and far between.[12] Ebert's occasional expansions of the sense are usually helpful, showing that he has been following the argument intelligently (for example, his translation of 'from the Emperor's consent' as 'ex tacito Imperatoris consensu').[13] And although Ebert's own Latin style, as displayed in his dedicatory epistle to the King of Prussia, was elaborate to the point of affectation, his rendering of Hobbes's English is reasonably straightforward — occasionally cumbersome, but never obfuscatory.[14] Nor does he intrude his own opinions on the text, except in one particular — and quite minor — instance. At one point, 'A' criticizes 'those princes that with preferment are forced to buy the obedience of their subjects', and offers an ironic interpretation of the story of Hercules and the Hydra: 'For Hercules at first did not cut off those heads, but bought them off; and afterwards, when he saw it did him no good, then he cut them off, and got the victory'. Ebert, apparently not recognizing the sardonic humour of this remark, adds a marginal comment: 'Here Hobbes goes against the meaning and the truth of the pagan fables, which do in fact teach something different'.[15] Otherwise, however, this is a sympathetic and faithful presentation of Hobbes's narrative in Latin, which could and should have

---

'posture'), 127v ('per mod[um] casus'), 236r ('vicarius Praetor') (Tönnies edn, 32, 72, 79, 99, 175).
11 SBB, MS Lat. 2o 129, fos. 11r (where the 1679 edition has 'Train'd-bands'), 86r, 93v (Tönnies edn, 2 (which has 'trained soldiers'), 63, 70).
12 SBB, MS Lat. 2o 129, fo. 21v (Tönnies edn, 9). Some omissions are ascribable not to the copyist but to the 1679 edition, e.g. fo. 112r: 'by the imprisonment of the Archbishop of Canterbury, and of Judge Bartlet, and the impeachment of other bishops and judges' (Tönnies edn, 85) is given as 'Archi-Episcopo autem Cantuariensi et judicibus in carcerem consectis', which correctly translates the truncated version in the 1679 edition (1161 (sig. F11v)). Much more puzzling is the translation of 'secular and ... regular priests' (Tönnies edn, 14) as 'sacerdotes eorumq[ue] amicos' (fos. 27v–28r), which has no warrant in the 1679 edition.
13 SBB, MS Lat. 2o 129, fo. 24r (Tönnies edn, 11).
14 One of the worst examples of cumbersomeness is his version of the opening phrase, 'If in time, as in place, there were degrees of high and low ...' as 'Siquidem tempora alia majoria alia minora aestimari merentur, quemadmodum spatiis locorum discrimen ejusmodi convenire videmus ...' (fo. 10r); the quality of the translation does improve thereafter.
15 Tönnies edn, 72; SBB, MS Lat. 2o 129, fo. 96r ('Hobbes hic sensui et veritati repugnat fabulis Ethnicis quippe aliud docentibus').

reached a wider European audience through the medium of print. Why, then, was it merely deposited in the King of Prussia's library?

III

Ebert's translation of Hobbes was not the only work of its kind to be passed by him to the Royal librarian. Between 1695 and 1725 he presented a total of twenty such manuscript volumes, consisting of his own translations (into Latin, from Spanish, English, French and Italian) of a variety of works, mostly historical or political.[16] The first of these was a version of one part of the biography of Charles V by Prudencio de Sandoval; four subsequent volumes (the last of them dated 1701) contained further extracts from Sandoval's work.[17] These were followed by an 'epitome' of Bayle's *Dictionnaire* (in 1702); Edward Herbert's *The Life and Raigne of King Henry the Eighth* (1706); a little-known work on the 'arcana' of Ottoman rule by Antonio Geropoldi, the *Bilancia historico-politica dell'impero ottomano* (1707); and then Hobbes's *Behemoth* (1708).[18] Four years later Ebert presented his translation of Luis de Cabrera de Cordova's life of Philip II, in four manuscript volumes; this was followed in 1717 by a large volume containing the principal works of Baltasar Gracián.[19] Three years after that, he produced a three-volume translation of d'Herbelot's *Bibliothèque orientale*, a ground-breaking encyclopaedia of Arabic and oriental scholarship; in 1722 he contributed a version of some of the works of the abbé de Brantôme; in 1723 a strange coupling of the life of Christopher Columbus by his son, and Gracián's treatise on the Eucharist; and finally, in 1725, another composite volume, containing a version of the oriental

---

16 See the listing in V. Rose, *Verzeichniss der lateinischen Handschriften der Königlichen Bibliothek zu Berlin*, 3 vols (Berlin: A. Asher & Co., 1893-1919), ii. 1406-10 (SBB, MSS Lat. 2o 101-5, 117, 120-30, 132, 177, and MS Theol. 2o 199). The evidence tends to suggest that all the volumes presented by Ebert have survived: in the dedicatory epistle to the penultimate volume (MS Lat. 2o 104, dated 1723), Ebert wrote that it would bring the total to nineteen (fo. 3v: 'ijs[que] augebunt novendecim Volumina manuscripta'), and this was followed by one volume presented in May 1725 (MS Lat. 2o 105). However, in the preface to his *Historia captivitatis* (see below, n. 27), he mentions one other manuscript prepared by him, a translation into French of the letters of Charles I to Henrietta Maria during the civil war (probably taken from *The King's Cabinet opened; Or, Certain Packets of Secret Letters & Papers, written by the King's own Hand, and taken in his Cabinet at Naseby-Field* (London, 1645)); this does not appear to have survived.
17 SBB, MSS Lat. 2o 132 (1695), 120-2, 123 (1701). The work by Sandoval was his *Historia de la vida y hechos del emperador Carlos V* (Pamplona, 1634).
18 SBB, MSS Lat. 2o 177, 128, 130, 129. Geropoldi's work (*Bilancia historico-politica dell'impero ottomano, overo arcani reconditi del maomettismo* (Venice, 1686)) is rare, and apparently not held by any British library; there is a copy in the Bibliothèque Nationale, Paris (pressmark J-3407).
19 SBB, MSS Lat. 2o 124-7; Theol. 2o 199 (containing Gracián's *El criticón; El discreto; El político Fernando; El héroe;* and *El oráculo*; Ebert had probably taken these from the two-volume collected *Obras* of Gracián published at Antwerp in 1669). The work by Cabrera de Cordova was his *Felipe segundo, rey de España* (Madrid, 1619).

fables *Kalilah ve Dimnah*, and the lightweight work by de Mailly, *Rome galante, ou histoire secrète*.[20]

The great majority of these manuscripts bear personal dedications to the king (or, before 1701, Elector); clearly, attracting favour and patronage must have been a primary aim of the entire enterprise. This was in fact a method of gaining attention which Ebert had developed at an early stage in his life. As his account of his youthful travels round Europe informs us, he ended his stay in England in 1678 by presenting his manuscript Latin translation of Cavendish's life of Wolsey to the Archbishop of Canterbury; and on his eventual return to Brandenburg-Prussia in 1680, he gave copies of his Latin version of Sir Kenelm Digby's *Observations on Religio medici* to the two senior preachers at the Elector's court in Berlin.[21] Another manuscript, dated 1696, ended up in the library of the Freiherr von Schwerin. (Unlike all the others, this appears to have been an original work, a critical and biographical survey of modern historical writers.)[22] This last item was also dedicated to the Elector; whether it was given directly to von Schwerin, or whether he merely failed to pass it on to its dedicatee, is not clear. What is evident is that Ebert was happy to kill more than one bird with such stones; his 'epitome' of Bayle, for example, which was presented to the Elector's library, bears a dedication to the state coun-

---

20 SBB, MSS Lat. 2o 101–3, 104, 105. On the significance of d'Herbelot's work see H. Laurens, *Aux Sources de l'orientalisme: la* Bibliothèque orientale *de Barthélemi d'Herbelot* (Paris: G. P. Maisonneuve et Larose, 1978). Gracián's *El comulgatorio de varias meditaciones de la sagrada comunion* was included in the two-volume *Obras* of 1669. The work known as *Kalilah ve Dimnah* has a complex textual history (see the Introduction to I. G. N. Keith-Falconer, *Kalilah and Dimnah, or, The Fables of Bidpai* (Cambridge: University Press, 1885)); the book translated by Ebert was the Spanish translation (by a Ragusan) of the first eight chapters of a Turkish version (the *Humayun-namah*): *Espejo politico, y moral, para principes, ministros, y todo genero de personas*, tr. 'Vicente Bratuti' [Vicko Bratutti], 2 vols (Madrid, 1654–58). On this translation see Keith-Falconer, op. cit., lxx, and H. F. von Diez, *Über Inhalt und Vortrag, Entstehung und Schicksale des königlichen Buchs, eines Werks von der Regierungskunst* (Berlin: In Commission der Nicolaischen Buchhandlung, 1811), 151. (Bratutti worked first as a dragoman for his native Ragusa in Istanbul, then for the Habsburgs in Austria and Spain, and died in 1678; I am grateful to Dr Robin Harris and Dr Nenad Vekaric for their help in identifying him.) The work by de Mailly was first published in Paris in 1685; its second edition was entitled *Amours des empereurs romains Iules César et Auguste* (Amsterdam, 1701).

21 [A. Ebert,] *Auli Apronii vermehrte Reise-Beschreibung, von Franco Porto der Khur-Brandenburg durch Teutschland, Holland und Braband, England, Frankreich ... ferner nach Turin, gantz Italien, Rom, Neapolis ... mitgehend besondere Discourse von Religion, privat- und publique Conduite, wie auch galante und remarqvable Conversation, in Europa* (Frankfurt, 1724), 1. 106; 2. 347.

22 This folio MS, which has not survived, is mentioned in G. G. Küster, *Des alten und neuen Berlin dritte Abtheilung* (Berlin, 1756), 551, where the title is given as 'Prodromus bibliothecae Parnassi complexus examen, vitasque historicorum, qui lingua latina, Germanica, Belgica, Anglica, Gallica, Italica, Hispanica & Portugallica duobus adhinc seculis gesta Regum Europae quam optime illustrarent' ('A forerunner of the library of Parnassus, containing an examination, and the lives, of those historians who, writing in Latin, German, Dutch, English, French, Italian, Spanish and Portuguese, might best illuminate the actions of European kings in the last two centuries.')

sellor Baron von Iljen, and the composite Columbus-Gracián volume, dedicated to the king, is accompanied by a letter to the royal minister Baron von Prinzen, which asks him to pass it first to Baron Cocceji (President of the royal council), and only thereafter to deliver it to the king's library.[23]

But the potential readers of these volumes were more than just multiple potential patrons. In several of the manuscripts one finds, after the elaborate and honorific dedicatory epistle, a quite separate 'Preface to the Reader' — just as one might expect to find in a printed book.[24] And there is some evidence that Ebert did intend, or at least hope, that some of these manuscripts would be printed. The reason he gave for donating his translation of the life of Wolsey to the Archbishop of Canterbury was that he knew that his continuing travels would prevent him from making arrangements to get it printed at that time.[25] The dedicatory epistle placed before his translation of Geropoldi (1707) declared (with some metaphorical awkwardness): 'These are just some of the flowers that perfume the field which dares to invite Your Majesty to walk in it — Your Majesty, all your Court, and, if you wish, all the Republic of Letters' — the last phrase clearly implying that Ebert hoped the king would sponsor the work's publication in print.[26] In 1715 Ebert did publish a book containing some extracts from his translations of Sandoval, Cabrera de Cordova and Herbert.[27] And ten years later, when he had completed his translation of *Kalilah ve Dimnah*, he went to the trouble of announcing, in a Leipzig journal, that he intended to have it printed.[28]

---

23 The letter to von Prinzen (5 November 1723) is tipped in at the start of SBB MS Lat. 2o 104, and has been numbered as fo. 1 (fo 1r: 'Apret [sic] l'avoir communiqué aussi a Mon Le Baron Cocceji Le President, je vous supplie, Monseigneur, de le livrer a la Bibliotheque Royale').
24 For example, SBB MSS Lat. 2o 101, fos. 9v–11; 128, fo. 4; 130, fo. 8r.
25 Ebert, *Auli Apronii vermehrte Reise-Beschreibung*, 106 ('weil den *Authoren* die *Continuation* seiner Reise nach Frankreich und anderen Landschafften darinnen jetzo verhinderte dermahleins zum Druck zu befördern').
26 SBB, MS Lat. 2o 130, fo. 7r ('Ceux cy sont en partie les fleurs dont respire le camps qui ose inviter Votre Majesté a la Promenade, Toute sa Cour, et si Vous voulez, toute la Republique des Lettres').
27 A. Ebert tr., *Historia captivitatis Francisci I. Galliarum regis, nec non vitae Caroli V. Imper. in monasterio, additâ relatio vitae mortisque Caroli Infantis Philippi II. Regis Hispaniarum filii: authoribus Prudentio de Sandoval ... et Ludovico de Cabrera de Cordua* ('Milan' [Frankfurt an der Oder?], 1715). The brief specimen of his translation of Herbert consists of a speech by Cardinal Wolsey (367–72 [mispaginated '370']).
28 von Diez, *Über Inhalt und Vortrag des königlichen Buchs*, 152 ('Ebert hatte auch den Druck seiner Übersetzung durch die leipziger Zeitungen von 1725 angekündigt'). In 1731 an edition appeared at Frankfurt an der Oder of another work which Ebert had translated, Gracián's *Oráculo*, under the title *Aulicus, sive de prudentia civili et maxime aulica liber singularis*. However, this translation is quite different from Ebert's, being taken from the French version by Amelot de la Houssaie (see below, n. 95), and the translator is identified on the title page as 'Franc[iscus] Glarianus Meldenus, Constantiensis'.

Why were most of these works never printed? One slightly puzzling piece of evidence is supplied by the littérateur Gottlieb Stolle, who recorded, after Ebert's death, a conversation he had had with him in 1704 about his version of Sandoval's life of Charles V: 'Hereupon he told me that he translated this Spaniard's biography of Charles V from the Spanish, but that the King of Prussia had some scruple about allowing it to be printed, so the manuscript passed to the library in Berlin'.[29] The implied suggestion seems to have been that this text was thought to be sensitive and unsuitable for general consumption; this fits (as we shall see) Ebert's own obsession with the *arcana imperii*, but hardly fits the nature of the work itself, which had in any case been in print for many decades. A simpler explanation might be that Ebert had wanted the Elector to sponsor the publication in practical and financial terms, and that the Elector had doubted whether it was worth the trouble. Nevertheless, it is Ebert's own scruples that matter most of all in this story, as they seem to have determined his strategy of conveying works on statecraft to his ruler, and leaving it to the ruler's judgement to decide what level of readership they should be allowed to enjoy. (Compare the gradations of readership set out in the dedicatory epistle quoted above: 'Your Majesty, all your Court, and, if you wish, all the Republic of Letters'.) And a similar point is made in the dedicatory epistle which Ebert placed before his translation of Hobbes:

> Indeed, Hobbes not only adapted his efforts to demonstrating the savagery of rebellious injustice, but also ... wanted to make known the arts by which Cromwell, that unparalleled politician, climbed to the top of the ruins of royal power, admired by all the world. So, kneeling before your throne, I present this offspring of my industry to you, most sacred King; it would be most useful to have it committed to general publication, to defend the security of princes, which is apt to be undermined either by ignorance of the art of ruling, or by envy of royal power (dressed up as 'the right of the people'). If, indeed, you consider, once again, that such publication would be inadvisable for it, I beg you to store away this translation in your Royal library.[30]

---

29 G. Stolle, *Anmerckungen über D. Heumanns Conspectum reipublicae literariae, allen Liebhabern der Historie der Gelahrheit zu Liebe an den Tag gegeben* (Jena, 1738), 610 ('Hierauf erzehlte er, dass er dieses Spaniers Lebensbeschreibung Kayser Carls des V. aus dem Spanischen vertiret, doch habe der König in Preussen Bedencken getragen, es drucken zu lassen, daher das Mst. in die Bibliothec zu Berlin gekommen').

30 SBB, MS Lat. 2o 129, fos. 5–6r ('Labores vero suos aptavit *Hobbesius* non modo ad demonstrandam injustitiae rebellantis immanitatem, sed et ut ... vulgarentur illae artes, quibus *Politicus sine Exemplo*, Cromvellus ille, regio rudere fastigium omni admirabile mundo evexit. Curvus igitur genu Solio Tuo hosce industriae meae foetus offero *Rex Sacratissime* utilissimos typis committi generalibus, ut incolumitas vindicetur Principum, quam vel inscitia regnandi vel livor Regiae Magnitudinis obtentu *Juris Populi* solet attentare. Quod si vero iisdem annuere denuo inconsultum, supplico, ut *Regiâ* versionem hanc recondas *Bibliothecâ*.')

'Inadvisable' here ('inconsultum') appears to mean something a little more than 'undesirable'; the implication is that what is involved is an exercise of royal prudence, perhaps even political judgement. A common theme in the literature on 'reason of state' and the *arcana imperii* was the question of whether it was prudent to allow the general population to know about such matters; the standard response was a qualified 'yes' (the theorists giving this response were, after all, usually doing so in books that were on sale to the public), but the qualification was that due deference must be paid to the ruler's political needs and requirements.[31] In some cases, the rulers did decide that publication would not be in their interest. (A classic example was the decision by the authorities in Venice to suppress the manuscript of Boccalini's great commentary on Tacitus: the officials who scrutinized it in 1627 produced a report stating that 'I am not sure how useful it would be for it to be distributed in the hands of the people, given that one may read in it about those *arcana* of rulers which it would be much better to have kept safely in private studies than seen and sold in shops'.)[32] The safest solution for a deferential author, therefore, was to let the ruler make the decision himself; but at the same time the most self-gratifying way of doing this was to donate the work to a library which, although under the ruler's direct control, was nevertheless a semi-public place.

As recent studies of 'scribal publication' have shown, the distinction which now seems so absolute between the worlds of print and manuscript was far from clear-cut in the early modern period.[33] Only in modern and colloquial usage does 'to publish' function as a synonym of 'to print'. To deposit a manuscript in a library could also be a form of publication; indeed, it might be described as the converse of scribal publication, involving not a multiplicity of copies being made (typically) for individual readers, but rather a multiplicity of readers coming to make use of an individual copy. Early modern writers might consign manuscripts of

---

31 See, for example, the comments to this effect by Ebert's teacher Johann Christoph Beckmann: *Conspectus doctrinae politicae brevibus thesibus earumq[ue] demonstrationibus propositus* (Frankfurt an der Oder, 1691), 5, 1213.

32 Report by Girolamo Lando and Vincenzo Gussoni, cited in H. Hendrix, *Traiano Boccalini fra erudizione e polemica: ricerche sulla fortuna e bibliografia critica* (Florence: L. S. Olschki, 1995), 144 ('non saprei quanto fosse utile che ella si spargiesse per le mani de' popoli, si perche in essa leggono quegli arcani de principi che molto meglio stanno custoditi nelle secrette che nelle botteghe veduti et venduti'). The work was eventually published (incompletely and inadequately) in 1677 and 1678. Ebert, who was an enthusiast for both Tacitus and Boccalini, would no doubt have taken a special interest in the story of its suppression.

33 See, for example, H. Love, *Scribal Publication in Seventeenth-Century England* (Oxford: Clarendon, 1993); W. Speed Hill ed., *New Ways of Looking at Old Texts* (Binghamton, NY: Renaissance English Text Society, 1993); A. F. Marotti, *Manuscript, Print, and the English Renaissance Lyric* (Ithaca, NY: Cornell University Press, 1995).

their writings to libraries for a variety of reasons. Modesty — the feeling that the work did not merit the more definitive method of publication in print — was one: for example, the Swiss mathematician Johann Heinrich Rahn explained in the preface to his 'Algebra speciosa seu introductio in geometriam universalem' (1667) that he knew that distinguished men in England and Holland were working on the same topic, and that he had therefore decided to deposit his work in the Zurich city library instead of having it printed.[34] Other reasons might include a desire to preserve a controversial text for posterity without giving immediate offence to certain people (where the text included personal criticisms or accusations), and, more generally, a desire to make available to suitable researchers the raw materials for future works by others.[35] In all cases, what was intended was not non-publication, but publication of a specially qualified kind.

The Royal Library in Berlin was also a 'public repository'. In c.1661 the practice had been adopted of allowing the public to consult items in the Elector's library in the afternoons — or, at least, not the general public, but approved individuals such as court officials and administrators, clerics, professors and scholars. A full-time librarian was employed, and thanks to a very active acquisitions policy the collection held, by 1688, no fewer than 20,600 volumes.[36] By 1715 this figure had risen to roughly 50,000.[37] Many scholars — for example, the orientalists Christian Ravius, Hiob Ludolf and Andreas Acoluthus — did make regular use of the library; access was also easily gained by visiting men of letters such as John Toland, who reported in 1702 that 'In the Palace is a Library, which has an annual Fund to augment and to maintain it. The Books are well chosen, numerous, and in good case'.[38] In 1693 the hours of the reading-room had been extended to mornings as well as afternoons; however, after some misuse, automatic access was restricted in 1710–11 to state counsellors and members of the 'Societät der Wissenschaften'. (Others had to apply to

---

34 Zentralbibliothek, Zurich, MS C 114a, fo. IIIv.
35 Both of these motives were at work in John Aubrey's decision to consign his MSS to a 'public repository': see K. Bennett, 'John Aubrey's Collections and the Early Modern Museum', *The Bodleian Library Record*, 17 (2001), 213–45, esp. 216–18.
36 E. Paunel, *Die Staatsbibliothek zu Berlin: ihre Geschichte und Organisation während der ersten zwei Jahrhunderte seit ihrer Eröffnung, 1661–1871* (Berlin: De Gruyter, 1965), 17–18, 23. See also K. Tautz, *Die Bibliothekare der churfürstlichen Bibliothek zu Cölln an der Spree: ein Beitrag zur Geschichte der Preussischen Staatsbibliothek im siebzehnten Jahrhundert* (Leipzig: O. Harrassowitz, 1925), 23–37.
37 F. Wilken, *Geschichte der Königlichen Bibliothek zu Berlin* (Berlin: Duncker und Humblot, 1828), 87.
38 Ibid., 38–40; Küster, *Des alten und neuen Berlin*, 23; J. Toland, *An Account of the Courts of Prussia and Hanover, sent to a Minister of State in Holland* (London, 1705), 13 (letter dated 18 August 1702).

a state counsellor to obtain permission.)[39] A senior court official was entrusted with the post of 'Patronus' or overseer of the library: holders of this office included Otto, Freiherr von Schwerin (from 1697 until his death in 1705); Marquard Ludwig, Freiherr von Prinzen (from 1709 until his death in 1725); and Samuel, Freiherr von Cocceji (from 1730 until his death in 1755) — three of the other people whose attentions were solicited by Ebert.[40] The Royal Library was thus an institution closely tied to the court, and its users could be presumed to consist of people authorized (either directly or indirectly) as readers by the king and his immediate circle of political advisers.

How justified that presumption may have been, in practice, is hard to judge. Probably any educated person, with a suitable contact in Berlin society, could obtain access. And once access was gained, the reader would have found that there were few formal restrictions on the use that could be made of the library's materials; with the good will of the librarian, a manuscript might even have been copied *in toto*. There is no direct evidence to show that any further copies of Ebert's *Behemoth* translation were ever made; but there is one piece of indirect evidence, a suggestive chronological near-coincidence. In 1711 the Leipzig publisher Thomas Fritsch was planning to produce a new edition of Hobbes's works, and was chivvying Leibniz for the loan of his copy of his 'book about liberty' (either *Of Libertie and Necessitie* or, more probably, *The Questions concerning Liberty, Necessity, and Chance*).[41] Fritsch's ambitious project thus included the issuing of translations of works that had hitherto been available in English only. As Gottlieb Stolle later recalled, commenting on Hobbes's *Opera philosophica, quae latinè scripsit, omnia* of 1668: 'the writings which he left behind in his mother tongue are not included in it. Thomas Fritsch wanted to issue these in a Latin translation, and publish these *Opera* together with them, but this project made no progress, because he was not able to get hold of all of them'.[42] Another reason for the non-appearance of Fritsch's edition was that in October 1711 the Elector

---

39 Paunel, *Die Staatsbibliothek*, 34.
40 Ibid., 25; above, at nn. 22, 23.
41 J. Burckhard, *Historia bibliothecae Augustae quae Wolffenbutteli est*, 2 vols (Leipzig, 1744–46), ii. 336 (Leibniz to Hertelius, 23 July 1711: '*M. Fritsch m'ayant fait presser pour l'Ouurage de Hobbes sur la Liberté*').
42 Stolle, *Anmerckungen*, 975 ('die Schrifften, so er in seiner Muttersprache hinterlassen, stehen nicht mit darunter. Thomas Fritsch wollte dieselben lateinisch übersetzen lassen, und diese *Opera* damit gantz heraus geben, allein, wie er sie nicht alle erhalten können [sic], so ist dieses Vorhaben Krebsgängig worden'). Puzzlingly, Stolle mis-dates the *Opera philosophica* to 1684. In a previous discussion of Fritsch's project I commented that he had 'perhaps' planned to commission translations into German, French or Latin (*Aspects of Hobbes* (Oxford: Clarendon, 2002), 462); this evidence from Stolle, which was not known to me then, shows that Latin was the intended language.

of Saxony instructed the book-licensing authorities in Leipzig to suppress it; intriguingly, his instructions mentioned that Fritsch was planning to include 'several manuscripts which have not previously been printed'.[43] The identity of these manuscripts (presumably, translations into Latin of English-language texts by Hobbes) cannot be ascertained. But it must seem possible — likely, even — that one of them was a copy of Adam Ebert's complete translation of *Behemoth*, which had become available to interested members of the public, in the neighbouring territory of Brandenburg-Prussia, just three years before.

IV

What was the nature of Ebert's own interest in Hobbes? In order to answer this question, it is necessary first of all to fill in some of the details of the story of Ebert's life.

Adam Ebert was born in Frankfurt an der Oder, some time between 1653 and 1657.[44] He came from a prominent local family, which had supplied Lutheran clerics and intellectuals to that city for more than a century. His great-great-grandfather had been Frankfurt an der Oder's first Lutheran minister; his great-grandfather had been Rector of the city's University in 1593, 1605 and 1613; his grandfather was a Lutheran minister, and a brother of a Professor of Hebrew at the University; and his father, Gottlieb, was a merchant and city councillor.[45] Given this family background, there could be little doubt as to which university Adam Ebert would attend. He was first registered at the University of Frankfurt an der Oder — as, in effect, an auditor — in 1665; whether he was as young as eight or as old as twelve, he must have been a very precocious child. His matriculation took place in December 1674.[46] This university was of a modest size, and would soon be overshadowed, in the Elector of

---

43 Sächsisches Hauptstaatsarchiv, Dresden, MS 10753 (Oberkonsistorium, Büchersachen, vol. ii (1711-13)), fo. 18, copy of letter from Elector to 'Büchercommissarien', 11 Oct. 1711 ('worzu itzo noch etliche Manuscripta, so vorhero nicht in druck gewesen, kommen wären').

44 Modern reference works such as the *Allgemeine deutsche Biographie* (see above, n. 3) give his date of birth as 1653. The text (by Georg Gottfried Küster) in M. F. Seidel, *Bilder-Sammlung, in welcher hundert gröstentheils in der Mark Brandenburg gebohrne, allerseits aber um dieselb wohlverdiente Männer vorgestellt werden* (Berlin, 1751), gives 1656 (45). In the preface to his account of his travels in 1678, 1679 and 1680, however, Ebert refers to himself as aged 21, 22 and 23, which would imply that he was born in 1657; and in the text he refers to the start of his 22nd year (i.e. his 21st birthday) in the autumn of 1678 (Ebert, *Auli Apronii vermehrte Reise-Beschreibung*, sig. π4v; 1. 116). In view of his early registration at the university, however, it may be suspected that he was understating his age in these later writings.

45 Seidel, *Bilder-Sammlung*, 45 (Gottlieb); J. C. Beckmann ['Becmanus'], *Notitia Universitatis Francofurtanae, una cum iconibus personarum aliquot illustrium* (n.p., n.d. [Frankfurt an der Oder, c.1706]), 50-1, 71, 116-20 (other ancestors).

46 E. Friedländer ed., *Ältere Universitätsmatrikeln der Universität Frankfurt an der Oder*, 3 vols (Leipzig: S. Hirzel, 1887-91), ii. 108.

Brandenburg's territories, by the new foundation at Halle in the 1690s; it also represented a stricter, more old-fashioned brand of Lutheranism. But it did possess some intellectual luminaries — among them, the law professors Johann Brunnemann and Samuel Stryk, and the historian Johann Christoph Beckmann.[47]

Ebert graduated in 1677; he then set off on the first of his travels, a round trip to Vienna, passing through Silesia on the way there and returning via Prague. In the Viennese bookshops he found a satirical pamphlet on the fall from favour of Leopold I's minister, Prince Wenzel Lobkowitz, written as if by Boccalini (in the manner of his *Ragguagli di Parnasso*).[48] Ebert may have been already familiar with Boccalini's work, which was still highly popular throughout Europe, but this was perhaps his first encounter with the genre of pseudo-Boccalinian writing, to which he himself would later contribute. In January 1678 he travelled to Hamburg, to take a boat to Amsterdam. While in Hamburg he met a Major-General von Bülow, who discussed with him, over dinner, people of exceptional intelligence who had suffered for their cleverness: Machiavelli, Cardano, Boccalini and Campanella. The Major-General also recommended Bacon's *Sermones fideles* (the Latin version of his *Essays*) and Cardano's *Arcana prudentiae* (his treatise on behaviour in society, *Proxeneta, sive de arcanis prudentiae civilis liber singularis*).[49] Ebert's destination in Holland was Leiden, where he had planned to study jurisprudence; but he was quickly disappointed by the quality of the law professors, and abandoned the idea. He returned to Amsterdam, where he bought both of the books by Cardano and Bacon: the latter he 'read through three times in two months'. Then he took a boat to England, arriving in London on Easter Saturday.[50]

Thanks to the help of the Freiherr von Schwerin, who was then the Elector of Brandenburg's envoy in London, Ebert obtained a letter of introduction to the Oxford mathematician John Wallis; his aim was to study under him 'the science of encrypting letters in unbreakable code'. But when he met Wallis, at his farm outside Oxford, Wallis demanded such exorbitant

---

47 See C. R. Hausen, *Geschichte der Universität und Stadt Frankfurt an der Oder* (Frankfurt an der Oder: F. Apiz, 1800), 17–20.
48 Ebert, *Auli Apronii vermehrte Reise-Beschreibung*, 1. 18–19. The pamphlet appeared first in 1674 as *Der gewonnene Aussgang und plötzliche Fall des … Fürst Lobkowitzens … geschrieben aus dem Parnas von Trajano Boccalini*; it was reissued in both German and Latin in 1675 (see P. Stötzner, 'Der Satiriker Trajano Boccalini und sein Einfluss auf die deutsche Litteratur', *Archiv für das Studium der neueren Sprachen und Litteraturen*, 103 (1899), 107–47; here 144–5).
49 Ebert, *Auli Apronii vermehrte Reise-Beschreibung*, 1. 29–30.
50 Ibid., 1. 51, 58 ('die er dreymahl in 2. Monathen durchgelesen'), 60.

fees that Ebert decided immediately to return to London.[51] There he visited the Royal Society, which did not impress him, and the bookshops, which did; he bought (among other things) Edward Herbert's life of Henry VIII, Jeremy Taylor's *Ductor dubitantium* and a commentary on Tacitus.[52] More surprisingly, he also paid a visit to Thomas Hobbes. This meeting — one of the very last documented encounters that anyone had with the elderly philosopher — has remained unknown to Hobbes scholars; indeed, it has always been assumed, on the basis of a statement by Aubrey, that Hobbes left London in 1675 and spent the rest of his life in Derbyshire.[53] Ebert's account (in which he refers to himself in the third person) is therefore worth reproducing in full.

> He also paid his respects to the world-famous Thomas Hobbes, who, at a great age, was lodging with a maker of mathematical instruments, Robert Joyle, not far from Fleet Bridge. He expressed his esteem for him, and that of all Germany; but he [Hobbes] was so ill and incapable that he could scarcely enter into relations with him. He was a tall man, with fair or sun-bleached hair. He had to endure many misfortunes during Cromwell's time, especially where Dr Wallis was concerned at Oxford University — in such a manner that he was also threatened with imprisonment in that very place. After that, he betook himself to King Charles II in France, and taught him mathematics, giving him such pleasure that the King, at his restoration, not only greeted him while making his first entry into London (when he saw him at the window), but also, thereafter, had his portrait put up in all his palaces.[54]

'Robert Joyle' here was Robert Jole or Choule, a scientific instrument maker who was active in London between 1664 and 1704; Ebert's account is confirmed by the fact that Jole is known to have had an address in Fleet

---

51   Ibid., 1. 61 ('wegen der Wissenschaft Brieffe in unauflöselichen Characteren zu verhehlen'), 64. Wallis's activity as a code-breaker on behalf of the Parliamentarian authorities during the civil war was one of the things harped on in Hobbes's polemics against him.
52   Ibid., 1. 70, 73, 106, 109–10.
53   J. Aubrey, *'Brief Lives', chiefly of Contemporaries, set down by John Aubrey, between the years 1669 & 1696*, ed. A. Clark, 2 vols. (Oxford: Clarendon, 1898), i. 346 ('1675, mense ... [sic], he left London *cum animo nunquam revertendi* ['with the intention of never returning'], and spent the remaynder of his dayes in Derbyshire').
54   Ebert, *Auli Apronii vermehrte Reise-Beschreibung*, 1. 78–9 ('Er hat auch dem Welt-berühmten Th. *Hobbes reverenciret* / als er sehr alt zu Londen bey einem *Mechanico Mathematischer Instrumenten*, *Robert Joyle*, nicht weit von Fleetbridge logirt. Er trug ihm sein *Estim*, so in gantz Teutschland / vor; allein er war so kranck und unvermögend / dass er sich wenig einlassen konte; ein langer Mann / gelb oder *basané*. Er hatte zu *Cromvels* Zeiten viel *Dessastres* aussszustehen gehabt / absonderlich auff der *Universität* zu Ochsfort mit *Doctor Vallis*, dergestalt / dass er auch mit dem *Carcer* daselbst *scandalisirt*. Nachdem begab er sich in Franckreich zum König *Carolo II.*, *informirte* ihn *in Mathematicis* mit solchem Vergnügen / dass der König bey seiner *Restitution* ihn nicht allein grüssete / als er seinen ersten Einzug in Londen that und ihn im Fenster erblickete / sondern auch nachmahls sein Bildnüss in allen seinen Pallästen auffrichten liess.')

Street in 1672.[55] But what his connection was with Hobbes, or why Hobbes was lodging with him at this time, remains quite obscure. Some of the details about Hobbes's life given here are evidently rather confused, in matters of both fact and chronology; nor is it clear whether they are based on what Hobbes told Ebert on that occasion, or on other sources of information (the most likely being hearsay, the 'Hobbianae vitae auctarium' by Aubrey and Blackburne, and Sorbière's published account of his visit to England). If they derive from Ebert's conversation with Hobbes, then the cause of the confusion may have been Hobbes's illness (only a temporary one, however, as we know that he was capable of perfectly lucid argument one year later); or, more probably, it may have been linguistic, given the rustiness of Hobbes's Latin and the fact that Ebert had been learning English for only a matter of weeks or months.[56] That Wallis could have threatened to have Hobbes imprisoned in Oxford seems unlikely; but perhaps there was some other legal threat by him, the details of which have otherwise not survived. One thing at least is clear: Ebert was happy to express his admiration of Hobbes, even though he was well aware of his controversial reputation. Not long afterwards, when he was returning to London after a trip to Windsor, he had an agreeable Englishwoman as his travelling companion. 'But when she came to talk about the world-famous Thomas Hobbes, she exclaimed against him as a child of the devil; something for which he was also denounced throughout England, especially by theologians — in the pulpit, at any rate'.[57]

Ebert left England in the autumn of 1678, and spent the next seven months in Paris. There he visited Colbert's house, and studied the 'Testaments politiques' of both Colbert and Louvois; he also got to know the historian Antoine Varillas at the Bibliothèque Saint-Victor, who advised him

---

55 For what little is known of Jole, see J. Brown, 'Guild Organisation and the Instrument-Making Trade, 1550–1830: The Grocers' and Clockmakers' Companies', *Annals of Science*, 36 (1979), 1–34 (here, 31); G. Clifton, *Dictionary of British Scientific Instrument Makers, 1550–1851* (London: Zwemmer in association with the National Maritime Museum, 1995), 152.

56 Quentin Skinner has recently demonstrated that Chatsworth Hobbes MS D 5, which contains a fragment of a series of dictated responses by Hobbes to questions by the fourth Earl of Devonshire, was a product of the Exclusion Crisis of 1679 (T. Hobbes, Writings on Common Law and Hereditary Right, ed. A. Cromartie and Q. Skinner (Oxford: Claendon, 2005), 155–76). So whatever Hobbes's medical problems may have been in these final years, it is clear that they did not include senility. Hobbes's spoken Latin was already unusably rusty by 1652: see L. Huygens, *The English Journal, 1651–1652*, ed. and tr. A. G. H. Bachrach and R. G. Collmer (Leiden: E. J.Brill/Leiden University Press, 1982), 75, 218.

57 Ebert, *Auli Apronii vermehrte Reise-Beschreibung*, 1.105 ('Als sie aber zu reden gekommen von dem Weltberühmten Th. Hobbes, schalt sie denselben vor ein Teuffels-Kind / davor er auch in gantz England / absonderlich von den Theologis, allerdings auff der Cantzel aussgeruffen ward.')

to read the works of Sandoval.[58] On one occasion he visited Versailles, where, in the gardens, he caught a glimpse of the *Roi soleil*, in clothes glittering with pearls and jewels.[59] In the summer of 1679 he returned briefly to Holland, and then began a long tour of the French coast, starting in the north-west; for the first part of this journey he had a travelling-companion, an English merchant, who described himself as a cousin of Cromwell. This man was, it seems, a source of 'many' stories about the Protector and his family; the only one Ebert preserved for posterity concerns Charles II summoning one of Cromwell's daughters to an audience soon after the Restoration, at which he pinched her nose and repeated the words of the popular song, 'Oliver, Oliver, lend me your nose'.[60] Ebert was evidently fascinated by Cromwell; in England he had acquired a book about him, and in Holland he bought a medal which had the Protector's head on one side, and an olive-tree on the other, with (according to Ebert) the motto 'Nunquam tibi deficient oliva'. With a slight frisson, Ebert recalled in his travel-book that he had been told 'in secret' by the seller that this medal was in fact made not in 1658 (the date it bore) but in 1678, 'because England was not very satisfied with Charles II, and wanted thereby to let him know, indirectly or ambiguously, that there could soon be another Oliver Cromwell, if he did not improve his rule'.[61]

Ebert's tour of French coastal towns took him as far as Marseille and Toulon; from there he travelled to Lyon, and from Lyon he set off for Italy. He settled for a while in Turin, where he paid a Genoese man to instruct him in Italian—not so much because he needed language lessons, as

---

58   Ibid., 116, 153, 156. Varillas had previously been Royal librarian in Paris (1655–62), and had published his most famous work, *Politique de la maison d'Autriche*, in 1658.

59   Ibid., 145. Thirty-six years later Ebert would refer to this encounter when addressing one of the three dedications of his translation of Cabrera, Sandoval and Herbert (see above, n. 27) to Louis XIV (the others being to the Kings of Prussia and Spain): Ebert tr., *Historia captivitatis Francisci I*, 'II'.

60   Ebert, *Auli Apronii vermehrte Reise-Beschreibung*, 1. 162 (Holland), 192 (story).

61   Ibid., 1. 107 (book), 108–9 ('in geheim'; 'da England auf König Carolo II. Nicht wohl zu Muth; diesem *oblique* oder halb und halb dadurch zu verstehen zugeben, es könte sich bald ein neuer Olivarius Cromvel finden / wan er nicht besser *regirte*'). Ebert's memory was faulty, and his version of the inscription ungrammatical: the medal, dated 3 September 1658 (the date of Cromwell's death) in fact bears a picture of a young olive tree glowing close to the dead stump of an old one, with the motto 'NON. DEFITIENT. OLIVA' ('They [sc. the people] shall not lack an olive-tree')—referring to Richard Cromwell. The medal was genuinely issued in 1658, by the well-known artist Thomas Simon, but two imitations of it were made later in Holland (see H. W. Henfrey, *Numismata cromwelliana* (London: J. R. Smith, 1877), 167–72; E. Hawkins, *Medallic Illustrations of the History of Great Britain and Ireland to the Death of George II*, 2 vols (London: Printed by order of the Trustees of the British Museum, 1885), i. 433–5). Ebert also noted (*Auli Apronii vermehrte Reise-Beschreibung*, 1. 202) that the 'cousin' of Cromwell looked just like the portrait on the medal. He refers to the book as 'the Mistakes of Cromvel'; in a subsequent comment (2. 348) he appears to identify this with the German book *Politicus sine exemplo*, which was a translation of the anonymously published work by Henry Fletcher, *The Perfect Politician* (see below, n. 99).

because the man was secretary to a senior minister, and was able to tell him 'the most secret things, which had just become known at Court'.[62] He also patronized an Italian musician who had recently moved to Turin from England, giving him money because he liked to hear his stories about the courts where he had worked. Unfortunately, he just missed Richard Cromwell, who came to Turin at about this time; by then, Ebert himself was on his travels again.[63] He went first to Venice; anti-Roman books in his luggage were confiscated at the border, but he persuaded the authorites to give them back. He enjoyed the carnival there; then he travelled to Florence (where he admired the manuscripts of Tacitus, Apuleius and Virgil in the Medicean library) and on to Rome.[64] After further trips to Naples and Palermo, he returned to Venice; from there he travelled north, through Austria, to his home town, arriving in the summer of 1681.[65] He was soon calling on various dignitaries in Berlin: the court preachers (to whom he gave his translation of Digby), the secretaries of state (to whom he presented copies of a book about Cromwell), and the Elector's chief minister, Friedrich von Jena. To the last of these, Ebert had written a long letter from Toulon, giving his observations on the strength of France's coastal and naval defences; it thus seems that Ebert's French tour had incorporated an element of amateur espionage. And on the strength of this, he obtained an audience with the Great Elector himself, who was so charmed by his young subject that he invited him back for further discussions on three separate occasions.[66]

Given his fascination with courts and politicians, it might have been expected that Ebert would now embark on a political career himself, perhaps as a secretary to some important courtier or minister. That his own interests lay in that direction was confirmed by the publication, two years later, of his first book, *Quinquagenta relationes ex Parnasso* — a spirited imitation of Boccalini's *Ragguagli di Parnasso*, discussing history, philosophy, political theory and political practice from a wide range of countries and periods. Contemporary politics was not excluded: one 'relatio' analysed the reasons for the excessive power of France (relative to Spain and England), and another contained a discussion of the recent Treaty of Nijmegen — to which Ebert appended the text of his long letter to von Jena

---

62 Ibid., 1. 257–91 (Marseille-Lyon); 2. 22 ('die geheimsten Dinge, so zu Hoff nur *eclatirten*').
63 Ibid., 2. 11, 33.
64 Ibid., 2. 41–6 (books), 120 (Florence), 127 (Rome).
65 Ibid., 2. 151 (Naples), 175 (Palermo), 258 (Venice), 347 (Frankfurt an der Oder). (The date of arrival is given as July '1680', but this appears to be a misprint, given the chronology up to that point.)
66 Ibid., 2. 347–51.

about French ports and the French navy.[67] Overall, this book was a work of some youthful exuberance, containing such things as an apologia by Attila the Hun, an argument between St Paul and Numa Pompilius, a reply by Tacitus to his critics, and a dialogue between Thales and Campanella; the only modern scholar to have commented on the quality of Ebert's work judges it too harshly when he says that it 'completely lacks' the vigour and vivacity of Boccalini's own *Ragguagli*.[68]

At the end of the list of contents of this book, Ebert gave a listing of the works he planned to produce: these included an edition of Tacitus (with a 'supplement' to the *Annals*), a work entitled 'XXXIV. Libri Historiarum Europae, a primordio hujus seculi ad Pacem usque Noviomagensem' ('Thirty-four books of the histories of Europe, from the beginning of this century to the Peace of Nijmegen'), and one called 'Pallium Religionis fraudes Gentilium, Judaeorum, Christianorum & Mahumetanorum obtegens' ('The cloak of religion, which covers up the frauds of the heathen, the Jews, the Christians and the Muslims').[69] None of these, however, was to see the light of day. And instead of pursuing a career as a littérateur, composing these or other such works on history, politics and religion, Ebert returned to the University of Frankfurt an der Oder to undertake a doctorate in law. This was accomplished in 1685, under Professor Stryk; Ebert's doctoral dissertation, 'De eo quod fit ipso jure', was an ambitious study of the concept (in Roman law) of that which is done 'by right itself', as opposed to that which is done by either the right of a minister of the state, or the right of a subject. Published thirteen years later, it filled more than 200 pages; characteristic touches included references to Taylor's *Ductor dubitantium* (on Mosaic law) and an opening section based on Tacitus's account of the origin of law in book 3, chapter 26, of the *Annals*.[70] In the following two years Ebert presided over the presentation of two other substantial dissertations, on diplomatic immunity and

---

67 A. Ebert, *Quinquagenta relationes ex Parnasso de variis Europae eventibus* (Hamburg, 1683), 1–7, 242–9, 250–8.

68 Stötzner, 'Der Satiriker Trajano Boccalini', 146 ('Seinem Vorbilde aber steht Ebert weit nach, es fehlt ihm völlig die Frische und Lebhaftigkeit, die an Boccalini so wohl gefällt').

69 Ebert, *Quinquagenta relationes*, sig. *7v. The other works included a treatise on the relatedness of the Romance languages, and one on shorthand.

70 J. C. Beckmann ['Becmanus'], *Catalogus bibliothecae publicae Universitat. Francofurtanae* (Frankfurt an der Oder), 92, gives its date of publication as 1698 (in '*Voll. Dispp. Francoff.*'). No copy of this edition is known to me. A 2nd edition ('denuo ed.') was published in 1699: *Tractatus de eo, quod fit ipso iure* (Frankfurt an der Oder); there is a copy in the Universitäts- und Landesbibliothek, Münster, pressmark Ia 4097+ a-5, 12. Another edition ('Revisus & denuo editus' ('revised and re-published')) was issued in Hanover and Leipzig in 1699 (203 pp.); there are multiple copies of this in the Universitäts- und Landesbibliothek, Halle. I have used the later printing in S. Stryk, ed., *Dissertationum juridicarum francofortensium volumen novissimum sive Vtum, ex jure publico, privato, feudali et statutario materias exhibens* (Frankfurt an der Oder, 1744), 374–460: see 374 (Tacitus), 402–3 (Taylor).

on the legal justification of the policies of Philip II of Spain; and in October 1686 he was appointed 'professor extraordinarius' in the faculty of law.[71] But after giving a course of lectures on the whole of Grotius's *De jure belli ac pacis*, he 'preferred to move on', as he would later put it, 'to studying the ways in which not only natural law but also the law of nations and civil law were put into practice by kings'.[72] In some of his later accounts he gave the impression that he had been put off, either by the 'thorny and useless' nature of Roman law, or by the fact that the theoretical basis of civil law had plenty of teachers already.[73] But in moving away from pure theory, he was simply renewing his long-standing interest in the study of political action. In his preface to the dissertation on diplomatic immunity of 1686, he had announced that he would embark on a series of studies of the 'jus' (right, or legality) of the actions of great princes down the ages; the long list of suitable subjects which he appended there included Xerxes, Alexander the Great, Julius Caesar, Charles V, Mehmet II, Süleiman the Magnificent, Henry VIII, Philip II, Mazarin, and Queen Christina of Sweden.[74]

None of these studies (with the exception of his pupil's dissertation on Philip II, to which Ebert may have contributed substantially) ever appeared.[75] Instead, Ebert's work in this field seems to have been con-

---

71 The dissertations are: *Dissertatio de immunitate legatorum, quam ... praeside Dn. Adamo Eberto, J.U.D & P.P. in auditorio Jctorum ad diem XXVI. Augusti anno MDCLXXXVI. ... sistit aut. & resp. Andreas Johann Liscovius Cöslino-Pom.* (n.p, n.d. [Frankfurt an der Oder, 1686]); *Dissertatio academica, de justitia actionum Philippi II. Hispaniae & Indiarum regis, quam Adamo Eberto, D. & professore juris extraordinario 1687. ad diem 28. Maj. Publicae eruditorum censura exhibiturus Gustavus Andreas Bornemann, Wernigerodensis* (Frankfurt an der Oder, n.d. [1687]). The titles indicate that Ebert's appointment as professor took place between those two dates; a four-page prospectus of his inaugural lecture (dated 31 October) was printed as *Ab augusto sereniss. & potentissimo domino Friderico Wilhelmo, Electore Brandenburgico ... professionem iuris extraordinariam clementissime demandatam iussa solennitate auspicandi ad explicationem tituli imperatoris Iustiniani die 31. octobris in auditorio publico proponendam ... invitat Adam Ebertus D.* (Frankfurt an der Oder, n.d. [1686]). (There is a copy in the Sächsisches Landesbibliothek – Staats- und Universitätsbibliothek, Dresden, pressmark Coll. Diss. B. 129, misc. 19.) The title 'professor extraordinarius' signified merely that he was outside the offical complement of law professors, which was fixed by the statutes at no more than five (G. Kaufmann and G. Bauch, eds., *Acten und Urkunden der Universität Frankfurt a. O.*, Heft 3, 'Die Facultätsstatuten und Ergänzungen zu den allgemeinen Statuten der Universität Frankfurt a. O.', ed. P. Reh (Breslau, 1900), 50). Under these statutes, the curriculum concentrated solidly on the Pandects, Institutes, and other texts of Roman law (52–3).

72 Ebert, tr., *Historia captivitatis Fransisci I.*, sig. * 2v ('ad *Praxin* transgredi *Regiam* placuit, JURIS NATURAE nimirum, GENTIUMQUE & CIVILIS').

73 The former comment ('Spinosa ac inutili jurisprudentia') is from a note added by Ebert to the end of his 1685 dissertation: Stryk, ed., *Dissertationum juridicarum*, 460. The latter is contained in a brief autobiographical text by Ebert, printed in Seidel, *Bilder-Sammlung*, 45.

74 Ebert, praes, *Dissertatio de immunitate legatorum*, sigs. 2A1–2.

75 The dissertation was attributed to Ebert by Stolle: *Anmerckungen*, 609. According to Küster, Ebert's manuscript works did include a life of Alexander the Great (as well as a commentary

fined to extending his knowledge of the historical-political literature, and, as we have seen, translating some specimens of it, for the benefit of his royal patron and others. In 1715, the year in which he published extracts from his translations of Sandoval, Cabrera de Cordova and Herbert, a new edition of his *Quinquagenta relationes ex Parnasso* also appeared; and eight years later he published the long account of his youthful travels, *Aulii Apronii Reise-Beschreibung*.[76] (His nom-de-plume, 'Aulus Apronius', was adapted from the name of a minor character in the *Annals* of Tacitus, Lucius Apronius.)[77] A certain element of boastfulness was apparent in the preface to this last book. Ebert remarked that some people might wonder whether a young man of 21, 22 or 23 could have had the intellectual ability to observe and understand all the things contained in the book, but retorted: 'Where then did the *Relationes ex Parnasso* come from in 1681?'[78] Some readers found an answer to that question: seizing on a passage in the travel-book in which Ebert said that he had gained material for his *Relationes ex Parnasso* from the Italian musician whom he had cultivated in Turin, they supposed that that work was little more than a piece of plagiarism. The accusation was made after Ebert's death by the bibliophile E. G. Rinck, whose general verdict on Ebert was that 'he was tormented by enormous ambition'.[79] Ebert's reputation did not improve with time; an anonymous owner of the British Library copy of the 1715 edition of the *Relationes ex Parnasso* wrote that 'He was a most extraordinary man, having almost become deranged in consequence of an excess of vanity and self-importance'.[80] But those who had known him personally wrote about him in a way that, while making allowance for his stylistic exuberance, treated him with respect and admiration. Gottlieb Stolle, writing soon after Ebert's death in 1735, noted his love of 'the high-faluting, affected style of the Spanish', and observed that 'he therefore cultivated a concentrated way of writing'; Samuel Strimesius, writing twelve years earlier,

on the *Annals* of Tacitus, and several legal treatises): Seidel, *Bilder-Sammlung*, 46. But those manuscripts have not survived.

[76] The 2nd edition of the *Quinquagenta relationes* was entitled *Anecdota sive historia arcana Europae* ('Cosmopolis' [Amsterdam?], 1715). Copies of the 1st edition of *Auli Apronii Reise-Beschreibung* (Frankfurt an der Oder) are rare; there is one in the Niedersächsische Staats- und Universitätsbibliothek, Göttingen, pressmark 8 ITIN, 164 EXE: 02. I have used the more common 2nd (and enlarged) edition, *Auli Apronii vermehrte Reise-Beschreibung*.

[77] See Tacitus, *Annals*, 1. 29 and 3. 64.

[78] Ebert, *Auli Apronii vermehrte Reise-Beschreibung*, sig. π4v ('wo sind dann Anno 1681. die Relationes ex Parnasso ... hergekommen?'). Ebert had mis-remembered the date of publication, perhaps substituting inadvertently the date of composition.

[79] A. F. Glafey ed., *Bibliotheca rinckiana, seu suppellex librorum quos ... collegit ... Eucharius Gottlieb Rinck* (Leipzig, n.d. [1747]), 240 ('enormi ambitione vexabatur'), 847-8 (plagiarism). The statement made by Ebert about his debt to the musician does not begin to support such a charge.

[80] Ebert, *Anecdota*, BL pressmark 9073 b. 13, note on blank leaf before title page.

had praised him for possessing 'a pen wonderfully skilled in European and learned languages'.[81]

V

Some of the elements of Adam Ebert's intellectual formation will already be apparent from this brief sketch of his life. From his early adulthood onwards, he had been influenced by what seemed to him a particular tradition, even a canon, of political writers. The canon is delineated most clearly in his *Quinquagenta relationes*, where Apollo, giving advice on reading to a group of German 'studiosi', lists Machiavelli, Cardano and Bacon as the greatest writers on 'civil prudence', and declares that the best theorists on politics are Machiavelli, Cardano, Bacon and Campanella: Cardano and Bacon taught people how to advise themselves, he explains, while Machiavelli and Campanella taught them how to advise princes. Exercising some prudence of his own, Ebert also announced that the best guide to morals was the Bible; but he added, significantly, that the truth of the Christian religion 'is simple, nor would there ever have arisen any controversies about it, except where they were needed for domination'.[82] Interest was the driving force of all political action, and in order to attain mastery in the art of politics it was necessary to study all the stratagems and devices by means of which successful rulers ensured that their own interest prevailed. Such a study was necessarily historical; and of all the historians who had written about politics, none was more important than Tacitus, the veritable lode-star of Ebert's intellectual life. He worked for many years on an edition of, 'supplement' to, and/or commentary on Tacitus; he took his own nom-de-plume from a Tacitan character; his *Quinquagenta relationes* were modelled on the writings of Boccalini, the most prominent of modern literary Tacitists; and in his travel-book he not only mentioned his inspection of the Medicean manuscript in Florence, but also cited and discussed Tacitus' works repeatedly.[83] Tacitus appears several times in the *Quinquagenta relationes*, defending himself from not very substantial criticisms by two writers who were themselves heavily influenced by him, Justus Lipsius and Virgilio Malvezzi. Blamed for teaching the secrets of rulers to all and sundry, he explains that he never teaches such 'arcana' directly, but uses phrases which lead the intelligent

---

81 Stolle, *Anmerckungen*, 609 ('die hochtrabenden gezwungnen Manieren der Spanier'; 'einer tiefsinnigen Schreibart beflissen'); Strimesius, quoted in Küster, *Den alten und neuen Berlin*, 550 ('eine in den Europäischen und gelehrten Sprachen wunder-erfahrne Feder'). Strimesius had been Rector of the University of Frankfurt an der Oder in 1688, 1694 and 1699.

82 Ebert, *Quinquagenta relationes*, 180–1 ('simplex est, *nec unquam de eadem motae fuissent controversiae nisi ubi illis indiguerit Dominatio*').

83 Ebert, *Auli Apronii vermehrte Reise-Beschreibung*, 1. 208, 268; 2. 122, 144, 232, 239.

reader to search them out; and in any case, the 'arcana imperandi' can never be understood by the vulgar.[84]

Ebert was thus a late representative of the Tacitist tradition — a tradition which, thanks to writers such as Arnold Clapmarius in the early seventeenth century, had become closely intertwined with a particular branch of the Machiavellian tradition, identifying the stratagems of the Machiavellian prince with the Tacitan 'arcana imperii'.[85] It was no less closely connected with the theory of 'reason of state', which justified the exceptional measures taken by rulers to defend the state, and/or preserve their own rule. (Ebert's own most striking use of this phrase was in the long essay which he appended to his *Quinquagenta relationes*, entitled 'Ratio status Davidis, Judaeorum regis' ('The reason of state of David, king of the Jews') — a study of the political arts by which David came to power.)[86] The general assumptions of anyone who adhered to these interconnected traditions in the seventeenth century might be summarized as follows. 'Interest' is the driving force not only of politics, but of all human affairs. The common people, though always eager to advance their own crude interests, are stupid, and easily tricked. An ambitious demagogue can deceive them, making them think that they will advance their interests when they will in fact only promote his; and a wise ruler can, and in some ways should, deceive them, both by keeping them in awe of unknown powers, and by giving them those 'simulacra' of liberty which will make them content. Much of the art of ruling thus consists of knowing how to simulate and how to dissimulate. This does not mean that ruling is unconnected with moral values, merely that, in order to further those values, it is necessary for the wise man to adapt his actions to the conditions of cupidity and stupidity that prevail among the people. Similarly, the interests of the state can properly be furthered by actions which would otherwise, without such a justification, be immoral. In the case of some writers, this pattern of thought enjoyed an affinity with neo-Stoicism; it encour-

---

84 Ebert, *Quinquagenta relationes*, 135–46 ('arcana', 143), 182, 197, 269–78 (reply to criticism).
85 On this identification see especially P. S. Donaldson, *Machiavelli and Mystery of State* (Cambridge: Cambridge University Press, 1988), 110–40. On Tacitism see J. von Stackelberg, *Tacitus in der Romania: Studien zur literarischen Rezeption des Tacitus in Italien und Frankreich* (Tübingen: Max Niemeyer, 1960); E.-L. Etter, *Tacitus in der Geistesgeschichte des 16. und 17. Jahrhunderts* (Basel: Helbing & Lichtenhahn, 1966); G. Spini, 'The Art of History in the Italian Counter Reformation', in E. Cochrane ed., *The Late Italian Renaissance* (London: Macmillan, 1970), 91–133 (esp. 114–33); K. C. Schellhase, *Tacitus in Renaissance Political Thought* (Chicago: University of Chicago Press, 1976); the essays by P. Burke, 'Tacitism', in T. A. Dorey ed., *Tacitus* (London: Routledge & K. Paul, 1969), 149–71, and 'Tacitism, Scepticism, and Reason of State', in J. H. Burns and M. Goldie eds., *The Cambridge History of Political Thought, 1450–1700* (Cambridge: Cambridge University Press, 1991), 479–98; and R. Tuck, *Philosophy and Government, 1572–1651* (Cambridge: Cambridge University Press, 1993), 31–136.
86 Ebert, *Quinquagenta relationes*, 317–76.

aged a separation between an inner world of belief and intention, where true virtue is located, and an outer one, where actions must inevitably be compromised by circumstance. And this set of attitudes also tended to promote a view of true religion as an essentially internal affair: all the externalities of religion, meanwhile, needed to be placed under the ruler's control, since religion would otherwise be too powerful a tool in the hands of demagogues and plotters intent on gaining political power for themselves.

For writers who held such assumptions, the issue of whether it was right to expose the stratagems of statecraft to public view was not just a matter of authorial prudence; it raised much larger political or ideological questions. One classic study divides the authors of this period into 'black' and 'red' Tacitists — in other words, monarchical and popular.[87] The former wrote about the devices and deceptions used by skilful monarchs to show that they were necessary and justified; the latter wrote about them to teach the people how not to be deceived. Naturally, there were many possible gradations between the red and black ends of this spectrum. So-called 'liberal' monarchist Tacitists, for example (such as Malvezzi) wrote essentially from the monarchical point of view, but advised the ruler that it was against his interests to thwart the interests of his people; the German professor of politics and counsellor to the Count of Hesse Cyriacus Lentulus used Tacitus — in his *Princeps absolutus* (Herborn, 1663) — to teach the ruler the difference between a 'princeps bonus', such as Trajan, and a 'princeps pessimus', such as Nero.[88] On the 'red' side of the argument, by far the most influential writer was Boccalini; but his own precise place on the spectrum was hard to locate, thanks to the stylistic devices (of irony, the dramatization of argument, and so on) which rendered his most widely-read work, the *Ragguagli*, so piquant and intriguing. Throughout that work, a parallelism operates between Tacitus and Machiavelli, and while the latter is denounced at the surface level of the text, he is nevertheless implicitly commended as a truthful writer; both Tacitus and Machiavelli are accused (by other, hostile speakers — this is one of Boccalini's literary devices) of endangering princes by unmasking their devices. (The charge against Machiavelli is that he has taught sheep the tricks of dogs; that against Tacitus is that he has given the people 'political spectacles', which have enabled them to see through the pretences of princes.)[89] That Boccalini opposed the Spanish monarchy and favoured

---

87 G. Toffanin, *Machiavelli e il 'tacitismo'* (Padua, 1921).
88 Tuck, *Philosophy and Government*, 74–8 (Malvezzi); Etter, *Tacitus in der Geistesgeschichte*, pp. 167–8 (Lentulus).
89 See T. Boccalini, *Ragguagli di Parnasso*, ed. G. Rua and L. Firpo, 3 vols (Bari: Laterza, 1910–48), i. 326–8 (cent. 1, rag. 89); ii. 247–9 (cent. 2, rag. 71). The most penetrating study of Boccalini's

the Venetian republic was clear enough from the text appended to his *Ragguagli*, the *Pietra del paragone politico*; on this basis, his work was often used or adapted by anti-absolutist writers in northern Europe in the two or three generations after his death.[90] But the passionately anti-monarchical nature of his thinking became fully apparent only when substantial parts of his commentary on Tacitus were finally published in Switzerland in 1677 and 1678. 'So beware,' he wrote, 'you who negotiate with princes, of their malicious thoughts, and of the poultice of their soft words; for when they sing sweetly, they are weaving cruel spells. Their tongues are moved by interest, not by justice, nor by love of the public good'.[91]

It might be thought, therefore, that in producing a work so closely modelled on Boccalini in 1683, Adam Ebert was signalling an anti-monarchic ideological position. This would have been a strange tactic, however, for someone who had gone to such trouble to ingratiate himself not only with senior courtiers in Berlin, but also with the Great Elector himself. In fact there is nothing anti-monarchical in his *Quinquagenta relationes*; a text which includes a very reasonable-sounding apologia by Attila the Hun is unlikely to be read as a denunciation of the cruelty of princes. Instead, Ebert finesses the red-black problem by adopting a distinctive shade of grey: in his view, the essential function of Tacitus' historiography and analysis is neither to justify princes nor to give power to the people, but rather to instruct 'courtiers'—a category that appears to include all politicians operating under a monarchy—in the arts of survival and self-promotion. Thus Apollo declares that 'Tacitus described the *arcana* of courtiers'; and he also recommends that among the Latin historians, 'Tacitus and Justinus should be read carefully—the former because he would teach the reader how to be a courtier, the latter, how to be a counsellor'.[92] (This distinction seems to imply that a courtier is someone who acts in his own interest, as opposed to someone who attends to the interest of the monarch.) The only potentially subversive element here is the possibility that Tacitus teaches courtiers not merely how to survive, but how to usurp the power of the ruler; this is the main point at issue in the discussions Ebert presents between Tacitus and both Malvezzi and Lipsius, which focus on Tacitus' account of the rise to power of Sejanus. Thus Malvezzi says to Tacitus at one point: 'You, the leading writer at the court of the emperors of the human race, taught posterity the ways in which one can deceive kings and overcome one's equals'.[93] Lipsius accuses Tacitus of contradiction, since he writes at one point as if Sejanus brought about Tiberius's retirement to Capri, and at another point as if Tiberius willed it himself. Tacitus replies that Sejanus strengthened a pre-existing inclination on the emperor's part; but, with studied ambiguity, he explains his own role as follows. 'He did not describe what Sejanus did, but rather, taught what another person could have done. He recommended that art to every historian. For the writer should be concerned not so much with the history, as with the use of it'.[90]

An obsession with courtiers runs through all of Ebert's work; even his nom-de-plume converts the name taken from Tacitus, Lucius Apronius, into 'Aulus' Apronius. ('Aulus' was an authentic Roman name; but Ebert seems to have chosen it for its association with 'aula' (court) and 'aulicus' (courtier).) His selection of texts to translate was dominated by such concerns: Gracián's *Oraculo*, for example, taught the reader how to behave as a 'great man', whether courtier or ruler, and its popular French translation by Amelot de la Houssaie (who also translated Machiavelli and wrote a commentary on Tacitus) was entitled *L'Homme de cour*.[91] The role of 'ministers' attracted Ebert's special attention; his interest may have been first drawn to the Spanish version of *Kalilah ve Dimnah* by the fact that it was entitled *Espejo politico, y moral, para principes, ministros, y todo genero de personas* ('A political and moral looking-glass for princes, ministers and all sorts of people'). In his *Quinquagenta relationes* he strongly recommended the *Relaciones* and *Aphorismos* of Antonio Pérez, the minister of Philip II who had fallen from grace, been imprisoned, and subsequently fled to England; the *Aphorismos* in particular are full of advice on how a senior courtier should conduct himself.[92] And when characterizing his *Quinquagenta relationes* in 1715, Ebert described it—rather misleadingly—as 'comprising the *arcana* of the Minister, Count and Duke Olivares, Cardinal Richelieu and Cardinal Mazarin, the Earl of Clarendon, Griffenfeld, and others'.[93]

Oliver Cromwell, of course, could not be placed precisely in this category; his rise to power was not based on ministerial office. But he was, like the others just mentioned, someone who came to exercise state power

---

90 Ibid., 272 ('se non, quid fecerit Sejanus, scripsisse; sed quid alios facere posset, docuisse. Illamque artem se recommendare unicuique Historicorum. Nam non adeo Historiae quam ejusdem usui scriptorem decere esse intentum.')

91 B. Gracián, *L'Homme de cour*, tr. N. Amelot de la Houssaie (Paris, 1684); this was reprinted fourteen times between 1686 and 1716 (see B. Gracián, *The Oracle*, ed. and tr. L. B. Walton (London: Dent, 1962), 44). The first German translation, by J. L. Sauter, was similarly entitled *L'Homme de Cour, oder der heutige politische Welt- und Staats-Weise* (Frankfurt am Main, 1687). Gracián was himself deeply influenced by Boccalini: see Hendrix, *Traiano Boccalini*, 75–84.

92 Ebert, *Quinquagenta relationes*, 182, 204. On Pérez see G. Marañón, *Antonio Pérez (el hombre, el drama, la época)*, 7th edn, 2 vols (Madrid: Espasa-Calpe, 1963): for details of the original printings of these works see ii. 954–5. Ebert probably read the *Relaciones* and the various sets of *Aphorismos* in the 1676 Geneva edition, *Las obras y relaciones de Antonio Perez*; for examples of court-related aphorisms see 402, 404, 727, 731.

93 Ebert tr., *Historia captivitatis Francisci I.*, sig. *2r ('arcana Ministerii Comitis & Ducis OLIVARII RICHELIIQUE & MAZARINI Cardinalium, CLARENDONIIQUE Comitis & Greifenfeldii aliorumque complexae'). Peder Schuhmacher Griffenfeld was the powerful minister of the Danish kings Frederick III and Christian V.

through his own skill, not through the accident of inheritance. Indeed, he had gone much further than the others: he was a consummate usurper who had entirely supplanted the hereditary ruler, a Sejanus who had had Tiberius put to death. Ebert, who had been under Cromwell's spell for thirty years before he translated *Behemoth*, seems to have regarded him as the ultimate exponent of those arts and stratagems which ambitious courtiers and politicians needed to master: he knew how to deceive the people, how to enlist other holders of power in his own support, and how, in the end, to take that power from them.

Such, in fact, was the standard view of Cromwell in the writings about him published in continental Europe. Soon after his death, a popular satirical pamphlet by an anonymous German author presented a discussion between Cromwell and Oxenstierna in the underworld; this work, itself an imitation of Boccalini, was filled with references to Tacitus, and praised Cromwell as a master of the Tacitan arts of 'ratio status'. As one character remarks to Cromwell, discussing his retention of the House of Commons after he had abolished the House of Lords: 'For your Highness arranged for the English to have only "umbrae" and "simulacra", shadows and pictures, as Tacitus and Boxhorn (in his 17th Emblem) call them'.[94] Also widely read in Germany was a translation, published in 1663, of Henry Fletcher's *The Perfect Politician* (1660): this was the work to which Ebert referred, under the first part of its title, when he used the phrase *Politicus sine exemplo* in the dedication of his *Behemoth* translation.[95] Fletcher's book, which was written just before the Restoration, was a mainly positive appreciation of Cromwell's political skills.

> He shewed himself to be in *Policy* as far above the *Peoples Capacities*, as *Saul* in *Stature* was above the *Israelites* ... In his rise, he never cut down one step before another was built to support him ... Secrecy in carrying on Designs, is the principal part of a Prince: at this he was excellent.[96]

---

94 *Schreiben welches der vorlengst verstorbene hochgelahrte Herr Don Franciscus de Quevedo ... überschicket betreffende einige statistische ... Discursen so zwischen denen verstorbenen Hn: Protectore von Engellandt dem schwedischen Reichs-Cantzler Ochsenstern und Lilienströhmen* (n.p., 1659), e.g. sigs C3v (on Cromwell's arrangement of his son's succession, calling it 'ratio status'), C4r (on his gradual accumulation of power), C4v ('Indem Ew. Hoheit den Engelländern nur umbras und simulacra, nur Schatten und Bildnüsse, wie Tacitus und Boxhornius, Embl. 17. es nennen, hergemachet'). There were several editions and continuations of this work: see G. Berghaus, *Die Aufnahme der englischen Revolution in Deutschland, 1640-1669* (Wiesbaden: O. Harrassowitz, 1989), 316-19. Marcus Zuerius Boxhorn taught at Leiden University, and published an edition of Tacitus in 1643. This reference is to his *Emblemata politica*, 2nd edn (Amsterdam, 1651), 134-6.

95 [H. Fletcher,] *Politicus sine exemplo, oder kurtzer Begriff der Kriegs- und Staatshandlungen seiner Hoheit Olivier Cromwels*, tr. anon (Nuremberg, 1663). For Ebert's reference see above, n. 30.

96 [H. Fletcher,] *The Perfect Politician*, 2nd edn (London, 1680), 281. The German translator's Preface praises his political skills even more highly: *Politicus sine exemplo*, 1-2.

The beauty of this characterization of Cromwell was that it equally served the purposes of those who wished to damn him; thus the fervently pro-Royalist Ferrarese writer Alfonso Paioli could describe Cromwell as the incarnation of the Machiavellian Prince, a 'politico' *par excellence*, while not denying that 'he was a person of extraordinary talents'.[97] Such an attitude, hostile but at the same time admiring, was expressed in the two books that enjoyed the widest circulation in Europe: Ferdinand de Galardi's *La Tyrannie heureuse, ou Cromwel politique, avec ses artifices & intrigues* (Leiden, 1671), and the *Historia, e memorie recondite sopra alla vita di Oliviero Cromvele, detto il tiranno senza vizi, il prencipe senza virtù* (2 vols, Amsterdam, 1692), by Gregorio Leti, the editor of Boccalini's commentary on Tacitus. As Leti put it (quoting, as he claimed, his English patron, the Earl of Anglesey),

> the earth never had a ruler more prudent than he, nor a commander more skilled in advancing his own fortune ... He was a friend without loyalty, an enemy without rancour, a judge without justice, a great politician among disorders ... in short, he was a compendium of the worst evil, and a summation of the greatest good.[98]

VI

Such, then, was the fascination of Cromwell for Ebert, and, because of it, the appeal to him of Hobbes's work. But was Ebert responding, at the same time, to elements that are genuinely present in Hobbes's account? Is it possible that this Ebertian reading of *Behemoth* may have at least something positive to contribute to our understanding of that work? Behind such questions there lurks a larger one: should Hobbes's political thought be viewed as essentially a product of the Tacitist tradition?

To see Hobbes in this way would not be a novel development. One person who did so was the influential writer Johann Christoph Beckmann, who was first Professor of History, then Professor of Politics, at the University of Frankfurt an der Oder. Beckmann would write admiringly of Ebert when they were colleagues in later years; Ebert had probably attended Beckmann's lectures as a student, we may guess that it was thanks to Beckmann—one of the most outspoken defenders of Hobbes in

---

97 A. Paioli, *Vite del Turena, del Mazarini e del Cromvele* (Bologna, 1680), 234 (Machiavelli), 239 ('isquisitamente Politico'), 240 ('non può negarsi ch'egli fosse soggetto di straordinari talenti').

98 Leti, *Historia*, i. 5 ('la Terra non hebbe mai un Governatore più prudente di Lui, nè un Condottore più destro della sua propria fortuna ... Egli fu amico senza fede, nemico senza rancore, Giudice senza Giustitia, gran Politico tra li disordini ... & in somma un compendio del maggior male, & un'Epilogo del più gran bene.') It is also noteworthy that de Galardi defended the style he had adopted by reference to a French translation of Tacitus: *La Tyrannie heureuse*, sig. *5r. There is no general study of continental representations of Cromwell. For a very brief overview, see W. C. Abbott, *The Writings and Speeches of Oliver Cromwell*, 4 vols (Cambridge, Mass.: Harvard University Press, 1937–47), iv. 883–4.

Germany at the time — that he had acquired such a keen interest in Hobbes that he sought him out in London in 1678.[99] In his *Meditationes politicae* (1674), Beckmann tried to weld together Hobbesian natural law theory and the entire Tacitist tradition of political analysis. His list of recommended modern writers on politics included Bacon, Boccalini, Boxhorn and Clapmarius, and culminated in Grotius, Hobbes and Pufendorf; substantial parts of the book were devoted to the defence and praise of Hobbes, whom he called 'ingeniosissimus'. His chapter on 'ratio status' began by explaining that while the name was new (invented, he said, by Italians in modern times), the theory was ancient, and could be found in the works of Tacitus.[100] As an exposition of it he recommended the *Dissertatio academica, cuius pars prima de ratione status* ... by Wilhelm von Schröder, a highly controversial work which had been denounced on its first appearance as an extreme statement of 'Hobbism'.[101] Beckmann's own argument, which followed quite closely in Hobbes's tracks, was that people act out of interest; that individual interests necessarily clash; that self-preservation is an overriding interest, which requires human beings to create sovereign authority; and that that authority can and should then act in whatever ways are necessary to advance the interest of the whole state.

Put in those terms, Hobbes's theory does seem to flow quite naturally from a Tacitist world-view. We can be confident, too, that Hobbes had read not only Tacitus, but also the works of some of the key writers in the modern Tacitist tradition. In the Chatsworth library catalogue which he drew up in the late 1620s (making some further additions in the early 1630s), we find, for example, 'Ammiratus in Tacitu[m]' (Scipione Ammirato, *Dissertationes politicae, sive discursus in C. Tacitum* ('Helenopolis', 1609), the

---

99 On Beckmann see C. G. Jöcher, *Allgemeines Gelehrten-Lexicon*, 4 vols (Leipzig, 1750-51), i. cols. 994-5, and F. Palladini, *Discussioni seicentesche su Samuel Pufendorf: scritti latini, 1663-1700* (n.p. [Bologna]: Il Mulino, 1978), 284-5. For his praise of Ebert see his *Notitia universitatis francofurtanae*, 118-19. Beckmann may also have given Ebert the idea of becoming a translator of politically interesting texts: he published a translation of James I's *Basilikon doron* (*Jacobi donum regium, sive de institutione principis* (Frankfurt an der Oder, 1679)).

100 J. C. Beckmann, *Meditationes politicae, iisdemque continuandis & illustrandis addita politica parallela* (Frankfurt an der Oder, 1679), 5-7 (writers), 24 ('Ingeniosissimum Hobbes), 31 ('ratio status'), 47-53, 85-6, 417-18 (defence of Hobbes). (This edition, the third of the *Meditationes*, includes the first printing of a second work, the *Politica parallela*.) All references to Hobbes were omitted from his later political treatise, *Conspectus doctrinae politicae*, but the essential theory remained unchanged; and that work did also include the statement that 'Machiavelli too is not as bad as he is popularly supposed to be' ('*Machiavellum quoq[ue] tam malum non esse, qvam vulgo creditur*', p. 6).

101 W. von Schröder ['Schröter'], *Dissertatio academica, cuius prima pars de ratione status, altera de nobilitate, tertia de ministrissimo* (Jena, 1663); this dissertation was presided over by S. C. Olpe, Rector Magnificus of the University of Jena, and Beckmann refers to it as his work (*Meditationes*, 44). On the reaction to it see Malcolm, *Aspects of Hobbes*, 512-13.

Latin version of his *Discorsi sopra Cornelio Tacito* (Florence, 1594)); 'Cleland. Institution of a Nobleman' (John Cleland, *Propaedeia, Or, The Institution of a Young Noble Man* (London, 1607) — a work written by the tutor of the young Prince Charles, which draws moral advice from Tacitus); 'Lipsij opera'; 'Lipsij Politica'; 'Tacitus English' (*The Annales of Cornelius Tacitus*, tr. R. Greenwey (London, 1598)); 'Ammirato. Discorsi sopra Tacito'; 'Boccalinj Ragguaglij di Pernasso'; 'Boccalinj Pietra di Parangone' [sic]; 'Tacito Lat. Italian by Dati. 2. vol.' (*C. Cornelij Taciti opera latina, cum versione italica* (Frankfurt, 1612), which included the translation by G. Dati, first published in Venice in 1563); 'Tacito Ital. by Politi' (*Annali, et istorie, di G. Cornelio Tacito*, tr. A. Politi (Venice, 1615–16)); 'Tacitus wth Aphorismes in Spanish' (*Tacito español, ilustrado con aforismos*, tr. B. Alamos de Barrientos (Madrid, 1614)); and 'Tacitus in french' (*Les Oeuvres de C. Cornelius Tacitus*, tr. C. Fauchet and E. de la Planche (Paris, 1584)).[102] When Hobbes's pupil William Cavendish (the future second Earl of Devonshire) published — anonymously — a book of his essays in 1620, it included a 'Discourse upon the Beginning of Tacitus'; although the claim by its two modern editors that this discourse was written by Hobbes may be doubted, the work nevertheless provides important evidence of the intellectual preoccupations of the person to whom Hobbes was most closely attached at that time.[103]

Many of the assumptions of the Tacitists, about human nature in general and political action in particular, can be found in Hobbes's works, implicitly or explicitly; and in few works are they more explicit than in *Behemoth*.[104] Of the Scottish gentry, 'B' remarks that 'in their lives they were just as other men are, pursuers of their own interests and preferments'; and more generally he insists that 'people always have been, and always will be, ignorant of their duty to the public, as never meditating anything but their particular interest'.[105] In some cases the pursuit of such interest is crude and straightforward (as with the soldiers who supported Cromwell only because 'they aimed at rapine and sharing the lands and goods of their enemies'); in other cases, while it rests on equally obvious foundations, it may have gained a little superstructure of pseudo-justification (as with the merchants who support rebellions because their 'pro-

---

102 Chatsworth, MS Hobbes E 1 A (unfoliated; the entries are given here in the order in which they appear). A forthcoming edition of this MS, by the late Richard Talaska, has been promised by the Philosophy Documentation Center, Bowling Green, Ohio.

103 The claim is made in 'T. Hobbes' (attrib.), *Three Discourses: A Critical Modern Edition of Newly Identified Work of the Young Hobbes*, ed. N. B. Reynolds and A. W. Saxonhouse (Chicago: University of Chicago Press, 1995). For the original text of this discourse see Anon. [W. Cavendish], *Horae subsecivae: Observations and Discourses* (London, 1620), 223–324.

104 See also Richard Tuck's comments in his 'Hobbes and Tacitus', in G. A. J. Rogers and T. Sorell, eds., *Hobbes and History* (London: Routledge, 2000), 99–111, esp. 109.

105 Tönnies edn, 29, 39.

fession is their private gain', but who claim to be taking a principled stand against the 'grievance' of taxation).[106]

However, in many cases—above all, the religious demagogues, on whom Hobbes lays the primary blame for the civil war—the pseudo-justification seems to have corrupted even the understandings of those who use it, so that it becomes hard to tell whether they are cynical hypocrites fooling the people, or whether they have, so to speak, fooled themselves, thereby becoming sincere fanatics. Thus on the one hand 'A' explains that the Presbyterians were 'impious hypocrites' who sought political power in order to 'fill their purses'; yet on the other hand he declares that 'this was the design of the Presbyterian ministers, who taking themselves to be, by divine right, the only lawful governors of the Church, endeavoured to bring the same form of government into the civil state'.[107] Fixated as he is on the idea that everything in the political realm depends, in the end, on the beliefs that exist in people's heads, Hobbes cannot operate with a simple dichotomy between the foolish multitude, whose beliefs are subject to manipulation, and their manipulators, the clever politicians, who act on a clear-sighted view of their own advantage—for the latter may also have beliefs in their heads that lead them to act in irrational ways.[108] When 'B' exclaims, 'What silly things are the common sort of people, to be cozened as they were so grossly!', 'A' replies: 'The craftiest knaves of all the Rump were no wiser than the rest whom they cozened. For the most of them did believe that the same things which they imposed upon the generality, were just and reasonable ... '.[109] His interest in this issue thus seems to have propelled Hobbes some way beyond the Tacitist position.

There are, it is true, plenty of passages in *Behemoth* which consist of analyses of political 'arts', 'artifices', deceptions and tricks, performed—sometimes with real skill—by both Presbyterians and Parliamentarians. Such passages do indeed show what a Tacitist grounding there was to Hobbes's understanding of political action. But as the work progresses, the Parliamentarians are increasingly shown to have been dupes themselves, always liable to be fooled or out-manoeuvred by others; and the Presbyterians are increasingly depicted as driven by an almost frenzied malice. Only one figure emerges on the rebel side who

---

106 Ibid., 126, 136,
107 Ibid., 26, 75, 89.
108 For a valuable analysis of how non-rational behaviour can be found at all levels of Hobbes's argument, see S. Holmes, 'Political Psychology in Hobbes's *Behemoth*', in M. G. Dietz ed., *Thomas Hobbes and Political Theory* (Lawrence, Kansas: University Press of Kansas, 1990), 120–52.
109 Tönnies edn, 158.

seems, for the most part, to have been neither a fool nor a fanatic: Oliver Cromwell. Here was someone who had both a long-term aim (to take sovereign power from the king and exercise it himself: 'His main end was to set himself in his place') and an interim strategy of self-advancement ('I cannot believe he then thought to be King; but only by well serving the strongest party, which was always his main polity, to proceed as far as that and fortune would carry him').[110] Hence the passages illustrating Cromwell's political skill, to which Ebert drew special attention with his marginal notes—above all, those describing his manoeuvrings in the period 1647-8, in what Hobbes portrays, in a grand extended metaphor, as 'a game at cards' between Cromwell and parliament. Here Ebert was responding to elements that are genuinely present in the text—even though he may not have appreciated all the nuances of Hobbes's writing. (When he translated 'This was the first trick Cromwell played' using the word 'artificium', and repeated it in his marginal note, he probably did not notice the card-game metaphor at work.)[111]

However, although Hobbes is happy to credit Cromwell with considerable political skill, he is far from portraying him as 'the perfect politician'. Even during that crucial political card-game, Cromwell is shown to have made a potentially devastating mistake, when he arranged for the king to escape from captivity; had the king actually fled abroad, he might have returned with a victorious French army, and it was only the unexpected actions of the Governor of the Isle of Wight that prevented that from happening.[112] Nor was Cromwell's judgement faultless in military affairs: Hobbes goes out of his way to emphasize that, during his last Scottish campaign, 'all his glories had ended in shame and punishment, if fortune and the faults of his enemies had not relieved him'.[113] And although Hobbes says almost nothing about Cromwell's religious convictions, he does allow 'B' to comment that he was 'superstitious' in his belief in 3 September as a lucky day—which suggests that there was room for at least some foolish beliefs in Cromwell's otherwise calculating brain.[114] The

---

110 Ibid., 143, 147. Both statements are by 'A', and the apparent contradiction between them is largely mitigated by the comments with which he introduces the latter statement: Cromwell had a series of necessary steps to take before he could seize kingly power, each of them difficult and risky, so that his strategy involved pitching his ambitions no higher than one step at a time.

111 Ibid., 138 (and see also the continuation of the metaphor on 139: 'These were the articles that put them to their trumps'); SBB, MS Lat. 2o 129, fo. 179r. Tuck notes parallels between Hobbes's treatment of Cromwell here and that of Augustus by Tacitus, as commented on in the 'Discourse upon the Beginning of Tacitus' ('Hobbes and Tacitus', 109–10).

112 Tönnies edn, 143–4.

113 Ibid., 167.

114 Ibid., 183.

overall assessment of Oliver Cromwell seems to be that he was a flawed but great politician: he may never have achieved any one thing quite so magnificent as Monck's march on London ('the greatest stratagem that is extant in history'), but he did display impressive political skills in a whole series of contests for power over a long period. (And, it must be said — though Hobbes does not of course make the comparison explicitly — he is shown to have been a much more skilled politician than Charles I, who failed to take the initiative at crucial moments, and allowed his advisers to talk him into pursuing a hopeless strategy of would-be negotiation.)[115]

One key term is used to characterize Cromwell's undoubted talent for power-politics: Hobbes refers to it as 'wit'. Describing Cromwell's seizure of sovereign power from parliament, 'A' remarks: 'Therefore he called a Parliament, and gave it the supreme power, with condition that they should give it to him. Was not this witty?'[116] The adjective may have overtones of humorous ingenuity, but the substantive stands for an important human attribute, a kind of natural prudence or cunning. In an earlier passage, 'A' described the plans of the Presbyterians to engineer a transfer of power from the king to the House of Commons, which they were confident they could control: 'wherein they were deceived, and found themselves outgone by their own disciples, though not in malice, yet in wit' — those disciples being, apparently, first the Independents, and then Cromwell.[117] The significance of this particular human attribute is brought home most strongly in an important speech delivered by 'A' near the beginning of the fourth dialogue:

> You may perhaps think a man has need of nothing else to know the duty he owes to his governor, and what right he has to order him, but a good natural wit; but it is otherwise. For it is a science, and built upon sure and clear principles, and to be learned by deep and careful study, or from masters that have deeply studied it ... Your calling the people silly, obliged me by this digression to show you, that it is not want of wit, but want of the science of justice, that brought them into these troubles. Persuade, if you can that man that has made his fortune, or made it greater, or an eloquent orator, or a ravishing poet, or a subtle lawyer, or but a good hunter or a cunning gamester, that he has not a good wit; and yet there were of all these a great many so silly, as to be deceived by the Rump and yet were members of the same Rump. They wanted not wit, but the knowledge of the causes and grounds upon which one person has a right to govern, and the rest an obligation to obey; which grounds are necessary to be taught the people, who without them cannot live long in peace amongst themselves.[118]

---

115 Ibid., 102–3, 125.
116 Ibid., 181.
117 Ibid., 75.
118 Ibid., 158–60.

The inclusion of cunning gamesters in this list of people with 'a good wit' is also significant: it reminds us that Hobbes's metaphor of the Cromwellian game of cards was not chosen lightly. Throughout his political writings, Hobbes resorts to metaphors of games of chance or skill (or some combination of the two) to characterize what true politics is not. In *De cive* he observes that wars of aggression are like games with dice ('sicut alea'), in most cases making the aggressors poorer in the long run.[119] And, famously, in *Leviathan* he declares:

> The skill of making, and maintaining Common-wealths, consisteth in certain Rules, as doth Arithmetique and Geometry; not (as Tennis-play) on Practise onely: which Rules, neither poor men have the leisure, nor men that have had the leisure, have hitherto had the curiosity, or the method to find out.[120]

This, surely, is where Hobbes departed from — and went far beyond — the Tacitist tradition. That tradition was fixated on the study of political history, because it did not believe that there was any 'method' that would yield certain rules for political action comparable to the rules of arithmetic and geometry; the most that any method could achieve was to extract maxims and aphorisms from a comparative study of discrete units of political experience. Hobbes, on the other hand, believed in the possibility of working out a true civil 'science' — a system of certain knowledge, not a mere accumulation of prudence. And he believed not only that that possibility had been realized (in his own writings), but also that it was necessary to teach the basic conclusions of that science to the people, so that they would have a clear understanding of their own political duties. That is the central theme of *Behemoth*; and every passage, every comment that emphasizes the importance of people's beliefs as the basis of their actions is itself an expression of that theme.

Hobbes made large claims about the ability of his 'science' to furnish all the essential principles needed for 'maintaining', as well as 'making', commonwealths: in other words, he seems to have thought that it could provide not only a formal system of rights and duties, but also, in some ways at least, the actual contents of governmental policies. Nevertheless, he did not exclude the need for knowledge of contingencies, or for the prudential skills required to manage them. Listing the qualities of a good 'Counsellor' in *Leviathan*, he put first a true understanding 'of the Rights of Government' (i.e. his 'science of justice'), and then added that knowledge was also required of 'the Strength, Commodities, Places, both of their own Country, and their Neighbours' — which, he said, 'is not

---

119 Hobbes, *De cive* (Paris, 1642), XIII. 14.
120 T. Hobbes, *Leviathan* (London, 1651), 107.

attained to, without much experience'. He concluded: 'When for the doing of any thing, there be Infallible rules ... all the experience in the world cannot equall his Counsell, that has learnt, or found out the Rule. And when there is no such Rule, he that hath most experience in that particular kind of businesse, has therein the best Judgement, and is the best Counsellour'.[121] At one point in *Leviathan* he even seemed to imply that governing a state consisted, most of the time, of the exercise of such prudence: 'To govern well a family, and a kingdome', he suggested, were both applications of prudence, albeit 'to different sorts of businesse'. That was the prudence which he had just defined as follows:

> When the thoughts of a man, that has a designe in hand, running over a multitude of things, observes how they conduce to that designe; or what designe they may conduce unto; if his observations be such as are not easie, or usuall, This wit of his is called PRUDENCE; and dependeth on much Experience, and Memory of the like things, and their consequences heretofore.[122]

In this sense, the story of how Cromwell exercised his political 'wit' may well have had some value, in Hobbes's eyes, as an example of how natural prudence could adapt to circumstances and carry an agent through to his long-term goal. But this can only have been a secondary purpose for Hobbes—not a primary one, as Ebert's re-titling of the entire work seemed to imply. If there was any didactic value in the story of Cromwell's prudential actions, it lay only in exhibiting the general functioning of such prudence (and at the same time, as we have seen, qualifying it as no guarantee of success); it did not consist, as Ebert and the Tacitists would have supposed, in furnishing a set of specific tricks and manoeuvres. For, as 'A' puts it in a dismissive comment about the Parliamentarians, 'If craft be wisdom, they were wise enough. But *wise*, as I define it, is he that knows how to bring his business to pass (without the assistance of knavery and ignoble shifts) by the sole strength of his good contrivance.'[123] Prudence is easily converted into craft by knavery: 'To Prudence, if you adde the use of unjust, or dishonest means ... you have that Crooked Wisdome, which is called CRAFT'.[124] The politician who based his actions on 'the science of justice', however, could never be perverted in this way; his actions—which, of course, might well be described as 'tyranny' by those who disliked their effects—would, by definition, never make use of unjust means. The Tacitist description of a world of craft and deception was not dismissed out of hand by Hobbes. On the con-

---

121 Ibid., 134-5.
122 Ibid., 34.
123 Tönnies edn, 38.
124 Hobbes, *Leviathan*, 34.

trary, he recognized it as a description of the real world—the reality of which had been made painfully clear in the British Isles between 1642 and 1660. But instead of trying to extract, from such a description, a set of techniques of deception which had proved successful before and might possibly be successful in the future, he aimed at something quite different: a true science of politics, which would guarantee the certainty of success for future rulers by systematically undeceiving the people. Tacitism mattered for Hobbes, but it did so only because it described the problem. To that problem, he offered a fundamentally different solution.

Paul Seaward

'Chief of the ways of God'
Form and Meaning in the 'Behemoth' of Thomas Hobbes

Behold now behemoth, which I made with thee;
   He eateth grass as an ox.
Lo now, his strength is in his loins,
   And his force is in the muscles of his belly.
He moveth his tail like a cedar:
   The sinews of his thighs are knit together.
His bones are as tubes of brass;
   His limbs are like bars of iron.
He is the chief of the ways of God:
   He only that made him can make his sword to approach unto him.
Surely the mountains bring him forth food;
   Where all the beasts of the field do play.
He lieth under the lotus trees,
   In the covert of the reed and the fen.
The lotus trees cover him with their shadow;
   The willows of the brook compass him about.
Behold, if a river overflow, he trembleth not;
   He is confident, though Jordan swell even to his mouth.
Shall any take him when he is on the watch,
   Or pierce through his nose with a snare?[1]

I

Behemoth is perhaps the oddest and most obscure of Hobbes's major works. Some of the oddness is explained by its difficult publishing history. One of a group of works written in the 1660s, the decade after the Restoration, it was not published then — apparently because the king refused to allow it to be — but it circulated in manuscript and eventually appeared in print in 1679 without Hobbes's authorisation and in a particularly poor version. Even the text Hobbes's publisher issued in 1682 after

---

1 Job 40: 15-24.

the philosopher's death was in places confused. Yet the difficulties with the text go much deeper than the vicissitudes of the press. The title by which the work is usually known suggests an antithesis with the Leviathan (the other overwhelmingly powerful beast described in Job), but nowhere does Hobbes indicate how this is meant to be read and, indeed, it is unclear whether this title was one which had Hobbes's sanction — or in fact what title he intended it to have. The work purports to be a relatively straightforward account of the English civil wars and their aftermath, the period between the mid to late 1630s and 1660. In fact it draws together a narrative largely borrowed from other publications with a summary of the views its author expounded in other works — particularly in the *Leviathan*. Moreover, the narrative is developed in the course of a dialogue between two people, marked 'A' and 'B', a form which seems peculiarly ill-adapted for conveying the hard facts of historical discourse. The effect is rather as if an originally stimulating and opinionated, though slightly one-sided, discussion in a pub has degenerated as one interlocutor virtually abandons the struggle in the hope of persuading his companion to shut up and go home.

It is difficult to fit Behemoth into any obvious context. A good proportion of Hobbes's work of the late 1660s was defensive, as, notoriously, Hobbes felt somewhat beleaguered after the Restoration. The reconstruction of the Church of England had restored to ecclesiastical and political power his main polemical opponents of the 1650s, a group of people who regarded him as uniquely dangerous to religion and government.[2] The views of Churchmen and their supporters would help to prevent almost all of his works from securing the licence required for publication after the passage of the Licensing Act 1662. Hobbes also felt under threat of being proceeded against for heresy, and devoted a considerable amount of his energy in the period to writing about the current enforceability of the law on the subject: apart from the *Historical Narration Concerning Heresie*, he handled it in the *Dialogue ...of the Common Laws*, in one of the appendices to the latin edition of *Leviathan*, and in *Behemoth*. However, as Philip Milton has shown, the threat was considerably greater in Hobbes's imagination than it was in reality. Hobbes's fears were centred on the bishops, whom he regarded — according to those who recorded his views during the decade — as the authors of a heresy prosecution in parliament. As Milton points out, although there was a resolution in the Commons in October 1666 which was intended to lead to an attack on *Leviathan*, it amounted to far less than a charge of heresy against the book's author. A

---

2   See Philip Milton, 'Hobbes, Heresy and Lord Arlington', *History of Political Thought* 14 (1993), 504–8, for Hobbes's relationship with the bishops, especially John Bramhall and Seth Ward.

bill ultimately issued from the Commons against atheism and profaneness, although it became embroiled in legal argument in the Lords and the text that emerged (but was nevertheless not passed) would not have helped anyone to prosecute Hobbes for heresy.

Richard Tuck has suggested a rather wider context for these works of the late 1660s, and has argued that they were meant as a contribution to the debates which took place in the House of Commons from 1667 to 1670 about whether to permit comprehension or toleration.[3] Philip Milton has also answered this point: Hobbes

> never mentioned the Act of Uniformity, the Conventicle Acts or any of the other measures against dissenters, and I very much doubt whether he disapproved of them. As Behemoth so clearly shows, he shared to the full the royalist view that dissenting conventicles were seed-beds of rebellion, and he would have few if any qualms about their suppression.[4]

Indeed, Hobbes condemns Independents and other 'enemies which arose against his Maiesty from the private interpretations of the Scripture exposed to every mans scanning in his Mother tongue'.[5]

Behemoth cannot be uncomplicatedly linked to any specific contemporary debate, and certainly not one about comprehension and toleration. Which is not to say that it does not engage with a number of contemporary ideas and polemics. *Behemoth*'s theme of the uses of eloquent demagoguery to lead people into discontent and violent disorder has been recognised by most commentators, and some scholars have fitted *Behemoth* into wider interpretations of Hobbes's work based on these lines. Stephen Holmes has read in it Hobbes's 'mature understanding of political breakdown and the reestablishment of authority'. The work provides insights into 'the subversion of rationality—into discombobulating passions, intoxicating doctrines, imposing names, and mesmerizing norms'.[6] Quentin Skinner has found in it an analysis of the destructive power of misdirected eloquence—the 'victory for irrational but overwhelming power of neo-classical and antinomian rhetoric' (of the 'democraticall gentlemen' and Presbyterian preachers) over the 'small power of science and rationality'; 'faced with interest and ignorance, reason and science have little chance of being heard'.[7] But its themes seem general, dis-

---

3 Richard Tuck, 'Hobbes and Locke on Toleration', in *Thomas Hobbes and Political Theory*, ed. M. G. Dietz (Lawrence: University Press of Kansas, 1990).
4 'Hobbes, Heresy and Lord Arlington', 532.
5 St John's College, Oxford, MS 13 [hereafter MS], fo. 2v; *EW* 6. 167.
6 Stephen Holmes, 'Political Psychology in Hobbes's Behemoth', in *Thomas Hobbes and Political Theory*, ed. M. G. Dietz.
7 Quentin Skinner, *Reason and Rhetoric in the Philosophy of Hobbes* (Cambridge: Cambridge University Press, 1996), 435, 433.

persed, and largely derived from Hobbes's more famous philosophical works. As a result, for most writers on Hobbes the work has been of relatively marginal interest in the canon. With little new material, and no very clear link to a political context, it is tempting, indeed, to regard Hobbes's account of the civil war as a confused and comparatively incoherent work of the philosopher's dotage. Can anything more be made of *Behemoth*?

II

Hobbes did provide some indication of what he was up to in *Behemoth*. The manuscript of the work, in the hand of Hobbes's amanuensis, James Wheldon, and preserved in the library of St John's College, Oxford, contains a dedication to the secretary of state, Lord Arlington, in which he presents his patron with what he describes as 'four short dialogues concerning the memorable Ciuill Warre in his Maiesties Dominions from 1640 to 1660'. Although there are four dialogues, the work falls more naturally into three sections. The first of the dialogues, he goes on to say, 'containes the seed of it, certaine opinions in Diuinity and Politicks'. The second dialogue 'hath the growth of it in Declarations, Remonstrances, and other writings between the King and Parliament published'. The third and fourth parts are 'a very short Epitome of the Warre it selfe, drawne out of Mr. Heath's Chronicle'.[8]

This final section relies very heavily on James Heath's *Brief Chronicle of the Late Intestine VVarr in the Three Kingdoms of England, Scotland and Ireland*, originally published in 1662, and apparently largely compiled from newsbook reports. From about a quarter of the way through Hobbes's third dialogue until the end of the book, beginning with the king's setting up of his standard at Nottingham on 23 August 1642, his text is indeed for much of the time an epitome of Heath's, borrowing many of the same words. It adopts similar breaks as Heath's text, ending part 3 as Heath does a section, after the execution of the king. Heath's text is, of course, vastly more detailed than is Hobbes's — the précis is often very severe; and where Hobbes pauses to provide more detail, the departures from his model are naturally significant. At their mildest, they slant the interpretation, sometimes only just noticeably. On the fight at Brentford shortly after Edgehill, for example, Heath writes separately of the preparations made by parliament before the battle, and then the effects of the news of the battle itself, which 'brought a general consternation upon the City of *London*, all shops were shut up, and all the Regiments, both Trained Band and Auxiliaries were drawn out, so that the Earl of *Essex* had a most compleat and numerous Army of a sudden'. Hobbes elides the informa-

---

8   MS, fo. 1v; *EW* 6. 166.

tion about preparation for the battle and the effect of the news to imply panic at the approach of the king: parliament 'caused all the Trained Bands and the Auxiliaries of the City of London (which was so frighted as to shut vp all their shops) to be drawn forth, so that there was a most compleat and numerous Army, ready for the Earle of Essex that was crept into London iust at the time to head it'.[9] Heath was himself capable of sardonic asides; but Hobbes frequently picks them up to make them much more rhetorically effective. On Fairfax's summons to the Trained Bands of counties adjoining London to join the army in response to the Presbyterian coup of July 1647, Heath notes that 'such Bands were not under pay of the Parliament, and so not under any Command of the General by any Order of Ordinance. But armed violence was not to be stopt with Lawyers niceties'. Hobbes has:

> B: Were the Trayned Soldiers part of the Generalls Army?
>
> A: No, nor at all in pay, nor could be without an order of Parliament. But what might not an Army doe after it had mastered all the Laws of the Land?[10]

Hobbes is sometimes provoked by Heath's account into a more elaborate digression. Explaining the easy collapse of the same coup, Heath says that 'the wealthier sort began to flinch from those resolutions of adhering to their Engagement to save their bags, nothing being more vogued among the people then that the City would be plundered, as it was given out by some of the Grandees of the Army'.[11] Hobbes takes a longer detour from his narrative, twisting the same point into an attack on the values of the City:

> I consider the most part of rich subiects, that haue made themselues so by craft and trade as men that neuer look vpon any thing but their present profit, and who to euery thing not lying in that way are in a manner blind, being amazed at the very thought of plundering. If they had vnderstood what vertue there is to preserue their wealth in obedience to their lawfull Soueraigne, they would neuer haue sided with the Parliament, and so we had had no need of arming. The Mayor and Aldermen therefore being assured by this submission to saue their goods, and not sure of the same by resisting, seeme to me to haue taken the wisest course.[12]

One of the most striking passages of this kind comes when both authors open their accounts of 1648 with a description of the parliamentary visita-

---

9 James Heath, *A Brief Chronicle of the Late Intestine War* (London, 1633) [Wing H1319][hereafter Heath], 70; MS fo. 59; *EW* 6. 315.

10 Heath, 249–150 [recte 250]; MS fo. 67v; *EW* 6. 339.

11 Heath, 247.

12 MS fo. 68; *EW* 6. 240.

tion of the University of Oxford. Heath had himself been ejected during this process, from a studentship of Christ Church, Oxford, and not unnaturally injects into his account a strong sense of personal loss and grievance, lamenting the removal of 'the most eminent for Learning, and Piety and Duty to the Church'. Parliament had resolved, he writes,

> to put out (as the accursed *Philistians* did to *Samson*) the eyes of the Kingdome, that so they might make sport with our Laws, Franchises, and Priviledges, and then ruin and fatally destroy us, at last separating the Head from the Body Politique in their ensuing monstrous Regicide.

One can almost hear Hobbes's snort of derision as he comes across the passage. His version reports that the Parliamentary Commission had:

> turned out all such as were not of their faction, and all such as had approued the vse of the Common Prayer booke; as also diuers scandalous Ministers and Schollars (that is, such as customarily without need took the name of God into their mouths, or vsed to speake wantonly, or haunt the company of lewd women). And for this last I cannot but commend them.

An untraditional view from a royalist, to say the least. Hobbes turns then to a long condemnation of the Universities not only as nurseries of vice, but also because they provided the clergy with a platform from which they could disseminate their views: 'certainly an Vniuersity is an excellent seruant to the Clergy, and the Clergy if it be not carefully look'd to (by their dissentions in doctrins, and by the aduantage to publish their dissentions) is an excellent means to diuide a Kingdome into factions'.[13]

Heath cannot quite be Hobbes's sole source for the third and fourth dialogues, for there are differences in some details, although usually minor ones. The account of the king's trial and execution may owe something to a separate collection of documents. Some divergences from Heath's account may be explainable by Hobbes's own connections — for example his claim that the Earl of Newcastle had in late 1642 'made himselfe in a manner master of all the North': Heath in fact gives the contrary impression.[14] Some others are difficult to explain, however. The account, for example, in the fourth dialogue of the treason and summary execution of Manning, Cromwell's spy at the royalist court, contains a number of details which are not derived from Heath, and presumably come from personal information.[15] Sometimes Hobbes alters the order in which he deals with events, presumably to maintain his narrative more effectively, although this can have a somewhat confusing effect. Often he compresses

---

13   MS fo. 70– v; *EW* 6. 347.
14   Heath, 71; MS fo. 59v; *EW* 6. 316.
15   MS fo. 88; *EW* 6. 394.

the narrative severely — this is particularly noticeable where he discusses the events leading up to Pride's Purge and the execution of the king — and as a result produces a garbled or confused account.

The second part of *Behemoth* is derived from a different source. He described it as providing an account of the development of the confrontation between king and parliament 'in Declarations, Remonstrances, and other writings'. It is in fact only about half way through the Second Dialogue that Hobbes begins to describe these exchanges in detail — just at the point where the fullest collection of printed documents, that published by Edward Husbands, begins with the Grand Remonstrance of December 1641. From this point Hobbes goes systematically through all of the significant documents in the collection, describing and commenting on them: Husbands' collection becomes, in fact, the sole basis of his account for the period leading up to the outbreak of war. His own responses to the parliamentary texts he describes are often based on the king's responses printed in the same volume. Understandably much of the detail of the increasingly complex exchanges is omitted or compressed; but at some points Hobbes becomes either disingenuous or cavalier with his sources. Towards the end of the second dialogue, for example, as he discusses the addresses, answers and replies which flew with exceptional velocity around the time of the defence of the king by Sir John Hotham at Hull, Hobbes attributes to parliament certain propositions which were in fact ironically given to it in one of the king's Answers — in *His Majestie's Answer to a Printed Booke*, one of the works of royalist propaganda drafted by Hobbes's former acquaintance, now Lord Chancellor, Edward Hyde, which provoked one of parliament's own most famous polemics, Henry Parker's *Observations upon some of his Majesties late Answers and Expresses*. B's response to Hyde's tendentious summary of parliamentary political philosophy that 'This is plain dealing and without hypocrisie', echoes the words of the king's reference to parliament's Remonstrance of 26 May 1642, which ironically commends the 'plaine dealing and ingenuity of the Framers and Contrivers of that Declaration' — but fails to recognize the fact that the text he cites came not from parliament, but its enemies.[16]

Much of the text of *Behemoth* after the middle of the second dialogue is in some sense a commentary on Heath and Husbands, and it is tempting to imagine the old man sitting with the two books open in front of him, dictating to James Wheldon his summaries and comments as he leafs through the pages. There are, perhaps, some affinities with his procedure in the *Dialogue between a philosopher and a student of the Common Laws of England*, another work of the 1660s, which treats Coke on Littleton and a

---

16 MS fo. 50v; *EW* 6. 292.

set of the statutes in much the same way. In some ways this makes it seem an unambitious text—a work perhaps like the *Epitome* of Thomas May's *History*, produced presumably more for commercial than intellectual reasons. But it is clear that Hobbes thought of his text as considerably more serious and significant than was conveyed by the word 'epitome' which he used for the third and fourth dialogues—not just because Heath and Husbands are used to spark off reflections on the history of the period, but also because more than three-eighths of the work is constructed in a rather different fashion. The first of the dialogues, in fact, is much less closely tied to facts and events: indeed, it is only around half-way through the dialogue that Hobbes mentions a specific event—the attempt to introduce the Book of Common Prayer into Scotland in 1637—and only around three and a half pages out of 38 are taken up with a narrative. The business of the first and second dialogues is weighted towards analysis, rather than reportage; not so much (in the words of B's request at the beginning of the work) an account of the 'actions you then saw', but of their 'causes, pretensions, iustice, order, artifice, and euent'.[17] It is also the polemical heart of the work, in which is contained what appears to be the admonitory message which Hobbes wanted to convey.

III

The first dialogue launches quickly into a discussion of the causes of the collapse of royal authority in 1642. The typology of 'seducers' who had 'corrupted' the people which is sketched out by the main speaker, labelled as 'A', is a familiar one from the views of other royalist commentators: Ministers 'pretending to have a right from God to governe every one his Parish' (in other words Presbyterians); Roman Catholics; Independents and other sectaries; gentlemen who had read too deeply in the classics and 'became thereby in love with their formes of government'; the City of London and other large towns, who saw the prosperity of the low countries and expected that a change to republican government would produce the like in England; the ambitious, who 'hoped to maintain themselves ... by the lucky choosing of a party to side with'; and the people generally, who

> were so ignorant of their duty, as that not one perhaps of ten thousand knew what right any man had to command him, or what necessity there was of King or Commonwealth, for which he was to part with his money against his will; but thought himselfe to be so much master

---

17 MS fo. 2; *EW* 6. 163.

of whatsoever he possest, that it could not be taken from him upon any pretence of common safety without his own consent.[18]

Hobbes continues by discussing, apparently in the order given above, these various groups and how they had gone about corrupting the people. Much of about the first two-fifths of the first dialogue consists of a discussion of the practices of the Pope and the Roman Church in establishing their power over secular rulers, a discussion which very largely repeats and expands on the points made in the last Chapter of *Leviathan*. Then 'B' turns 'A''s attention to the Presbyterians, asking him 'how came their Power to be so great, being of themselves for the most part but so many poor Schollers?'[19] In the course of this discussion, 'A' refers also to the fourth sort of seducers, the gentlemen who read too deeply in the classics; but the argument hinges largely on the Presbyterians' powers of rhetoric and the effectiveness of their persuasion. At this point, the dialogue starts to move towards narrative, with explanations of the Scottish resistance to the Prayer Book and episcopacy, as well as a lengthy digression concerning nationality rights for the Scots in England. It returns to the analysis when Hobbes criticises the opposition to Ship Money in the late 1630s and the leadership of some of the gentry who sat in the House of Commons, who were capable of drawing with them not only other Members of Parliament, but also the common people as a whole.

Having established the main causes of the events of 1640 and afterwards, the discussion turns naturally to how to avoid a repetition of the chain of events that produced the War: 'A' argues that it comes down to education, that people should be 'taught their duty, that is the Science of Just and Vniust, as diuers other Sciences haue been taught from true Principles, and euident demonstration'; 'B' does not demur, but doubts how these things can effectively be taught 'when it is against the interest of those that are in possession of the power to hurt him?' Hobbes explains through 'A', with transparent self-advertising intent, that

> The Rules of Just and Vniust sufficiently demonstrated, and from Principles euident to the meanest capacity, haue not been wanting; and notwithstanding the obscurity of their Author, haue shined not onely in this, but also in forraigne Countries to men of good education.[20]

But as he goes on to say, disseminating these principles can only be done through the pulpit—precisely the source of so much of the teaching that had caused the trouble in the first place: 'And therefore the light of that

---

18 MS fo. 2v–3; *EW* 6. 167.
19 MS fo. 11; *EW* 6. 190.
20 MS fo. 19v; *EW* 6. 212–13.

Doctrine has been hitherto couer'd and kept vnder here by a cloud of aduersaries which no priuate mans reputation can break through, without the Authority of the Vniuersities'.[21] There follows an explanation of the creation of the universities and the way that they had instituted a form of learning designed to maintain the power of the Pope and clergy, bending the Logic, Physics and Metaphysics of Aristotle to their purposes. 'A' then discusses Aristotle's *Ethics*, indicating that he regards there to be a difference between the ethical virtues of subjects and those of sovereigns, and concluding, against Aristotle, that 'all actions and habits are to be esteemed good or euill, by their causes and vsefullnesse in reference to the Common wealth, and not by their mediocrity nor by their being commended'.[22] 'B' objects that he has not considered Religion to be a virtue, though it should be the greatest. 'A' responds, but only after a short passage explaining the relevance of the discussion which would appear to be a digression—a passage which must be intended to flag up that the next few pages are particularly significant. He tells 'B' that 'all vertue is comprehended in obedience to the Laws of the Common wealth, whereof Religion is one'; and therefore 'I haue placed Religion amongst the Vertues'. In view of the uncertainty of what God has actually instructed men to do, it is necessary that people should recognize some human authority in the matter. In any question where people's duty to God and the king is involved, they should therefore accept the word of the sovereign — or the law — rather than the preaching of their fellow subjects or of a stranger. 'B' leaps to the conclusion that he is meant to draw: 'if the King giue vs leaue, you or I may as lawfully preach as any of them that doe. And I beleeue we should performe that office a great deale better, then they that preach'd vs into the Rebellion'.[23] 'A' goes on to describe the principal virtues as conceived by the Church of Rome: 'to obey their Doctrine though it be Treason; and that is their Piety and Liberality. To be beneficiall to the Clergy, that is to be Religious. And to beleeue vpon their word that which a man knows in his Conscience to be false; which is the faith they require'.[24]

So far, this is not significantly further than Hobbes went in *Leviathan*; and the more specific comments on the clergy are directed pretty clearly at the Church of Rome. But at this point, 'B' asks, reasonably enough, whether it might also be held to apply to the established clergy in England: 'what is the Morall Philosophy of the Protestant Clergy in England?'

---

21 Ibid.; *EW* 6. 213.
22 MS fo. 22; *EW* 6. 220.
23 MS fo. 22v; *EW* 6. 221.
24 MS fo. 23; *EW* 6. 221–2.

'A' is understandably cautious, and answers (though with a sting in the tail) 'so much as they shew of it in their life and conuersation is for the most part very good, and of very good example, much better then their writings'. His next step is cast as a question — in other words, the point is made as deniably as possible:

> Doe the Clergy in England pretend, as the Pope does, or as the Presbyterians doe to haue a right from God immediately to gouerne the King and his subiects in all points of Religion and Manners? If they doe you cannot doubt but that if they had number and strength, which they are neuer like to haue, they would attempt to obtaine that power, as the others haue done.

Without responding to this, 'B' says that he would like to 'see a Systeme of the present Moralls written by some Diuine of good reputation and learning, and of the late Kings party'. 'A' directs him to *The Whole Duty of Man* — 'the best that is extant, and such a one as (except a few passages that I mislike) is very well worth your reading'. *The Whole Duty of Man*, now assumed to be by Richard Allestree, Provost of Eton from 1665 and Regius Professor at Oxford, was perhaps the best-selling manual of practical theology published in the seventeenth century, and a classic statement of Anglican devotion. Yet 'A' goes on to say, now more daringly, that 'if the Presbyterian ministers, euen those of them which were the most diligent Preachers of the late Sedition were to be tryed by it, they would go neer to be found not guilty'.[25]

'A' aims to show, in short, how the Anglican version of the subject's duty is entirely consistent with the doctrine of Presbyterians. Their interpretation of the attributes of God are the same; they acknowledge the word of God to be the same books of Scripture, and if (as 'B' objects) it is 'according to their own interpretation', this is no different to the approach of the Bishops and the loyal party. On that basis it was impossible to accuse them of acting against God's will, for as 'B' acknowledges, 'Hypocrisy hath indeed this great Prerogatiue aboue other sins, that it cannot be accused'. 'B' follows by recognizing that 'the Loyall party and the Presbyterians haue always had an equall care to haue Gods House free from profanation, to haue Tiths duly paid, and Offerings accepted, to haue the Sabbath day kept holy, the Word preached, and the Lord's Supper and Baptisme duly administred', implying that these are services to God which happen to be in the interests of the clergy of whatever persuasion. 'B' moves quickly on to the main point — the duty that is owed to the king. 'A' quotes Allestree to say that active obedience is owed to rulers in the case of all lawful commands, when the magistrate commands some-

---

25 MS fo. 21; *EW* 6. 223.

thing that is not contrary to some command of God. But when the magistrate commands something that *is* contrary to what God has commanded, then

> we may, nay we must refuse thus to act (yet here we must be very well assured that the thing is so contrary, and not pretend conscience for a Cloak of Stubbornesse) we are in that case to obey God rather then men. But euen this is a season for the passiue obedience, we must patiently suffer what he inflicts on us for such refusall, and not, to secure our selues, rise vp against him.[26]

'B' reasonably asks why this doctrine should give any excuse for rebellion, or be linked to it; 'A' responds that even if it does not apparently justify rebellion, nevertheless, like the Presbyterian doctrine, it claims to set the individual's interpretation of God's word above the determination of the Sovereign.

> If it be lawfull then for subiects to resist the King when he commands any thing that is against the Scripture, that is contrary to the Command of God, and to be Judge of the meaning of the Scripture, it is impossible that the life of any King or the peace of any Christian Kingdome can be long secure. It is this Doctrine that diuides a Kingdome within it selfe, whatsoeuer the men be Loyall or Rebells that write or preach it publickly.[27]

Whether or not the resistance is violent, in short, it still undermines the authority of the sovereign; besides, Hobbes doubts that passive obedience can ever be a realistic doctrine:

> He that means his suffering should be taken for Obedience, must not onely not resist, but also not fly, nor hide himselfe to auoid his punishment. And who is there amongst them that discourse thus of passiue obedience, when his life is in extreme danger that will voluntarily present himselfe to the Officers of Justice? Doe not we see that all men when they are led to execution are both bound and guarded. And would break loose if they could, and get away? Such is their passiue obedience.[28]

'B' does not object to this claim, but does point out that Allestree at least insists that before refusing active obedience to the king on the grounds that it would be contrary to God's law, the refuser must be 'very well assured that the thing is so contrary'. 'A' tells him that

> because men do for the most part rather draw the Scripture to their owne sense, then follow the true sense of the Scripture, there is no other way to know certainly and in all cases what God commands or forbids vs to doe, but by the Sentence of him or them that are constituted by the King to determine the sense of the Scripture vpon hearing

26 MS fo. 24; *EW* 6. 225.
27 MS fo. 24v; *EW* 6. 226.
28 MS fo. 24v; *EW* 6. 226.

of the particular case of Conscience which is in question. And they that are so constituted are easily knowne in all Christian Common wealths, whether they be Bishops, or Ministers, or Assemblies that gouerne the Church vnder him or them that haue the Soueraigne Power.[29]

There is an insinuation here that Allestree's attempted reassurance that the refuser needs absolute certainty of the rightness of his refusal is no reassurance at all, for the judge in these circumstances is likely to be the Church itself. 'B' raises the objection that in that case, why were the Scriptures translated into English; and what right had the apostles to defy the high priest? In the latter case, answers 'A', their knowledge that they had received a revelation from God provided them with just cause; and he argues that the benefits of the Scriptures being in English, in terms of the lessons they can provide in both 'faith and manners' much outweigh the disadvantages.

At this point the argument shifts away from the discussion of Anglican political theology and back to the issue about education, how to teach the science of just and unjust. 'A' expands on the benefits of reading Scripture, and claims that men who 'are of a condition and age, fit to examine the sense of what they read, and that take a delight in searching out the grounds of their duty, certainly cannot chuse but by their reading of the Scriptures, come to such a sense of their duty, as not onely to obey the Laws themselues, but also to induce others to do the same.'[30] 'B' leaps to the conclusion that he means those learned in Greek and Latin, who are 'such as love knowledge and consequently take delight in finding out the meaning of the most hard Tests, or in thinking they have found it, in case it be new, and not found out by others', people who have 'had their breeding in the Vniuersities', where they are exposed to both pointless controversies about the nature of God and seditious discussions about the rights of civil and ecclesiastical government; he goes on to argue that reform of the universities to bring them to 'such a compliance with the actions of state, as is necessary for the business' is essential for the maintenance of peace.[31] 'A' responds in an arch fashion that since the universities had so effectively served the authority of the Pope against the right of Kings and contrary to the law, 'why can they not as well, when they haue all manner of Laws, and Equity on their side, maintaine the Rights of him that is both Soueraigne of the Kingdome, and Head of the Church?' 'B' asks why did this not happen at the Reformation, when Henry VIII became head of the Church; 'A' tells him that this is because the Bishops contrived, rather

---

29 MS fo. 25– v; *EW* 6. 228.
30 MS fo. 26v; *EW* 6. 231.
31 MS fo. 27; *EW* 6. 233.

than abandoning the powers and rights that the Pope had lost, to take them over themselves: 'For though they were content that the Diuine Right which the Pope pretended to in England, should be denyed him; yet they thought it not so fit to be taken from the Church of England, whom they now supposed themselves to represent'.[32]

At this point Hobbes seems to try to divert attention from the bitterness with which he is assailing the Church of England by returning to the Presbyterians and their hypocrisy. But he quickly returns to the universities and the need for their reform: he recommends that they were

> not to be cast away, but to be better disciplin'd, that is to say, That the Polyticks there taught be made to be (as true Polyticks should be) such as are fit to make men know that it is their duty to obey all Laws whatsoeuer shall by the Authority of the King be enacted, till by the same Authority they shall be repealed; such as are fit to make men vnderstand that the Ciuill Laws are Gods Laws, as they that make them are by God appointed to make them; and to make men know that the People and the Church are one thing, and haue but one Head the King, and that no man has title to gouerne vnder him, that has it not from him. That the King ows his Crowne to God onely, and to no man Ecclesiastick or other. And that the Religion they teach there, be a quiet waiting for the comming againe of our blessed Sauiour, and in the mean time a resolution to obey the Kings Laws (which also are Gods Laws) to iniure no man, to be in charity with all men, to cherish the poor and sick, and to liue soberly and free from scandall.[33]

Given that 'B' has already suggested that he and 'A' could preach as effectively as the clergy, it seems clear that Hobbes is suggesting nothing less than a repeat of the purge of the Universities which he praises in the third dialogue, but one guided by himself—or at least by his doctrine. Peace demands, in effect, the takeover of the higher education system by the secular authorities, and its reform on lines drawn up by Hobbes. Only this will overcome the power of the Clergy, as dangerous in Anglican hands as in Roman Catholic or Presbyterian ones.

In short, within the first dialogue of *Behemoth*, there exists a carefully constructed and very specific argument and message. The doctrine of the Church of England threatened the peace and stability of the kingdom just as significantly as did that of the Presbyterians (or indeed the Romanists); and that peace and stability could not be guaranteed without the civil power seizing control of the system which educated those who wielded social and educational influence. The clergy of the Church of England and the universities are not, it is true, *Behemoth*'s only targets—the text throughout is particularly virulent on Presbyterianism and on the

---

32 MS fo. 27v; *EW* 6. 234.
33 MS fo. 28- v; *EW* 6. 236.

common-law culture of mid-seventeenth century England—but the attacks on them do form the most original aspects of the work. *Leviathan* had mounted an assault on priestcraft; it had not, however, specifically or directly attacked the Church of England, largely, no doubt, because during the 1650s Anglicanism was almost irrelevant (as Hobbes pointed out). It had also made a number of references to the role of papally instituted universities in upholding clerical power and had (in the Review and Conclusion) advertised his own doctrines as the antidote. But the point had been made there much less vigorously than in *Behemoth*. This part of *Behemoth*'s message, at any rate, was not missed by contemporaries. A member of the Privy Council, Sir Thomas Chicheley, noticed its appearance in 1679, telling a friend 'I think [it] as well worth your reading as any thing you have read a great while there is no fault in it but his animosity to the universityes'.[34]

IV

Why, though, is this argument juxtaposed with a more straightforward narrative of the civil war, its origins and its consequences? It may be explained by a very specific set of circumstances, which ties *Behemoth* not to a particular contemporary political debate, but with one of Hobbes's ongoing controversies; it also, I think, increases the likelihood that *Behemoth* was the title intended by Hobbes. Towards the end of the discussion outlined above Hobbes uses a peculiar and apparently irrelevant quotation. As 'B' talks about the continuing inadequacies of Presbyterians he quotes a phrase from Book IV of Virgil's *Aeneid*: 'haeret lateri letalis harundo' ('fast to her side clings the deadly shaft', according to the Fairclough translation).[35] The phrase comes as part of a simile about the lovelorn Dido, who is compared to a hind, already mortally wounded by an arrow, running about in a frenzied attempt to escape. It would naturally, I suppose, be taken to refer to the following sentence: 'The Seditious Doctrine of the Presbyterians has been stuck so hard into the peoples heads and memories (I cannot say into their hearts, for they vnderstand nothing in it, but that they may lawfully Rebell) that I fear the Common wealth will neuer be cured'.[36] Yet the phrase seems forced in this context, and it does, in fact, have a much more precise significance.

Bramhall's 1658 review of *Leviathan*, *The Catching of Leviathan or the Great Whale*, was the target of one of Hobbes's other works of the late

---

[34] Legh MSS, John Rylands Library (unnumbered). I am grateful to Mark Knights for this reference.
[35] Virgil, *Aeneid*, IV. 73 (Loeb ed., vol. I. 400).
[36] MS fo. 28; *EW* 6. 235.

1660s. There is some evidence that this text was in Hobbes's mind in 1668, about the same time as he was working on *Behemoth*. In the preface to his response to Bramhall, Hobbes writes that although Bramhall's text was published ten years previously, he had seen it for the first time only three months before. If this comment is not mistaken or disingenuous (both of which are possible), it dates the *Answer* to 1668. This seems confirmed by the fact that he was corresponding with the Under secretary of state, Joseph Williamson, in June 1668 about alterations to the text of his *Historical Narrative concerning Heresy*—a work which was eventually published with and appears to be linked to the answer to Bramhall. Bramhall's work has a preface, addressed 'to the Christian Reader', in which the Bishop plays with the image of Leviathan at some length, applying it to Hobbes himself—'The Leviathan doth not take his pastime in the deep with so much freedom, nor behave himself with so much height and insolence, as T.H. doth in the Schooles, nor domineer over the lesser fishes with so much scorn and contempt, as he doth over all other authors'. Hobbes is not so absolute a sovereign as he imagines himself to be: 'Our Greenland fishers have found out a new art to draw him out of his Castle, that is, the deep, though not with a fish hook, yet with their harping irons'. Three of these harpoons have been provided (by Bramhall of course): the first is aimed at his heart, the theological part of his discourse, to show his principles are not consistent with Christianity or any other religion; the second at the backbone, the political part of the discourse, to show that his principles are 'pernicious to all forms of government and all societies'; and the third at his head, or the 'rational part of his discourse', to show that his principles are inconsistent with themselves and contradict one another. Bramhall concludes with the warning 'Let him take heed, if these three darts do pierce his Leviathan home, it is not all the Dittany which groweth in Creet that can make them drop easily out of his body, without the utter overthrow of his course', and the quotation: 'haerebit lateri lethalis arundo'.[37] Hobbes's use of this quotation ten years later in *Behemoth*, with its reference to doctrines being stuck hard into people's heads, memories and hearts, show, I think, that he is making a deliberate and teasing reference here to Bramhall's words; moreover, the fact that it is Presbyterian doctrines which are stuck is perhaps intended to back up the main thesis —that Anglican views on matters of clerical power are no different in practice from Presbyterian ones.

That this is the essential message of *Behemoth* is, I think, clinched by the work's odd title—a subject on which it is the controversy with Bramhall,

---

37 John Bramhall, *The Catching of Leviathan*, preface, in *Castigations of Mr. Hobbes his last animadversions in the case concerning liberty and universal necessity* (1657).

again, that casts some light. That the title was intended by Hobbes has been doubted: he never referred to it by this name, and complained of its 'foolish title' when it emerged in its unauthorised state in 1679.[38] Yet the title he must have been referring to the was not *Behemoth* but the *History of the Civil Wars of England*, the title borne by the unauthorised printings of 1679; the St John's manuscript does bear the title *Behemoth*, apparently in Wheldon's hand, as does Crooke's 1682 edition. Hobbes's use of the word in his earlier controversy with Bramhall in the 1650s — published as *Liberty, Necessity and Chance* — is relatively well known. Archbishop Bramhall said that two of his own Church were busy preparing answers to *Leviathan*, and offered to write one himself, to show how Hobbes's principles 'are pernicious both to piety and policy, and destructive to all relations'. Hobbes responded that '*I desire not that he or they should so misspend their time; but if they will needs do it, I can give them a fit title for their book, Behemoth against Leviathan*'.[39] When he came to read *The Catching of Leviathan* in 1668 he would have been reminded of the comment, for Bramhall alludes to it there, in the same preface as he uses the Virgilian quotation referred to above.

In the remark in the controversy with Bramhall, the word Behemoth is used to mean the Church: the clerical estate against the civil power. Hobbes was not the first to use the word in this way, or close to it. Patricia Springborg has emphasised how Reformation writers such as Beza and Calvin avoided allegorical interpretations of Job, and stressed instead a more naturalistic interpretation, but Mornay's anti-papal tract *The Mystery of Iniquity* (to which Hobbes makes a gratuitous reference in *Behemoth*) quotes allegorical uses in pre-Reformation texts.[40] One of St Bernard's sermons refers to Behemoth (according to Mornay) as antichrist, who 'hath devoured the flouds of the Wise, and the streams of the mightie', and 'trusteth that he can draw up Jordan into his mouth, that is the simple and humble that are in the Church'.[41] Mornay also quoted Matthew of Paris's account of the prophecy of Robert Grosseteste, Bishop of Lincoln in the time of Henry III:

> he did manifest by what meanes the Roman Court, like as Behemoth (in Iob) promised to swallow up all Iordan in this throat, might usurpe unto herselfe the goods of all intestates, and distinct legacies,

---

38 Letter 208, *Correspondence of Thomas Hobbes*, ed. Noel Malcolm (Oxford: Clarendon, 1994), vol. 2. 772.
39 *The Questions concerning Liberty, Necessity and Chance*, EW 5. 27.
40 Patricia Springborg, 'Hobbes's Biblical Beasts: Leviathan and Behemoth', *Political Theory* 23 (1995), 357–60.
41 Philip Mornay, *The Mysterie of Iniquitie: That is to say, the Historie of the Papacie, englished by Samson Lennard* (London, 1612), 304.

> and for the more licentious performance hereof, how she might draw
> the King to be a partaker and consort with her, in her rapine.⁴²

In these examples, the word is used to describe the Roman Church, or various manifestations of it. But I think that, as Hobbes's reference to the word during the mid-1650s implies, we should read it as referring to the Church of England and its episcopate.

An objection to this interpretation is that the title used in the St John's manuscript—*Behemoth or the Long Parliament*—seems to suggest that Behemoth should be taken as meaning the Long Parliament, and some commentators have viewed it in this way.⁴³ Such a meaning need not be excluded: Hobbes enjoyed creating ambiguity, and he may well have intended that Behemoth could be taken to mean either the Long Parliament or the Church—whether Roman or Anglican—either because both are aimed at in the text, or else because he was keen to confuse his critics. It is also the case that Hobbes used the word in the *Historia Ecclesiastica* in a different sense: here Leviathan *and* Behemoth are depicted as both being ensnared by their common enemy, the papacy:

> But now the Pope his end completely gains
> And leads the People, and their Prince, in Chains:
> Now vast *Leviathan* the Hook receives,
> And *Behemoth* his wounded Nostrils grieves:
> All gently own the Pope's Imperial Sway
> Where'r the *Roman* eagles wing their Way.⁴⁴

Again, I don't believe that this should prevent us from interpreting Hobbes's use of the word in *Behemoth* in a different sense: Hobbes makes use of the phrase as his polemical or rhetorical requirements take him, and in the verse ecclesiastical history he plainly wished to pick up on the idea that here were two beasts described in Job as impossible to capture, which the papacy had succeeded in taming. Other interpretations have been advanced: Luc Borot has suggested that 'the fact that the word behemoth is in the plural, and connected to the explanation of the behaviour of groups makes me think that there is a connection—one that takes account of one of the most fundamental assumptions of the way of thinking of the time'—in other words Behemoth represents the turbulence of the common people. While plausible, and, as Borot says, consonant with contemporary ideas of the nature of popular interventions in political life, I can find no evidence in the text to support it.⁴⁵ Using Behemoth as the title for

---

42 Ibid., 400.
43 Patricia Springborg, 'Hobbes's Biblical Beasts', 368.
44 Quoted in ibid., 363.
45 Luc Borot, 'Hobbes's *Behemoth*', in *Hobbes and History*, ed. G. A. J. Rogers and T. Sorrell (London: Routledge, 2000).

the dialogues seems intended by Hobbes as a sort of joke, offered in a spirit of some ambiguity, but containing a message meant to be in line with significant parts of the text: Behemoth, the 'chief of the ways of God', is to be read as an ironic reference not just to the Church, but more specifically to the Church of England, its hierarchy and to one of its chief defenders, Archbishop Bramhall.

V

Behemoth remains an ambiguous work, so oddly put together that it is worth considering whether its gestation is more complex than at first appears. Karl Schuhmann speculated that *Behemoth* was the work that Hobbes told Du Verdus about in a lost letter of 1666.[46] If this is right, if *Behemoth* does contain references made in response to *The Catching of Leviathan*, and if that response can be dated to 1668, then it seems conceivable that it was originally a relatively straightforward narrative work—though with some commentary—onto which Hobbes grafted, somewhat uncomfortably and well after it was begun, some elements of a response to Bramhall. This interpretation would certainly fit with the fact that Hobbes referred in his letter to Du Verdus to an 'epitome', and described the third and fourth dialogues in his dedication to Arlington as an 'epitome', yet did not use the word to describe the work as a whole.

It also seems possible that the work—or at least these polemical parts of it—may be associated with a particular moment and opportunity. The fall of the Earl of Clarendon in August 1667 was widely seen as removing from power one of the Church's principal defenders and allowing the re-opening of the debate on the Restoration ecclesiastical settlement. One result was the sporadic debates on comprehension and toleration which ensued. While *Behemoth* seems clearly not to be designed as a contribution to those debates, it may stem from the same moment—a moment which may have seemed to Hobbes particularly apt to offer his thoughts on the need for a revision of the relationship between Church and State.

These are speculations. But it is clear that some of the most significant parts of *Behemoth* do constitute a shrewd and provocative assault on the central claims of the Restoration Church of England to a close alliance with the monarchy of Charles II, coupled with a recommendation that the

---

46 In a review of 'Thomas Hobbes, *Oeuvres'*, *British Journal for the History of Philosophy* 4, no. 1 (1996). The letter referred to is Letter 180, *Correspondence*, vol. 2, 697-8. Du Verdus writes in April 1668 in reply to a letter of Hobbes of 20 July 1666 (which he had only recently received). He says 'O que je jouirous aussi avec tres grand plaisir de votre Epitome de vos Troubles si vous le donies au public et qui'il pleut a Dieu qu'il me vint' (If only I might also have the very great pleasure of reading your Summary of your Tribulations, if you were to publish it and if it pleased God to let me have a copy.)

universities, controlled by the clergy, should be radically reformed. The discussion of *The Whole Duty of Man* and the points that it provokes occupy only about seven pages out of 38 in the first dialogue, or out of about 140 in the whole work. Yet it seems to me to be central to Hobbes's agenda in *Behemoth*: to demonstrate to the King and others that the Anglican clergy, who trumpeted their loyalty to the monarchy and their political reliability, on whom the state relied for the education of the people in their political duties, were essentially as untrustworthy as all other clergy, Roman or Presbyterian. Though the Church tried strenuously to insist that it and the State were inseparable allies and that the viability of the state depended on the survival of the Church, it was already nervous, only a few years after the Restoration, that the State held a very different perspective on the problem; twenty years later such intense pressure would be placed on the political loyalty of the Church of England that Hobbes's dissection of the meaning of its doctrine of passive obedience might have appeared apt and prescient.

Johann P. Sommerville

'Behemoth', Church-State Relations and Political Obligation

This chapter is about Hobbes's ideas on church-state relations and political obligation, especially as they are expressed in *Behemoth*. It has been said that *Behemoth* 'appears to sit oddly with the rest of the Hobbes canon'.[1] A leading purpose of this essay is to compare what Hobbes says there with the views he propounded in *Leviathan* and, indeed, in his other writings. Many of the issues that Hobbes addresses in *Behemoth* also feature in other works which he wrote during the last two decades of his life. For example, he discusses the nature of heresy in *Behemoth* and also at length in the Appendix to the Latin *Leviathan*, in his *Dialogue between a Philosopher and a Student of the Common Laws*, in *An Historical Narration concerning Heresy*, and in the *Historia Ecclesiastica*.[2]

The latter book is especially close to *Behemoth*, though it is in Latin verse, not English prose. In some ways, *Behemoth* can be seen as a continuation of, or a sequel to the *Historia*. In the *Historia*, Hobbes chronicles the cheats of power-hungry priests from the earliest times to the Lutheran Reformation. There, and again in *Behemoth*, he goes well back before the Christian era, arguing that 'in most ancient kingdoms of the world' 'philosophy, together with divinity, have very much conduced to the advancement of the professors thereof to places of greatest authority, next to the authority of kings themselves'. Indeed, in some places they effectively took power from their monarchs, as in ancient Egypt. In Ethiopia

---

1   Fritz Levy, 'The background of Hobbes's *Behemoth*', in *The Historical Imagination in Early Modern Britain: History, Rhetoric, and Fiction, 1500–1800*, eds D. R. Kelley and D. H. Sacks (Cambridge: Woodrow Wilson Center Press and Cambridge University Press, 1997), 243–66, at 243.
2   Thomas Hobbes, *Behemoth or the Long Parliament*, ed. Ferdinand Tönnies, with an introduction by Stephen Holmes (Chicago: University of Chicago Press, 1990), 8–10; *Leviathan, sive de materia, forma, et potestate civitatis ecclesiasticae et civilis*, in *OL* 3. Appendix, ch. 2; *A Dialogue between a Philosopher and a Student of the Common Laws of England*, ed. Joseph Cropsey (Chicago: University of Chicago Press, 1971), 122–32; *An Historical Narration concerning Heresy*, in *EW* 4. 385–408; *Historia Ecclesiastica*, in *OL* 5. 341–408, especially at lines 423–4, 451–2, 511–12, 613–16, 647–71, 1129–40.

the priests had long exploited popular superstition to establish a custom that the king would take his own life when they sent him an order to do so. But King Ergamenes executed the priests and took back authority. Much bloodshed would have been prevented, Hobbes suggests in a strikingly Machiavellian passage of *Behemoth*, if Charles I had similarly killed the seditious Presbyterian ministers. In both books, he drew heavily on the ancient Greek historian Diodorus Siculus—'the greatest antiquary perhaps that ever was'. In *Behemoth* Hobbes recapitulates some of the ancient and medieval material covered in the *Historia*, but his main concern is to analyze what happened in England after the point where the *Historia* rather abruptly stops—the Reformation.[3]

Behemoth lays the blame for the English civil war on the continued deceits and plots of clerics, and especially of Presbyterian ministers.[4] These men, together with their equally grasping allies the democratical gentlemen of the House of Commons, seduced people from their allegiance to the king so that they could gain power for themselves. Having gained it, they fell out with each other. The gentlemen outwitted the Presbyterian ministers, and were in turn outwitted by Oliver Cromwell and his Independent supporters, who used his army to seize power. They purged parliament, executed Charles I, and established the republican rule of the Rump. But soon Cromwell used force to oust the Rump, and later take power for himself. After his death, another general—George

---

3   Hobbes, *Behemoth*, 90 (professors of philosophy and divinity); 91–2 (Egypt); 93–5 (Ethiopians, Ergamenes and Presbyterians); 91 (greatest antiquary); *Historia*, lines 191–212 (Ethiopians and Ergamenes); 219–70 (Egypt). Hobbes also tells the story of Ergamenes in *Ten Dialogues of Natural Philosophy*, in *EW* 7.74. A contemporary English version of Diodorus Siculus's work is *The History of Diodorus Siculus*, trans. Henry Cogan (London: John Macock for Giles Calvert, 1653); in *Behemoth*, 91–4, Hobbes includes a number of quotations from Diodorus in a translation that seems to be his own; it differs from the renditions of the same passages in *The History of Diodorus Siculus*, 240, 50–2, 90, 97, 115–16. The passage from Diodorus on how the Egyptians decided law cases by using a jeweled necklace or collar which they pretended had magical properties (*Behemoth*, 92; *Historia*, lines 226–70) is also discussed in Hugo Grotius, *De Imperio Summarum Potestatum circa Sacra* (Paris, 1647), 124. Grotius argues that the Egyptians derived their customs from the Jews; Hobbes in *Behemoth*, 92 n. 1, is noncommittal on whether the Jews influenced the Egyptians or vice versa; but in *Historia*, lines 149–88, he vigorously asserts the Africanist thesis that the arts began in Ethiopia and then spread to Egypt, Greece and Rome. David Wootton argues that *Behemoth* is a Machiavellian work in 'Thomas Hobbes's Machiavellian Moments', in Kelley and Sacks, *The Historical Imagination*, 210–42, especially 227, 238. But it is worth noting that at *Behemoth*, 58, Hobbes insists that the sovereign should 'put none to death without actual committing such crimes as are already made capital by the laws', and decries extralegal political assassination as 'horrible, unchristian, and inhuman'. Presumably the Presbyterians would have been tried for plotting treason, and only then executed.

4   Deborah Baumgold, 'Hobbes's Political Sensibility: The Menace of Political Ambition', in *Thomas Hobbes and Political Theory*, ed. M. G. Dietz (Lawrence: University of Kansas Press, 1990), 74–90, at 82–4, argues that Hobbes explains the civil war in terms of self-interest, as do modern 'revisionist' scholars, and not of ideas. This is true of the hypocritical leaders of rebellion in Hobbes's account, but not of their deluded followers, who are deceived by false ideas. Robert P. Kraynak, *History and Modernity in the Thought of Thomas Hobbes* (Ithaca: Cornell University Press, 1990), interestingly argues that intellectual vanity was the fundamental cause of the war.

Monck—performed 'the greatest stratagem that is extant in history'[5] by marching his army from Scotland to London, restoring the excluded members to parliament, and bringing back the King Charles II.

In *Behemoth*, Hobbes has a great deal to say against Roman Catholics and their ideas on church-state relations. This is true also, of course, of *Leviathan*, where the forty-second chapter, which is directed largely at the theories of Cardinal Bellarmine, takes up more than an eighth of the entire book. There is something of a puzzle about why Hobbes spent so much ink on popish ideas in *Behemoth*, however, for the English Catholics did not in fact lead the rebellion against the king, and most parliamentarians were their enemies, not their friends.[6] The first section below discusses Hobbes's arguments on Catholics, arguing that they have much in common with standard seventeenth-century Anglican views. The Anglicans, who defended the established church against the criticisms of Protestant dissenters as well as Catholics, commonly argued that the dissenters' political ideas were essentially popish. In *Behemoth*, as in *Leviathan*, Hobbes likewise assimilates the theories of the Catholics to those of the Presbyterians and other non-conforming Protestant groups. His rhetorical strategy is to begin by attacking the principles of the widely disliked Catholics, and then to show that the others shared their fundamental principles.

The second section below discusses Hobbes's attitudes to the Presbyterians, Independents, and other sects, and also to Oliver Cromwell. It was the Independents, together with Cromwell and the army, who were responsible for cutting off the king's head in 1649. But in *Behemoth* Hobbes lays the blame for the regicide on the Presbyterians as well as the Independents. Some modern commentators have claimed that by the early 1650s Hobbes had moved close to Independency on the question of church-state relations. Perhaps his affection for the Independents is reflected in the relative leniency with which they, and Oliver Cromwell, are treated in *Behemoth*. The material below will cast doubt on these suggestions, and show that Hobbes was never particularly close to the Independents except in his dislike for Presbyterianism—a dislike which he also shared with Anglicans and others. Nor does he depict Cromwell very favorably in *Behemoth*.

Hobbes argues that the Protestant dissenters held political ideas that were just as dangerous as those of the Catholics. His position on this point is not all that far from traditional royalist and Anglican views. Indeed, on many questions he took much the same broad line as such hawkish royal-

---

5 Hobbes, *Behemoth*, 204.
6 Catholicism did cause problems in Ireland, however, as Hobbes notes in *Behemoth*, 163.

ists as Sir Robert Filmer, Peter Heylyn, and Roger Maynwaring. But he broke decisively with Anglican and royalist thinking in what he had to say about two tenets dear to many royalists, namely passive obedience and divine right episcopacy. On both these questions, his teaching remained unchanged in *Behemoth*. As in *Leviathan*, he extended his critique of Catholic and Presbyterian ideas on church-state relations to undermine the views of Anglicans as well. The Anglican theory of divine right episcopacy, he claimed, was close to the Catholic theory of the papal deposing power. Hobbes's own views on church-state relations, expressed in *Leviathan*, *Behemoth* and elsewhere, were broadly Erastian in sympathy. Erastians advocated state control of ecclesiastical affairs. But such control could be exercised in very different ways—loosely and tolerantly, for example, or alternatively in a rigorous and intolerant fashion. Modern commentators are more or less agreed on Hobbes's Erastianism, but divided on whether he was a supporter or an opponent of toleration. The third section of this chapter is about Hobbes's attitudes to Anglicanism and to toleration.

I have claimed above that Hobbes shared many key views with royalist writers like Filmer. But a well-known interpretation of *Leviathan* holds that it was written to defend 'the so-called Oath of Engagement'. On 11 October 1649, so this interpretation runs, the Rump Parliament 'called on virtually the entire literate population to swear' the Oath, 'requiring them to be 'true and faithful to the Commonwealth of England, as it is now established, without a King or House of Lords'. In response to this, the account proceeds, Hobbes rapidly penned *Leviathan*, which was 'a uniquely important contribution to the lay defence of engagement'. By 1651, there was 'nothing specifically royalist' about Hobbes's political theory, and he felt—correctly, as it turned out—that 'the eirenic message of *Leviathan* was likely to be warmly received by supporters of the Rump.[7] If this account holds water, then there is at least one extremely stark difference between *Leviathan* and *Behemoth*, for by no stretch of the imagination can the latter work be construed as a defense of the 'Oath of Engagement', or as anything other than a blistering attack on the Rump and the Long Parliament in general. The fourth and final section below discusses the question of whether the two books do indeed adopt radically divergent positions on the Rump. It concludes that they do not, for Hobbes did little to defend the Rumpers in *Leviathan*. Nor are there compelling reasons to believe that Hobbes abandoned royalist principles when he wrote *Leviathan*, only to take them up again when he wrote *Behe-*

---

7 Quentin Skinner, 'Conquest and Consent: Hobbes and the Engagement Controversy', in *Visions of Politics* (Cambridge: Cambridge University Press, 2002), 3. 19, 306, 20.

moth. The Hobbes who wrote *Behemoth* was an older and perhaps more disillusioned man than the author of *Leviathan*, but both maintained the same fundamental principles.

Catholics

In *Behemoth*, Hobbes tells us that in order to make the people hostile to the king, parliament encouraged them to believe that he intended 'to introduce and authorize the Roman religion in this kingdom: than which nothing was more hateful to the people'.[8] Perhaps mindful of the popularity of anti-popery, Hobbes began his account of the seditious doctrines that had led to the civil war by discussing the papists. In keeping with Protestant tradition, he argued that the history of Catholicism was a story of clerical fraud and ambition. By deluding the ignorant, the pope and his allies had striven to gain power for themselves. To ensure the success of their plan, they needed to keep people in the darkness of ignorance and superstition. Hobbes declared that 'there was never such another cheat in the world' as the Roman church.[9] The detection of popish cheats is a common theme in the writings of Hobbes's contemporaries. For example, Samuel Harsnett—an Anglican and bishop and archbishop whose high views on royal power resembled Hobbes's—decried 'egregious popish impostures' and called Catholicism a 'mimic superstition' intended to 'catch fools, children, and women' by pretended magic.[10] Hobbes argued that the Catholic church tolerated and Christianized pagan practices in order to make converts.[11] Harsnett asserted that 'papism' was 'naught else but a perfect apism and imitation of Gentilism and heathenish superstition,' constructed

> to gull, terrify, and amaze the simple ignorant people, and by bringing them into an admiration of the power of their priesthood, the sanctity of their attire, and the divine potency of their Romish Catholic

---

8   Hobbes, *Behemoth*, 60. Discussing bishops, ibid., 89, Hobbes argues that the House of Commons was so hostile to them because it hoped 'to make the King and his party odious to the people'. A strikingly similar viewpoint is expressed in John Selden, *Table Talk of John Selden*, ed. Sir F. Pollock (London: Quaritch, 1927), 99: 'Wee charge the prelaticall Clergie with popery to make them odious though wee know they are guilty of no such thing.' According to Thomas Tenison, *The creed of Mr. Hobbes examined* (London: Francis Tyton, 1670), 188, Hobbes seemed to have 'swallow'd down' Selden's Erastian doctrines 'along with the good provisions of his Table'. The Erastian principles of Hobbes and Selden are compared and contrasted in Johann P. Sommerville, 'Hobbes, Selden, Erastianism, and the history of the Jews', in *Hobbes and History*, eds G. A. J. Rogers and T. Sorell (London: Routledge, 2000), 160–88.

9   Hobbes, *Behemoth*, 21. The fourth part of *Leviathan* of course contains a great deal of material on the papists' pious and not-so-pious frauds.

10 Samuel Harsnett, *A Declaration of egregious popish impostures* (1603), in F. W. Brownlow, *Shakespeare, Harsnett and the Devils of Denham* (Newark: University of Delaware Press, 1993), 184–413, at 219. There is material of Harsnett's political ideas in Johann P. Sommerville, *Royalists and Patriots: Politics and Ideology in England, 1603–1640* (Harlow: Longman, 1999), 124, 150.

11 Hobbes, *Historia*, lines 1327–54.

church, by this means to enchant and bewitch their innocent simple souls, and so to offer them up for a prey to their great idol at Rome.[12]

Amongst many others who shared Hobbes's objective of exposing the forgeries and falsifications perpetrated by papists were the churchman William Crashaw, and Bodley's first librarian, Thomas James.[13]

Hobbes insisted that early church councils had been convoked by the emperors, who confirmed their decrees.[14] This was the standard Anglican position, repeatedly expressed in anti-papal and anti-Presbyterian polemics.[15] Many Catholics argued that the pope does not have direct temporal power over Christian sovereigns, but that his spiritual primacy confers upon him *indirect* temporal power, which he can use to promote the spiritual good. So popes could depose kings if they thought such action would advance the spiritual interests of Christians, but not otherwise. Hobbes held that this theory of the indirect deposing power effectively deprived kings of all their authority, since it granted the pope alone the right to decide what constituted the spiritual good.[16] Again, this was a commonplace of anti-papal literature.[17]

Protestants were of course agreed that the Roman church had become corrupt, and that the Reformation had therefore been necessary. They differed on the date at which the corruption had begun. Hobbes set the date rather early, arguing that already in Constantine the Great's time the pope claimed supremacy over emperors, though he prudently failed to inform Constantine about this.[18] Hobbes also gives an atypically early date for the first use of the papal deposing power. Most English Protestants claimed that it was only in the eleventh century that the pope first attempted to depose a secular ruler, but Hobbes—like such Catholics as Cardinal Bellarmine and Francisco Suárez—claimed that the practice had begun much earlier, for in the eighth century Pope Zachary (or Zacharias) had deposed Chilperic (or Childeric), the last Merovingian king of

---

12 Harsnett, *Declaration*, 271.
13 William Crashaw, *Falsificationum Romanarum: et catholicarum restitutionum* (London: Richard Field for Matthew Lownes, 1606); Thomas James, *Bellum Gregorianum siue Corruptionis Romanae in operibus D. Gregorii M.* (Oxford: Joseph Barnes, 1610).
14 Hobbes, *Behemoth*, 10; *Leviathan*, ed. R. Tuck (Cambridge: Cambridge University Press, 1991), 326 (1651 edn, 286–7).
15 e.g. Lancelot Andrewes, *A sermon preached before the Kings Maiestie at Hampton Court, concerning the Right and Power of calling Assemblies* (London: Robert Barker, 1606), especially 37–8, 51; Richard Harris, *The English Concord, in Answer to Becane's English Jarre* (London: H. Lownes for Matthew Lownes, 1614), 97, 165, 158.
16 Hobbes, *Behemoth*, 6, 41; *Leviathan*, 396 (1651 edn, 315).
17 Johann P. Sommerville, *Thomas Hobbes: Political Ideas in Historical Context* (Houndmills: Macmillan, 1992), 116.
18 Hobbes, *Behemoth*, 11.

France.[19] Hobbes was also unusual in the rigor with which he decoded Catholic doctrines to show that their purpose was to increase the power and wealth of the clergy. And finally, Hobbes diverged from practically all Protestant (and, of course, Catholic) writers in claiming that kings have all the powers of bishops.[20] For the most part, however, what Hobbes said in *Behemoth* about Catholic theory was perfectly compatible with standard Anglican teaching. The same goes for *Behemoth*'s treatment of the Presbyterians and Independents.

Presbyterians, Independents, the sects, and Oliver Cromwell

Hobbes blames the civil war most of all on the Presbyterians, whose seditious preaching moved many to join in the rebellion against the king. Presbyterians claimed that by divine right the church ought to be governed by elected ministers, elders, and councils, and not by the civil magistrate. Kings ought to obey the church in religious affairs. Presbyterian ministers, said Hobbes, aimed to establish equality in the church and to overthrow the power of the bishops; they also 'endeavoured to bring the same form of Government into the civil state'. Ambitious gentlemen allied with them to further this objective, aiming to win sovereignty for the House of Commons.[21] The Presbyterians, like the friars in the Middle Ages, used preaching to spread their message, and skillfully deployed voice and gesture to act 'the part of a right godly man', persuading the people of their zeal and holiness.[22] Catholics controlled opinion by punishing heterodox views as heresy, and dominating the universities. Presbyterians similarly used the universities to spread their ideas, and tried to suppress true learning.[23] The ministers hoped that once the king was defeated, they would dominate the Commons, 'wherein they were deceived, and found themselves outgone by their own disciples, though

---

19   Ibid., 12; *Leviathan*, 396 (1651 edn, 315). Cardinal Robert Bellarmine, *Tractatus De Potestate Summi Pontificis in Rebus Temporalibus*, in *Opera Omnia* (Naples: G. Giuliano, 1856–62), 4. 2, 257–344, at 274; Francisco Suárez, *Defensio Fidei Catholicae*, III. 23, 15, in *Opera Omnia* (Paris: Vivès, 1856–78), 24. 319. The standard English Protestant view that popes deposed kings only from the time of Gregory VII is expressed in e.g. William Goodwin, *A Sermon preached before the Kings most excellent Maiestie at Woodstocke* (Oxford: Joseph Barnes, 1614), 26; Francis White, *A Replie to Iesuit Fishers Answere* (London: Adam Islip, 1624), 572. English Protestants, and some French Catholics, held that Childeric was deposed by the French people and not by the pope. In the *Historia Ecclesiastica*, lines 1727–38, Hobbes relates how the pope deposed Childeric for stupidity; at lines 1823–46 he argued that popes later extinguished true learning by introducing scholasticism and that then kings in general became stupider than Childeric.

20   Hobbes, *Behemoth*, 14; in *Leviathan*, 374 (1651 edn, 297), Hobbes similarly argues against the conventional idea that there are some powers which only churchmen, and not the sovereign, can exercise.

21   Hobbes, *Behemoth*, 75, 23, 119.

22   Ibid., 24.

23   Ibid., 57–8, 96.

not in malice, yet in wit'.²⁴ But though they had been defeated, their seditious principles lived on.²⁵

The idea that Presbyterianism in the church led to democracy in the state was an Anglican commonplace. Once 'an equalitie ... among the Clergie' had been introduced, said the Elizabethan John Whitgift (who became Archbishop of Canterbury), it would 'not be long' before the Presbyterians tried to introduce 'the same among the laytie'.²⁶ Whitgift's successor as Archbishop of Canterbury was Richard Bancroft, who in 1593 convicted the Presbyterians of sedition and rebellion against secular governments in *Daungerous Positions and Proceedings, published and practised within this Iland of Brytaine, under pretence of Reformation, and for the Presbiteriall Discipline*, and of greed, hypocrisy, and fraud in his *Survay of the pretended Holy Discipline*.²⁷ Charles I's chaplain Peter Heylyn penned a history of the Presbyterians in which he inveighed against their 'pious frauds' and 'godly pretences'. Heylyn argued that the civil war resulted from a plot to destroy the monarchy and raise a 'new commonwealth' on its ruins. The plotters used the Presbyterian ministers 'as the fittest instruments for drawing the people to their side, and preaching up the piety of their intentions'. The war that resulted led to the loss of 'more than one hundred thousand lives' but did not achieve the Presbyterians' objectives, for they were driven out of power by the army and the Independents.²⁸

Hobbes's idea that the civil war was the result of a plot hatched by ambitious politicians and Presbyterian ministers accorded well with royalist and Anglican tradition, which had long stressed that Presbyterians were seditious, hypocritical and self-seeking. Some modern commentators have argued that Hobbes was much more lenient towards the Independents in *Behemoth*. It has been suggested that Hobbes in fact endorsed Independency – the theory that each congregation should be autonomous in church affairs – in *Leviathan*, and that although he dropped his explicit defense of Independent ideas after the Restoration, he continued to have some affection for them, and therefore in *Behemoth* suggestively 'played down' 'the triumph of Independency' and treated Oliver Cromwell 'with

---

24 Ibid., 75.
25 Ibid., 57.
26 John Whitgift, *An answere to a certen Libel intituled, An admonition to the Parliament* (London: Henrie Binneman for Humfrey Toy, 1572), 77; see also 133.
27 Richard Bancroft, *Daungerous Positions and Proceedings, published and practised within this Iland of Brytaine, under pretence of Reformation, and for the Presbiteriall Discipline* (London: John Wolfe, 1593); *A Survay of the pretended Holy Discipline* (London: John Wolfe, 1593).
28 Peter Heylyn, *Aerius Redivivus, or, the History of the Presbyterians* (Oxford: John Crosley, 1670), 278, 481–2.

considerable respect'.[29] There are two main problems with this thesis. The first is that it is difficult to see *Leviathan* as particularly supportive of Independent ideas. It is true that Hobbes, like the Independents, rejected the claims of Presbyterians and other ecclesiastics to have jurisdiction over the whole populace, and in that sense he did endorse Independency.[30] But on most other key questions he strongly opposed it. For example, Independents held that we must always follow our consciences even if this involves us in breaking the law, and they argued that a government which intrudes on our rights of conscience, or takes our property without consent, is tyrannical and may be actively resisted by its subjects. Hobbes, on the other hand, repeatedly declared that we have no right to follow our consciences against the law, that we have no right of property against our sovereign, and that subjects act criminally if they resist their sovereign.[31]

The second problem is that *Behemoth* is not in fact very sympathetic to the Independents, nor to Cromwell and the sects. Near the beginning of the book, Hobbes listed the 'divers sorts' of 'seducers' who 'corrupted' the people into rebelling against their king. The first two were Presbyterians and papists, while the third included Independents, Baptists, Quakers and others.[32] He claimed that all these groups were offshoots of the Presbyterians, styling them 'this brood of their own hatching', and asserting that they were 'commonly called by the name of fanatics'.[33] Hobbes insisted that 'the Presbyterian ministers, throughout the whole war, instigated the people against the King', but immediately added 'so did also independent and other fanatic ministers'.[34] Discussing the books of the Independent John Milton, who defended the trial and execution of Charles I on behalf of the Rump, and of the Presbyterian Claude de Saumaise (or Salmasius), who condemned the king's murder and wrote in the Stuart cause, Hobbes commented that

> They are very good Latin both, and hardly to be judged which is better; and both very ill reasoning, hardly to be judged which is worse; like two declamations, *pro* and *con*, made for exercise only in a

---

29 Richard Tuck, *Hobbes* (Oxford: Oxford University Press, 1989), 35; idem, *Philosophy and Government, 1572–1651* (Cambridge: Cambridge University Press, 1993), 343; Jeffery R. Collins, 'Christian Ecclesiology and the Composition of *Leviathan*: A Newly Discovered Letter to Thomas Hobbes', *Historical Journal* 43 (2000), 217–31, at 227–8; Royce MacGillivray, *Restoration Historians and the English Civil War* (The Hague: Martinus Nijhoff, 1974), 73, 80; Julius Lips, *Die Stellung des Thomas Hobbes zu den politischen Parteien der grossen Englischen Revolution: Mit erstmaliger Übersetzung des Behemoth oder das Lang Parlament* (Leipzig: Ernst Wiegandt, 1927), 96.
30 Hobbes, *Leviathan*, 479–80 (1651 edn, 385).
31 These points are discussed in greater detail in Johann P. Sommerville, 'Hobbes and Independency', in *Rivista di Storia della Filosofia* 21 (2004), 155–73.
32 Hobbes, *Behemoth*, 2–3.
33 Ibid., 136.
34 Ibid., 159.

rhetoric school by one and the same man. So like is a Presbyterian to an Independent.[35]

Hobbes did, indeed, reject the idea that 'the Independents were worse than the Presbyterians', arguing that they were equally bad: 'both the one and the other were resolved to destroy whatsoever should stand in the way to their ambition'.[36] A saying that circulated after the king's death was 'that presbiterians held him by the hayr, till independents cut off his head'.[37] Hobbes made a similar point when he declared that the Presbyterians 'sought only the subjection of the King, not his destruction directly,' while the Independents 'sought directly his destruction'. Folly, treason, vice, hypocrisy, and crime characterized both parties.[38]

Hobbes relates how Cromwell was largely responsible for the parliamentarian victory at Marston Moor, and how the parliament 'had very great confidence' in his 'conduct and valour'—'which they would not have done, if they had known him as well then as they did afterwards.'[39] Oliver turned his sword against them, and took the defeated king from their custody into his own. 'Here,' commented Hobbes, 'is perfidy upon perfidy: first, the perfidy of the Parliament against the King, and then the perfidy of the army against the Parliament'.[40] Cromwell disguised from parliament his ambition to be their master, and so the Presbyterian members foolishly trusted him and betrayed and sold the king to him and the other murderers.[41] Though in reputation as a general Cromwell was 'so much magnified for conduct', at Dunbar 'all his glories had ended in shame and punishment, if fortune and the faults of his enemies had not relieved him'. A few years later, Hobbes noted with some glee, six coach horses 'being as rebellious as himself' threw Cromwell out of his coach and almost killed him.[42] So Cromwell was a perfidious rebel and murderer. Elsewhere, he added that Oliver was mad. Vindicating his own reputation against Wallis's charges in 1662, Hobbes argued that it was Wallis and his Presbyterian allies who were to blame for the civil war—not because Cromwell was somehow innocent of the king's murder, but because he had acted on principles which Presbyterian ministers had taught him: 'you were guilty of all the Treasons, Murders and Spoil

---

35 Ibid., 163–4.
36 Ibid., 165.
37 Thomas Birch, ed., *A Collection of the State Papers of John Thurloe, Esq.* (London: for the executor of F. Gyles, 1742), 1. 764.
38 Hobbes, *Behemoth*, 195.
39 Ibid., 131.
40 Ibid., 138.
41 Ibid., 143, 155.
42 Ibid., 167, 185.

committed by *Oliver*, or by any upon *Oliver's* or the *Parliaments* Authority: For during the late trouble, who made both *Oliver* and the people mad, but the Preachers of your Principles?' It was the Presbyterians who put the army into Cromwell's hands, 'who before, as mad as he was, was too weak, and too obscure to do any great mischief'.[43]

It is true that in the early pages of *Behemoth* there is much about Catholicism and Presbyterianism, and relatively little about Independency and Oliver Cromwell. This does not at all indicate that Hobbes had any great sympathy for Cromwell and his Independent allies. Three points are in order here. Firstly, Cromwell and the Independents were not in fact very important in the period leading up to the civil war, nor in the first stages of the war itself. It is therefore not surprising that Oliver and the Independents do not feature much in Hobbes's explanation of why the war broke out. As Hobbes records, the Independents and the sects 'in the beginning of the troubles were not discovered'. Nor, as Hobbes noted, was Cromwell of any significance until he began to serve in the army of the Eastern Association in 1643.[44] Secondly, the main political principles on which Cromwell and the Independents acted had in fact earlier been lucidly expressed by Presbyterians. For example, Samuel Rutherford in his *Lex, Rex, or the Law and the Prince* (1644) argued that kings are bound by the covenants which they made with their subjects when they were first granted power, that they are under the law, and that if they abuse their power their subjects are perfectly entitled to wage war against them. Rutherford did indeed say that it was unlawful to kill a king, but he added that this was true only 'so long as he remaineth a king,' and argued that it was open to subjects to dethrone a monarch for 'such tyranny as is inconsistent with his royal office'.[45] Hobbes was right to think that when the Independents cut off Charles I's head they were acting on principles which Presbyterians had frequently voiced. Thirdly, when Hobbes wrote *Behemoth* in the 1660s, the Presbyterians were a far larger and more important group than the defeated Independents. The Restoration was engineered by royalists allied with Presbyterians against the Independents and the sects. After the Restoration, the question of what share in power should be given to the Presbyterians was very much alive, for they had helped to bring the king back. But the Independents had come to be politically irrelevant. For this reason too, it made sense for Hobbes to say more about the Presbyterians than the Independents. What he said about these

43 Hobbes, *Mr. Hobbes considered in his Loyalty, Reputation, and Manners* (London: for Andrew Crooke, 1662), 15; *EW* 4. 419.
44 Hobbes, *Behemoth*, 3, 122.
45 Samuel Rutherford, *Lex, Rex, or the Law and the Prince; a Dispute for the Just Prerogative of King and People* (Harrisonburg, Virginia: Sprinkle Publications, 1982), 54–62, 125–36, 148, 232.

groups, and about Cromwell, and about the Catholics was largely compatible with what he had already said in *Leviathan* and elsewhere, and also with royalist and Anglican thinking. What he said about Anglicanism, however, diverged emphatically from the thinking of most royalists, though it was predictable enough from the author of *Leviathan*.

Anglicanism and toleration

In the thirty-first chapter of Leviathan, Hobbes discusses 'the Kingdom of God by Nature', and outlines the ways in which God should be worshipped, claiming that 'in *Prayers, Thanksgivings, Offerings* and *Sacrifices*, it is a Dictate of naturall Reason, that they be every one in his kind the best, and the most significant of Honour'. So prayers ought to 'be made in Words and Phrases, not sudden, nor light, nor Plebeian; but beautifull, and well composed'. There ought, he insisted, to be public worship of God: 'But seeing a Common-wealth is but one Person, it ought also to exhibit to God but one Worship; which then it doth, when it commandeth it to be exhibited by Private men, Publiquely.' The essence of such worship, he remarked, 'is to be *Uniforme*', and he proceeded to spell out that 'where many sorts of Worship be allowed, proceeding from the different Religions of Private men, it cannot be said there is any Publique Worship, nor that the Commonwealth is of any Religion at all'. We ought to honor God in public worship. But it is the sovereign who decides what words and actions signify honor: 'those Attributes which the Soveraign ordaineth, in the Worship of God, for signes of Honour, ought to be taken and used for such, by private men in their publique Worship'. The sovereign could select from 'an infinite number of Actions, and Gestures, of an indifferent nature' and by ordering them to be used as signs of honor to God make it obligatory for his subjects to do so.[46]

This account of public worship was multiply incompatible with the ideas of puritans, whether Presbyterian, Independent, or sectarian. Puritans held that the civil magistrate could not add any rites of worship to those prescribed in the bible. Indifferent actions, they claimed, emphatically did not become obligatory if the sovereign commanded them.[47] Many favored extempore (or sudden, and often light and plebeian) prayer over so-called stinted prayer — Hobbes's well-composed prayers. Independents rejected the idea that the godly should worship uniformly throughout the commonwealth, allowing them to form their own inde-

---

46 Hobbes, *Leviathan*, 252–3 (1651 edn, 191–2).
47 Johann P. Sommerville, 'Conscience, Law, and Things Indifferent: Arguments on Toleration from the Vestiarian Controversy to Hobbes and Locke', in *Contexts of Conscience in Early Modern Europe, 1500–1700*, eds H. Braun and E. Vallance (Houndmills: Palgrave Macmillan, 2004).

pendent congregations. Hobbes views on worship were close to those of the Anglicans, however, and, indeed, to the Laudians, whom puritans especially disliked.[48]

In *Behemoth*, Hobbes stuck by his old position, and declared that Laud had wanted 'the service of God performed, and the house of God adorned, as suitable as was possible to the honour we ought to do to the Divine Majesty'. He defended Laud on other points, for instance (wrongly) suggesting that the story that Laud had been offered a cardinal's hat was false.[49] But he also criticized Laud, and, more generally Anglican ideas on church-state relations. He did not indeed blame the Anglican clergy for the war. It was, he said, the Presbyterians, Independents and other fanatics who had instigated the people against the king, while the rest of the clergy stayed in their parishes and preached 'points of controversy, to religion impertinent, but to the breach of charity amongst themselves very effectual; or else elegant things, which the people either understood not, or thought themselves not concerned in'. Unlike the Presbyterians, these Anglican preachers were not particularly harmful: 'as they did little good, so they did little hurt'.[50] Laud, however, did cause problems by his authoritarianism, for he stood 'upon punctilios concerning the service-book and its rubrics'. Moreover, he acted unwisely in bringing into the state his 'former squabblings in the University about free-will', which was foolish because such 'unnecessary disputes' have nothing to do with religion, and because Laud's stance on the question allowed his enemies to portray him as popish.[51]

But the main objections that *Behemoth* voices to Anglican theories were concerned with divine right episcopacy, passive obedience, and censorship. As in *Leviathan*, Hobbes held that clerics derive their power only from the sovereign, and not directly from God, though he seems to have intended to tone down his assault on divine right episcopacy for publication. He argued that all power to govern in church or state is derived from the sovereign. The bishops claimed that their authority to govern the church stemmed from God alone. In Hobbes's view, this was a false and

---

48 Sommerville, *Thomas Hobbes*, 155–6.
49 Hobbes, *Behemoth*, 73, 62. In fact, Laud *was* offered a cardinal's hat: Laud's diary, in William Laud, *Works*, eds W. Scott and J. Bliss (Oxford: John Henry Parker, 1847–60), 3. 131–255, at 219 (4 August and 17 August, 1633). At *Behemoth*, 72, Laud's death is misdated 1643 instead of 1645. This is probably an error of transcription, as is the printing of 'Calais' for 'Cadiz', ibid., 83, 111.
50 Hobbes, *Behemoth*, 159.
51 Ibid., 73, 61–2. Hobbes gives no hint here that he thought these 'unnecessary disputes' were in fact of central importance to establishing religious truth, but Martinich argues that that was nevertheless so, and that Hobbes sided strongly and to his personal cost with one side in the debate, namely the Calvinists. See A. P. Martinich, *The Two Gods of Leviathan: Thomas Hobbes on Religion and Politics* (Cambridge: Cambridge University Press, 1992), especially 334–5.

seditious idea, not all that far removed from the theory of the indirect papal deposing power.[52] Anglicans denied this, arguing that although the bishops receive their power directly from God, they cannot exercise it in any Christian state except with the permission of the sovereign. So *jure divino* episcopacy is compatible with the King of England's supremacy over the church, for bishops derive their right to exercise their powers, but not the powers themselves, from the sovereign.[53] Hobbes was well aware of this distinction between a right or power on the one hand, and its exercise on the other, but thought it absurd. Writing against Bishop Bramhall, he noted that Anglicans said bishops derive their power to ordain ministers from God, but can exercise it only with royal license, 'as if the right to ordain, and the right to exercise ordination, were not the same thing'. This was like saying that King David 'had a power to kill Uriah, but not to exercise it upon Uriah, that is to say, he had a power to kill him, but not to kill him, which is absurd'.[54]

While Presbyterians and Independents had allowed active resistance to the king, Anglicans permitted only passive obedience. That is to say, they held that if the king commands us to perform actions which are contrary to God's decrees, we must obey God and not the king, but we must also passively accept whatever punishment the king inflicts on us for our disobedience. In *Behemoth*, Hobbes went out of his way to challenge Anglican teaching on this point at some length, arguing that we cannot know what God commands except 'by the sentence of him or them that are constituted by the King to determine the sense of Scripture'. So we ought to obey actively, and passive obedience was in any case no kind of obedience.[55] He had also rejected the distinction between active and passive obedience in *De Cive*, but did not mention it in *Leviathan*.[56]

Hobbes opposed all efforts by clerics to assert power independent from the state. He resented and feared their attempts to control ideas, for he held that 'all true philosophy, especially civil and moral' would suffer. Both the Presbyterians and the Anglicans had used power to suppress all

---

52 Hobbes attacks divine right episcopacy in *Behemoth*, 6 and 95. The first of these two passages was erased in the manuscript, but nevertheless was printed, though in somewhat muted form; the second passage was excised and not printed. Sommerville, *Thomas Hobbes*, 120–1.

53 Sommerville, *Royalists and Patriots*, 196–9.

54 Hobbes, The questions concerning liberty, necessity, and chance, in *EW* 5. 143. Nevertheless, in *Behemoth*, 135, Hobbes himself somewhat anomalously distinguishes between the right to sovereignty and the exercise of sovereignty. Also rather anomalous are references in Behemoth to tyranny, for example of the major generals, ibid., 186–7. In *Leviathan* 130 (1651 edn, 95) tyranny is only monarchy misliked.

55 Hobbes, *Behemoth*, 49–52.

56 Hobbes, *De Cive*, ch. XIV, section xxiii; in *De Cive: The Latin Version*, ed. H. Warrender (Oxford: Clarendon Press, 1983), 217–18.

opinions that militated against their interests, and that included many that were true and useful. Hobbes records the formation of the Royal Society, but expresses skepticism about how much it was likely to achieve, given that 'the authority of licensing the books that are to be written of the subject, is not in them, but in some divines, who have little knowledge in physics, and none at all in mathematics'.[57] This sounds like a plea against censorship, but *Leviathan* is often seen as a manifesto of intolerance, and *Behemoth* has been portrayed in a similar light: 'the Hobbes of *Behemoth* wanted to impose a state religion on a country where there was a measure of toleration, and to impose a state ideology on universities in which a certain amount of intellectual diversity was permitted'.[58] Some scholars, however, have persuasively argued that Hobbes was an advocate of free speech and toleration.[59] Both views are partially true, for Hobbes thought that people's beliefs are easily and almost infinitely malleable, and that there are many self-seeking individuals ready to indoctrinate them with pernicious opinions. To prevent such indoctrination, the sovereign must take control of the means of persuasion, and most of all of the universities – the 'core of rebellion'. The universities, he argued, should teach the true and proven principles of politics, which he himself had demonstrated. The sovereign would also enforce a vague and undogmatic religion, though without standing upon punctilios. But on all matters that did not conflict with the subject's political duties, Hobbes advocated free speech and inquiry.[60] Hobbes famously saw the liberty of the subject as nothing more than freedom to do what the law allows. We tend to think of this as a narrow and slavish concept of liberty. But it is one for which Hobbes's generation had to struggle, for clerics were all too eager to impose restrictions on speech and action, though the state had imposed none.[61]

Though Hobbes rejected Anglican claims for divine right episcopacy, the political creed of *Behemoth* is far closer to that of royalists and Anglicans than it is to Catholicism, Independency, or Presbyterianism. *Behemoth* attacks parliamentarians throughout, but rarely criticizes royalists, except for being insufficiently hawkish. Yet *Leviathan* is often portrayed as a book which betrayed royalism and defended the Rump Parliament, and

---

57 Hobbes, *Behemoth*, 95–6.
58 Wootton, 'Thomas Hobbes's Machiavellian Moments', 240.
59 Alan Ryan, 'Hobbes, Toleration, and the Inner Life', in *The Nature of Political Theory*, eds D. Miller and L. Siedentop (Oxford: Clarendon Press, 1983), 197–218; Frank Lessay, 'Hobbes and Sacred History', in Rogers and Sorell, *Hobbes and History*, 147–59, especially 153–4.
60 Hobbes, *Historia Ecclesiastica*, lines 1129–40, 1173, 1177–82; Lessay, 'Hobbes and Sacred History', 153–4.
61 Hobbes, *Behemoth*, 39–40, 58, 70; *Leviathan*, 147–8 (1651 edn, 109).

in particular the Engagement oath. If that is so, then there is a fundamental incompatibility between the two books. The final section of this essay assesses the evidence for this.

Hobbes, the Rump and the Engagement

One highly influential interpretation of *Leviathan* contends that it was a defense of the Rump's 'Oath of Engagement' which was imposed upon 'virtually the entire literate population' on 11 October 1649. Hobbes, the argument runs, rapidly wrote *Leviathan* in defense of the oath. By this time, we are told, there was 'nothing specifically royalist' about Hobbes's political theory, and he calculated that *Leviathan*'s message was likely to be warmly received by supporters of the Rump, as indeed it was.[62] Not surprisingly, we are informed, 'royalists widely read' *Leviathan* 'as an apologia for the Commonwealth's bitterly detested Engagement oath'.[63]

There are a number of difficulties with this approach. Chronology is a problem. On 13 May 1650, Hobbes's friend Robert Payne recorded that Hobbes had written to him from Paris, telling him that he had completed thirty-seven chapters of an English book on politics—obviously *Leviathan*.[64] We do not know the date of Hobbes's letter to Payne, but it clearly cannot have been written much later than the beginning of May. On 11 October 1649, the Rump voted that its own members should take the Engagement, not that the population at large should do so.[65] The text of *Leviathan* does not suggest that Hobbes was at all concerned what the Rumpers chose to impose on themselves. In the 'Review, and Conclusion' at the end of the book, he declared that people become subject to a conqueror only when they submit to him, and observed that those who submit to 'the Enemy' actually help him less than those who do not, for the latter would lose only 'part of their estates' while the former would forfeit them all. Hobbes's argument is that since the Rump is now firmly in control in England, royalists may acknowledge it as the sovereign authority in the country, and compound with it for their estates—as Hobbes's patron and friend the Earl of Devonshire did. Alternatively, they could continue the war by living secretly in England and refusing to accept the Rump's protection, or by living abroad (as Charles II did).[66] Hobbes's key contention is that since the Rump has won the war, royalists can submit to

---

62 Skinner, *Visions of Politics*, 3. 19, 22.
63 Collins, 'Christian Ecclesiology and the Composition of *Leviathan*', 222.
64 Nicholas Pocock, 'Illustrations of the State of the Church during the Great Rebellion', in *The Theologian and Ecclesiastic* 6 (1848), 161–75, at 172 (letter 128).
65 Samuel Rawson Gardiner, *History of the Commonwealth and Protectorate, 1649–1656* (London: Longmans, Green, and Co., 1903), 1. 176.
66 Hobbes, *Leviathan*, 485–6 (1651 edn, 390–1).

'Behemoth', Church-State Relations and Political Obligation 109

it to regain their property. The Engagement (which was not an oath but a declaration and promise) was first imposed on males aged eighteen or more by an Act of 2 January 1650. That Act provided that the engagement be tendered to various categories of people, including officeholders and plaintiffs in lawsuits. But it was not until 26 February 1650 that the Engagement was imposed upon compounding royalists.[67] Since it is extremely unlikely that Hobbes could have written thirty-seven chapters between 26 February, or even 2 January, and the beginning of May, we may conclude that the original purpose of *Leviathan* was not to defend the Engagement, and that passages licensing ex-royalists to submit to the Rump are late additions.

It seems that until the Restoration, which brought the bishops back to power, remarkably few royalists connected Hobbes with the Engagement, or criticized *Leviathan* on the grounds that it was a defense of the Rump. There is no hint in the writings of Filmer, for example, that he read Hobbes in that way. Hobbes himself refers to the Engagement just once, in his response to Wallis of 1662. There he calls its imposition 'a very great Crime'. He also remarks that in *Leviathan* there is 'scarce a page' 'that doth not upbraid' both Cromwell and the Presbyterians with 'your abominable hypocrisie and villany'.[68] *Leviathan* does indeed argue that subjects should obey their sovereigns and not make war upon them. It asserts that by the law of nature we have a duty to protect in war the authority which protects us in peace, and claims that the English were mad to take up arms against their king.[69] Among the many specifically royalist tenets that Hobbes maintains in *Leviathan* are that 'Christian kings have their civil power from God immediately', and that 'the king, and every other sovereign, executeth his office of supreme pastor by immediate authority from God, that is to say, in God's right, or jure divino'.[70] The Rumpers thought kings were accountable to the people. In chapter twenty-nine of *Leviathan* Hobbes lists seditious doctrines which undermine government. Most were principles on which the Long Parliament in fact acted, as *Behemoth* was to show.[71] They did not receive *Leviathan* warmly, and apparently ignored it completely. It is true that in *Leviathan* Hobbes denies that hereditary right is indefeasible, but until Charles I's defeat few royalists

---

67 C. H. Firth and R. S. Rait, *Acts and Ordinances of the Interregnum, 1642–1660* (London: His Majesty's Stationery Office, 1911), 2. 325–9, 348–54.
68 Hobbes, *Mr. Hobbes considered*, 13, 8, in *EW* 4. 418, 415.
69 Hobbes, *Leviathan*, 484 (1651 edn, 390), 299–300 (1651 edn, 232), 54–5 (1651 edn, 36). These points are developed in Sommerville, 'Lofty Science and Local Politics', in *The Cambridge Companion to Hobbes*, ed. T. Sorell (Cambridge: Cambridge Univesity Press, 1996), 246–73 at 262–3.
70 Hobbes, *Leviathan*, 374 (1651edn, 296), 391 (1651 edn, 311).
71 Luc Borot, 'Hobbes's *Behemoth*' in Rogers and Sorell, *Hobbes and History*, 137–46, at 141.

claimed that it was, and Hobbes had already spelled out his position on this in his earlier political works. So it is hard to support the idea that Hobbes changed his fundamental political doctrines in *Leviathan* and then changed them back again in *Behemoth*, and hard, too, to show that Leviathan was intended as a defense of the Rump. Arguably, when Hobbes called the Engagement 'a very great Crime' he was doing no more than spelling out the principles of *Leviathan*. In the body of that book, we learn that 'the dispute of sword'[72] concerning sovereign authority amongst the English has not yet been decided. So the war was still going on. But in war we are bound to side with the power which protects us in peace—the king's power. And therefore the imposition of the Engagement was an act of treason. Much of *Leviathan* was written against the Rumpers's ideas. But after they had won the war, Hobbes defended submission to them. There is no serious incompatibility between *Leviathan* and *Behemoth*, for Hobbes was always an enemy to the Parliamentarians' principles.

---

[72] Hobbes, *Leviathan*, 311 (1651 edn, 241).

A. P. Martinich

Presbyterians in 'Behemoth'

Presbyterians and Puritans

Presbyterians play a large role in Hobbes's history of the English civil war, as one might expect. He thought that the corruption of the people was one of the causes of the English civil war, and that the Presbyterian clergy were one of the corrupting groups. Indeed, they are the first group that he mentioned in this regard. The Presbyterians are followed by Roman Catholics ('Papists'), Independents, university educated gentlemen, the city of London, spendthrifts, and people ignorant of their political obligations (2–3).[1] Hobbes's view contrasts with that of contemporary historians. Although Elizabethan Presbyterians are often mentioned for purposes of providing background, they are not mentioned as a cause of the civil war by standard books on that topic, for example, *The Causes of the English Revolution 1529–1642* by Lawrence Stone (1972), *The Causes of the English Civil War* by Conrad Russell (1990), and *The Causes of the English Civil War* by Ann Hughes (1991).[2]

If Hobbes is wrong to blame the Presbyterian clergy, as I shall show he was, why did he make this mistake? Perhaps the source for his history claimed that the Presbyterians were at fault. In a prefatory note to *Behemoth*, he says that he relied on 'Mr. Heath's chronicle'. This is James Heath's long treatment of the civil wars, *A Brief Chronicle of the Late Intestine War in the Three Kingdoms of England, Scotland & Ireland etc.* (1663), which exceeds 750 pages.[3] The mention of the three kingdoms in the title

---

1   Thomas Hobbes, *Behemoth or The Long Parliament*, ed. Ferdinand Tönnies (Chicago: University of Chicago Press, 1990). Page references to Behemoth are placed in the text. In the quotation above, Hobbes may be mimicking the Grand Remonstrance in which 'The Jesuited Papists', 'The Bishops, and the corrupt part of the Clergy', 'Councillors and Courtiers' are mentioned as the 'actors and promoters' of 'mischief'. S. R. Gardiner, ed., *The Constitutional Documents of the Puritan Revolution*, 3rd edn (Oxford: Clarendon Press, 1903), 206–7.
2   Others could be mentioned, e.g. Conrad Russell, *The Fall of the British Monarchies, 1637–1642* (Oxford: Clarendon Press, 1991).
3   The year before, Heath published *A Brief Chronicle of All the Chief Actions*, etc., which is about sixty pages long.

of Heath's book may make it appear much more astute than it actually was. It is largely a chronicle of the battles of the civil war; some attention is paid to political events; and almost no attention is paid to religious ones. The Presbyterians are rarely mentioned, and Heath excuses himself for not offering any causes of the wars:

> No higher or greater cause for this war can be assigned ... but the fate and catastrophe of Kingdomes and Monarchies, which do at certain periods of time tast [sic] of that vicissitude and mutability, to which all other sublunary things are more frequently subjected.
>
> The secondary causes of it, are so many and so uncertain, so variously reported and beleeved that it would spend the paper allotted to this Epitome in ascertaining them.[4]

So Hobbes's attribution of the causes, for good and for ill, are not Heath's, and we can say with confidence that they are his own. He had, for example, already been critical of Presbyterians in *Leviathan*.[5]

If Heath is not the cause of Hobbes's mistake, who or what is? I think much of the answer depends on semantics. Hobbes's use of the term 'Presbyterian' is misleading.[6] In today's usage, a Presbyterian is a Christian whose church has 'presbyters' and does not have bishops. Currently, 'Presbyterian' and 'episcopacy' are incompatible terms. The usage of the word in the early 1640s is more complicated. The most important point is that, although their beliefs and attitudes overlapped substantially, Presbyterians were not thereby puritans.

My main goal in this chapter is to discuss the accuracy of Hobbes's portrayal of the Presbyterian ministers because that is the group about which he says a great deal. It is fortunate that the topic can be restricted in this way because the Presbyterian ministers, along with the religious Presbyterians,[7] are easier to characterize and identify in the early 1640s[8]

---

4   Heath, *A Brief Chronicle of the Late Intestine War* (London: William Lee, 1662), 1-2.
5   *Leviathan*, ed. A. P. Martinich (Peterborough, Ontario: Broadview Press, 2001), 47. 4. References to *Leviathan* are to chapter and paragraph.
6   Is it possible that 'Presbyterian' was simply a name for the puritans in the early 1640s? Richard Baxter says, 'But the greatest Advantage which I found for Concord and Pacification, was among a great number of Ministers and People who had addicted themselves to no Sect or Party at all; though the Vulgar called them by the Name of *Presbyterians*.' Richard Baxter, *Reliquiae Baxterianae*, ed. M. Sylvester (London, 1696), 146. However, in this passage, written about 1654, Baxter is talking about the decade of the 1640s. Earlier he wrote, 'But the *generality* of the People through the Land ... who were then called Puritans, Precisions, Religious Persons, that used to talk of God, and Heaven, and Scripture, and Holiness, and to follow Sermons ... adhered to Parliament.' Baxter, *Reliquiae*, 31.
7   I will often use 'Presbyterians' to mean religious Presbyterians or the Presbyterian clergy. The context should indicate which meaning it has.
8   I use 'early 1640s' generally to denote 1639-42.

than the so-called political Presbyterians.⁹ For more than half a century, historians have been debating whether a helpful distinction can be made between religious and political Presbyterians, and if so, of what the distinction consists. This is half of a broader problem, namely, whether a helpful distinction can be made between religious and political Independents. Although the problem has been vigorously debated for decades, there is no consensus about exactly who or what 'Presbyterian' and 'Independent' denoted as regards clergy and MPs in the early 1640s. So, a large part of my discussion involves directly or indirectly the definition of a Presbyterian minister, although I do not pretend that I am advancing the general problem. In this regard, I am concerned principally with identifying whom Hobbes is talking about when he applies the term 'Presbyterian' to a minister.

Let's approach the characterization of the Presbyterians by beginning with a characterization of a puritan in the early 1640s, not as the word 'puritan' was used at that time, because its use was unbridled, but as I wish to use it to identify a certain set of beliefs. The puritans were those members of the Church of England of whom the following can be said: (i) they were Calvinists in theology, (ii) they favored simple ceremonies, in contrast with the elaborate ones of the Roman Catholic and the Laudian Church, (iii) they favored a national church, and (iv) they opposed the concept of *jure divino* episcopacy. Puritans as puritans wanted religious reform, not non-religious ones. Although many puritans were also dissatisfied with the king's policies, civil dissatisfaction is not a characteristic of the puritans as puritans.¹⁰

---

9   Fortunately, I rarely have to refer to the 'political Presbyterians', not to mention the correlative group, the 'political Independents'. Concerning the difficulty of defining these terms or identifying people who fit the description, see for example, J. H. Hexter, 'The Problem of the Presbyterian Independents', *The American Historical Review* 44 (1938), 29–49; reprinted with revisions in *Reappraisals in History* (New York: Northwestern University Press, 1962), 163–84; David Underdown, 'The Independents Reconsidered', *Journal of British Studies* 3 (1964), no. 2, 57–84; George Yule, 'Independents and Revolutionaries', *Journal of British Studies* 7 (1968), no. 2, 11–32; David Underdown, 'The Independents Again', *Journal of British Studies* 8 (1968), no. 1, 83–93; Valerie Pearl, 'The "Royal Independents" in the English Civil War', *Transactions of the Royal Historical Society*, 5th series 18 (1968), 69–96; Blair Worden, 'The Independents: A Reprisal in History', *Past and Present* 47 (1970), 116–122; Valerie Pearl, 'Exorcist or Historian: The Dangers of Ghost-Hunting', ibid., 122–7; David Underdown, 'The Presbyterian Independents Exorcised: A Brief Comment', ibid., 128–33; George Yule, 'Presbyterians and Independents: Some Comments', ibid., 130–3; J. H. Hexter, 'Presbyterians, Independents and Puritans: A Voice from the Past', ibid., 134–6; and Stephen Foster, 'A Rejoinder', ibid., 137–46.

10 One might object that many of the puritan ministers of the early 1640s were millenarians and hence both expecting and hoping for the overthrow of secular government and the establishment of the kingship of Jesus. However, I do not think that the millenarian attitude involves dissatisfaction with civil policies or a secular government in the sense that some other civil policy or secular government would be preferred. I cannot treat the millenarian

In characterizing the puritans, two possible features do not play any role: (a) adherence to the *classis*-system, and (b) sole jurisdiction of the Church over all religious matters. Anyone who, in addition to (i)–(iv), believed in (a) and (b) will count as a Presbyterian. Feature (b) alone is not sufficient to identify a Presbyterian since religious Independents also accepted (b), but not (a).

Although puritans had other dominant features, I do not think that it is necessary to include them in the characterization. One of these, however, deserves mention because Hobbes thought that it was the main way that his 'Presbyterians' stirred up trouble against the king. Puritans emphasized preaching. While Hobbes did not disapprove of preaching itself, he thought that 'much preaching an inconvenience' (64). He made his complaints specific in this passage:

> What needs so much preaching of faith to us that are no heathens, and that believe already all that Christ and his apostles have told us is necessary to salvation and more too? Why is there so little preaching of justice? I have indeed heard righteousness often recommended to the people, but I have seldom heard the word justice in their sermons. (63)

So far my characterization of religious Presbyterians in terms of (i)–(iv) and (a) has the consequence that all Presbyterians were puritans. In order to make the classes of puritans and Presbyterians disjoint, I will say that puritans do not accept (a). What this means is that many puritans of the early 1640s became Presbyterians when episcopacy was no longer a viable option, and Presbyterianism seemed to be the only way to preserve a national religion.

I have been at some pains to distinguish the Presbyterians from the puritans. One might object that the effort is all for naught, because Hobbes is justified in using the word 'Presbyterian' broadly enough to include puritans of the early 1640s even though they were not yet Presbyterians in the technical sense used here, as long as they eventually adopted the presbyterian system of church government, just as it is justified to use 'Augustus' to refer to Octavian in discussing events prior to his obtaining that title. The general point about the use of names and titles is correct. Nonetheless, I think Hobbes's use of 'Presbyterian' to refer to puritans of the early 1640s is misleading and probably unjustified.

Religious complaints

As the items characterizing them indicate, the puritans were agitated about the religion of England and not about the monarchy *per se*. They

---

aspect of puritanism here. See John F. Wilson, *Pulpit in Parliament* (Princeton: Princeton University Press, 1969), 223–30.

were angry with William Laud, his bishops, and many clergymen. Laud took the brunt of the anger because he seemed to be the driving force behind the imposition of a liturgy that the puritans considered for all intents and purposes Roman Catholic; and he seemed to be responsible for the harsh punishment inflicted on people who opposed him in the Church courts.[11]

The chief complaints against Laud's bishops were that they were haughty and corrupt. Dissatisfaction with the policies and lives of the bishops led to the London Root and Branch Petition of 1641, which is a potpourri of complaints. It said that 'the pride and ambition of the prelates ... [was] boundless', and that they were 'unwilling to be subject either to man or laws'.[12] The Petition objected to the episcopal claim of being *jure divino*; and it charged the bishops with encouraging clergymen to 'despise the temporal magistracy, the nobles and gentry of the land'. In various ways it complained that the Church of England had become too much like the Roman Catholic Church, and that this was preparation for the restoration of that 'superstitious religion'. Finally, it expressed the fear that the 'present wars and commotions happened between his Majesty and his subjects of Scotland', because of the bishops, and that the English would go 'to an utter ruin' unless the episcopacy was abolished.[13]

The Root and Branch petition fuelled anti-episcopal feeling, both in parliament and among the ministers. A newsletter reported, 'All the pulpits do now ring of the disorders of the clergy both in doctrine and discipline'.[14] Even moderate MPs joined in condemnation of the bishops. The speech of Harbottle Grimston in the House of Commons in early November, 1640, reflected the views of many: 'Who are they that of late years have been advanced to any preferment in the Church, but such as have been notoriously suspicious in their discipline, and for the most part vicious in their lives'.[15] John Culpepper, Lucius Cary, and Edward Hyde, all of whom aligned themselves with the king as war approached, criticized the bishops during the first month of the Long Parliament. Hobbes reported that 'in a manner all the people of England, were their [the bishops'] enemies, upon the account of their behavior, as being (they said) too imperious' (89). He indicated general agreement with the objections

---

11 See also Julian Davies, *Caroline Captivity of the Church* (Oxford: Clarendon Press, 1992).
12 J. P. Kenyon, ed. *The Stuart Constitution*, 2nd edn (Cambridge: Cambridge University Press, 1986), 156.
13 Ibid., 154–7.
14 Quoted from Anthony Fletcher, *The Outbreak of the English Civil War* (London: Edward Arnold, 1981), 108.
15 Quoted from William Shaw, *A History of the English Church During the Civil Wars and Under the Commonwealth, 1640–1660* (New York, 1900), 1. 11.

against the bishops and calls them 'supercilious'.[16] Commenting on the Nottingham petition, one of the thirteen county petitions that followed the Root and Branch Petition, Hobbes took a moderate position in a letter he wrote from Paris to the third earl of Devonshire. He said that the 'abundance of abuses committed by Ecclesiasticall persons and their Officers, w^{ch} ... cannot be denied or excused'. But, he added, 'that they proceed from y^e *Episcopacy* it selfe, is not so evidently proved'.[17] Hobbes's view is similar to that of Digby, who said,

> To strike at the root, to attempt a total alteration, before ever I can give my vote to that, ... [it] must be made manifest to me ...[that the] mischiefs which are felt under Episcopacy flow from the nature of the function [of episcopacy], and not from the abuse of it.[18]

The opposition to Laud and his bishops gave rise in puritans to disgust for the episcopacy as an institution. Abolishing episcopacy came to be seen as the easiest route to achieving the other reforms that disgruntled members of the Church of England wanted in liturgy, discipline, and governance. The Root and Branch Petition called for the abolition of the office of bishop and affiliated clergy. However, some of the MPs may have supported it as a tactical move against the liturgy being promoted by the bishops. Their opposition to the Laudian church and support of the Root and Branch Petition resulted in making some of the MPs seem more opposed to the bishops than they may have been. They went from being against the liturgy that the bishops supported to being against the bishops who supported the liturgy.

In addition to the reasons for abolishing the episcopacy already given, Hobbes adds his own psychological explanation. Motivating the Presbyterians was 'the delight of sharing in the government'. This delight gave them a sense of power, and with that sense of power they felt that they could take revenge on 'those that do not admire their learning' (89; see also 163, 172).[19] In making this comment, it is possible that Hobbes was thinking of the Laudian claim that bishops 'enjoyed ... inherently greater spiritual knowledge and grace, all apparently as a function of

---

16 Letter 37 in *The Correspondence of Thomas Hobbes*, ed. N. Malcolm (Oxford: Clarendon Press, 1994), 120.
17 Letter 37 in *The Correspondence of Thomas Hobbes*, 120. Johann Sommerville mistakenly maintains that Hobbes thought that 'lay commissioners would replace bishops in governing the church'. His judgment is based upon a misreading of the letter. Hobbes alludes to the fact that the new scheme is 'propounded', not 'likely'. See Johann Sommerville, 'Hobbes, Selden, Erastianism, and the History of the Jews', in *Hobbes and History*, eds G. A. J. Rogers and T. Sorell (London: Routledge, 2000), 161, 165.
18 Quoted from Shaw, *A History of the English Church*, 1. 3.
19 Hobbes did not admire their learning, but since he had left England in late 1640, one might think that he could not be thinking of himself. But he probably was since he feared that he had put himself in danger by circulating *The Elements of Law, Natural and Politic*, earlier in 1640.

their consecration'.[20] By referring to the learning of the Presbyterians, Hobbes may have been alluding to the fact that the Westminster Assembly of Divines consisted of the most part of ecclesiastical scholars. But in fact he denigrated their knowledge: 'For their learning, it amounts to no more than an imperfect knowledge of Greek and Latin, and an acquired readiness in the Scripture language, with a gesture and tone suitable thereunto ...' (172). They may also have had the reputation for learning.[21] He thinks their pretensions to learning gave them a false feeling of competence. He undercut that supposed competence with this argument: Either they were learned in politics or something else. It was not politics, because their specialty is called 'divinity'. So, if anything, they are learned in divinity. But if they were learned in divinity, then they would know that they should not have been causing controversy because 'religion itself admits no controversy'. Religion should be uncontroversial because religion is 'the law of the kingdom' (90). Hobbes is trading here on the conventionally accepted etymology of 'religion' from '*religare*' *to bind*. It is the king alone who, as the maker and judge of the law, can bind his subjects to a form of worship. In fact, Hobbes goes on, the divines do not tend to preach on religion at all but on philosophy (90). And on this subject the divines are obviously not competent. They merely think they are because they studied Latin and Greek and the ancient philosophers at their universities.[22]

Puritans and hierarchy

Notwithstanding the puritan opposition to the Laudian bishops, puritanism was compatible with episcopacy. Even puritans who eventually became Presbyterians were willing to accept a kind of episcopacy. This would be an institution in which the bishops would not be considered superior to other clergymen with respect to their ministry. The favored episcopacy was often called a 'primitive episcopacy'. In a word, the episcopacy would not be a 'prelacy', that is, a position of special authority.[23] The basis for their beliefs was the New Testament accounts of the early church, just as it was for the episcopal men and for the Independents.

---

20 Anthony Milton, *Catholic and Reformed: The Roman and Protestant Churches in English Protestant Thought, 1600–1640* (Cambridge: Cambridge University Press, 1995), 469.
21 Baxter, *Reliquiae*, 140.
22 The opposite view is presented later: 'Do not divines comprehend all civil and moral philosophy within their divinity?' (148).
23 'Prelacy' was sometimes identified with any episcopal rule, e.g. in 'The Solemn League and Covenant', Gardiner, *Constitutional Documents*, 268–9.

These puritans recognized that good order required some hierarchy.[24] But they did not think that the hierarchy needed to originate from the top down. It could, and according to the Presbyterians it did, come from the bottom up. The bottom up hierarchical system of the English Presbyterians was spelled out in this way. Each congregation would have a court consisting of the minister (or ministers) and the elders of the congregation. They would represent their congregation to a *classis* (or presbytery); each *classis* would elect representatives to a provincial synod, and each synod in turn would elect representatives to the General Assembly of the entire nation.[25]

Hobbes commented that this structure was tantamount to making 'the national assembly an archbishop and the provincial assemblies so many bishops' (89). His observation was apt. Although the source of the authority of the Presbyterian Church comes from the bottom and goes up, the exercise of authority goes from the top down, just like the system of archbishops and bishops. A higher level of authority of the Presbyterian Church could impose rules on the lower levels, in contrast with the Independent Churches, which made each congregation semi-autonomous. Hobbes could also recognize how neatly his theory of an artificial person describes the Presbyterian system. An artificial person acts with authority for some other entity, usually one or more other persons.[26] For Hobbes, it is not important whether that artificial person consists of one person, as a bishop does, or consists of many, as assemblies do. In either case, they count as one object.

As mentioned earlier, I suspect that Hobbes's use of 'Presbyterian' to refer to puritans of the early 1640s was not innocent. He wanted to project the militant attitudes of the mid-1640s onto the attitudes of people in the early 1640s. He did not discriminate between those who did not intend to oppose the king with force and those Presbyterians who supported militant opposition to the king. Also, Hobbes may have thought that the Presbyterians had already worked out a system of church governance without bishops substantially earlier than 1643. But Hobbes is wrong to think that prior to the opening of the Assembly of Divines, the members knew what system of church governance they were for. They were clear or unified in their thoughts only about what system they were against.[27]

---

24   Patrick Collinson, *The Elizabethan Puritan Movement* (Oxford: Clarendon Press, 1967), 103.
25   Robert S. Paul, *The Assembly of the Lord* (Edinburgh: T. & T. Clark, 1985), 103.
26   *Leviathan*, 16.
27   Paul, *The Assembly of the Lord*, 114–15, and Shaw, *A History of the English Church*, 1. 7. Some scholars today continue to write as if the puritan clergy going into the Westminster Assembly were already committed to a Presbyterian system. Johann Sommerville gives the mistaken impression that the puritan clergy began the Westminster Assembly committed to Presbyterianism (Sommerville, 'Hobbes, Selden, Erastianism', 163). See also Tai Liu, *Discord in*

Ironically, at one point Hobbes generalized this fact about the divines and attributed it to all the rebels: 'For from the beginning of the rebellion, the method of ambition was constantly this: first to destroy, and then to consider what they should set up' (192).

Intentionally or not, Hobbes exaggerated the aspirations of the Presbyterians. He thought that the Presbyterian system was part of a conspiracy as much to gain control over the government as to gain control over the Church. For him, the Presbyterian clergy were essentially rebels. He wanted to prove that the clergymen that supported the war against the king were committed to his overthrow at least a couple of years before the fighting began. They wanted the Christian religion to be independent of the monarch. In two earlier works, he had argued that making the Church independent is setting up a second sovereign and that no man can serve two masters.[28] (He also thought that the House of Commons had resolved by late 1640 to 'depose the King, or to let him have the title only so long as he should act for their purposes' (89).) One of his major complaints against the Presbyterians is expressed in the following passage, although he is speaking specifically of the Scots in 1651-2:

> This is a downright declaration to all kings and commonwealths in general: that a Presbyterian minister will be a true subject to none of them in the things of Christ; which things what they are, they will be judges themselves. What have we then gotten by our deliverance from the Pope's tyranny, if these petty men succeed in the place of it, that have nothing in them that can be beneficial to the public, except their silence? (172)

On this issue at least, Hobbes and Milton agreed:

> Your plots and packings worse than those of Trent,
> That so the Parliament
> May with their wholesome and preventive shears
> Clip you phylacteries, though balk your ears,
> And succour our just fears
>
> When they shall read this clearly in your charge:
> New *Presbyter* is but old *Priest* writ large.[29]

Speaking of July 1641, Hobbes says, it 'was the design of the Presbyterian ministers, who taking themselves to be, by divine right, the only lawful governors of the Church, endeavoured to bring the same form of

---

Zion: The Puritan Divines and the Puritan Revolution, 1640-1660 (The Hague: Martinus Nijhoff, 1973), 37.

28 *De Cive*, in *Man and Citizen*, ed. Bernard Gert (Indianapolis: Hackett Publishing, 1991), 6.11 and 9.1. References to *De Cive* are to chapter and paragraph. See also, *Leviathan* 20. 4, 29. 15, 42. 102, and 42. 123.

29 John Milton, 'On the New Forcers of Conscience under the Long Parliament', in *The Complete Poems*, ed. J. Leonard (London: Penguin Books, 1998), 87.

Government into the civil state' (75). He claimed that they intended to have the MPs under their thumb: 'as the spiritual laws were to be made by their synods, so the civil laws should be made by the House of Commons'. However, the ministers 'were deceived' in thinking that the MPs would be ruled by them (75). Alluding to the Assembly of Divines, Hobbes describes their plan: 'the State becoming popular [democratic], the Church might be so too, and governed by an Assembly; and by consequence (as they thought) seeing politics are subservient to religion, they might govern, and thereby satisfy not only their covetous humour with riches, but also their malice with power to undo all men that admired not their wisdom' (159; see also 195). As mentioned already, there was no significant Presbyterian group that was plotting an overthrow of religion, and certainly not an overthrow of parliament.

It is possible that Hobbes's belief that the Presbyterian had great power in the early 1640s was based on a belief that it was part of an unbroken movement that began in England during Elizabeth's reign. He mentions that when the protestants went to Geneva during the reign of Mary I, they saw how that city 'set up presbyteries for the government of their several churches' (136). The English exiles

> were much taken with this government, and at their return in the time of Queen Elizabeth, and ever since, have endeavored to the great trouble of the Church and nation, to set up that government here, wherein they countenanced sometimes in their frequent preaching, they introduced many strange and many pernicious doctrines. (136)

However, the Presbyterians movement had been broken by the end of her reign, and did not return during the reign of James. So it is a mistake to think of Charles's Presbyterians as continuous with Elizabeth's. Richard Baxter wrote:

> Though Presbytery generally took in Scotland, yet it was but a stranger here ... And when I came to try it, I found that most (that ever I could meet with) were against the *Jus Divinum* of Lay Elders, and for the Moderate Primitive Episcopacy, ... and for an accommodation of all Parties, in order to Concord, as well as myself. [30]

As part of his mistaken belief about the power of the Presbyterians in the early 1640s, Hobbes misjudged their numbers. He claimed that there were far more Presbyterians than Arminians right after the Synod of Dort (61). Even if we take 'Presbyterian' to mean 'puritan', it is still not obvious that he is right. Puritans were Calvinists, and there certainly were more Calvinists than Arminians in the 1610s and 1620s; but since not all Calvinists were puritans, it does not follow that the puritans outnumbered

---

30 Baxter, *Reliquiae*, 146. See also Collinson, *The Elizabethan Puritan Movement*, 448–67.

Presbyterians in 'Behemoth'

non-puritans. He said that 'the power of the Presbyterians was so very great, that, not only the citizens of London were almost all of them at their devotion, but also the greatest part of all other cities and market-towns of England' (23). He may have based this on the dozen or so petitions relating to abolishing the episcopacy that were sent from the counties to the House of Commons in the wake of the London Root and Branch Petition and on the arrival of those ministers from the country who preached before parliament. But these petitions against the bishops were not thereby petitions for Presbyterianism, and those ministers do not represent a fair sample of the population. Hobbes also unjustifiably attributes the passage of the Bishops' Exclusion Bill in February 1642 to the Presbyterians (89). The opposition to the bishops at that time was much more widespread than that.

Even if Hobbes's judgment about the power of the Presbyterians is based upon the power of the Presbyterian clergy in the Westminster Assembly, he would still be wrong in claiming a Presbyterian plot to take over the government. The Assembly did not have any intention of participating in the civil government of England. The divines wanted (and expected) only to dictate the form and discipline of the English Church. Even if the Presbyterian clergy had aspired to more, they would not have been able to achieve it. The House of Commons wanted nothing more from the Assembly than advice, and advice only about ecclesial matters.

Puritan ministers and the civil war

Given that Hobbes was wrong to blame the Presbyterians for the corruption of the people, was there a group of ministers whom Hobbes might have been referring to and who were a cause of the civil war? The short answer is 'yes'.[31] But, *pace* Hobbes, the Presbyterian ministers generally did not argue directly against the king until 1642, when armed conflict became inevitable. In late 1640 and 1641, in addition to sermons in London against the bishops and various abuses in the Church, they also preached against the secular government. Some of the most important of these sermons were the Fast Day sermons sponsored by the Long Parliament. The first two were preached by Cornelius Burgess and Stephen Marshall, both of whom later became members of the Assembly of

---

[31] Here as elsewhere Richard Baxter is level-headed: 'And whereas the Kings Party usually say, that it was the seditious Preachers that stirred up the People, and were the Cause of all this, I answer,
1. It is partly true, and partly not: It is not true that they stirred them up to War (except an inconsiderable Number of them, one perhaps in a County, if so much.) But it is true that they discovered their dislike of the Book of Sports, and bowing to Altars, and diminishing Preaching, and silencing Ministers, and such like; and were glad that the Parliament attempted a Reformation of them.' Baxter, *Reliquiae*, 34.

Divines and Presbyterians. Marshall's sermon was appropriate for a new parliament and was not inflammatory. Burges's sermon had more political substance. Ostensibly talking about a crisis in Judah, Burges's references to 'This Northern Army [Medes and Persians]' were easily taken as referring to the Scottish army ensconced in the north of England. This was confirmed when he went on about the deliverance of the Church depending upon 'a more solemne, strict, and inviolable Covenant' with God.[32] Near the end of his sermon, he urged the House of Commons to 'carefully reforme, or cast out all idle, unsound, unprofitable, and scandalous Ministers; and provide a sound, godly, profitable and settled Preaching Ministry in every Congregation through the land'.[33] This sermon fit the call for the reform expressed in the Root and Branch Petition. Its demand for clerical reform was a direct criticism of the current state of religion, but not of the king. (Of course, many of the reformers knew that Charles I was the problem.) Ministers not subject to the strictures of the Fast Sermons could speak or write with less restraint. The author of *A Glimpse of Sions Glory*, often attributed to Hanserd Knollys, a Baptist, wrote in 1641, 'It is the work of the day to cry down Babylon, that it may fall more and more ... *Blessed is he that dasheth the brats* of Babylon *against the stones:* Blessed is he that hath any hand in pulling downe *Babylon* ... [C]ry down Babylon, and the Prelacie'.[34]

Many of the sermons had substantial political content. In *The Troublers Troubled, Or Achan Condemned and Executed*, preached on April 4, 1641, Samuel Fairclough urged all 'the 'Joshuahs' of the parliament to seek out the 'Achans'.[35] Achan was an Israelite who was stoned to death for taking plunder (Joshua 7). Fairclough, who had an indirect connection with John Pym, was obviously urging that Strafford be punished. At this time, a sharp distinction was still made between the good king and his evil counsellors. Only the evil counsellors were the target of the dissidents. The

---

32 Quoted from Wilson, *Pulpit in Parliament*, 39.
33 Quoted from Wilson, *Pulpit in Parliament*, 39–40.
34 *A Glimpse of Sions Glory* (London, 1641), 2, 7. Knollys is referring to Psalm 137, lines 7-9: 'Remember, O Lord, the children of Edom in the day of Jerusalem; who said, "Rase it, rase it, even to the foundation thereof". O daughter of Babylon, who art to be destroyed; happy shall he be that rewardeth thee as thou hast served us. Happy shall he be that taketh and dasheth thy little ones against the stones.' See also Stephen Marshall's sermon of February, 1642, *Meroz Cursed* (London, 1641): 'It may be some of you may be called as souldiers, to spend your blood in the Churches cause: If you knew the honour to such a service, you would say, as the Martyr once, Had every haire on your head a life you would venture them all in the Churches cause' (53). Knollys calculates the beginning of the end to be 1650 (32). Wilson, *Puritan in Pulpit*, 224-7, says that Thomas Goodwin is probably the author of *A Glimpse of Sions Glory*, but he does not mention William Haller's arguments for attributing it to Knollys; see Haller's *The Rise of Puritanism* (New York: Columbia University Press, 1938), 396-7.
35 Wilson, *Pulpit in Parliament*, 44.

intention was reform, not revolution. Again, this is not to deny that these actions of the Puritan ministers, later to be Presbyterians, are part of the cause of the English civil war. It is rather to deny what Hobbes says or implies, that they were preaching revolution.

However, both Charles and Hobbes interpreted the actions of these ministers as revolutionary. Church and State, being united in England, were ultimately under the authority of the king. So any criticism of either the Church or the State was ultimately a criticism of the king. In his speech of 21 January 1641 to the Parliament, Charles said, 'Now I must clearly tell you, that I make a great difference between reformation and alteration of government; though I am for the first, I cannot give way to the latter.'[36] Although Charles seems to be talking more about the proposed religious reforms than the secular ones, he is comfortable using the word 'government' to cover both. In March 1642, Charles wrote, 'For my fears and doubts, I did not think they should have bin thought so groundless or triviall, while so many seditious Pamphlets & Sermons are looked upon'.[37] When the Parliament asked what pamphlets and sermons Charles meant, he mentioned *The Protestation Protested* by Henry Burton, *The Prentices Protestation*, and *To Your Tents O Israel*.[38] In a later address to his subjects, Charles said,

> When they had made this breach upon the Ecclesiasticall State, they took care (under pretence of incouragement of Preaching) to erect lectures in severall Parishes, and to commend such Lecturers as best suited their designes, men of no Learning, no Conscience, but furious promoters of the most dangerous Innovations which were ever introduced into any State, many of them having taken no Orders, yet recommended by Members of either House to Parishes ...; and when Mechanick persons have been brought before them for preaching in Churches, and confessed the same, the power of those Grand Reformers hath been so great, that they have been dismissed without punishment, hardly with reprehension ... [A]nd such men ... boldly and

---

36 'King Speech, 25 January 1641,' in Kenyon, *The Stuart Constitution*, 17.
37 *A Declaration of the Lords and Commons in Parliament ... Whereunto is annexed His Majesties Speech to the Committee* (London, 1641) [Speech of 9 March 1641 (old style)]. See also *The Journals of the House of Lords*, 4. 641.
38 *The Journals of the House of Lords*, 4. 686. Neither *The Prentices Protestation* nor *To Your Tents* in either Thomason Tracts, Wing Short-Title Catalogue or Early English Books Online. I assume 'The Prentices Protestation' refers to *The Apprentices Lamentation* (1641), though I do not have access to a copy of this work. Concerning the other, all copies of it seem to have been destroyed. See Ernest Sirluck, 'To Your Tents, O Israel: A Lost Pamphlet', *Huntington Library Quarterly* 10 (1956), 30-6. It is alluded to in Clarendon's description of Charles's departure from the House of Commons: 'the rude people [were] flocking together, and crying out, *'Privilege of parliament, privilege of parliament'*, some of them pressing very near his [the King's] coach, and amongst the rest one calling out with a very loud voice, "To your tents, O Israel"'. Edward [Hyde], *The History of the Rebellion and Civil Wars in England*, ed. W. Dunn Macray (Oxford: The Clarendon Press, 1888), 1. 486.

> seditiously preached against the Government of the Church, against the Book of Common Prayer, against Our Kingly Lawfull Power, and against Our Person ... ; All licence was given to those lewd, seditious Pamphlets, which despised the Government both of Church and State, which laid any imputations or scorns upon Our Person or Office, and which filled the ears of all Our good Subjects with lies, and monstrous discourses, to make them believe all the ill of the Government, and Governours of Church and State; Books against the Book of Common Prayer, and the established Laws of the Land suffered without reprehension to be dedicated to both Houses of Parliament ...[39]

Hobbes was to some extent right when he claimed that the MPs' accusation of misdeeds by 'the bishops, counselors, and courtiers' in the Grand Remonstrance of December 1641 was 'a more mannerly way of accusing the king himself, and defaming him to his subjects' (83). His claim is made plausible by the fact that both Strafford and Laud, not to mention Windebank, Finch and others, were out of the way, and the political conditions continued to deteriorate. However, when Hobbes reports the allegation that the bishops during the 1630s had been trying 'to suppress the purity and power of religion' as a way of suppressing 'the doctrine of the Presbyterians', he is again confusing certain puritans with Presbyterians (82).

Hobbes coupled his Presbyterians with the political opponents of the king. He represented them as acting in parallel with the 'great many gentlemen' who wanted 'a popular government in the civil state' (23). He suggested a coordinated action on the part of both groups by referring to them as a unit: 'presbyterian and other democratical men', 'the English Presbyterians and democraticals', 'the democratical and Presbyterian English', and 'the Presbyterians and men of democratical principles' (*Behemoth*, 20, 30, 31, 193).[40] The Presbyterians approximated to being democrats in religion. Hobbes also connected the Presbyterians and democrats to each other by pointing out that they have the same place of origin. Members of both groups acquired their beliefs in the universities (23). The clergy in the university is 'an excellent means to divide a kingdom into factions' (148).[41] Underlying these sentiments is an invalid argument:

---

39 *His Majesties Declaration to All His Loving Subjects. Of August 12, 1642*, 21-2. The same sentiment is expressed in other declarations, e.g. 'For we cannot without grief of heart, ... look upon the bold Licence of some men, in Printing of Pamphlets, in preaching and Printing of Sermons, so full of bitternesse and malice.' *His Majesties Declaration to His Loving Subjects by England and Wales Published with the Advice of His Privie Councell* (London, 1641), 11.

40 Hobbes also refers to men of the Protectorate as 'Presbyterian and men of democratical principles' (193).

41 Hobbes also criticizes the morals of students at universities: 'I have often heard the complaints of parents, that their children were debauched there to drunkenness, wantonness, gaming, and other vices consequent to these. Nor is it a wonder amongst so many youths, if they did corrupt one another in despite of their tutors, who oftentimes were little elder than themselves

Presbyterians and democrats believe that the king should not have absolute sovereignty; Presbyterians and democrats acquired their corrupt beliefs in universities. Therefore, the universities are corrupt.

Obviously some of the puritan ministers interacted with some MPs, and Trevor-Roper thought that Clarendon was right when he wrote: 'the first publishing of extraordinary news was from the pulpit; and by the preacher's text, and his manner of discourse upon it, the auditors might judge, and commonly foresaw, what was like to be next done in the Parliament or Council of State'.[42] Trevor-Roper gives a colorful description of Stephen Marshall's behavior:

> In the Long Parliament he would emerge as the inseparable political and spiritual ally of Pym, the interpreter of Pym's policy after Pym's death. At every stage of the revolution we can see him. Now he is thumping his pulpit on great occasions; now he is meeting with Pym, Hampden and Harley to prepare parliamentary tactics; now he is bustling through Westminster Hall to push voters into the Parliament before division; now he is retiring, exhausted, to recuperate in the well-appointed house of his good friend 'my noble Lord of Warwick.'[43]

Nonetheless, Hobbes, I think, exaggerated the connection and the influence of the ministers. The supposed parallelism of 'Presbyterian' and democratical action breaks down in various ways. As already indicated, the 'Presbyterians' were not advocating the overthrow of the monarchy in 1640–41. The ministers were helping the MPs gain more political power, rather than the reverse. They might participate in tactical discussions, but in their activities they were reflecting what should or would happen in the Parliament as dictated by certain MPs, not making the policy. Unlike the democratical men, the Presbyterians had no direct means of attacking the institution of the episcopacy. They had no power in Convocation, and little influence in the House of Lords. They had to work with members of the House of Commons.

I have been emphasizing that there was no substantial English Presbyterianism in the early 1640s. How then did it arise? The history is complicated, but the salient fact is the institution and operation of the Assembly of Divines. When fighting broke out between the king and the anti-royalist forces, Charles had the upper hand. The anti-royalist faction needed the support of the Scottish army; but the Scots would come to the aid of their Protestant brothers only on the condition that the members of the House of Commons promised to work for 'the reformation of religion

---

... [T]he Parliament did not much reverence ... the universities ... though many of them learned there to preach, and became thereby capable of preferment and maintenance' (147).

42 H. R. Trevor-Roper, 'The Fast Sermons of the Long Parliament', in *The Crisis in the Seventeenth Century* (New York: Harper & Row, 1968), 294.
43 Ibid., 297–8.

in the kingdoms of England and Ireland, in doctrine, worship, discipline, and government, according to ... the example of the best reformed Churches'.[44] Although parliament had been seriously considering setting up an assembly of divines to consider various aspects of religion in England, the call for the Assembly was put into action by the Parliament's need of the Scots.[45] An Ordinance calling for the Assembly was passed on June 12, 1643.[46]

About 120 divines, a dozen peers, and twenty members from the House of Commons were nominated to be members of the Assembly. More than thirty of these nominees never attended because of their loyalty to the king, who disapproved of the Assembly. One of these was Robert Sanderson, later bishop of Lincoln, who like Hobbes was Calvinist in theology and favored a church administered by bishops. So, from the beginning, the members that attended the Assembly favored some alternative to the Laudian episcopacy. One of these alternatives was Independency, according to which, each congregation was self-governing. Groups of congregations might be represented in associations or synods, but would not have jurisdiction over the individual congregation. To many, this arrangement seemed to spell the end of a national church. So the opponents of both a strong episcopacy and Independency looked for some middle ground to occupy. A form of Presbyterianism fit the bill. It had a hierarchy, which could exercise discipline on the Church from the top down, even though the origin of the hierarchy was bottom up.

Last remarks on the Presbyterians

Once Hobbes begins to describe the battles fought in 1642 through 1644, he rarely mentions the Presbyterians until he comes to the New Model Army. At that point he says that they were in control of the Parliament and in order to achieve their aims 'would fain have the king murdered' (131). This applies more to the 'political' Presbyterians than to the 'religious' ones that we have been discussing. In the same stretch of discourse, he alludes to the Assembly of the Divines as 'an Assembly of Presbyterian ministers' (131). By 1644, the Presbyterian *classis*-system had been worked out, and a majority of the members of the Assembly were religious Presbyterians. But there were some important dissenting ministers and

---

44 'The Solemn League and Covenant', in Gardiner, *Constitutional Documents*, 268. *The Solemn League and Covenant* was taken after the beginning of the Assembly of Divines. The Scots' insistence on reform of the English church antedates both.
45 Paul, *The Assembly of the Lord*, 63.
46 Kenyon, *The Stuart Constitution*, 237-8.

also some important 'Erastians' in the Assembly, most notably Hobbes's future friend, John Selden.[47]

Hobbes next mentions the 'political' Presbyterians in order to criticize them for bungling an attempt to restore the king: 'The Parliament, in which there were more [political] Presbyterians yet than Independents, might have gotten what they would of the King during his life, if they had not by an unconscionable and sottish ambition obstructed the way to their ends' (144–5). Perhaps Hobbes is holding the same view as that expressed in this 'Letter of Intelligence':

> The Scottish compliance of this city [London] will spoil both themselves and the kingdom—the kingdom at present, by corresponding with our taskmasters; and themselves in the end, when for this correspondence they will be rewarded with slavery; ... for they are led by the nose with their own principles by the Kirk of Presbyters in Scotland, by whose direction it is that they comply thus with the Independent party that Presbytery may be held up upon any terms in England, ... knowing this, that if the Royalists should prevail in England, then farewell Presbytery, and therefore they admitted of an Independent compliance as the least evil. Thus his Majesty is bought and sold still amongst the factions.[48]

Reflecting on the execution of the king, Hobbes lambastes the Presbyterians:

> What greater vices than irreligion, hypocrisy, avarice and cruelty; which have appeared so eminently in the actions of Presbyterian members and Presbyterian ministers? What greater crimes than blaspheming and killing God's anointed? Which was don by the hands of the Independents, but by the folly and first treason of the Presbyterians, who betrayed and sold him to his murderers? (155)

Hobbes's views about the Presbyterians during the civil war may be summed up in these passages:

> A great part of them, namely, the Presbyterian ministers, throughout the whole war, instigated the people against the King; so did also independent and other fanatic ministers ... The mischief proceeded wholly from the Presbyterian preachers, who, by a long practised histrionic faculty, preached up the rebellion powerfully ... Our late King ... was murdered, having been first persecuted by war, at the incitement of Presbyterian ministers; who are therefore guilty of the death of all that fell in that war? (159, 95.)

Here was their plan:

---

47 See Paul, *The Assembly of the Lord*, or W. M. Hetherington, *History of the Westminster Assembly of Divines* (New York: Mark H. Newman, 1843), for details.
48 Quoted from S. R. Gardiner, *History of the Great Civil War* (London: Windrush Press, 1987), 4. 129.

> the State becoming popular [democratic], the Church might be so too, and governed by an Assembly; and by consequence (as they thought) seeing politics are subservient to religion, they might govern, and thereby satisfy not only their covetous humour with riches, but also their malice with power to undo all men that admired not their wisdom. (159; see also 195.)

Notwithstanding his inaccuracies and exaggerations, Hobbes was right to identify actions by disgruntled clergy as one of the causes of the English civil war. He was a revisionist historian *avant là lettre*.

Gabriella Slomp

On Ambition, Greed, and Fear

Is *Behemoth* simply an attempt to apply the 'science of politics', as expounded in *De Cive* and *Leviathan*, to an historical event?[1] Or does it mark a significant development in Hobbes's ideas? Scholarship is divided on this issue. The terms of this long-standing debate can be encapsulated in the contrasting ways in which two Hobbesian interpreters have introduced recent editions of *Behemoth*: Maurice Goldsmith in 1968 and Stephen Holmes in 1990. On one side of the argument, Goldsmith in his brief but compelling Introduction puts forward the claim that Hobbes's intention in writing *Behemoth* was to provide a 'scientific' explanation of the phenomena leading to the English civil war. According to Goldsmith, *Behemoth* should be regarded as an application of Hobbes's 'science of politics' to history and in this application lies its greatness and importance.[2] Hobbes's account of the civil war, Goldsmith suggests, corroborates the argument in *Leviathan* that the causes of conflict among men are 'ideological'[3] and reside ultimately in 'men's passions'.[4]

On the other side, Stephen Holmes, in his in-depth Introduction to the 1990 reprint of *Behemoth*, indirectly but firmly challenges Goldsmith's view that *Behemoth* is a mere application of scientific principles to historical events. While agreeing with the latter part of Goldsmith's claim, namely that for Hobbes '[t]he causes of the upheaval were not economic and legal [...] but rather psychological and ideological',[5] and accepting

---

[1] I am very grateful to the Editor, Tomaž Mastnak, for his constructive comments on an earlier version of this essay and to Ruth Turner for her invaluable help with the style.

[2] Maurice Goldsmith, 'Introduction,' in Thomas Hobbes, *Behemoth or the Long Parliament*, ed. F. Tönnies (London: Frank Cass, 1969), ix–xi.

[3] 'The causes of the rebellion were neither economic nor social; they were ideological.' Goldsmith, 'Introduction', xiii. 'Unlike Harrington, he [Hobbes] perceived no shift in the balance of property [...] for Hobbes, history was not class war.' Ibid., xii.

[4] Ibid., xi.

[5] Stephen Holmes, 'Introduction', in Thomas Hobbes, *Behemoth or the Long Parliament*, ed. F. Tönnies (Chicago and London: University of Chicago Press, 1990), viii. All quotations from *Behemoth* are from this reprint of the 1889 edition.

that 'the psychological assumptions inspiring its historical narrative are ultimately indistinguishable from those expounded [...] in *Leviathan*', Holmes nevertheless maintains that in *Behemoth* Hobbes introduces new concepts and ideas and in particular a 'fine-grained account of human motivation' that gives a 'realistic' tone to the narrative. According to Holmes, Hobbes shows in his Dialogues on the civil war 'that many human beings are, first of all, incapable of calculative reasoning and, second, stupidly indifferent to self-preservation'. Holmes contends that a greater 'concreteness and color' are *Behemoth*'s distinctive features and that this realism enriches our understanding of Hobbes.[6]

The aim of this chapter is to make a contribution to this debate. It is argued that, broadly speaking, *Behemoth* is consistent with the arguments advanced by Hobbes in *De Cive* and *Leviathan* but also contains significant differences. It is suggested that, far from being an application of political science to history, *Behemoth* can be interpreted as a reflection on the historical function of political science. In a nutshell, then, it is not *Leviathan* that provides an explanation for *Behemoth*, but *Behemoth* that explains *Leviathan*.

The chapter explores in some detail whether and to what extent the account of human motivation offered by Hobbes in *Leviathan* provides an insight into, and a theoretical basis for the narrative of *Behemoth*. It takes as its point of departure Hobbes's well-known view, epigrammatically expressed in Chapter 13 of *Leviathan,* that 'in the nature of man, we find three principall causes of quarrel [...] First, Competition; Secondly, Diffidence; Thirdly, Glory. The first, maketh men invade for Gain; the second, for Safety; and the third, for Reputation'. My chapter then examines the role that these three passions (ambition, desire of gain and fear) play in the account of the civil war offered by Hobbes in *Behemoth*. Section 1 argues that in *Behemoth* Hobbes identifies ambition as the passion motivating the leaders of the rebellion, but adds the crucial proviso that this passion alone, without generalised ignorance about the meaning and value of civil obedience, would have found 'no hands'. Section 2 argues that (i) gain and money have a double function in *Behemoth* as motivation and opportunity of action and (ii) greed alone would not have led people to rebel had it not been for widespread ignorance about the role of the military, the function of taxation, and the purpose of sovereignty. Section 3 argues that regarding the most compelling human motivation, namely fear, we witness a major change in the transition from *Leviathan* to *Behemoth* in so far as Hobbes abandons the idea that fear is the passion to be 'reckoned upon'. He now believes that fear alone without knowledge of

---

6   Holmes, 'Introduction,' xlix.

the 'true science' of political obligation cannot protect against civil disorder. Section 4 summarizes the results of the previous sections' textual analysis and puts forward a tentative explanation for the different emphasis on the passions that one can find in *Behemoth* vis-à-vis previous writings. It also attempts to answer the question that opened the essay: whether or not *Behemoth* is just an attempt to apply the 'science of politics' to an historical event.

On ambition

The view that ambition was seen by Hobbes as a major cause of the English civil war is hardly contentious and can be supported by a wealth of textual evidence. In *Behemoth* Hobbes often reiterates his belief that ambition was the motivation of 'those that [...] were set upon the enterprise of changing the government'[7] and that

> the chief leaders [of the rebellion] were ambitious ministers and ambitious gentlemen, the ministers envying the authority of bishops whom they thought less learned and the gentlemen envying the privy-council and principal courtiers whom they thought less wise than themselves.[8]

In this section my aim is to examine the meaning and significance of ambition in *Behemoth*, to study the type of people that according to Hobbes were prone to being ambitious, and to explore how ambitious people tried to attain their objective.

Although, of course, in *Behemoth* Hobbes does not offer a definition of ambition, its meaning is easy to reconstruct since it is consistent with the use of this word in all his political works. In the *Elements of Law*, *De Cive*, and *Leviathan*, when naming the internal causes that bring about the dissolution of government,[9] Hobbes never fails to include ambition among the 'seditious attitudes of the mind'. Although ambition motivates people to surpass each other and thus is linked to the Hobbesian concept of glory, the two passions do not coincide. Glory in its various forms (vain glory, false glory, just esteem, pride) is discussed by Hobbes in his account of human nature and of the natural conditions of mankind and is described as the generic desire and pleasure of superiority. Ambition, instead, makes an appearance mainly in Hobbes's accounts of the political state and is used to signify the desire of a specific form of superiority and power: the political power of the ruler over the ruled — a definition that

---

7 *Behemoth*, 115–16.
8 *Behemoth*, 23.
9 Thomas Hobbes, *De Cive*, ed. H. Warrander (Oxford: Clarendon Press, 1983), ch. 12; Thomas Hobbes, *Elements of Law*, ed. F. Tönnies (London: Frank Cass, 1969), 270; Thomas Hobbes, *Leviathan*, ed. R. Tuck (Cambridge: Cambridge University Press, 1991), ch. 29.

Hobbes endorses also in *De Homine*. In *Behemoth*, glory is hardly mentioned as a motivational force, in contrast to ambition which instead looms large over the whole text. In *Behemoth*, when Hobbes does mention glory, the context is quite revealing, in so far as Hobbes ascribes glory-seeking behaviour either to states or nations[10] or to individuals whose aim is not political power, but economic superiority, e.g., the merchants.[11]

Ambition is the central passion in Dialogues 1 and 2 where the seed and growth of the rebellion are examined, and in Dialogues 3 and 4 it shares centre stage with another 'greatest thing', the desire of gain. In the narration, ambition is linked by Hobbes to a very long list of passions such as stubbornness and contumacy,[12] pride,[13] insolence and licentiousness,[14] impudence, envy,[15] vain glory,[16] presumption,[17] hypocrisy and revenge,[18] cruelty and finally to all sorts of 'follies', 'vices' and 'crimes'.[19]

To sum up: in *Behemoth* ambition is a sub-category of the desire of glory, meaning desire to rule, and its significance is central in so far as it is the major drive of the leaders of the rebellion.

As to the type of people who developed this passion at the time of the English civil war, Hobbes is slightly ambiguous. On the one hand, in the concluding Dialogue, teacher A remarks to pupil B: 'I believe it is the desire of most men to bear rule'.[20] This remark might suggest that *Behemoth* marks no change in this respect compared with *Elements of Law* and

---

10 For example, Hobbes explains the politics of the gentry and nobility of Scotland as motivated by 'emulation of glory between the nations' and desire 'to acquire some power over the English'. *Behemoth*, 30. He points out that 'that nation [the Scots] [...] always esteemed the glory of England for an abatement of their own,' and that 'it is commonly seen that neighbour nations envy one another's honour'. *Behemoth*, 32.

11 '[The merchants'] only glory being to grow excessively rich by the wisdom of buying and selling.' *Behemoth*, 126. According to Hobbes the merchants supported the rebellion only because, as private gain is their main motivation, 'they are naturally mortal enemies to taxes.'

12 '[T]his stubbornness and contumacy towards the king and his laws is nothing but pride of heart and ambition, or else imposture.' *Behemoth*,53. Elsewhere Hobbes claims that stubbornness, motivated by ambition, hinders ambitious people from attaining their aims and gives the example of Lord Strafford: 'I have observed often that such as seek preferment by their stubbornness have missed of their aim.' *Behemoth*, 72.

13 '[A]ll, such as had a great opinion of their sufficiency in politics, which they thought was not sufficiently taken notice of by the King.' *Behemoth*, 27.

14 Very often Hobbes describes the clergy as ambitious and insolent, for example, *Behemoth*, 18–19.

15 *Behemoth*, 23.

16 'I might add the folly of those fine men, which out of their reading of Tully, Seneca or other anti-monarchics, think themselves sufficient politics, and show their discontent when they are not called to the management of the state.' *Behemoth*, 155–6.

17 '[The two Houses] had always pretended to greater than ordinary wisdom and godliness.' *Behemoth*, 203.

18 '[P]ower to undo all men that admired not their wisdom.' *Behemoth*, 159.

19 *Behemoth*, 155.

20 *Behemoth*, 193.

De Cive where desire of superiority, or glory, is seen by Hobbes as the greatest motivation of most, if not all, individuals. On the other hand, it can be argued that the claim of a generalised desire to rule does not furnish a fully accurate account of the narrative in *Behemoth*, in so far as Hobbes stresses the point that the common people were the victims of ambitious individuals rather than being ambitious themselves. 'The common people' are described as not understanding the 'reasons of either party'.[21] According to Hobbes, merchants and tradesmen were also not interested in political ambition, absorbed as they were in the activity of buying and selling.[22]

Hobbes identifies five sets of agents whom he describes as prone to ambition: the clergy, the Parliamentarians, the well-educated, the army, and the nobility. I will examine these groups briefly in turn, bearing in mind that their membership is not mutually exclusive, so that, for example, according to Hobbes, the most active and influential members of parliament come from the group of the well-educated.

As far as the clergy is concerned, Hobbes regards it as unreservedly ambitious, irrespective of age, of hierarchical status[23] and of denominational affiliation ('[Do] not believe that the Independents were worse than the Presbyterians: both the one and the other were resolved to destroy whatsoever should stand in the way to their ambition').[24]

In Hobbes's account, ambition is all-pervasive also among the parliamentarians. Writes Hobbes:

> as for the men that did this [attempted to change the government] it is enough to say that [...] most of them were members of the House of Commons; some few also, of the Lords; but all had a great opinion of their sufficiency in politics which they thought was not sufficiently taken notice of by the King.[25]

To the Parliamentarians Hobbes attributes 'unconscionable and sottish ambition' that often obstructs 'the way to their ends'.[26] Their ambition takes the form of 'impudence' in democratic assemblies[27] and can lead to

---

21 *Behemoth*, 115.
22 *Behemoth*, 126.
23 Hobbes consistently attributes insolence, avarice and hypocrisy to the clergy, not only during the civil war but earlier too, from top ministers and bishops down to ordinary priests, monks, and friars. See, for example, *Behemoth*, 18–19.
24 *Behemoth*, 165.
25 *Behemoth*, 27.
26 *Behemoth*, 145.
27 *Behemoth*, 68. 'Impudence in democratic assemblies does almost all that's done; 'tis the goddess of rhetoric and carries proof with it. For what ordinary man will not, from so great boldness of affirmation, conclude there is great probability in the thing affirmed?' *Behemoth*, 68–9.

cruelty and perfidy.²⁸ Admittedly, not all parliamentarians are for Hobbes impudent or ambitious: in Dialogue 3 he suggests that many were simply deceived by their colleagues' motives and that it took them a long time to discover 'the hypocrisy and private aims of their fellows'.²⁹

The group of the highly educated, in Hobbes's view, also yields to the temptation of political ambition: 'out of these men were chosen the greatest part of the House of Commons, or if they were not the greatest part, yet, by advantage of their eloquence, were always able to sway the rest'.³⁰ Later in the Dialogue he explains: 'For it is a hard matter for men, who do all think highly of their own wits, when they have also acquired the learning of the university, to be persuaded that they want any ability requisite for the government of a commonwealth'.³¹

In the army ambition appears to be correlated to rank, in so far as Hobbes sees it as the motivation only of the top leaders and generals, whereas the rest are more interested in economic rewards. Hobbes speaks of the 'ambition of the great commanders'³² and resorts often to ambition to explain Cromwell's behaviour³³ as well as that of other generals. Even among the generals, however, not all desire to rule. If ambition is Cromwell's main hidden motivation and the open drive of General Lambert who always 'thought so well of himself',³⁴ the same cannot be said of General Monk who is described as having a different inclination, a different type of ambition.³⁵

Ambition and pride are also the key concepts used by Hobbes to explain the behaviour of the Scottish nobility and gentry who 'in their lives [...] were just as other men are, pursuers of their own interests and preferments'.³⁶ He adds that they, as 'men of ancient wealth and nobility [were] not apt to brook, that poor scholars should (as they must, when they are made bishops) be their fellows.'³⁷

Having examined briefly the groups of individuals who according to Hobbes were more tempted by ambition, the next step is to see how they managed to get a hold on the whole population, since, as Hobbes points

---

28 *Behemoth*, 138.
29 *Behemoth*, 139.
30 *Behemoth*, 3.
31 *Behemoth*, 23.
32 *Behemoth*,
33 *Behemoth*, 138-9, 143, 179.
34 *Behemoth*, 197, see also 198, 201.
35 'His ambition had not appeared here in the contentions for the government.' *Behemoth*, 198.
36 *Behemoth*, 29.
37 *Behemoth*, 29-30.

out, 'ambition can do little without hands'.[38] In view of the observation that 'from the beginning of the rebellion, the method of ambition was constantly this: first to destroy and then to consider what they should set up',[39] the question to address is how did ambitious people manage to convince the rest to 'destroy' the political order? The answer provided by Hobbes is best understood if broken down in three parts: (i) ambition is difficult to detect; (ii) ambitious individuals take advantage of people's ignorance about the meaning and function of civil obedience; (iii) ambitious individuals sabotage the very signification of language and thus confuse people.

As to (i) Hobbes claims in *Behemoth* not only that 'it is a hard matter or rather impossible to know what other men mean especially if they be crafty',[40] but also that even when people are not consciously misleading, 'we cannot safely judge of men's intentions'.[41] In other words, in *Behemoth* Hobbes is less convinced than in earlier works that it is possible to 'enter into other men's thoughts'.[42]

As to (ii), Hobbes reminds the reader repeatedly in *Behemoth* that people's ignorance had been the cause of all rebellions and seditions throughout human history.[43] Although he often attributes ignorance to 'the people in general'[44] and to the 'common people',[45] he contends that ignorance about the principles of political obligation is widespread also among educated people, among the Lords, and even among lawyers.[46] For Hobbes, 'it is not want of wit, but want of the science of justice, that brought [the English people] into these troubles'.[47] We have seen above that 'the common people' could not understand the 'reasons of either party', and yet

38 *Behemoth*, 70.
39 *Behemoth*, 192.
40 *Behemoth*, 37.
41 *Behemoth*, 72.
42 *Behemoth*, 29.
43 Hobbes mentions the seditions that afflicted ancient Greece and remarks that they materialised 'all for want of rules of justice for the common people to take notice of which if the people had known in the beginning of every of these traditions the ambitious persons could never had the hope to disturb their government after it had been once settled'. *Behemoth*, 70.
44 'The people in general were so ignorant of their duty as that not one perhaps of ten thousand knew what right any man had to command him, or what necessity there was of king or Commonwealth.' *Behemoth*, 4.
45 'Common people know nothing of right or wrong by their own meditation; they must therefore be taught the grounds of their duty and the reasons why calamities ever follow disobedience to their lawful sovereigns.' *Behemoth*, 144.
46 *Behemoth*, 155.
47 *Behemoth*, 159. 'They wanted not wit but the knowledge of the causes and grounds upon which one person has a right to govern and the rest an obligation to obey which grounds are necessary to be taught the people who without them cannot live long in peace amongst themselves.' *Behemoth*, 160.

they were extremely important, in so far as 'their hands were to decide the controversy'.[48] This ignorance, Hobbes tells us, was exploited, for example, by the Parliamentarians who aimed at increasing the 'people's disaffection' towards the king in order to enhance their own chances of becoming more powerful.[49]

As to (iii), namely the question of how the ambitious managed to take advantage of people's ignorance, Hobbes's answer is that the main weapon used to trick people into rebellion was language itself. Words were deployed to deceive and confuse. For example, we are told that the Rump 'meant that neither the king, nor any king nor any single person but only they themselves would be the people's masters and *would have set it down in those plain words if the people could have been cozened with words intelligible as easily as with words non intelligible*'.[50]

Language is used to manipulate and indoctrinate the common people. The received meaning of words, the very signification of language, is put in question. Hobbes tells us that 'disobedient persons [were] esteemed the best patriots',[51] and that 'by delinquent they meant only a man to whom they would do all the hurt they could'.[52] In this situation, civil disobedience is praised and civil obedience is labelled as pride: 'The Papists claim that to disobey the pope is pride and deserves death'.[53]

In many ways this reminds us of Thucydides's description of the progressive disintegration of common values, standards, and beliefs in Corcyra during the stasis. In the vibrant words of Hobbes's own translation of Thucydides's *History*: 'inconsiderate boldness, was counted true-hearted manliness: provident deliberation, a handsome fear: modesty, the cloak of cowardice: to be wise in everything, to be lazy in everything'.[54]

Although both Hobbes and Thucydides are reporting the crisis of signification of language during a state of civil war, Hobbes goes further. He is suggesting that those who manage to convince the common people that disobedient people are 'the best patriots', that 'wisdom' or 'gallantry' is in fact 'folly',[55] that 'private opinion' can be treated as 'heresy',[56] in effect

---

48 *Behemoth*, 115.
49 *Behemoth*, 60.
50 *Behemoth*, 164 (emphasis added).
51 *Behemoth*, 2.
52 *Behemoth*, 69.
53 *Behemoth*, 5.
54 Thomas Hobbes, *The History of the Grecian War written by Thucydides*, EW 8. 348. I have discussed some similarities between Hobbes and Thucydides in G. Slomp, 'Hobbes on Glory and Civil Strife', *The Cambridge Companion to Hobbes's Leviathan*, ed. P. Springborg (Cambridge: Cambridge University Press, 2007), 181–98.
55 *Behemoth*, 38.
56 *Behemoth*, 9.

acquire power over the common people. In Hobbes's narrative, the giving of names is not only arbitrary,[57] but a sign of power. The power to decide who is a spy,[58] who a traitor or a murderer[59] remains unchallenged where there is ignorance. Linguistic skills and techniques are used to control people so that 'a man unacquainted with such art could never suspect any ambitious plot in them to raise sedition against the state'.[60]

Not only public speakers but also writers are part of the conspiracy aimed at getting 'the hands' of the common people working for their own ambition: 'the schoolmen [...] learnt the trick of imposing what they list upon their readers and declining the force of true reason by verbal forks; I mean distinctions that signify nothing, but serve only to astonish the multitude of ignorant men'.[61]

In closing this section, we can conclude that in *Behemoth* ambition, or desire to rule, grows among those circles of people who because of their social status (clergy) or their education, on the one hand, develop more 'insolence' than the rest about their own wisdom and ability to rule, and, on the other hand, can take advantage for their own ends of the ignorance of the people about the dangers of civil disobedience. Hobbes's message is that during the English civil war ambition alone could not ruin a whole nation; but the ambition of some individuals combined with the ignorance of most people could and did.

On greed and money

In *Behemoth* we can find a plethora of references to money and to money-related terms, such as booty, plunder, pay, tax, subsidies, coffers, etc. A better understanding of the role played by money and greed can be gained by distinguishing the two main forms under which money enters Hobbes's narrative, namely: (i) as objective or motivation of action; and (ii) as means or opportunity for action.

We may begin by examining in *Behemoth* in what sense money can be regarded as motivation of action. This function is particularly clear in Dialogues 1 and 2, where desire of money, plunder, monetary rewards, and

---

57 '[M]en may give to their assembly what name they please, what signification soever such name might formerly have had; and the Rump took the name of Parliament, as most suitable to their purpose, and such a name, as being venerable amongst the people, had for many hundreds years countenanced and sweetened subsidies and other levies of money, otherwise very unpleasant to the subject.' *Behemoth*, 155.
58 *Behemoth*, 128.
59 *Behemoth*, 154. The king is called 'tyrant, traitor, murderer' by the 'wicked Parliament'. *Behemoth*, 149.
60 *Behemoth*, 24.
61 *Behemoth*, 41.

relief from taxation are concepts used by Hobbes to explain why many agents behaved in the way they did.

As ambition is attributed by Hobbes to different types of agents, from single individuals, to social groups, to entire nations, so are desire of gain and greed.[62] However, there is a difference between the role of these two passions in the dynamics of the rebellion: whereas ambition (or desire to rule) is reckoned by Hobbes to be the main drive in the leaders of the rebellion, greed instead is singled out as the strongest passion in their followers. In the Dialogues, greed is ascribed to the common people,[63] to the army (be it led by the king, the Parliamentarians, or Cromwell[64]), to the 'most part of rich subjects',[65] to the merchants[66] and tradesmen (who see taxes as 'grievances'), to the 'men of ancient wealth and nobility of Scotland',[67] to the Scots in general,[68] to the clergy, to the Rump,[69] to big cities (such as London), and to even entire nations.[70]

In some agents ambition and greed are equally strong passions. A prime example is provided by the Presbyterians, who were 'aiming at seeing politics subservient to religion' so that 'they might govern and

---

[62] In Dialogue 1 Hobbes writes: 'there were a very great number that had either wasted their fortunes or thought them too mean for the good parts which they thought were in themselves; and more there were, that had able bodies, but saw no means how honestly to get their bread. These longed for a war and hoped to maintain themselves hereafter by the lucky choosing of a party to side with, and consequently did for the most part serve under them that had greatest plenty of money.' *Behemoth*, 4.

[63] '[T]here were few of the common people that cared much for either of the causes but would have taken any side for pay or plunder.' *Behemoth*, 2.

[64] This applies to all armies, irrespective of their allegiance. For example, in the kings's army 'the best and forwardest of his soldiers [...] looked for great benefit by their service out of the estates of the rebels in case they could subdue them'. *Behemoth*, 115. In Cromwell's army, 'there were in the army a great number (if not the greatest part) that aimed only at rapine and sharing the lands and good s of the enemies'. *Behemoth*, 136.

[65] 'I consider the most part of rich subjects that have made themselves so by craft and trade as men that never look upon anything but their present profit and who [... are] amazed at the very thought of plundering.' *Behemoth*, 142.

[66] According to Hobbes for this class of people taxation is a reason for civil disobedience: 'Grievances are but taxes, to which citizens, that is merchants, whose profession is their private gain are naturally mortal enemies; their only glory being to grow excessively rich by the wisdom of buying and selling.' *Behemoth*, 126.

[67] That these people hope for in the war is 'some great sum of money as a reward of their assistance beside great booty'. *Behemoth*, 30.

[68] Who are said to be 'animated [...] with a promise of reward and hope of plunder'. *Behemoth*, 31. Not so much as a matter of principle, but 'upon the payment of 200,000l, the King was put [by the Scots] into the hands of the commissioners' of the English parliament. *Behemoth*, 134.

[69] 'They [the Rump] give one another money and estates, out of the lands and goods of the loyal party.' *Behemoth*, 164.

[70] On the 'greed of the Dutch', see *Behemoth*, 174.

thereby satisfy not only their covetous humour with riches but also their malice with power to undo all men that admired not their wisdom'.[71]

We saw in the previous section that, according to Hobbes, ambition as a motivation is difficult to detect. The same applies to greed. Not surprisingly, some individuals enrich themselves by taking advantage of this and of people's ignorance, vulnerability, and good faith. The behaviour of the clergy provides Hobbes with many examples. In Dialogue 1, the teacher explains: '[preaching friars] privately insinuated themselves with women and men of weak judgment, confirming their adherence to the Pope, and urging them, in the time of their sickness, to be beneficial to the Church'.[72] In a similar vein, Hobbes believes that both before and during the rebellion the contents of the sermons of most ministers can be explained in terms of greed, covetousness, or hope of financial gain: 'they [ministers] did never in their sermons or but lightly inveigh against the lucrative vices of men of trade or handicraft [...] which was a great ease to the generality of citizens and the inhabitants of market-towns and no little profit to themselves'.[73] It is no coincidence, Hobbes tells us, that in these sermons neither greed nor fraud was condemned but only 'carnal lust and vain swearing' and 'nothing else was sin'.[74] By exploiting people's fears of '[t]he estate of man's soul after death, in heaven, hell and purgatory [...] every man knows, how great obedience, and how much money they [the clergy] gain from the common people'.[75]

In Hobbes's account, the clergy's attempt to convince people that to be charitable means to be liberal with the Church is not merely motivated by greed but also by the knowledge that in war money is necessary to victory — a view that permeates the whole discussion in *Behemoth*. This hints at the second function of money mentioned in the opening paragraph of this section: in addition to motivating people to action, money opens up opportunity for action. This latter function appears particularly clear in Dialogues 3 and 4 where it is shown how in war victory goes to the richest contender. Even in Dialogue 1, however, we are told that 'if the King had had money, he might have had soldiers enough in England' as most of the 'common people [...] would have taken any side for pay or plunder'. From the very inception of the rebellion the key concern of the king was how to find revenues to raise and keep an army. His enemies, of course, had the same concern, but they were successful to attract 'plentiful contri-

---

71   *Behemoth*, 159.
72   *Behemoth*, 16.
73   *Behemoth*, 25.
74   *Ibid.*
75   *Behemoth*, 42.

bution' from London and other rich cities with the promise to ease people from taxes.[76]

In Hobbes's explanation of the civil war, the main reason why the king was unable to suppress the rebellion when it first started was his lack of money and conversely the motivation why a large number of people joined the parliamentarian cause was their reluctance or resistance to pay subsidies or taxes to the king. Both circumstances, the speaker tells us, materialised because of people's ignorance. Hobbes argues that all agents (from the common people to the Lords, from the merchants and the tradesmen to the nobility and the king himself) were unaware of the link between sovereignty and the command of the military. Because of widespread ignorance, representatives in parliament were selected on the ground of their commitment to protect people from taxation: the general trend was 'to choose as near as they can such as are most repugnant to the giving of subsidies'[77] as if taxation were a royal caprice and the ultimate control of the military irrelevant to the order and peace of the commonwealth. Hobbes attributes short-sightedness to the merchants, who 'are said to be of all callings the most beneficial to the commonwealth',[78] but in fact do not realise that without commonwealth there is no trade and to all tradesmen who failed to understand 'what virtue there is to preserve their wealth in obedience to their lawful sovereign'.[79] More generally, Hobbes decries the ignorance of those who, while thinking they were pursuing their own self-interest, in fact were not, in so far as, by neglecting the beneficial effects of living in the safety of the commonwealth, they failed to consider their own long-term advantage.[80]

To conclude, when speaking of greed as a motivation for civil disobedience, Hobbes makes clear that greed alone could have not led people to ruin. It was because of widespread ignorance about the value of peace and the function of subsidies and taxation that greed contributed to the collapse into civil war.

On fear

Having examined the role played by ambition and greed in Hobbes's account of the English civil war, the next step is to examine the importance in *Behemoth* of the remaining crucial motivation of human behaviour listed in *Leviathan*, namely fear. My aim in this section is to show that

---

76 *Behemoth*, 2.
77 *Behemoth*, 121.
78 *Behemoth*, 126.
79 *Behemoth*, 142.
80 *Behemoth*, 54. '[Every man] reads that covetousness is the root of all evil; but he thinks, and sometimes finds, it is the root of his estate.' Ibid.

the transition from *Leviathan* to *Behemoth* marks a major change about the significance of fear in Hobbes's political theory. We may begin by considering the different object of fear in *Leviathan* and *Behemoth*. In Chapter 13 of *Leviathan* Hobbes maintains that in natural conditions the greatest object of fear is violent death by the hand of others; in Chapter 14 he adds two further objects of fear—one natural the other artificial—facing individuals who live within political associations, namely, fear of 'Spirits Invisible', and fear of punishment, and he suggests that the latter is usually stronger than the former. In his words:

> [Fear has] two very general Objects: one, The Power of Spirits Invisible; the other, The Power of those men they shall therein Offend. Of these two, though the former be the greater Power, yet the fear of the later is commonly the greater Feare. The Feare of the former is in every man, his own Religion: which hath place in the nature of man before Civill Society. The later hath not so.

In *Behemoth* we are told a different story. On the one hand, fear of violent death and fear of punishment are hardly mentioned in the four Dialogues; on the other hand and in contrast with the view expressed in *Leviathan,* fear of eternal damnation turns out to be 'the greater fear' at the time of the civil war. As one of the speakers explains 'as much as eternal torture is more terrible than death, so much they would fear the clergy more than the king'.[81] A qualification, though, is in order. Whereas in *Leviathan* Hobbes suggests that in the state of nature fear was universal, in *Behemoth* he eschews any claim of universality. On the contrary, he points out that 'common people' did not care much about the dispute and were willing to take either side for hope of plunder.[82] This would suggest that fear of damnation was not equally strong in everyone.

As the object of fear is different in *Leviathan* and *Behemoth,* so is its role. Both in *Behemoth* and in *Leviathan* Hobbes resorts to the notion of fear to elucidate the causes of conflict. In *Leviathan* fear explains not only the dynamic of the state of nature and the escalation from diffidence to anticipation and first strike, but also why subjects refrain from breaking the laws within the political state. In *Behemoth*, however, Hobbes limits the role of fear only to showing how it led to civil disobedience and disorder.

It can be argued that in *Leviathan* 'continuall fear' is the passion that according to Hobbes describes most accurately the relationship between individuals in the state of war 'where every man is enemy to every man'. Not so in Hobbes's account of the English civil war. Although in *Behemoth,* too, we are told that 'no man was so blind as not to see they were in an

---

81 *Behemoth*, 14–15.
82 *Behemoth*, 2.

estate of war one against another',[83] Hobbes does not pinpoint fear as the dominant passion during the rebellion. Instead, we are told that the enemy aroused spite,[84] or scorn,[85] or even hatred, but not fear. In Dialogue 3, one of the speakers remarks that the parliament's army 'had that in them, which in time of battle is more conducing to victory than valour and experience both together; and that was spite'.[86] Even when describing the war between the Rump and the Dutch, Hobbes does not mention fear as playing any role in the conflict.[87]

Moreover, in *Leviathan* fear enables individuals to understand the benefits of peace and eventually to create the social contract. As Hobbes puts it in Chapter 13: 'Feare of Death' is one of the passions that 'encline men to Peace'. Although in *Behemoth* Hobbes on occasions does mention that it was concern for personal safety that eventually led some (e.g., the tradesmen) to see sense, on the whole he does not suggest that people were enlightened by fear as to the benefits of living in a peaceful commonwealth. He suggests that nothing, neither painful experience,[88] nor reflection,[89] 'neither wit nor prudence nor diligence',[90] nor 'natural reason'[91] can make individuals understand their duties as subjects. Only knowledge of 'the true science of equity and justice'[92] can:

> They wanted not wit, but the knowledge of the causes and grounds upon which one person has a right to govern, and the rest an obligation to obey; which grounds are necessary to be taught the people, who without them cannot live long in peace amongst themselves.[93]

It is difficult to overemphasise the significance of fear in *Leviathan* in so far as this passion is the cornerstone of Hobbes's political construct. As Hobbes himself unambiguously states in Chapter 14, 'the Passion to be reckoned upon, is Fear', as it leads Hobbesian individuals to be afraid of punishment and to obey the laws. In contrast, the significance of fear in *Behemoth* is much more modest. It is, of course, true that Hobbes makes a number of remarks that are consistent with his earlier views. For example,

---

83 *Behemoth*, 117.
84 *Behemoth*, 169, 110.
85 *Behemoth*, 180, 174.
86 *Behemoth*, 110.
87 'The true quarrel, on the English part, was that the proffered friendship was scorned, and their ambassadors affronted; on the Dutch part, was the greediness to engross all traffic, and a false estimate of our and their own strength.' *Behemoth*, 174.
88 *Behemoth*, 39.
89 *Behemoth*, 41.
90 *Behemoth*, 70, 158–9.
91 *Behemoth*, 144.
92 *Behemoth*, 70.
93 *Behemoth*, 160.

he claims that 'all the kingdoms of the world [...] proceed from the consent of people, either for *fear* or hope'.[94] He explains that 'it happens many times that men live honestly for *fear* who if they had power would live according to their own opinions',[95] and, not unlike Machiavelli, he points to 'coffers and early severity'[96] as the most reliable cures for commonwealths. However, although there is room for debate, the balance of evidence suggests that in *Behemoth* fear is no longer the passion that Hobbes 'reckons upon'. On the contrary, Hobbes is at pains to make his readers realise that people are easily deceived, not simply by experienced speakers but also by vulgar 'fortune-tellers,' 'astrologers' and 'prophets'[97] and induced to fear the 'wrong things' or fear the right things in the 'wrong order'.

Sometimes because of malice and bad faith, sometimes because of mere ignorance, people are led to fear the 'wrong things' as when members of the two Houses fear 'absolute obedience'[98] because they are unclear about the meaning and function of political obligation, or when the merchants and tradesmen abhor taxation[99] because they are ignorant about the long-term utility of living in a peaceful commonwealth; or when men and women 'of weak judgement' are afraid of obeying the king because they are misguided about their duties as Christians.[100]

So whereas in *Leviathan* Hobbes relies on fear to deliver individuals from destruction and civil war, in *Behemoth* he stresses the view that unless ignorance is replaced with knowledge about the principles of political obligation, fear alone can offer no salvation. For the State to rely on fear is not only ineffective, but also dangerous in so far as for example '[s]uppression of doctrine does but unite and exasperate, that is, increase both the malice and power of them that have already believed them'.[101]

To conclude, in *Behemoth* fear is no longer the building block of the political order in so far as Hobbes makes clear that fear alone without knowledge of the 'true science' of political obligation cannot protect from civil disorder and therefore cannot be relied upon for the maintenance of future peace.

---

94 *Behemoth*, 12 (emphasis added).
95 *Behemoth*, 47.
96 *Behemoth*, 57.
97 *Behemoth*, 187–8.
98 *Behemoth*, 125.
99 *Behemoth*, 126.
100 *Behemoth*, 46, 50–1.
101 *Behemoth*, 62.

Conclusion

It is time to gather the loose threads of the arguments of this essay and to address the question I raised in the opening paragraph, namely whether *Behemoth* should be interpreted as an historical application of the principles of political science expounded in *De Cive* and *Leviathan* or as something different.

On the one hand, the textual analysis contained in previous sections has shown that the account of the English civil war offered in *Behemoth* is consistent with Hobbes's claim in Chapter 13 of *Leviathan* that conflict among men is the outcome of their passions and in particular of their ambition, greed and fear.

On the other hand, textual analysis has also shown that in *Behemoth* Hobbes conveys the view that the passions alone can neither condemn people to civil war nor save them from it. In Section 1 we have seen that, according to Hobbes, ambitious people would have been unable to 'find hands' and would have failed to challenge the political order had it not been for widespread ignorance about the foundations of political obligation. Moreover, in Section 2 it was noticed that greed alone, too, could not have led people to civil disobedience. Rather, it was because of generalized ignorance about the role of the military, of the importance of the link between sovereignty and ultimate control of the military, and of the long-term utility of subsidies and taxation that greed contributed to the collapse into civil war. Finally, in Section 3 we argued that in *Behemoth* Hobbes's message is that fear alone without a sound knowledge of the principles of political obligation cannot and does not deliver people from the evil of civil war.

Already in *De Cive* and *Leviathan* Hobbes had highlighted the importance of education in restraining human passions and singled out ignorance as a major contributor to social disorder. It was not until *Behemoth*, however, that Hobbes advanced the stronger claim that ignorance is a *necessary* condition for the collapse of a political state into civil war.

At this stage, it is natural to ask why there should be a difference between *Behemoth* and previous writings vis-à-vis the relative importance they place on the role of the passions and of ignorance in fomenting civil unrest. This can be answered in a number of different ways.

First of all, it can be argued with some confidence that Hobbes's views on human nature changed over time and that in the transition from *Elements of Law* to *De Homine* the Hobbesian man emerges progressively as a product of nurture rather than as a product of nature.[102] It can be claimed that *Behemoth* marks a step in this development: Speaker A emphasizes that bad books, bad priests, bad teachers, bad universities rather than bad human nature were responsible for the English civil war.

Moreover, the more limited role played by the passions in *Behemoth* can be imputed to the different methodology that Hobbes adopts in this later work: unlike Hobbes's argument in *De Cive* and *Leviathan*, the narrative in *Behemoth* is unconstrained by the logic of rigid dichotomies of cause and effect, of assumptions and deductions, of axioms and conclusions of reason. Speaker A in *Behemoth* has much greater liberty than Hobbes in *Leviathan* to bring to light the various layers and facets of human conflict and to uncover the multiple motivations, the complex intentions, the hidden agenda that induced diverse people and cities to act in a way that contributed to the final breakdown of the political order.

Indeed, Hobbes's methodology in *Behemoth* has attracted much attention among interpreters and although its proper analysis is completely outside the scope of this chapter, I would suggest that the methodological reflections advanced by Eric Voegelin in *The Science of Politics* can shed some light on the result of our textual analysis of *Behemoth*. Voegelin famously contrasts the 'positivist' method that he dislikes with the 'Aristotelian' approach that he recommends; he claims that the positivist scientist begins his analysis with *tabula rasa* whereas the Aristotelian philosopher engages typically with three contexts: the world of 'existence', the 'self-interpretation' of society where he lives, and the 'theoretization' of past political science.[103]

Although there is room for disagreement, it can be claimed that in *De Cive* and in *Leviathan* Hobbes adopts an approach that is close to what Voegelin terms as 'positivism': Hobbes starts with abstract definitions or axioms about man in isolation and about men in relation with each other; he then imagines men in a hypothetical state of nature and deduces the consequences of their interaction. The argument marches logically from assumptions to conclusions. Of course, both *De Cive* and *Leviathan* contain much more than a logical demonstration; indeed especially in *Leviathan* one can trace other narratives that run parallel to Hobbes's demonstration and that emphasize, among other things, the need to educate the Hobbesian citizen. Even so, the logical demonstration in *Leviathan* can be

---

102 I argue this claim in G. Slomp, *Thomas Hobbes and the Political Philosophy of Glory* (Houndmills: Macmillan, 2000).
103 Eric Voegelin, *The New Science of Politics* (Chicago: The University of Chicago Press, 1952).

isolated from the rest of the argument, as many game-theorists have succeeded to show.[104]

By contrast, the narrative in *Behemoth* is organized into a series of two-speaker dialogues in which Speaker A explains the causes and dynamics of the English civil war to Speaker B. Many scholars have investigated the identity of Speaker A. For present purposes it suffices to point out that Speaker A approaches his material in a different way from both the 'positivist' theorist of *Leviathan* and, perhaps more surprisingly, the unbiased historian whose analysis of the Peloponnesian war Hobbes so greatly admired: whereas Thucydides rarely commented on the events he reported and displayed a commitment to impartiality that Hobbes regarded as rare, Speaker A does not hesitate to voice his disapproval of his countrymen and to lament their ignorance and stupidity.

So, rather than the political scientist of *Leviathan* or the historian of the Peloponnesian war, Speaker A has far more in common with the 'Aristotelian theorist' described by Voegelin. Like the Aristotelian philosopher, Speaker A engages with three different contexts: first, he considers the 'world of experience' and describes what his countrymen did before and during the civil war; next, he examines 'the self-interpretation' of the society of the time and spells out how his countrymen interpreted their own actions; then he considers the 'theoretisation' of the world of experience inherited from the past and spells out how the well-educated, the schoolmen and the teachers interpreted political events through the lenses of their education.

In *Behemoth* Speaker A brings to light the disconnectedness between what people did—they disobeyed the law—and what people thought they were doing: they thought that they were defending their property or ensuring their salvation. He shows that such disconnectedness was reinforced by the bad faith and ignorance of the intellectuals of the time: the priests, the teachers and the men of the universities not only failed to correct the delusions of the common people but in fact fed and reinforced those delusions insofar as they made people think that by disobeying the law and the king they were in fact exercising their right as citizens and their duty as Christians.

Speaker A shows that the civil war occurred not as a mere result of human passions but because of the failure of both the common people and the well-educated to grasp and understand the true meaning and implications of their actions. Speaker A's message seems to be that only by

---

104 I have discussed and critiqued game-theoretical applications to Hobbes's *Leviathan* in G. Slomp, 'Hobbes, Harsanyi and the Edge of the Abyss' (joint with M. La Manna), *Canadian Journal of Political Science* 29 (1996), no. 1, 159–72.

re-connecting the world of existence and the self-interpretation of society can order and peace be attained and maintained. But no such re-connection is possible until ignorance is challenged and bad theorizing is replaced by true political science. In this way *Behemoth* asserts the paramount significance of *Leviathan*.

To conclude, this chapter has argued that although the ingredients that bring about political disorder are the same in *Behemoth* as they are in previous writings, the relative balance of these ingredients is different as *Behemoth* places less weight on the role of people's passions. Instead, *Behemoth* focuses more on the part ignorance plays in undermining the political order. This shift of emphasis is amenable to different yet compatible explanations all of which suggest that *Behemoth* in fact marks an important development in Hobbes's reflections on human nature, social nurture, methodology and the role of political science.

Patricia Springborg

'Behemoth' and Hobbes's 'science of just and unjust'

A. Why may not men be taught their duty, that is, the science of just and unjust, as divers other sciences have been taught, from true principles, and evident demonstration; and much more easily than any of those preachers and democratical gentlemen could teach rebellion and *treason*?[1]

Introduction

This chapter advances the following set of arguments, although not necessarily in this order: First, that we must take seriously Hobbes's claim in *Behemoth* that 'the science of *just* and *unjust*' is a demonstrable science, accessible to those of even the meanest capacity. Second, that *Leviathan* is the work in which this science, intended as a serious project in civic education, is set out. Third, that Hobbes is prepared to accept, like Plato and Aristotle, 'giving to each his own' as a preliminary definition of justice, from which, however, he draws some very un-Aristotelian conclusions. Fourth, that though in Hobbes's theory '*just* and *unjust*' are equivalent to 'lawful and unlawful', this is far from being a simple statement of legal positivism, but rather the conclusion of a practical syllogism. The first term of this syllogism is that *jus,* or right, is the foundation of justice; the second term is that justice only obtains between men in the state of society; and the third term, or conclusion, is that, because justice can only obtain where *jus* or right, has been converted into *lex*, or law, justice is therefore synonymous with lawful, injustice with unlawful. Fifth, that the impediments to this demonstrable science of justice being universally accepted, on Hobbes's account, are twofold, explained in terms of religion and the role of preachers and educators produced by the universities, on the one hand, and by the activity of 'democratical gentlemen' and classi-

---

1 *Behemoth, or The Long Parliament*, ed. F. Tönnies (London, 1889, facsimile ed., ed. S. Holmes, Chicago: University of Chicago, 1990), 39. All citations to *Behemoth* are to this edition.

cal republicans dominating parliament, on the other. Sixth, that Hobbes's account of the transition from *jus* to *lex*, specified in terms of a transition from the state of nature to that of civil society, although Epicurean in origin, is much closer to a conventional civil law position than is usually noted.

Behemoth may be seen as an extended disquisition on 'the science of *just* and *unjust*,' inserted into a history of the Long Parliament and the conduct of the English civil war from 1640 to 1660. Indeed, so literally does Hobbes intend his claim that the English civil war is to be read as the miscarriage of justice as a science, and one which requires the reform of the universities, hitherto so delinquent in their duty to teach this science, that he takes, as he admits, a long digression from the history of the civil war to set it out.[2] In the Dedication to Henry Bennet, Lord Arlington, Hobbes had already presented 'his four short dialogues concerning the civil war' in the following terms:

> the first contains the seed of it, certain opinions in divinity and politics. The second hath the growth of it in declarations, remonstrances, and other writings between the King and Parliament published. The two last are a very short epitome of the war itself, drawn out of Mr. Heath's chronicle.[3]

Behemoth, like the other late works that it most closely resembles,[4] the *Dialogue between a Philosopher and a Student of the Common Laws of England*,[5] the *Historia Ecclesiastica*,[6] and the 1668 Appendix to the Latin *Leviathan*,[7] is cast in dialogue form. The dialogue, like the invective, from which it was sometimes indistinguishable, was a favoured literary form of the Renaissance. In all three cases the dialogue is conducted between two interlocutors A and B. If, as Edwin Curley cautions in the case of the 1668

---

2 Ibid., 40–59. The interlocutors, having discussed at great length the rise of the universities, the student concludes (59): 'I am therefore your opinion, both that men may be brought to a love of obedience by preachers and gentlemen that imbibe good principles in their youth at the Universities and also that we never shall have a lasting peace, till the Universities themselves be in such manner, as you have said reformed.'
3 Ibid., iv.
4 Hobbes's *Dialogue of the Civil Wars of England* was completed around 1668, and is therefore contemporaneous with the final form of the Latin *Leviathan*.
5 Drafted in 1666, published in 1681.
6 Aubrey reports on the progress of the poem from 1659 and we have a record of its completion in the account books at Chatsworth in 1671, but it was first published in 1688. See Patricia Springborg, 'Introduction' to Hobbes, *Histioria ecclesiastica*, eds P. Springborg, P. Stablein and P. Wilson (Paris: Homoré Champion, 2008), ch. 2, 'Text and Timeframe: Material Evidence', 77–100. Translations are from this edition.
7 For translations of the 1668 Latin Appendix, see Thomas Hobbes, *Leviathan, with selected variants from the Latin edition of 1668*, ed., with introduction and notes, E. Curley (Indianapolis: Hackett, 1994), 498–48; as well as George Wright's excellent translation with notes, 'Thomas Hobbes: 1668 Appendix to *Leviathan*', *Interpretation* 18 (1991), no. 3, 324–413.

Appendix, we cannot assign either A or B as a personal spokesman for Hobbes, who is referred to by both in the third person, this is not the case with *Behemoth*, where A is a teacher who seems clearly to represent Hobbes, and B is an unidentified pupil.[8] These three works taken together not only contextualize *Leviathan*, cast in the classical form of a philosophical treatise, but they also cast important light on its theses. Moving between genres, as he does in the late dialogues, Hobbes buttresses the claims of *Leviathan* with the legal case method of the *Dialogue concerning the Common Law*, the ecclesiology of the *Historia Ecclesiastica*, presented in Latin hexameters, and the historiography of *Behemoth*.

In all three, as we shall see, Hobbes is concerned with heresy as false opinion, with sectarianism as a form of sedition, and with democracy as the pretension to power that carries these seeds of destruction with it. Heresy was on Hobbes's mind. His desire to vindicate himself against the charge of heresy in general, and charges that the parliament was prepared to lay against him in 1666-7 with respect to *Leviathan*, specifically, had precipitated a flood of works in those years, abating around 1670. These works, all of which address heresy more or less directly, comprise his *Historia Ecclesiastica* (written between 1659 and 1674, but published only in 1688); *A Dialogue between a Philosopher and a Student of the Common Laws of England* (drafted in 1666, but published only in 1681); Hobbes's *Answer to Bishop Bramhall's The Catching of Leviathan*, published together with his *An Historical Narration Concerning Heresy* (1668); the Latin *Leviathan*, including a new Appendix (1668); and other short manuscripts on heresy (1668). To this series of works, *Behemoth* (completed in 1670, but published only in 1679) belongs; and it is here that Hobbes explicitly stakes his claim to authorship of a 'science of *just* and *unjust*' as the lesson to be learned from civil war and the means to alleviate its causes.

As in the case of *Leviathan*, *Behemoth* is the Hebrew name for beasts from the book of Job and, even if not in this case Hobbes's chosen title,[9] it plays

---

[8] As we can gather, for instance, by A's reference to his Hobbes's patron, William Cavendish, as 'My Lord of Newcastle'. See *Behemoth*, 122. In the case of the *Historia Ecclesiastica*, the distribution of the dialogue, which is in any case uncertain on textual grounds, also cannot be assigned with confidence. See Springborg, 'Introduction' to Hobbes, *Histioria ecclesiastica*, Appendix A, 277-9.

[9] *Behemoth* was not the name Hobbes gave it, and was not the title of the first three unauthorized 1679 editions. In August 1679 Hobbes complained to Aubrey 'I have been told that my booke of the Civill Warr is come abroad, and I am sorry for it, especially because I could not get his majestye to license it, not because it is ill printed or has a foolish title set to it, for I believe that nay ingenious man may understand the wickednesse of that time, notwithstanding the errors of the presse.' See *The Correspondence of Thomas Hobbes*, ed. N. Malcolm (Oxford: Clarendon1994), 2. 772. Malcolm notes, ibid., 773 n. 4, that Hobbes's complaint about the title could not refer to *Behemoth*, which was not yet used, but might rather refer to the famous lines from Lucretius, *De Rerum Natura*, 83, 101, which Voltaire believed would last as long as

an important role in his lexicon.¹⁰ *Behemoth* is, however, plural for *Behema*, defined in Cooper's *Thesaurus* of 1565 as 'the dyvell, and signifieth a beaste'.¹¹ The plural is significant, for *Behemoth* to Hobbes represents the many-headed hydra of democracy, or government by opinion. The opinions that are so dangerous involve the conjunction of philosophy and divinity, which in turn breed sects, and the Greek word for sect is *haeresis*, the same as heresy. So, for instance, when, in the 1668 Appendix to the Latin *Leviathan*, A asks B, 'What is heresy?', B answers, 'The term is Greek, meaning the doctrine of any sect'. And when A asks, 'What is a sect?', B answers, 'A sect is a number of men who follow the same master in the sciences, one whom they have chosen for themselves, at their own discretion'. 'Heresy is a word which, when it used without passion, signifies a private opinion', the teacher claims in *Behemoth*. 'So the different sects of the old philosophers, Academicians, Peripatetics, Epicureans, Stoics, etc. were called heresies'.¹² This, it turns out, is the nub of it and, for Hobbes, the greatest failing of sectarianism, like democracy, is the fact that it represents choice by those who have no authority to choose.

Beginnings are significant and Hobbes chooses for *Behemoth* a Machiavellian opener:

> A. If in time, as in place, there were degrees of high and low, I verily believe that the highest time would be that which passed between the years 1640 and 1660. For he that thence, as from the Devil's Mountain, should have looked upon the world and observed the actions of men, especially in England, might have had a prospect of all kinds of injustice, and of all kinds of folly, that the world could afford, and how they were produced by their dams hypocrisy and self-conceit, whereof the one is double iniquity, and the other double folly.¹³

---

history, and which the editors of the pirated editions had appended: 'Religio pepercit Scelerosa atque impia Facta', and 'Tantum Religio potuit Suadere Malorum' ('religion was the mother of wicked and impious deeds', and 'Such was the evil which religion led men to commit'). However, in Hobbes's *Historia Ecclesiastica*, more or less completed, it appears, at the time as *Behemoth*, both the names *Leviathan* and *Behemoth* appear in conjunction, although not in the Grund ms, which the copyist tells us was made from the copy in 'My Lord Vaughan's library,' probably the presentation copy. The names appeared, rather, as an interpolation in the 1668 printed edition in the Harleian 1844 Ms. See Springborg, 'Introduction' to Hobbes, *Histioria ecclesiastica*, ch. 2, 'Text and Timeframe: Material Evidence', 97–100, and Appendix A, 275–7.

10   See Hobbes, *Historia Ecclesiastica*, line 1229 (Springborg et al., 453–5 and notes), where with reference to the machinations of the Pope he comments: 'Leviathan, like Behemoth, had again taken the hook in the nose; both the king and the people were slaves.'

11   See Thomas Cooper and Sir Thomas Elyot, *Thesaurus Linguae Romanae & Britannicae* (London, 1565).

12   *Behemoth*, 8–9.

13   Ibid., 1. See Springborg, 'Review Article: The View from the "Divell's Mountain"; Review of Quentin Skinner, *Reason and Rhetoric in the Philosophy of Hobbes*', *History of Political Thought* 17 (1996), no. 4, 615–22.

Hobbes's perspective is strikingly reminiscent of Machiavelli who begins the *Prince* 1. 2 by offering a short defense of why he, an ordinary citizen, should know more than rulers about the art of ruling, in terms of the analogy of a person standing on a mountain, as best positioned to survey the landscape below, compared with a person standing below, as best positioned to survey the mountain. From which he concludes, 'to comprehend fully the nature of people, one must be a prince, and to comprehend fully the nature of princes one must be an ordinary citizen'.

The pupil, B, of *Behemoth*, responds in the same idiom: [14]

> B. I should be glad to behold that prospect. You that have lived in that time and in that part of your age, wherein men used to see best into good and evil, I pray you to set me (that could not then see so well) upon the same mountain, by the relation of the actions you then saw, and of their causes, pretensions, justice, order, artifice and event.

Machiavellian *topoi* on the role of good men, good arms and good laws, as well as the problem of Christianity, as a religion of salvation, compared with the civil religions of antiquity, dominate *Behemoth*.[15] Hobbes's historiography of the English civil war is less concerned with the detail, which in exile in France he was not present to observe, than with these principles, as he notes, acknowledging, 'I shall only make use of such a thread, as is necessary for the filling up of such knavery, and folly also, as I shall observe in their several actions', 'in what is intended only the story of their injustice, impudence and hypocrisy'.[16]

On the subject of good men and good laws, he considers first how it was that in such short span of time the people were seduced from support of their king, 'a man that wanted no virtue ... in the well governing of his subjects', and how 'the people were corrupted generally, and disobedient

---

14 *Behemoth*, 1.
15 See Patricia Springborg, 'Hobbes on Civil Religion', in *Pluralismo e religione civile: una prospettiva storica e filosofica: Atti del Convegno Vercelli (Università del Piemonte Orientale), 24–5 giugio 2001*, eds G. Paganini and E. Tortarolo (Milano: B. Mondadori, 2004). Hobbes's indebtedness to Machiavelli has often been underestimated. *Leviathan* chapter 2, 'Of Man,' for instance, includes an allusion to the centaur, compounded of horse and man, which suggests Machiavelli's trope of the centaur as reflecting the duality of human nature in the Prince chapter 18. It is a trope which Machiavelli goes on to rework in the famous metaphor of the wolf and the fox, a notion famously redescribed by Hobbes himself in the concept *homo homini lupus*. Nor could Hobbes have been unaware of his patron, William Cavendish, Duke of Newcastle's famous princely mirror, his *Advice to Charles II*, which so closely follows Machiavelli's Prince. See *Ideology and Politics on the Eve of Restoration: Newcastle's Advice to Charles II*, transcribed by Thomas P. Slaughter (Philadelphia: American Philosophical Society, 1984.)
16 *Behemoth*, 119–20. For the details, he refers his pupil to 'the history written at large', presumably Clarendon's *History of the Rebellion*. See, Edward Hyde, First Earl of Clarendon, *The History of the Rebellion and Civil Wars in England, begun in the Year 1641. With the precedent Passages, and Actions, that contributed thereunto, and the happy end, and Conclusion thereof by the King's blessed Restoration, and Return upon the 29th of May, in the Year 1660* (Oxford, 1660).

people esteemed the best patriots'.[17] He gives a preliminary catalogue of 'the seducers' and then goes on to consider the role of arms, and control of the military, as well as the specific laws in terms of which the corruption of sovereignty was made possible. 'The seducers were of divers sorts,' the teacher claims, and proceeds to give a catalogue that includes ministers, first Papists, then Presbyterians and third, Independents, Fifth-monarchy-men, Quakers and Adamites, all of whom claimed an independent, and in some cases a democratic, authority.[18] Fourthly came the parliamentarians characterized by the educated gentry, classical republicans if not democrats, citing Greek and Roman precedents for 'popular government ... extolled by the glorious name of liberty, and monarchy disgraced by tyranny'.[19] Fifth were 'the city of London and other great towns of trade, having in admiration the great prosperity of the Low Countries after they had revolted from their monarch, the King of Spain', and who thought that they likewise might profit from a change of government.[20] Sixth were those who thought they could profit from war; and seventh and last, 'the people in general...so ignorant of their duty...or what necessity there was of King or Commonwealth...they had no rule of equity, but precedents and custom...whence crept in the pretences of that Long Parliament, for a democracy'.[21]

Parliament is characterized variously, as in the power of 'democratical gentlemen ... whose design of changing the government from monarchical to popula ... they called liberty',[22] as 'attempting the change of government from monarchical to democratical',[23] as ruled by 'Presbyterians and democraticals,'[24] and as 'animated by the democratical and Presbyterian English'.[25] It is the thread of the triple threats of heresy, sectarianism and democracy on which the argument is chiefly strung, leading the student to conclude:

> I see by this, it is easier to gull the multitude, than any one man amongst them. For what one man, that has not his natural judgment depraved by accident, could be so easily cozened in a matter that concerns his purse, had he not been passionately carried away by the rest

17 *Behemoth*, 2.
18 Ibid., 2–3.
19 Ibid., 3.
20 Ibid., 3–4.
21 Ibid., 4–5.
22 Ibid., 26.
23 Ibid., 27.
24 Ibid., 30.
25 Ibid., 31.

to change of government, or rather to a liberty of every one to govern himself?[26]

The pupil summarizes the lessons Hobbes drew from Thucydides, of whom he claimed in his *Vita*:

> There's none that pleas'd me like Thucydides.
> He says Democracy's a foolish thing,
> Than a republic wiser is one king.[27]

It is in this context that the teacher in *Behemoth* is prompted to ask:

> A. Why may not men be taught their duty, that is, the science of just and unjust, as divers other sciences have been taught, from true principles, and evident demonstration; and much more easily than any of those preachers and democratical gentlemen could teach rebellion and treason?[28]

The student is skeptical:

> B. But who can teach what none have learned? Or if any many have been so singular, as to have studied the science of justice and equity; how can he teach it safely, when it is against the interest of those that are in possession of the power to hurt him?[29]

And the teacher replies:

> A. The rules of just and unjust sufficiently demonstrated, and from principles evident to the meanest capacity, have not been wanting; and notwithstanding the obscurity of their author, have shined, not only in this, but also in foreign countries, to men of good education.[30]

Hobbes, as interlocutor A, undoubtedly refers to his own *Leviathan*, and its continental reception. Moreover, he presages the important role of education in inculcating the 'science of the just and the unjust', and the delinquency of the universities which, he claims, have failed in the task:

> And, therefore, the light of that doctrine has been hitherto covered and kept under here by a cloud of adversaries, which no private man's reputation can break through, without the authority of the Universities. But out of the Universities, came all those preachers that taught the contrary. The Universities have been to this nation, as the wooden horse was to the Trojans.[31]

It is as a project for the universities, or a theory of civic education, that Hobbes presents his 'science of *just* and *unjust*'. *Leviathan*, as Hobbes made clear, was intended as a text for university instruction, and there, as

---

26 Ibid., 38.
27 Hobbes, *Verse Autobiography*, lines 84–6, reproduced in *Leviathan*, ed. Curley, lvi.
28 *Behemoth*, 39.
29 Ibid.
30 Ibid.
31 Ibid., 40.

in the *Historia Ecclesiastica*, he gives substantially the same account of the development of the universities as initially papal foundations intended for religious indoctrination which might, however, be reformed to serve the state.³² As it stands, however, when men had 'grown weary at last of the insolence of the priests', they turned instead to 'the democratical principles of Aristotle and Cicero, and from the love of their eloquence fell in love with their politics, and that more and more, until it grew into the rebellion we now talk of'.³³ Hobbes implies that university reform is now imperative, and it is not difficult to see the entire project of *Leviathan* and *Behemoth* as an exercise in civic education.

Hobbes is careful to distinguish the Republican Aristotle, ushered in by the Renaissance, from the Aristotelianism of the Schools. And while it is against the Aristotelianism of the Schoolmen that he directs most of his ire, the republican Aristotle, famous in the *Politics*, for the definition of citizenship as the right to rule and be ruled, is a specific target in *Behemoth*:

> The virtue of the subject is comprehended wholly in obedience to the laws of the commonwealth. To obey the laws, is justice and equity, which is the law of nature, and, consequently, is civil law in all nations of the world; and nothing is injustice or iniquity otherwise than it is against the law. Likewise, to obey the laws, is the prudence of a subject; for without such obedience the commonwealth (which is every subject's safety and protection) cannot subsist.³⁴

Hobbes refers in this context to Aristotle's doctrine of the mean, which he derides as the rule of mediocrity: 'In sum all actions and habits are to be esteemed good or evil by their causes and usefulness in reference to the commonwealth, and not by their mediocrity'.³⁵ And he seems to lay the fall of the monarchy to the door of the theory of mixed government, or 'mixarchy', the classical republican doctrine of government balanced between monarchical, aristocratic and democratic principles, to be found first in Aristotle, that captivated not only the civil war parliamentarians but also the king's councillors.³⁶ A doctrine shared by Clarendon and

---

32 Hobbes, *Historia Ecclesiastica*, lines 1847–82 (Springborg et al., 535–9), closely parallels the account in *Behemoth*, 40–1, of the rise of the universities, beginning with Paris and followed by Oxford, as papal instruments and seats of theology.
33 *Behemoth*, 43.
34 Ibid., 44.
35 Ibid., 45.
36 The official theory of the 'balanced' or 'mixed' constitution of 'three estates', king, lords and commons, was set out in the *Answer to the XIX Propositions*, issued in June 1642 on behalf of Charles I and against his parliamentary opponents. Recent scholars have debated to what degree this is an expression of classical republican theory. At the time the statement was read less as empowering king or commons than as empowering bishops, the lords spiritual, and counterpart to the lords temporal, of the second estate, under attack in the parliament of 1640–41. Clarendon supported the independent authority of the Anglican church and was the principal advocate of 'mixarchy'. He was the unnamed target of Hobbes's

Royalists, as well as by Republicans, the theory of mixed government called for divided sovereignty and ineffective government, in Hobbes's view, a topic to which he many times returns in the course of *Behemoth*.

The possibility of a 'science of just and unjust'

Two commonplaces about Hobbes's political theory have obscured the significance of Hobbes's important claim in *Behemoth* that 'the science of *just* and *unjust*' is a demonstrable science, and that the principles of this science are 'evident to the meanest capacity'. The first concerns his nominalism and the second his legal positivism. Hobbes is deemed a nominalist by virtue of his subscription to the principle that right and wrong, good and bad, just and unjust do not exist in nature but are judgments of men. And he is deemed a legal positivist by subscribing to the view that 'justice is whatever the law says it is' and an 'unjust law' is simply an oxymoron.[37]

But such a simple understanding of Hobbes's position defies his notion of 'the science of just and unjust', variously expressed as the 'true science of equity and justice' (*EW* 6. 251), the 'true principles of duty' (*EW* 6. 253), the 'causes and grounds of duty' (*EW* 6. 363), the 'science of the laws of nature' (*EW* 3. 146), the 'science of virtue and vice' (*EW* 3. 146), and the 'true doctrine of the laws of nature' (*EW* 3. 166).[38] It is noteworthy that among modern accounts of Hobbes's science of justice and its sources, one of the most succinct and compelling is that of Reinhart Koselleck, student of Carl Schmitt, legal theorist of the Third Reich whose *Leviathan*[39] heralded a new and disturbing *Realpolitik* in the principles of *Freund und Feind*, an extrapolation from Hobbes's characteristic use of the old aphorism *homo homini lupus*.[40] Emphasizing the civil war context for Hobbes's political theory, Koselleck notes that Hobbes, in his search for a fundament on which to ground peace and security, rejects 'the laws and customs of one's country', as a starting point, on which Descartes, by con-

---

attacks on the doctrine, and its role in the fall of Charles I, in *Behemoth*. See Michael Mendle, *Dangerous Positions: Mixed Government, the Estates of the Realm, and the Answer to the XIX Propositions* (Tuscaloosa, Al.: University of Alabama Press, 1985); and the review of Mendle by Richard Tuck, *Journal of Modern History* 59 (1987), no. 3, 570–2.

37 Among legal theorists, the Viennese Hans Kelsen is most well known for the 'hard positivist' position that positive law needs no further justification: there are no universal facts about morality, or objective measures of what the law ought to be like. The origins of positive law are explained either in terms of command theory (Jeremy Bentham, John Austin), or social convention theory (Kelsen, H. L. A. Hart). The latter see Hobbes as a legal positivist in this sense.

38 For the purposes of easy comparison I list the references according to *EW*.

39 Carl Schmitt, *The Leviathan In The State Theory of Thomas Hobbes* (1938), trans. G. Schwab and E. Hilfstein (Westport, Conn.: Greenwood Press, 1996).

40 See the seminal piece by François Tricaud, '"Homo homini Deus", "Homo homini Lupus": Recherche des sources des deux formules de Hobbes', in *Hobbes-Forschungen*, eds R. Koselleck, and R. Schnur (Berlin: Duncker & Humbolt, 1969), 61–70.

trast, had insisted. Hobbes devoted chapter 11 of *Leviathan*, 'Of the Difference of Manners', to a polemic against 'Custome and Example', or *jus gentium*, as adequate to such a task. As early as *De Homine* (10. 5), Hobbes had insisted that politics and ethics, or the science of just and unjust, equality and inequality, is a science demonstrable *a priori* ('politica et ethica, id est scientia justi et injusti, aequi et iniqui, demonstrari a priori potest'), precisely because it is we who make cases of justice, just as to be sure we make the laws and pacts themselves ('justitiae causas, nimirum leges et pacta ipsi fecimus').[41] If civil war is due initially to the failure of philosophers and theologians to put truth above sectarianism ('non partium, sed pacis studio'), as Hobbes diagnoses in *Behemoth*, it is only in the course of the experience of war that sectarian interests, of individuals, parties and churches are progressively unmasked to disclose desire and fear ('appetitus et fuga') as the ultimate causes of war and peace.[42]

Indeed, one may argue, the monsters from the book of Job, *Leviathan* and *Behemoth*, make their appearance in the titles of Hobbes's works precisely to signal two things: first that right and wrong, good and bad, just and unjust are judgments that only men can make; and second that *Leviathan*, a human artifice constructed on the basis of fear, is indeed a *mortal* god, and *Behemoth*, civil war, is the story of its *mortality*.[43] If the main support for the state is the power of reason that brings it into being, the main threat to the state is religion, also born out of fear. It is primarily due to religion, in the form of priestcraft, and its specific bearer, the universities, he claims, that the science of justice has been subverted and the realm imperiled. Hobbes's position on reason as the power to make the state and religion as the power to unmake it, is classically Epicurean and does not involve the simple nominalism or legal positivism that have been ascribed to him. Understanding Hobbes as a latter day Epicurean allows us to take seriously his 'science of just and unjust'. It gives us important hints about the provenance of some of the characteristic features of his theory, notions of the state of nature, contract, the role of fear, religion as a prophylactic, and right reason as a route to peace. And it allows us to see the ingenuity with which Hobbes advances 'the science of *just* and *unjust*' along Epicurean lines.

There was a long tradition of treating justice as conventional, which included not only the sceptics but also the dogmatists, and even Aristotle

---

41 See Reinhart Koselleck, *Critique and Crisis: Enlightenment and the Pathogensis of Modern Society* (Cambridge, Mass.: MIT Press, 1988), ch. 2, 'Hobbesian Rationality and the Origins of Enlightenment', 23–4, and notes.

42 Ibid., 24, citing *Leviathan*, book 1, ch. 6.

43 See Job 30: 29; 40; 41; 42: 6, etc.; see also Patricia Springborg, 'Hobbes's Biblical Beasts: Leviathan and Behemoth', *Political Theory* 23 (1995), no. 2, 353–75.

had remarked that justice was a matter of law and custom and not by nature. But Epicurus managed successfully to combine the view of justice as conventional with emphasis on the therapeutic value of philosophy, which presupposed an objective measure of human betterment, or the Good. The notion that justice was conventional, arising from pacts between men, is explicitly elaborated in the important Sentences (*Ratae Sententiae*) XXXI to XL of Epicurus' *Principal Doctrines* (*Kuriai Doxai*).[44] So *RS* XXXI states: 'the justice which arises from nature is a pledge of mutual advantage to restrain men from harming one another and save them from being harmed'; *RS* XXXII states: 'For all living things which have not been able to make compacts not to harm one another or be harmed, nothing ever is either just or unjust; and likewise too for all tribes of men which have been unable or unwilling to make compacts not to harm or be harmed'; and *RS* XXXIII states: 'Justice never is anything in itself, but in the dealings of men with one another in any place whatever and at any time it is a kind of compact not to harm or be harmed'.

Justice may be conventional, but Epicurus reserves for harm and benefit a privileged status. If justice concerns benefit and injustice concerns harm, nevertheless justice 'arises from nature', even though if it is always mediated through compacts and is not, therefore, available to men in the natural state. This is precisely the structure of Hobbes's own theory. He may seem to repeat arguments that suggest the appellations good, bad, just and unjust are arbitrarily chosen terms, and that there is no measure by which to determine the difference in meaning between them. So, for instance, in the *Historia Ecclesiastica* he repeats an argument to be found in *Behemoth* in a more developed form:

> The crowd has no known measure of good and evil, and regard justice and injustice as mere words.
>
> Everyone calls 'just' whatever he can get away with; and whatever he suffers unwillingly, he considers a crime against God.[45]

What appears at first sight as a cynical acknowledgement of the conventional nature of justice turns out, upon analysis, to be a protest against the general failure to understand 'the measure of good and evil', of justice and injustice. To what cause is this general failure due? It comes about through the conjunction of democracy and sectarianism. Only at the behest of demagogues and false prophets do men fail to calculate their interest by *ratio*, the measure of harm and benefit. So, in *Behemoth*, where as so often he describes civil war as a 'world turned upside down' in

---

44 For *Ratae Sententiae* XXXI-III, I have used the English translation of Cyril Bailey in *Epicurus, the Extant Remains* (Oxford: Clarendon Press, 1926), 103.
45 Hobbes, *Historia Ecclesiastica*, lines 2155-58 (Springborg et al., 568-9).

remarkably Thucydidean terms, he claims: 'it is easier to gull the multitude, than any one man amongst them'.[46] It is precisely due to preachers and demagogues that men can be seduced so easily from their interests, and even their pecuniary interests.

'Good is to everything, that which hath active power to attract it locally, *Malum*, therefore, to everthing is that which hath active power to repel it', Hobbes declared as early as the *Short Tract* (c. 1630).[47] He had refined the thesis in *De Cive* (1642) and the *Philosophical Rudiments* (1651), claiming in the latter, 'For every man is desirous of what is good for him and shuns what is evil, but chiefly the chiefest of natural evils, which is death; and this he does by a certain natural impulsion of nature, no less than that whereby a stone moves downward'.[48] The thesis that good and evil are names for the attraction of pleasure and the avoidance of pain, natural impulses activated by human judgment, had been formulated by Lorenzo Valla and Juan Luis Vives, probable sources for Hobbes.[49]

> Therefore we say that such-and-such things exist or do not exist, or are these and those, of such or a different kind, we reckon on the basis of our belief, not of the things themselves. It is not they that constitute their measure for us, but our mind. For when we call things good, bad, useful, useless, we are not speaking according to things, but according to ourselves.[50]

Views about the conventional nature of judgments of good and bad, useful and useless, are to be found across the range of philosophical traditions, and are not peculiar to the Epicureans. The Sophist Protagoras had epitomized the view that the measure of truth was political, what men collectively decide (*Theaet.* 167c), although, like Democritus, he thought 'a basis for the judgments of "better" and "worse" is to be found in the effi-

---

46 *Behemoth*, 38.
47 See, Ferdinand Tönnies, 'A Short Tract on First Principles', in Tönnies, ed. *The Elements of Law*, including 'A Short Tract on First Principles', (New York, 1969), 208-9. For the debate about Hobbes's authorship of the 'Short Tract', see the late Karl Schuhmann's seminal piece, 'Le Short Tract, première oeuvre philosophique de Hobbes', *Hobbes Studies* 8 (1995), 3-36.
48 *EW* 2. 8.
49 For Hobbes and Valla, see Gianni Paganini, 'Hobbes, Valla e i problemi filosofici della teologia umanistica: la riforma 'dilettica' della Trinità', in *Dal necessario al possibile: Determinismo e libertà nel pensiero anglo-olandese del XVII secolo*, ed. L. Simonutti (Milan: Franco Angeli, 2001), 11-45; and idem, 'Thomas Hobbes e Lorenzo Valla: Critica umansitica e filosofia moderna', *Rinscimento, Rivista dell' Instituto Nazionale di Studi sul Rinascimento*, 2nd series, 39 (1999), 515-68.
50 See Juan Luis Vives, *De prima philosophia*, in his *Opera* (Basle, 1555), 1. 532-3, trans. Richard Waswo, *Language and Meaning in the Renaissance* (Princeton: Princeton University Press, 1987), 128-9. For a more extensive discussion of Hobbes and Vives, see Patricia Springborg, 'Hobbes and Epicurean Religion', in *Der Garten und die Moderne: Epikureische Moral und Politik vom Humanismus bis zur Aufklärung*, eds G. Paganini and E. Tortarolo (Stuttgart: Rommann-Holzboog, 2004).

cacy of "art"'.⁵¹ But for Democritus, as Gregory Vlastos points out, 'man is the measure' in a very different sense: 'His physical concept of the soul defines a unitary human nature which affords a basis for universally valid judgments'.⁵² 'Man is the measure', because the good for man is not given but must be created, through 'art'.⁵³ In this way man can truly be said to make himself.

The content of Hobbes's 'science of justice': jus to lex

The Latin term for 'the measure', so central to Hobbes's science of justice, was *ratio*, whose more concrete meaning, a system of calculation, has been overtaken by the figurative meaning, reason.⁵⁴ This system of calculation, reason, was in Hobbes's view, so straightforward that the simplest men could grasp it, and there are various remarks to this effect in *Behemoth*, as we have noted. His science of just and unjust, like Epicurus' *Principal Doctrines* (*Kuriai Doxai*), take the form of *Ratae Sententiae*, renamed by Hobbes Laws of Nature. It has been customary to compare these principles with Grotius's concept of natural right (*jus naturale*), and for good reason. Hugo Grotius (1583-1645), jurist and politician, was among the first early modern thinkers to derive particular moral axioms from general principles of reason in this way. So, for instance, Hobbes's definition of *jus naturale* as 'the liberty each man hath to use his own power, as he will himself, for the preservation of his own nature', appears to rephrase Grotius, who declared: 'Natural right (*jus naturale*) is a dictate of right reason indicating that some act is either morally necessary or morally shameful, because of its agreement or disagreement with man's nature as a rational and social being'.⁵⁵ In this respect Hobbes belongs to the long history of the reception of Roman law concept of *jus*, mediated by Canon law and the efforts of Glossators and Postglossators, to produce elaborate legal theory, differentiated in terms of *jus naturale* and *jus gentium*, as the basis for justice in 'right' (*jus*), on the one hand, and its expression in the positive law of nations (*lex*), on the other.⁵⁶

---

51 Gregory Vlastos, 'Ethics and Physics in Democritus, I', *The Philosophical Review* 54 (1945), 591.
52 Gregory Vlastos, 'Ethics and Physics in Democritus, II', *The Philosophical Review* 55 (1946), 53.
53 Ibid., 64.
54 For definitions of *ratio* see Lewis & Short's standard *Latin Dictionary* and Cooper's *Thesaurus Linguae Romanae & Britannicae* (London 1565):
55 Hobbes, *Leviathan*, ch. 14, 1, ed. Curley, 79. Curley notes the parallel to Grotius, *De jure belli ac pacis* 1. 1. 10. 12.
56 For Roman Law concepts of *jus* and *lex*, see H. F. Jolowitz, *A Historical Introduction to the Study of Roman Law*, 2nd ed. (Cambridge: Cambridge University Press, 1967). For the development of modern natural rights theory out of Roman Law *jus naturale* and *jus gentium*, see M. P. Gilmore, *Argument for Roman Law in Political Thought, 1200–1600* (Cambridge, Mass.: Harvard

'Behemoth' and Hobbes's 'science of just and unjust'   161

While this is indeed the legacy to which Hobbes's science of just and unjust belongs, the peculiar character of his own particular doctrines and the important role of social contract, as the vehicle by means of which *jus* can be converted into *lex*, are best explained with reference to Epicurus' *Ratae Sententiae* XXXI to XXXIII that we have already mentioned. Indeed, it is Pierre Gassendi, Hobbes's important contemporary, with whom he was closely associated in Paris, who was at the time putting together his great Latin compilation of Epicurean sources, whom Hobbes most likely followed in defining justice as conventional. A letter dated 10 October 1644 from Charles Cavendish, Hobbes's patron, to John Pell, the mathematician, reports: 'Mr Hobbes writes Gassendes his philosophie is not yet printed but he hath reade it, and that it is big as Aristotele's philosophie, but much truer and excellent Latin'.[57] Cavendish refers to Gassendi's *Life of Epicurus* and *Animadversions on the Ten Books of Diogenes Laertius* published in 1649.[58] The Hobbes-Gassendi dialogue was not all one way, however. Gassendi made an important concession to Hobbes by including his famous aphorism, 'homo homini lupus' in his comment to Epicurus *Ratae sententiae* XXXIII late in the *Animadversions*, to illustrate human aggressivity in the state of nature.[59] It is perhaps not surprising then, that when in *Leviathan* Hobbes first introduces the concept of Justice, his argument should follow the same structure as Epicurus' *Principal Doctrines*, read through Gassendi's eyes, which we may restate in the form of a syllogism:[60] (1) that justice, although arising from nature, is a pact of

University Press, 1961), and Richard Tuck, *Natural Rights Theories, their Origin and Development* (Cambridge: Cambridge University Presss, 1981).

[57] Published in J. O. Halliwell, *A Collection of Letters Illustrative of the Progress of Science in England from the Reign of Queen Elisabeth to that of Charles the Second* (London, Historical Society of Science, 1941), 85, and cited in Gianni Paganini, 'Hobbes, Gassendi e la psicologia del meccanicismo', in *Hobbes Oggi: Atti del convegno internazionale di studi promosso da Arrigo Pacchi, Milano-Locarno 18–21 maggio 1988*, ed. A. Napoli (Milan: Franco Angeli, 1990), 351–445 n. 12.

[58] Gassendi's 'dialogue at a distance' with Hobbes has now been documented by Gianni Paganini, 'Hobbes, Gassendi et le *De Cive*', in *Materia Actuosa: Antiquité, Âge Classique, Lumières; Mélanges en honneur d'Olivier Bloch*, eds M. Benitez, A. McKenna, G. Paganini, J. Salem (Paris: Champion, 2000), 183–206. In the ethical part of the *Syntagma*, dating to the years 1645–6, after the publication of the first edition of Hobbes's *De Cive* in 1642, and before the second, which Gassendi helped his friend Samuel Sorbière promote, Gassendi made transparent reference to Hobbes on freedom in the state of nature, as Paganini argues. For further elaboration on Hobbes's debt to the Epicureans see Arrigo Pacchi's seminal piece, 'Hobbes e l'epicureismo', in *Rivista Critica di Storia della Filosofia* 33 (1975), 54–71.

[59] This was noted by Paganini, 'Hobbes, Gassendi e la psicologia del meccanicismo', 438; a discovery made simultaneously by Olivier Bloch in his 'Gassendi et la théorie politique de Hobbes', in *Thomas Hobbes, Philosophie première, théorie de la science et politique: Actes du Colloque de Paris*, eds Y.-Ch. Zarka and J. Bernhardt (Paris: Presses Universitaires de France, 1990), 345.

[60] Gassendi's Latin translation of Epicurus *RS* XXXIII, indicated in italics, with his own interpolations in roman, reads: '*Iustitia per se* (et quatenus quidem id quod heic est iustum, illeic est iniustum) *nihil est; ac in homine solitariè spectato reperitur nulla, sed* dumtaxat *in mutuis hominum societatibus, pro ea cuiusque regionis amplitudines in qua possunt pacta de non*

mutual restraint against harm and being harmed (*RS* XXXI); (2) that 'for all tribes of men which have been unable or unwilling to make compacts not to harm or be harmed ... nothing ever is either just or unjust' (*RS* XXXII); and (3) that, therefore, 'Justice never is anything in itself, but in the dealings of men with one another in any place whatever and at any time it is a kind of compact not to harm or be harmed' (*RS* XXXIII).

We can reconstruct the logic of Hobbes's theory of Justice in terms of a parallel syllogism:[61] (1) 'To obey the laws, is justice and equity, which is the law of nature, and, consequently, is civil law in all nations of the world; and nothing is injustice or iniquity otherwise than it is against the law'. (2) In the state of nature, 'this war of every man against every man, this also is consequent: that nothing can be unjust. The notions of right and wrong, justice and injustice, have there no place'.[62] (3) Therefore: 'Where there is no common power, there is no law; where no law, no injustice'.

The conclusion to Hobbes's syllogism may suggest a legal positivist position: no *jus* without *lex*. But this is not the burden of his argument taken as a whole, which was rather to assert the classic position assumed by Aristotle as well as by Epicurus, that justice is relational, and not the virtue of the solitary man. Against Plato's theory of innate ideas, Hobbes concurs with Aristotle: 'Justice and injustice are none of the faculties neither of the body, nor mind. If they were, they might be in a man that were alone in the world as well as his senses and passions. They are qualities that relate to men in society, not in solitude'.[63] But if justice is in practice always a question of what is lawful, it cannot be reduced to a legal positivist principle, nevertheless. In fact Hobbes is harsh in his criticism of those who would reduce *jus* to *lex*, insisting: 'For though they that speak of this subject used to confound *jus* and *lex* (*right* and *law*), yet they ought to be distinguished, because RIGHT consisteth in liberty to do or to forbear, whereas LAW determineth and bindeth to one of them'.[64] So, in *A Dialogue between a Philosopher and a Student of the Common Laws of England* he explicitly accused Coke for confusing *jus* and *lex*,[65] a charge he might well have levelled against Grotius, for whom *jus* retained the idea of right as a

---

inferendo, accipiendove nocumento iniri.' See Gassendi: *Animadversiones in decimum librum Diogenis Laertii, qui est de vita, moribus, placitisque Epicuri* (first published 1649, 1675 ed.), 2. 302a, cited by Paganini, 'Hobbes, Gassendi et le De Cive', 188-9.

61 *Behemoth*, 44.
62 *Leviathan*, ch. 13, §13, ed. Curley, 78.
63 Ibid.
64 *Leviathan*, ch. 14, §3, ed. Curley, 79, where Curley notes that John Finnis, *Natural Law and Natural Rights* (Oxford: Clarendon Press, 1980), 205-10, emphasizes the parallel between Hobbes's position and that of Suarez (*On Laws and God the Lawgiver*, 1. 2. 5).
65 *EW* 6. 73, see Curley, 79 n. 4.

liberty, but who nevertheless defined *jus naturale* as a command or prohibition.[66]

For Hobbes, as for Epicurus, justice is not simply defined with reference to our interests. But Hobbes does not move as quickly as Epicurus to a conventional definition of justice. If it is in the nature of man as a social being to arrive at justice through covenants for Epicurus, for Hobbes the route to justice is through the laws of natural reason. Like Grotius Hobbes arrives, by a slightly longer route, at the conclusion that it is in man's nature to seek justice through covenants, due to rational theorems forced upon him by the war of all against all: 'reason suggesteth convenient articles of peace, upon which men may be drawn to agreement. These articles are they which otherwise are called the Laws of Nature',[67] which he then goes on to itemize: the first being to seek peace, the second contract as a means to peace, the third and subsequent being Laws of Nature concerning the laying down of a right, the renouncing of a right, and the transferring of a right.[68] It follows from these laws, and their implications in terms of obligation and duty, that *Injustice* is injury, or a form of malfeasance:

> And when a man hath in either manner abandoned or granted away his right, then is he said to be OBLIGED or BOUND not to hinder those to whom the right is granted or abandoned from the benefit of it; and [it is said] that he *ought*, and it is his DUTY not to make void that voluntary act of his own, and that such hindrance is INJUSTICE and INJURY, as being *sine jure* [without right], the right being before renounced or transferred. So that the *injury* or *injustice*, in the controversies of the world is somewhat like to that which the disputations of scholars is called absurdity. For as it is therefore called an *absurdity* to contradict what one maintained in the beginning, so in the world it is called injustice and injury voluntarily to undo that which from the beginning he had voluntarily done.[69]

If justice is honouring contracts and obedience to the law, injustice the failure to live up to the terms of the contract or, worse, efforts to retract rights that have already been contracted away, injustice is therefore an absurdity. But this fact alone is not sufficient to deter individuals from unlawful or unjust behaviour. It is in the nature of rational theorems that they bind *in foro interno*, in the internal court of reason, without necessarily binding *in foro externo*, in the external court of human affairs.[70] To prevent precisely this form of malfeasance the act of contract must be paralleled by an act of authorization, which empowers a sovereign to con-

---

66 Grotius *De jure belli ac pacis* 1. 1. 5, noted by Curley, 79.
67 *Leviathan*, ch. 13, §14, ed. Curley, 78.
68 Ibid., ch. 14, §§4–7, ed. Curley, 80–1.
69 Ibid., ch. 14, §7, ed. Curley, 81.
70 See *De Cive* (*EW* 2. 45–6).

vert *jus* into *lex*. Hobbes, like Machiavelli, argues the priority of the *princeps* as lawgiver, claiming in the *Dialogue between a Philosopher and a Student of the Common Laws* that lawmakers and laws are logically prior to justice and injustice:

> Laws are in their nature antecedent to justice and injustice. And you cannot deny that there must be law-makers before there were any laws, and consequently before there was any justice (I speak of human justice); and that the law-makers were before that which you call own and property of goods or lands, distinguished by meum, tuum, alienum.[71]

Discovering that the student takes as a definition of Justice the definition of Aristotle and the Common Lawyers, of 'giving to every man his own', the Philosopher in the *Dialogue* embraces this principle as his point of departure for 'the science of *just* and *unjust*', pointing out that the very substance of Justice depends on the particular laws of 'propriety' (property) that a sovereign has set up. This is simply a restatement of Hobbes's position in *Leviathan*, where he develops his case more fully, once again with reference to the Aristotelians:

> And this is also to be gathered out of the ordinary definition of justice in the Schools. For they say that *justice is the constant will of giving to every man his own*. And therefore where there is no *own*, that is, no propriety, there is no injustice; and where there is no coercive power erected, that is where there is no commonwealth there is no propriety; all men having right to all things; therefore where there is no commonwealth there is nothing unjust. So that the nature of justice consisteth in keeping of valid covenants; but the validity of covenants begins not but with the constitution of a civil power sufficient to complete men to keep them; and then it is also that propriety begins.[72]

It is in this way that *jus* and *lex* are mutually entailed and we can show that Hobbes, far from being a legal positivist in the ordinary sense, is closer in fact to Scholastic thought:

> The law of nature and the civil law contain each other, and are of equal extent. For the laws of nature, which consist in equity, justice, gratitude, and other moral virtues on these depending, in the condition of mere nature (as I have said before in the end of the 15th chapter) are not properly laws but qualities that dispose men to peace and obedience. When a commonwealth is once settled, then are they actually laws, and not before; as being then the commands of the commonwealth; and therefore also civil laws; for it is the sovereign power that obliges men to obey them. For in the differences of private men, to declare what is equity, what is justice, and what is moral virtue, and to make them binding, there is need of the ordinances of sovereign power, and punishments to be ordained for such as shall break them;

---

71   *EW* 6. 29.
72   *Leviathan*, ch. 15, §3, ed. Curley, 89.

which ordinances are therefore part of the civil law. The law of nature therefore is a part of the civil law in all commonwealths of the world.[73]

In *Leviathan* Hobbes goes out of his way in fact to rebut the legal positivist position that 'justice is whatever the law says it is' and an 'unjust law' is simply an oxymoron. He makes witty play on Psalm 14: 1-3 'The fool says in his heart, "There is no God"', to argue precisely the foolishness of arguing 'there is no such thing as justice', or that justice is whatever men decide conduces to their benefit. He makes the argument, significantly, in the context of broken covenants in general, and with reference to '*Coke's Commentaries on Littleton*', which make the case for setting aside a king, in particular:

> The fool hath said in his heart: 'there is no such thing as justice'; and sometimes also with his tongue, seriously alleging that: 'every man's conservation and contentment being committed to his own care, there could be no reason why every man might not do what he thought conduced thereunto, and therefore also to make or not make, keep or not keep, covenants was not against reason when it conduced to one's benefit'.[74]

Edwin Curley in his commentary notes that 'the position Hobbes ascribes to the fool is very like the one Grotius ascribes to Carneades, whom he takes as representative of those who deny natural law'; and he points to an inconsistency between *Leviathan* and *De Cive*, where Hobbes's position appeared to be close to Carneades' in claiming that 'in the state of nature profit [*utilitas*] is the measure of right [*jus*].[75] It is true that in *De Cive* Hobbes gives a curious redescription of his claim that 'The laws of nature oblige *in foro interno*: that is to say, they bind to a desire they should take place, but *in foro externo*: that is to putting them in act, not always', when he makes the following addendum: 'Briefly in the state of nature, what is just and unjust, is not to be esteemed by the actions, but by the counsel and conscience of the actor'.[76] But this is to emphasize that only in the state of nature, before the conversion of *jus* into *lex*, can justice be attributed to *jus* – *and then we might rather say that it is an impulse to justice, rather than justice as such*. It is a position that Hobbes explicitly abandons in *Leviathan*, where he says of the state of nature: 'The notions of right and wrong, justice and injustice, have there no place'.[77] Rather than being an inconsistency then, as Curley claims, Hobbes's position has in fact changed between the work of 1640 and that of 1652. It is likely that the

---

73 Ibid., ch. 26, §8, ed. Curley, 173.
74 Ibid., ch. 15, §4, ed. Curley, 90.
75 Curley, note to *Leviathan*, ch. 15, §4, ed. Curley, 90; see also *De Cive* (*EW* 2. 46).
76 *De Cive* (*EW* 2. 45-6).
77 *Leviathan*, ch. 13, §13, ed. Curley, 78.

course of the civil war, in many respects an analogue for the state of nature, may have impressed upon him the necessity to close any window that would open the opportunity to challenge the prevailing rule of law (*lex*) in the name of right (*jus*) or justice in the abstract. More importantly, Hobbes's doctrine of simultaneous authorization and consent, developed between *De Cive* and *Leviathan*, forbids it. *Jus* and *lex* now lie in different zones and the rights due to individuals in principle in the state of nature, once exchanged for *lex* under the terms of the social contract, can never be retracted.[78]

Hobbes's 'science of justice' and civil law

Hobbes presents himself, in fact, as a theorist in the civil law tradition, opposed to 'the ancient constitution' and, where he treats it *in extenso*, he tends to subsume feudal law under civil, as we shall later see.[79] When, as we have noted, the student, B, poses to the teacher, A, the Aristotelian question whether a differentiation can be made 'between the ethics of subjects and the ethics of sovereigns', A gives a civil lawyer's response: 'To obey the laws, is justice and equity, which is the law of nature, and, consequently, is civil law in all nations of the world; and nothing is injustice or iniquity otherwise than it is against the law'.[80] In other words, he appears to put the legal positivist position. But in fact, as we have seen, Hobbes's position is more complicated, and he argues justice as *lex* only as the conclusion of a syllogism that includes as its first premise the distinction between *jus* and *lex*. To accept the distinction between *jus* and *lex*, he argues, is to accept that *jus* is justiciable only in terms of *lex*, and that what justice *in practice* means, therefore, is that which is lawful, and injustice, that which is unlawful. It follows from the conversion of natural right (*jus naturale*) into the law of nations (*jus gentium*), as the necessary condition for a legally enforceable peace, that 'to obey the laws, is the prudence of a subject; for without such obedience the commonwealth (which is every subject's safety and protection) cannot subsist'.[81]

For all Hobbes's complaints about infatuation with the Greek and Latin tongues as signalling 'democratical principles', or the commitment of the gentry to Ciceronian republicanism, on the one hand, Aristotelianism and the philosophy of the Schools, on the other, it is precisely the Greek natu-

---

78   I have developed this argument elsewhere. See Patricia Springborg, '*Leviathan*, the Christian Commonwealth Incorporated', *Political Studies* 24 (1976), no. 2, 171–83; reprinted in *Great Political Thinkers*, eds J. Dunn and I. Harris (Cheltenham: Elgar, 1997), 2. 199–211).
79   See J. G. A. Pocock, *The Ancient Constitution and the Feudal Law* (Cambridge: Cambridge University Press, 1957).
80   *Behemoth*, 44.
81   Ibid., 44.

ral law and Roman civil law traditions, mediated through early modern thinkers like Bodin and Grotius, to which he in fact turns for his theory of justice. Much of the content of *Behemoth* is concerned with showing how the power of preachers and parliamentarians has succeeded in replacing 'the science of *just* and *unjust*', argued from Reason, with amorphous concepts of 'righteousness' extrapolated from the Bible. He complains that 'though in the Latin and Greek Bible the word *justice* occur exceeding often, in the English, though it be a word that every man understands, the word righteousness (which few understand to signify the same, but take it rather for rightness of opinion than of action or intention), is put in the place of it', concluding, ironically, that 'the writings of the heathens, Greek and Latin ... were not at all behind us in point of virtue and moral duties, notwithstanding that we have had much preaching, and they none at all'.[82]

One is impressed at the degree to which 'the science of *just* and *unjust*', set out programmatically in *Leviathan*, is contextualized in the later works, *Behemoth* and the *Dialogue between a Philosopher and a Student of the Common Laws*, in terms of prevailing legal debates over the relative merits of feudal practice, Common Law and Civil Law. This is not to say that Hobbes resolves all these issues — sometimes his position is ambiguous, as in the case of his attitude to feudal law. For instance, in *Behemoth* he characterizes the stance of 'the people' in the civil war, as 'in general ... so ignorant of their duty, as that not one perhaps of ten thousand knew what right any man had to command him, or what necessity there was of King or Commonwealth'. Their ignorance of the logic of sovereignty bespoke a feudal mentality: 'King, they thought, was but a title of the highest honour, which gentlemen, knight, baron, earl, duke, were but steps to ascend to, with the help of riches; they had no rule of equity, but precedents and custom'.[83]

Hobbes's polemic against 'precedents and custom' extends to the ancient constitution itself. While refraining from disparaging *Magna Carta* itself, which he deems a form of 'statute law', and to which, therefore, obedience is compulsory, the teacher, A, mocks its claims[84] to ancient liberty. He points specifically to 'the article wherein a King heretofore hath granted that no man shall be distrained, that is, have his goods taken from him, otherwise than by the law of the land'.[85] 'For, where was the law of the land, then?', he asks. 'Did they mean another *Magna Charta*, that was

---

82   Ibid., 63.
83   Ibid., 4.
84   Ibid.
85   Ibid., 35.

made by some King more ancient yet?' It was precisely the vulnerability of the law of precedent to infinite regress upon which the Parliamentarians had played in their effort constantly to expand their own scope for action. The people were unwitting victims, whom parliamentarians and preachers have intentionally misled, and who remain in ignorance of 'the rules of *just* and *unjust*', even though they have been 'sufficiently demonstrated' by Hobbes himself.[86]

It is not too much to claim that 'the science of *just* and *unjust*' in *Leviathan* precisely amounts to a theory of how the conversion of *jus* into *lex* takes place, explicated in terms of theories of natural right and Roman law, as we have seen. The state of nature is intolerable, precisely because there no generally accepted legal conventions obtain. And one of the most forceful reasons for erecting a sovereign, is that the concept of Justice in Natural Law has no content, and is practically inoperable, until the sovereign, with authority to define legal terms, is established. Hobbes adopts the Roman Law attribute of the sovereign as the source of all laws of property, [87] in a very strict sense, then.[88]

Justice according to reason and Aristotle 'giving to every man his own', is a vacuous imperative until the relevant terms have been defined by statute. In *Leviathan* Hobbes specifies Roman law as the source of this legal theory:

> For before constitution of sovereign power (as hath already been shown) all men had right to all things, which necessarily causeth war; and therefore, this propriety, being necessary to peace, and depending on sovereign power, is the act of that power, in order to the public peace. These rules of propriety (or *meum* and *tuum*) and of *good, evil, lawful* and *unlawful* in the actions of subjects are the civil laws; that is to say, the laws of each commonwealth in particular (though the name of civil law be now restrained to the ancient civil laws of the city of *Rome*, which being the head of a great part of the world, her laws of that time were in these parts the civil law). [89]

Hobbes had made a considerable advance on the social contract theory of Epicurus. The intervening millennium had seen, first the development of legal codifications, and later the recovery of the Roman law tradition and its and civil law practice. The thirteenth-century rediscovery of the Institutes of Justinian, which heralded the era of the humanist Glossators

---

86   Ibid., 39.
87   See M. P. Gilmore, *Argument for Roman Law*, 97, who dicusses the sovereign as the source of legal proprietary rights in Roman law.
88   'Laws are in their nature antecedent to justice and injustice. And you cannot deny that there must be law-makers before there were any laws, and consequently before there was any justice (I speak of human justice).' *EW* 6. 29.
89   *Leviathan*, ch. 18, §10, ed. Curley, 114.

and Postglossators had seen the gradual co-optation of theories of Natural Right by Canon Law. One cannot underestimate the ingenuity with which Hobbes melded these traditions in a theory of sovereignty which, although anticipated by Machiavelli and Bodin, constituted a systematic and demonstrable science of justice, richly contextualized in terms of feudal and civil law. To the man best known for the concept of the 'war of all against all', we owe in fact a 'science of *just* and *unjust*' fundamental to the modern theory of rule of law, and one which has now been extended from the sovereign nation state to the international system, where Hobbes believed the writ of law could not run. It is to defend this achievement, by means of which rule of law can be upheld across borders, across nations and even across cultures, that we wish to hold to account those who would let Behemoth loose. Leviathan, 'mortal god and king of the proud', with incomparable power on earth, is the nation state whose sovereignty we still defend in the name of peace.

Geoffrey M. Vaughan

The Audiences of 'Behemoth' and the Politics of Conversation

Behemoth presents its reader with a problem: what is this book? The title reminds one of *Leviathan* while the topic it covers, the civil war, was a central event in Hobbes's life, both personally and intellectually. And yet neither association seems to help. The problem with the book arises on two levels. First, as a dialogue rather than a treatise, *Behemoth* seems out of place in Hobbes's corpus of political philosophy.[1] This leads us to the second and more pressing problem: is it even related to political philosophy? It is difficult to see how *Behemoth* adds to or even confirms what Hobbes argued in his treatises. Whereas behemoth was 'the chief of the ways of God' (Job 40: 19), where *Behemoth* fits into the ways of Hobbes is unclear. It is the contention of this chapter that the problems of interpretation arise because we fail to apprehend the intended audience of the argument in *Behemoth*. What makes *Behemoth* so difficult to interpret and so unusual is the fact that there are two audiences. There is the audience of the narrative itself, the character 'B', and there is the audience of the metanarrative, the reader of the book. Once we realize that these two audiences are distinct, we shall be able to see that *Behemoth* both confirms and completes what Hobbes had maintained in his treatises regarding the transmission of political knowledge.

As a dialogue, Thomas Hobbes's *Behemoth* has a different character from his philosophical treatises. This fact, obvious as it may be, has been

---

[1] Hobbes wrote several dialogues, and increasingly so during his later lifetime. Many were devoted to scientific topics, such as *Dialogus Physicus* (1661), *Problemata Physica* (1662), and *Decameron Physiologicum* (1678). Three others were on church history and theology: 'On the Nicene Creed' and 'On Heresy' (as appendices to the 1668 Latin *Leviathan*), and *Historia Ecclesiastica Dialogus* (1688). The Latin *Leviathan* also included in the Appendix the dialogue 'On Certain Objections against *Leviathan*'. Finally, the only other dialogue to be published on its own and receive any scholarly attention is his *Dialogue Between a Philosopher and a Student of the Common Laws of England* (1666), ed. Joseph Cropsey (Chicago: University of Chicago Press, 1971). I return to the significance of the dialogue form below.

little noticed by its interpreters. Failure to account for the dialogue form, or to understand it, has led to a series of misinterpretations, misinterpretations that leave one with the impression of a book not worth reading. I intend to correct the predominant contention that *Behemoth* is primarily an Hobbesian account of historical events by considering the role the dialogue form plays in the history it recounts. When compared to other Restoration histories of the war and even to the historiographical debates of the seventeenth century in which Hobbes was immersed, we shall see that *Behemoth* stands apart as a different kind of text. More important than this, we shall see that the presentation and use of history in *Behemoth* runs counter to Hobbes's own writings on the proper work of history, writings spanning a period from 1629 with the publication of his translation of Thucydides (and possibly as early as 1620[2]) to 1674 and his translation of the *Iliad* and *Odyssey*.

The history of *Behemoth*

Hobbes's *Behemoth* has received increased attention in recent years, despite the fact that the only available editions are problematic. The version found in Molesworth's nineteenth-century collection of the works of Hobbes contains a less than critical edition of *Behemoth*. At the end of that same century Ferdinand Tönnies published his transcription of a much more authoritative manuscript copy held by St. John's College, Oxford.[3]

2 This date refers to the publication of the anonymous *Horae Subsecivae*. Following upon a suggestion of their Hobbesian character by Leo Strauss, some of the essays in this collection have been attributed to Hobbes. See Leo Strauss, *The Political Philosophy of Hobbes*, trans. Elsa M. Sinclair (1936; reprint Chicago: University of Chicago Press, 1984), xii–xiii. Arlene W. Saxonhouse renewed interest in these essays with her 'Hobbes & the *Horae subsecivae*,,' *Polity* 13 (1981), 541–67. Statistical analysis has led Noel B. Reynolds and John L. Hilton, 'Thomas Hobbes and the Authorship of the *Horae subsecivae*', *History of Political Thought* 14 (1993), 361–80, to conclude that three of the essays were written by Hobbes. Saxonhouse and Reynolds have worked together to publish these three essays along with an interpretive essay and explanations of the statistics used in Thomas Hobbes, *Three Discourses: A Critical Edition of Newly Identified Work of the Young Hobbes*, eds N. B. Reynolds and A. W. Saxonhouse (Chicago: University of Chicago Press, 1995). Acceptance of the evidence is not universal, however. See especially John C. Fortier, 'Hobbes and "A Discourse of Laws": The Perils of Wordprint Analysis', *Review of Politics* 59 (1997), 861–87. Hilton, Reynolds, and Saxonhouse responded with 'Hobbes and "A Discourse of Laws": Response to Fortier', *Review of Politics* 59 (1997), 889–903. Fortier was given a 'Last Word' in the same issue, 906–14. An earlier debate on the same topic without the statistical analysis can be found between F. O. Wolf, *Die neue Wissenshaft des Thomas Hobbes* (Stuttgart-Bad Cannstatt: Frohmann-Holzboog, 1969) and Douglas Bush, 'Hobbes, William Cavendish, and "Essays"', *Notes and Queries* 20 (May 1973), 162–4.

3 The St. John's College MS is apparently written in the hand of Hobbes's amanuensis with marginal corrections in Hobbes's own hand. The handwriting and the fact that *Behemoth* seems to have been published without Hobbes's permission (more below) make this a far more authoritative version of the book than the one Molesworth reproduced in the 1840s. According to the records of St. John's Library, the MS came to them from Revd Charles

Unfortunately, Tönnies modernized the spelling and punctuation, and committed some errors in transcription. His edition has been reprinted twice in the twentieth century with its faults left uncorrected.[4] Yet, whatever current revival of interest in *Behemoth* there may be, it is nothing like the interest sparked when the book was first published in 1679, in the middle of the Exclusion Crisis. Within just over a year it had gone through five editions and elicited one direct rebuttal: J. Whitehall, *Behemoth Arraigned or, a Vindication of Property Against a Fanatical Pamphlet Stiled Behemoth* (London, 1680).[5]

Behemoth, or to give it its full title, *Behemoth or the Long Parliament*, has a frustratingly convoluted history which is not at all unusual for Hobbes's books. It was probably written between 1668 and 1670, although we do not find a printed edition until 1679. There are five manuscript versions other than the one at St John's College, Oxford, but we do not know their dates. Given the cost of transcription and the multiple editions following 1679, however, it would be safe to assume that they predate the first printed edition.[6] We have three surviving letters from Hobbes in which

---

Wheatly, who matriculated 28 March 1705, and died 13 May 1742. How it came into Wheatly's hands is still unknown. I would like to thank the Librarian and Fellows of St. John's College, Oxford, for the opportunity to examine the manuscript in their care.

[4] The editions from this century are Thomas Hobbes, *Behemoth, or the Long Parliament*, ed. Ferdinand Tönnies, with an introduction by M. M. Goldsmith (New York: Barnes and Noble, 1969) and Thomas Hobbes, *Behemoth, or the Long Parliament*, ed. Ferdinand Tönnies, with an introduction by Stephen Holmes (Chicago: University of Chicago Press, 1990). All page references are to the Holmes edition, although pagination is consistent throughout both. Much more attention has gone into the French and Italian translations of the book. See *Béhémoth ou le long parliament*, ed. and trans. Luc Borot (Paris: Librairie Philosophique J. Vrin, 1990), and *Behemoth*, ed. and trans. Onofrio Nicastro (Rome: Editori Laterza, 1979).

[5] See Hugh Macdonald and Mary Hargreaves, *Thomas Hobbes: A Bibliography* (London: the Bibliographical Society, 1952), 64 ff. David Wootton makes the provocative suggestion that Locke and his associates sponsored the publication of some or all five of these editions in an attempt to expose the logic of absolutism. David Wootton, 'Thomas Hobbes's Machiavellian Moments', in *The Historical Imagination in Early Modern Britain*, eds D. R. Kelley and D. H. Sacks (Cambridge: Cambridge University Press, 1997), 241. There is no evidence of this, but there is certainly evidence that Locke was alerted to the existence of *Behemoth* several years before it was published: 'You may there see likewise his History of England from 1640 to 1660 about a quire of paper, which the King haz read and likes extremely, but tells him there is so much truth in it he dare not license for feare of displeasing the Bishops.' *The Correspondence of John Locke*, ed. E. S. De Beer (Oxford: The Clarendon Press, 1976), letter 268, Aubrey to Locke, 11 February 1673.

[6] See Peter Beal, *Index of English Literary Manuscripts, 1625–1700* (New York: Mansell Publishing Ltd., 1987), 2.1 A–K, 577. There are five other MSS of *Behemoth* in existence, but none bear the hand of Hobbes or his amanuensis. See Beal, *Index of English Literary Manuscripts*, 2.1. 577. On the history of Hobbes's manuscript and printed texts and his authorized and pirated texts, see Joseph Cropsey's Introduction to Thomas Hobbes, *A Dialogue Between a Philosopher and a Student of the Common Laws of England*; Richard Tuck, 'Warrender's *De Cive*', *Political Studies* 33 (1985), 308–15; M. M. Goldsmith, 'Hobbes's Ambiguous Politics', *History of Political Thought* 11 (1990), 639–74; and Philip Milton, 'Did Hobbes Translate *De Cive*?' *History of Political Thought* 11 (1990), 627–38.

he mentioned *Behemoth* (although there are no surviving letters in which he used that title), each of which expressed his intentions not to publish it. In a letter to his usual publisher, William Crooke, Hobbes wrote on 19/29 June, 1679,

> I would fain have published my Dialogue of the Civil Wars of *England*, long ago; and to that end I presented it to his Majesty: and some days after, when I thought he had read it, I humbly besought him to let me print it; but his Majesty (though he heard me gratiously, yet he) flatly refused to have it published … Therefore I pray you not to meddle in the business.[7]

It is interesting that Hobbes would write Crooke in 1679 when we have evidence that Crooke possessed a copy of this work as early as February, 1673.[8] Yet almost exactly one month after the original letter Hobbes wrote again to Crooke, this time thanking him for not publishing this book: 'I thank you for taking my advice in not stirring about the printing of my Book concerning the Civil Wars of *England*'.[9] The reason he saw fit to thank his publisher was that a pirated edition of the book was being printed and sold against his will. We know this from his letter to John Aubrey of the same day: 'I have been told that my booke of the Civill Warr is come abroad, and am sorry for it, especially because I could not get his majestye to license it, not because it is ill printed or has a foolish title set to it …'.[10] Hobbes, it seems, wanted this book published but he did not want to defy the king's commands. Although such obedience is consistent with Hobbes's political philosophy, we might also consider that in the period after 1675 Hobbes was petitioning Charles II for a renewal of his pension.[11]

Whatever might have been Hobbes's immediate reasons for not wishing to see his *Behemoth* in print in 1679, he had much earlier intended to print it and, had the king approved, would have been happy to see it when it finally did come out. The question remains, however, why did he want to publish *Behemoth*? Because this book was written near the end of his life, and because the title forces one to make a comparison with Hobbes's much more famous work, *Leviathan*, it is difficult to consider *Behemoth* as a freestanding work of history. Nevertheless, it is, with a few

---

7 *The Correspondence of Thomas Hobbes*, ed. Noel Malcolm (Oxford: The Clarendon Press, 1997), 2. 771, letter 206.
8 Aubrey to Locke, see note 5 above.
9 *The Correspondence of Thomas Hobbes*, 2. 744, letter 209, 18/28 August, 1679.
10 Ibid., 2. 772, letter 208. The foolish title probably refers to the title of the first three pirated editions published in 1679, *The History of the Civil Wars of England From the Year 1640, to 1660*. See Macdonald and Hargreaves, *Thomas Hobbes*, 64–5. It should also be noted that none of these other manuscripts bear the full title found on the St John's MS, *Behemoth or The Long Parliament*. See Beal, *Index of English Literary Manuscripts*, 2. 1. 577.
11 See Hobbes to King Charles II, *The Correspondence of Thomas Hobbes*, 2. 774–5, letter 210 and the editor's suggested dating of the letter.

exceptions, an account of the causes and events of the civil war and, therefore, must be read within the context of seventeenth-century historiography. This is what most commentators have done, with varying success. But it is my contention that in reading *Behemoth* as a history alone, and not also as a dialogue, even the most successful interpretations have failed to give an adequate account of the book.

Behemoth as history

Insofar as the content of *Behemoth* is the history of the English civil war, it must be understood within the context of Restoration history. The most notable comparison to *Behemoth* is the account of the period written by Edward Hyde, first Earl of Clarendon, Lord Chancellor, and Hobbes's political adversary.[12] Clarendon's *The History of the Rebellion and Civil Wars in England* was written intermittently from 1649 to 1672 and published posthumously in 1702-04. But Hobbes did not come so late to history as *Behemoth*. The first book he published under his own name was a translation of Thucydides in 1629. In his introduction he called the author 'the most politic historiographer that ever wrote'.[13] Hobbes's praise for Thucydides rested upon the historian's presentation of the facts of history without interposing his own interpretation between the events and the reader. Thucydides' procedure, he argued, allows the reader to uncover the causes for himself.[14] Hobbes returned to this praise for factual reporting without interpretation at the end of his career as an historian. In his 1673 translation of *The Iliads and Odysseys of Homer* he wrote: 'For both the poet and the historian writeth only, or should do, matters of fact'.[15] These two statements, although written fifty years apart, mark Hobbes's place in a long-standing debate among seventeenth-century English historians. Some, like Hobbes, argued that the historian's task was to relate the facts without partiality. These same historians accused anyone who might

---

12 On the relationship between Hobbes and Clarendon, see Richard Tuck, *Philosophy and Government 1572–1651* (Cambridge: Cambridge University Press, 1993), 320–36.

13 Thomas Hobbes, 'To the Readers', *The History of the Grecian War written by Thucydides*, in *EW* 8. viii. One of the essays in the *Horae subsecivae* (1620) is entitled 'Of Reading History'. No one is willing to attribute this essay to Hobbes. Rather, the likely author was William Cavendish, his student. If Hobbes had an influence on the topic, perhaps even suggesting it, we might push Hobbes's interest in history back to 1620 or earlier, even if his direct authorship of the three essays in question in *Horae subsecivae* remains in doubt. On this essay and its place in contemporary historiographical debates, see Levy, 'The Background of Hobbes's *Behemoth*', in *The Historical Imagination in Early Modern Britain*, 248–50.

14 Hobbes, 'To the Readers', and 'Of the Life and History of Thucydides', *The History of the Grecian War written by Thucydides, EW* 8. viii, xxii.

15 *EW* 10. vi. Quoted in Springborg, 'Mythic History and National Historiography', in *The Historical Imagination in Early Modern Britain*, 294.

allow partisanship or even explanation to enter an account to be far more of a rhetorician than an historian.[16]

Hobbes's place in the historiographical debate, that is, his emphasis on facts over interpretation, is hard to square with what is presented in *Behemoth*. Far more causes are presented than facts, and even the facts are given an interpretation. Within the dialogue itself the character 'B' announces this clearly when responding to 'A': 'for I suppose, your purpose was, to acquaint me with the history, not so much of those actions that passed in the time of the late troubles, as of their causes, and of the councils and artifice by which they were brought to pass'.[17] We can find, however, the same admission being given by Hobbes in the dedicatory letter to Henry Bennet, Baron of Arlington. He explained that the first two dialogues uncover the 'seed' of the war in 'certain opinions in divinity and politics' and its 'growth' 'in declarations, remonstrances, and other writings between the King and Parliament published'.[18] To further distance himself from the facts of the case alone, he then revealed that the last two dialogues are brief accounts of the war 'Drawn out of Mr. Heath's chronicle'. Royce MacGillivray has pointed out that this chronicle is one of two books, either Heath's *A Brief Chronicle of All the Chief Actions* (1662) or, more likely, his *A Brief Chronicle of the Late Intestine War in the Three Kingdoms* (1661).[19] Curiously, even here Hobbes is negligent of the facts. First of all, he used Heath's book inconsistently.[20] Secondly, in the matter of the king travelling to Edinburgh after the First Bishop's War to yield to the abolition of the Scottish episcopacy, Hobbes's character 'A' gets the story wrong whereas Heath had it right.[21] If Hobbes was sincere in his

---

16   For the general terms of the debate and Hobbes's place in it, see James Sutherland, *English Literature of the Late Seventeenth Century* (Oxford: Oxford University Press, 1969), 280-8, and Springborg, 'Mythic History', 267-79. For the debate over the differences between poetry and history among Hobbes's contemporaries see Levy, 'The Background of Hobbes's *Behemoth*', 251-6. Any mention of Hobbes and rhetoric cannot overlook Quentin Skinner's *Reason and Rhetoric in the Philosophy of Hobbes* (Cambridge: Cambridge University Press, 1996). The first part of the book is an exhaustive an illuminating account of rhetoric in Renaissance England. The second part is a problematic account of Hobbes's fluctuating acceptance and rejection of rhetoric. See my objections to Skinner in 'Quentin Skinner's *Reason and Rhetoric in the Philosophy of Hobbes*', *The Journal of the History of European Ideas* 23 (1997), 35-43.
17   Hobbes, *Behemoth*, 45.
18   The letter is reproduced in the Tönnies's editions of *Behemoth*. In the St John's MS this letter is found on the back of the title page, facing the first page of the text, and is undated.
19   MacGillivray, 'Hobbes's History of the English Civil War: A Study of *Behemoth*', *Journal of the History of Ideas* 31 (1970), 182.
20   One possible reason Hobbes used Heath's *Chronicle* is that Henry Bennet gave Heath his permission to print the book in 1663. See James Heath, *A Brief Chronicle of the Late Intestine War in the Three Kingdoms of England, Scotland & Ireland with the Intervening Affairs of Treatises, and other Occurrences relating thereunto* (London: J. Best for William Lee, 1663), i.
21   See Hobbes, *Behemoth*, 29 and 75, and Heath, *Chronicle*, 17-20. MacGillivray, 'Hobbes's History', 182, points this out as a blunder on Hobbes's part. The comments on this event in

praise of Thucydides and his description of the historian's art, *Behemoth* is not a very good history. There is little evidence that Hobbes was insincere and a good deal that *Behemoth* is not a good history.

Further complicating an interpretation of *Behemoth* as history is the fact that it not only defies Hobbes's own apparent criteria for a good history, it defied all established conventions. As David Wootton has remarked, it is difficult for the modern reader to appreciate how eccentric the content of Hobbes's history was for the time. Instead of recounting events and telling the stories of great men, as historians from Livy and Tacitus to Guicciardini and Clarendon had done, Hobbes wrote about 'causes and consequences, about long-term factors and short-term triggers'.[22] *Behemoth* was, therefore, a much more modern history than should be expected.[23] Hobbes's contemporaries went to great lengths to show their readers that they could be trusted because they were present at the events. These were not interpretations, therefore, but factual accounts by eyewitnesses. One can see this from the titles alone. Consider as examples James Heath's *A Brief Chronicle of the Late Intestine War in the Three Kingdoms* (1661), *A Brief Chronicle of All the Chief Actions* (1662), and *A Brief Chronicle of the Late Intestine War* (1663), Gilbert Burnet's *Memoirs of the Dukes of Hamilton* (1676) and *History of My Own Time* (published posthumously in 1723), Edmund Ludlow's *Memoirs* (published posthumously in 1698-9), Clarendon's *The History of the Rebellion and Civil Wars in England* (published posthumously in 1702-04), John Nalson's *An Impartial Collection of the Great Affairs of State* (1682), and Bulstrode Whitelocke's *Memorials of the English Affairs* (1682). Clarendon, of course, was Lord Chancellor and Ludlow one of the judges to condemn Charles I. As for the others, they insisted that they were chronicling, impartially collecting, and remembering what they saw. By contrast with these overt attempts to demonstrate credibility, Hobbes's *Behemoth* is an anachronism.

Behemoth come in the first two dialogues, not the last two which were supposed to come from Heath's *Chronicle*. Perhaps Hobbes did not misread Heath, but why he would claim to use a source and use it only intermittently requires an explanation (see n. 20). In a later work on the same subject, however, MacGillivray points out that Charles did contemplate going to Edinburgh and that Hobbes might have misremembered. See MacGillivray, *Restoration Historians and the English Civil War* (The Hague: Martinus Nijhoff, 1974), 66. On other historical mistakes and Hobbes's use of Heath's *Chronicle*, see Nigel Smith, *Literature and Revolution in England 1640–1660* (New Haven: Yale University Press, 1994), 354f.

22 Wootton, 'Hobbes's Machiavellian Moments', 220.
23 For an account of the historiographical debates of the seventeenth century and the dominant model of history for the time, see Levy, 'Background of Hobbes's *Behemoth*'. However, Levy makes the claim that Francis Bacon had a strong influence on Hobbes's understanding of the work of the historian, 248–50. For a useful survey of other histories of the same period from Hobbes's time see James Sutherland, *English Literature of the Late Seventeenth Century*, 271–88.

There is one other anachronistic characteristic of *Behemoth*. Royce MacGillivray has pointed out the fact that, unlike his contemporaries, Hobbes did not attribute divine intervention to any of the events of the war.[24] Although MacGillivray claims that references to divine intention were incidental to the histories written by Hobbes's contemporaries, there was often little other explanation for the course of events. The Royalists believed that God returned the world to its proper order once the sins of his people had been expiated by suffering, whereas the Republicans believed that God revoked his kingdom of righteousness and returned the king because of, again, his people's sinfulness.[25] In *Behemoth*, however, there are no attributions of divine intervention or a providential plan. The causes are much more mundane. Again, they are much more modern.

It is not only the book's place in the historiographical debate of the seventeenth century that marks it as peculiar. Beyond the content, the style of *Behemoth* stands out as unique when placed alongside other Restoration histories. Hobbes chose the unusual practice of writing a dialogue history of the war. Dialogues were not unknown at the time, of course, but they tended to be used only as a device to add drama to scenes of persecution. This was especially true of the Royalist hagiographies of the time. Two notable examples include James Heath's *New Book of Loyal English Martyrs and Confessors* (1663), and David Lloyd's *Memoires of the Lives, Actions, Sufferings, and Deaths of those noble, reverend and excellent personages that suffered by death, sequestration, decimation, or otherwise in our own late intestine Wars* (1668). Short dialogues appear in both but only as tropes, not as the format for an entire book.[26]

It is impossible not to approach *Behemoth* as a puzzle. It stands-out against the background of the seventeenth century as a book out of place. And, as we shall see, it takes some work to explain how it fits into Hobbes's philosophical and political project.

Various interpretations of *Behemoth*

Between its initial publication in 1679 and the publication of Tönnies's edition in 1889, *Behemoth* was largely ignored. Between then and Goldsmith's reissue of the text in 1969, any mention of *Behemoth* was usually as an aside in a discussion of *Leviathan*. Royce MacGillivray discussed the

---

24 MacGillivray, 'Hobbes's History', 180.
25 See Earl Miner, 'Milton and the Histories', in *Politics of Discourse: the Literature and History of Seventeenth-Century England*, eds K. Sharpe and S. N. Zwicker (Berkeley: University of California Press, 1987).
26 For a discussion of these books see D. R. Woolf, 'Narrative Historical Writing in Restoration England: A Preliminary Survey', in *The Restoration Mind*, ed. W. Gerald Marshall (Cranbury, NJ: Associated University Presses, 1997), 228–9.

book for its own merits in the early seventies and Robert Kraynak wrote an important article on the book in 1982. Most of the literature on *Behemoth*, however, dates to the 1990s. Despite the long time it has taken scholars to turn to this work with any great interest, the vast majority of commentators explain *Behemoth* as an application of Hobbes's theoretical principles to real, historical events. Indeed, there are only two exceptions: Robert Kraynak and David Wootton, both of whom make important advances in our understanding of this book.

The dominant interpretation of *Behemoth* as a theoretically inspired interpretation of recent political history reads the book on the model of Marx's *The Eighteenth Brumaire of Louis Bonaparte*. According to this interpretation, Hobbes attempted to vindicate the political philosophy he presented in *Leviathan* with the empirical evidence he would present in *Behemoth*. In the words of A. P. Martinich, 'To some extent then, *Behemoth* is an elaborate "I-told-you-so"'.[27] Less provocatively, perhaps, Finlayson writes that '*Behemoth* was a practical demonstration of the truth of Hobbism'.[28] The first problem with this interpretation is that it renders *Behemoth* a very uninteresting book. If it is merely the application of Hobbes's ideas to a particular event, the ideas are still far more interesting than the application. This is probably why it has received such little attention. The second, and far more interesting problem with this general line of interpretation is that the theoretical arguments so familiar to readers of *Leviathan*, *De Cive*, and *The Elements of Law*, are absent from *Behemoth*. Hobbes did not do in *Behemoth* what so many of its readers claim he did.

The state of nature, the laws of nature, and the move to civil society do not play a central, if any, role in *Behemoth*. Certainly the conclusions reached in the book are consistent with Hobbes's general political philosophy. For instance, the character 'A' asserts that 'there can be no government where there is more than one sovereign'.[29] Yet nowhere in the discussion preceding or following this assertion is there mention of the fundamental Hobbesian doctrine of authorship, that is, the principle that

---

27 A. P. Martinich, *Thomas Hobbes* (London: Macmillan, 1997), 115.
28 Michael G. Finlayson, *Historians, Puritanism, and the English Revolution: The Religious Factor in English Politics before and after the Interregnum* (Toronto: University of Toronto Press, 1983), 49. For other interpretations in line with this general view see Richard Peters, *Hobbes* (Westport, Conn.: Greenwood Press, 1979), 64; Goldsmith, 'Introduction,' in Thomas Hobbes, *Behemoth*, xi; Royce MacGillivray, 'Hobbes's History', 179–83; idem, *Restoration Historians and the English Civil War*, 67; R. C. Richardson, *The Debate on the English Revolution* (London: Methuen & Co. Ltd., 1977), 21; Stephen Holmes, 'Introduction' in Thomas Hobbes, *Behemoth*, vii–viii; William R. Lund, 'Hobbes on Opinion, Private Judgment and Civil War', *History of Political Thought* 13 (1992), 72; and D. R. Woolf, 'Narrative Historical Writing', 212.
29 Hobbes, *Behemoth*, 77. For Hobbes's doctrine of undivided sovereignty, see especially *Leviathan*, chs 18 and 29.

at the founding of any civil society is the reduction of all the various wills to one will,

> which is as much as to say, to appoint one Man, or Assembly of men, to beare their Person; and every one to owne, and acknowledge himselfe to be Author of whatsoever he that so beareth their Person, shall Act, or cause to be Acted, in those things which concerne the Common Peace and Safetie.[30]

Instead, the only argument provided for the unity of the sovereign in *Behemoth*, if it can even be called an argument, is the history of the early German tribes, of Saxon and Angle history, and of the Norman practices of government. This is a very different argument from that presented so powerfully in his treatises.

It is true that the doctrine of undivided sovereignty as presented in *Behemoth* is consistent with the doctrine as presented in Hobbes's treatises. We should be amazed if it were not. But the doctrine is not reached in anything like the same manner as Hobbes's philosophical works. If *Behemoth* were truly an application of Hobbes's philosophical principles to this historical event, we should be able to see those principles applied to the events in a way consistent with their derivation in the philosophical texts. We do not see this. Instead, we see the same conclusions, but we see them explained in terms of history, not philosophy.

Kraynak and Wootton take the historical content of *Behemoth* far more seriously as a central concern for Hobbes, and not merely as a convenient exemplar of his wisdom. As a result, they draw far more interesting conclusions from the book and reveal that it is a text worth reading. Neither one, unfortunately, pays sufficient attention to the dialogue form in which it is written and, therefore, they do not make the most of their insights.

Kraynak argues that Hobbes's primary access to political phenomena was through the study of history. Previous students of Hobbes's work have missed this fact, he argues, because *Behemoth* is temporally out of place in Hobbes's corpus. Accordingly, 'Hobbes's histories are logically prior to his treatises because they present the problem of traditional politics and science, whereas the treatises present the solution'.[31] When Kraynak turns his attention to *Behemoth*, he argues that its 'purpose is to teach the reader lessons about the defect of contemporary political authority and to explain specifically why King Charles I was incapable of

---

30 Thomas Hobbes, *Leviathan*, ed. R. Tuck (Cambridge: Cambridge University Press, 1996), 120, ch. 17.
31 Robert Kraynak, *History and Modernity in the Thought of Thomas Hobbes* (Ithaca: Cornell University Press, 1990), 32. See also Kraynak, 'Hobbes's *Behemoth* and the Argument for Absolutism', *American Political Science Review* 76 (1982), 837.

maintaining his power and preserving civil peace'.[32] This is a very insightful suggestion, but it ignores the fact that Hobbes could have accomplished his educational purpose much more directly in a treatise. Perhaps Hobbes was reticent to put his ideas into print. This is a plausible suggestion, especially when we consider the uncertainties authors could face under the Restoration government. However, this argument would have to overcome a great deal of evidence to the contrary. Hobbes was rarely reticent. And although he was often careful to protect himself — burning all of his papers, for instance — he did not shy away from putting his bold ideas in print.

Rather than looking to the political climate in which Hobbes wrote *Behemoth*, it would be far better to search for a reason for using the dialogue form within the book itself. If we take Kraynak's suggestion that a lesson was being taught in *Behemoth* and look to the interaction between the two characters rather than the relationship between author and reader, we see a far more likely location for education. By taking Kraynak's insight and turning it back into the dialogue between the characters we will have to reject many of his conclusions, but we shall find a way to read *Behemoth* that accounts for the dialogue form.

David Wootton also pays attention to the historical content of *Behemoth* and develops some worthwhile insights as a result. The main difference between their arguments is that where Kraynak thinks *Behemoth*, as a history, is logically prior to Hobbes's treatises, Wootton claims that it is a work of philosophical history in the tradition of Tacitus, Machiavelli, and Lipsius.[33] In his own words, Wootton substitutes 'Kraynak's claim that Hobbes's theory of the state of nature derives from his study of history the more specific claim that it derives from a study of Machiavelli'.[34] Nevertheless, Wootton makes an argument about the teaching role of *Behemoth* that is not too dissimilar from Kraynak's. According to Wootton, Hobbes wrote his history in order to influence the king's actions. '*Behemoth* was nothing less than an appeal to the king to reform the church, the universities, and the political principles of the nation by requiring that Hobbesian philosophy be taught throughout the land'.[35] More specifically, the book itself was to provide the type of education needed. 'In *Behemoth* Hobbes offers, above all, interpretation, so that those who experienced the war but failed to learn from it can be taught the right conclusions'.[36] This is similar

---

32 Kraynak, *History and Modernity*, 33.
33 Wootton, 'Hobbes's Machiavellian Moments', 211.
34 Ibid., 231.
35 Ibid., 229.
36 Ibid., 220. The parallels Wootton draws between Hobbes's *Behemoth* and Machiavelli's *Prince* are particularly interesting. See ibid., 225–8.

to Kraynak's conclusion that *Behemoth* had a teaching role. It is also similar in that the two authors overlook the dialogue form and move the activity of teaching, which is clearly present in the book, outside of the dialogue itself to a relationship where it is less clearly present.

Kraynak and Wootton go well beyond the standard interpretations of *Behemoth* and their failure to account for it being a dialogue does not detract significantly from the important insights each has made. However, if we are to come to grips with what this peculiar book is about we must understand it in the form Hobbes gave it to us, that is, as a dialogue.

Almost everyone who has commented on *Behemoth* has agreed with Martinich, that the characters, 'A' and 'B', are as nondescript as their names and both represent Hobbes.[37] The contempt for Hobbes's literary or dramatic abilities is remarkable, if a reduction of the dialogue form to some sort of cheap trick is any indication of the reaction to it. According to Fritz Levy, the dialogue form diffuses the authorial voice, but serves no other purpose.[38] Even Kraynak and Wootton, in their otherwise excellent studies, give the drama very little consideration. According to Kraynak, Hobbes's use of dialogue allows him to attack his opponents rather than demonstrate his own arguments, while it also allows him to comment on their hidden motives.[39] Wootton, on the other hand, argues that the dialogue form of *Behemoth* arises out of the underlying uncertainty of knowing what power is.[40] Stephen Holmes, at least, has found some use in it: 'Unlike a straightforward narrative, the dialogue format allowed Hobbes to dispel the naïveté of an inexperienced listener, while drawing useful lessons from events'.[41] Thus most comments on the dialogue form follow those of Hobbes's rival, John Wallis, in his personal attack on Hobbes's dialogues on the physics of Robert Boyle. Wallis wrote his *Hobbius Heauton-timorumenos or A Consideration of Mr Hobbes his Dialogues* in 1662 and had this to say about Hobbes's use of the dialogue: 'He found out a middle course, by way of Dialogue, between A and B (*Thomas* and *Hobs*;) Wherein *Thomas* commends *Hobs*, and *Hobs* commends *Thomas*, and both commend *Thomas Hobs* as a third Person; without being guilty of self-commendation'.[42] Although Wallis wrote this in regards to a series of dia-

---

37 Martinich, *Thomas Hobbes*, 117. See also S. A. Lloyd, *Ideals as Interests in Hobbes's Leviathan* (Cambridge: Cambridge University Press, 1992), 190.
38 Fritz Levy, 'The Background of Hobbes's *Behemoth*,' 250.
39 Kraynak, *History and Modernity*, 34.
40 Wootton, 'Hobbes's Machiavellian Moments', 225.
41 Holmes, 'Introduction', viii.
42 John Wallis, *Hobbius Heuton-timorumenos. Or A Consideration of Mr HOBBES his Dialogues*, Addressed to the Honourable Robert Boyle, Esq. (London, 1662). The title of this work comes from the play by Menander, *Heuton-timorumenos* (*The Self-Punisher*).

logues Hobbes wrote on scientific experiments, the general reaction has been the same. Hobbes's use of the dialogue form has not been considered important to understanding those works he has wished to present as dialogues.

Noam Flinker pointed out in an essay in 1989 that most discussions of *Behemoth* fail to distinguish between the characters when quoting from the text.[43] Since the publication of his essay this should no longer be possible. In a very close study of the dramatic tension in the dialogue, and admitting that it is not one of the great literary works of the seventeenth century, Flinker points out that the characters become more individuated as the dialogue proceeds.[44] He also points out that the younger character, 'B', fails to become intellectually independent of 'A' by the end of the book.[45] At the same time, Flinker is able to demonstrate that the drama of the dialogue reveals an educational project, not the kind suggested by Kraynak or Wootton, but a project within the dialogue itself. In other words, the educational project taking place within *Behemoth* is the education of 'B' by 'A', not the education of the reader by the author, that is, us by Hobbes. We must, therefore, make a distinction between the narrative and the metanarrative.[46]

Conversation and audiences

Why would Hobbes go to the trouble of writing a dialogue that shows one person being educated by another? What could this teach? It certainly does not confirm or add to any of the arguments he made in his treatises, at least, not obviously. What it does, however, is provide an example of how to educate people. Hobbes maintained in all three of his treatises that the opinions of the people had to be educated. The best statement comes from *Leviathan*: 'And the grounds of these Rights, have the rather need to be diligently, and truly taught; because they cannot be maintained by any

---

43 Noam Flinker, 'The View from the "Devil's Mountain": Dramatic Tension in Hobbes's *Behemoth*', Hobbes Studies 2 (1989), 10. Flinker points to Goldsmith, *Hobbes's Science of Politics* (New York: Columbia University Press, 1966); Strauss, *The Political Philosophy of Hobbes: Its Basis and Its Genesis*, trans. E. M. Sinclair (1936; reprint Chicago: University of Chicago Press, 1959); and Howard Warrender, *The Political Philosophy of Hobbes: His Theory of Obligation History and Modernity* to (Oxford: The Clarendon Press, 1957), but, had he waited a year, could have added Kraynak's this list.
44 Flinker, 'The View from the "Devil's Mountain"', 10.
45 Ibid., 21.
46 For a good accounting of the interaction between narrative and metanarrative in eighteenth-century dialogues, a century after the period we are interested in here, admittedly, see Clare Brant, '"What Does That Argue for Us?": The Politics of Teaching and Political Education in Late Eighteenth-Century Dialogues', in *Pedagogy and Power: Rhetorics of Classical Learning*, eds Y. L. Too and N. Livingstone (Cambridge: Cambridge University Press, 1998).

Civill Law, or terrour of legall punishment'.⁴⁷ Although it is often overlooked, Hobbes concluded that the fear of punishment was not enough to maintain peace. People had to be educated to understand the rights of the sovereign and the duties of the subject. But how?⁴⁸

Educating an entire population is a daunting task, even with the educational systems now in place throughout modern societies. Although the population of England was well-educated for the time, there was not nearly the same system then as is now in place. Even with the educational system of a twenty-first century nation state, using the schools to educate a population in its political duties and rights is no easy matter.⁴⁹ So how did Hobbes think this might be done in the seventeenth century? We find his best and most vivid explanation in his justification for why *Leviathan* should be taught in the universities of England:

> For seeing the Universities are the Fountains of Civill, and Morall Doctrine, from whence the Preachers, and the Gentry, drawing such water as they find, use to sprinkle the same (both from the Pulpit, and in their Conversation) upon the People, there ought certainly to be great care taken, to have it pure, both from the Venime of Heathen Politicians, and from the Incantation of Deceiving Spirits.⁵⁰

Some have argued that Hobbes wanted *Leviathan* to be taught in the universities.⁵¹ And he certainly did. But this was only the beginning. The universities, and ultimately *Leviathan*, would be the source of the doctrines, but only the source. Not enough people went to universities (or go now to study *Leviathan*) to make a direct impact. The education of the

---

47   *Leviathan*, 232. See also *Leviathan*, 127 and 133; *De Cive*, eds R. Tuck and M. Silverthorne (Cambridge: Cambridge University Press, 1998), 80, 146; *The Elements of Law Natural and Politic*, ed. F. Tönnies (New York: Barnes and Noble, 1969), 183.
48   I provide a much more complete account of the questions involved and the answers to be found in Hobbes's philosophy regarding the educating of citizens in my '*Behemoth' Teaches 'Leviathan': Thomas Hobbes on Political Education* (Lanham, Maryland: Lexington Books, 2002).
49   Among the many studies of this issue see Michael X. Delli Carpini and Scott Keeter, *What Americans Know about Politics and Why It Matters* (New Haven: Yale University Press, 1996); Robert D. Putnam, *Bowling Alone: The Collapse and Revival of American Community* (New York: Simon & Schuster, 2000); Nicholas Zill, 'Civics Lessens: Youth and the Future of Democracy', *Public Perspective* (January/February, 2002); Norman Nie et al., *Education and Democratic Citizenship in America* (Chicago: The University of Chicago Press, 1996); Norman Nie and D. Sunshine Hillygus, 'Education and Democratic Citizenship', in *Making Good Citizens: Education and Civil Society*, eds D. Ravitch and J. Viteritti (New Haven: Yale University Press, 2001); Judith Torney-Purta, 'The School's Role in Developing Civic Engagement: A Study of Adolescents in Twenty-Eight Countries', *Applied Development Science* 6 (2002), 203–12; Richard Niemi and Jane Junn, *Civic Education: What Makes Students Learn* (New Haven: Yale University Press, 1998); and *Rediscovering the Democratic Purposes of Education*, eds L. M. McDonnell, P. M. Timpane, and R. Benjamin (Lawrence, Kansas: University Press of Kansas, 2000).
50   *Leviathan*, 491. See also *De Cive*, 140; *Behemoth*, 23, 71.
51   For instance, Tracy B. Strong, 'How to Write Scripture: Words, Authority, and Politics in Thomas Hobbes', *Critical Inquiry* 20 (1990), 128–59.

people would have to be transmitted through those who have been educated in the universities.

The image Hobbes used in *Leviathan* was of the preachers and gentry spitting the waters of doctrinal heterodoxy—but maybe orthodoxy?—upon the people. While this might seem distasteful, it is a useful image. According to Hobbes, people absorb doctrines from their education. They might even absorb sensibilities from what they read. He was certain, for instance, that reading Greek and Roman histories inspired rebellion against monarchs.[52] It was the education men received in the universities that most troubled him. In *Behemoth* his character 'A' states, 'But out of the Universities, came all those preachers that taught the contrary. The Universities have been to this nation, as the wooden horse was to the Trojans'.[53] The universities would have to be reformed. But in *Behemoth* we see what the consequences of a reformed university education would be. Instead of sprinkling tainted water on his interlocutor, 'A' sprinkles him with the pure water of obedience. And even though there is hardly a trace of Hobbes's philosophical arguments in the dialogue, 'B' holds all the right opinions by the end.[54] 'B' learned from his conversation with 'A'. So, too, can others learn. Hobbes made this point several times in his earlier treatises.[55] *Behemoth*, therefore, provides the reader with an example of how someone might learn political lessons through a conversation.

This brings us to the question of the intended *reader*, that is, the audience outside of the dialogue. We now know that 'B' was the intended audience of 'A's narrative. But who was supposed to read the dialogue between these two men? Given that the dialogue presents an example of educating through conversation, the intended audience must be those who might learn how to teach others through conversation. This would be the gentry, and perhaps even the preachers. The preachers have the opportunity of the pulpit, of course, but they might also be able to teach through conversations. The point is, however, that the book was intended to be read by those who might reproduce in their acquaintances what 'A' produced in 'B'. And so Hobbes's politics would be implemented through conversation.

---

52 See *Leviathan*, 225.
53 *Behemoth*, 40.
54 Perhaps the only mention of Hobbes's philosophy in *Behemoth* is the reference 'A' makes to the rules of just and unjust that have become famous, 'notwithstanding the obscurity of their author.' *Behemoth*, 39.
55 See *Leviathan*, 211, 236–7, 491; *De Cive*, 140, 146; *The Elements of Law*, 184. See also Wootton, 'Hobbes's Machiavellian Moments', 238.

Conclusion

There are two audiences in *Behemoth*. 'B' is the first audience; he is the audience of the history, the audience of the narrative. The reader is the second audience; he or she is the audience of the dialogue, the audience of the metanarrative. Understanding that there are two audiences reveals a great deal about the book. It helps explain why it was so different from contemporaneous histories. Simply put, it was not a history. This also helps us understand its place in Hobbes's philosophical and political project. *Behemoth* was not a mere confirmation of his theories, that is, a grand, historical I-told-you-so. *Behemoth* was an attempt to put some of those ideas into practice. At the end of Part II of *Leviathan*, Hobbes despaired in the following terms: 'I am at the point of believing this my labour, as uselesse, as the Common-wealth of *Plato*'.[56] He then recovered some hope, he wrote, in thinking that a sovereign might take-up his book, 'and by the exercise of entire Soveraignty, in protecting the Publique teaching of it, convert this Truth of Speculation, into the Utility of Practice'. If *Behemoth* is the project that I have argued it is, Hobbes again turned to despair.

Although Hobbes sought royal permission to print *Behemoth*, he did write it prior to any command of the sovereign to do so. True, he did not want it published without permission, as the several letters attest. But that he wrote it unprompted reveals that he lost patience and thought he might turn the truth of speculation into the utility of practice on his own initiative. This must have been an uncomfortable decision for Hobbes, the great proponent of obligation and deference to one's sovereign. Yet it was surely in keeping with his character. What we know of Hobbes is that he was pugnacious and impatient. It may be comforting to know that he retained these qualities to the end, and that they produced such a fascinating book.

---

56 *Leviathan*, 254.

Michael A. Soubbotnik

De la montagne du diable à la vérité de la loi

Sur la 'montagne du diable' Hobbes place deux interlocuteurs anonymes, deux entendements curieux et obéissants: A, le 'témoin' instruit en droit, en histoire, en philosophie ; B, le plus jeune, versé en théologie. Nulle conversion, dans le *Behemoth*, de l'un des interlocuteurs à la puissance démonstrative de l'autre, comme c'est le cas dans le *Dialogus Physicus*, mais une coopération inquisitive, inégale, certes, en ce qui concerne le déroulement factuel, mais interprétativement substantielle : l'apport de B est décisif en matière théologique et ses questions orientent le dialogue vers les motifs et les conséquences. S'offre donc le 'spectacle' de vingt années de discorde féroce et de leurs origines.[1] Toutefois, l'accent de l'incipit porte moins sur le spectacle lui-même que sur le désir de le contempler. Le 'spectacle de toutes les sortes d'injustice et de toutes les formes de folie' n'est rien sans le *désir* de l'observer et de le 'considérer'.[2]

L'analyse historique du *Behemoth* est avant tout le fait d'esprits *curieux*. Véritable moteur du dialogue, la *curiosité* est cette passion qui sous-tend le comput de la raison et l'entreprise à la fois épistémologique et politique d'une *éducation* à l'obéissance civile. Dans le chapitre VI du *Leviathan*, Hobbes définit la curiosité comme le désir intellectuel de 'connaître le pourquoi et le comment', qui, avec la raison, distingue radicalement l'homme des bêtes brutes. Cette 'passion singulière' est 'une concupiscence [*lust*] de l'esprit qui, par la perpétuation de la volupté dans l'inlassable et continuelle génération du savoir, excède la

---

1   B I. 165. Nous nous référons ici à la traduction française du *Behemoth* (*B*) par Luc Borot, qui en fournit la meilleure édition critique à ce jour. Par commodité, la pagination est celle de l'édition Molesworth, tome VI des *English Works*. Les références au *Leviathan* (*L*) renvoient à l'édition McPherson, Pelican Books 1968. EL désigne les *Elements of Law*, DC le *De Cive*, DCorp. le *De Corpore*

2   B I. 165.

brève véhémence de tout plaisir charnel'.³ L'excès de volupté mentale, lié à la perpétuation de l'objet, est distinctif de l'humain. La brute, enfermée dans le temps bref de l'appétit sensible et de la consommation destructrice de son objet, ignore 'le souci de connaître les causes'. La volupté incessante qui accompagne la curiosité et l'entretient naît, par contre, de l'attente 'qui vient de ce qu'on voit par avance l'aboutissement, la conséquence de certaines choses', qu'elles 'procurent ou non un plaisir sensible'. Hobbes employait déjà des termes semblables dans une lettre de 1646 au marquis de Newcastle⁴. Après avoir constaté que lorsque la curiosité animait un homme, cette passion ôtait proportionnellement autant de force à la *convoitise*, il concluait que le désir de connaissance et le désir des vaines richesses étaient mutuellement incompatibles. Or, il y a un lien évident entre *convoitise* et discorde pour autant que 'les hommes se disputant [les richesses], il déplaît à chacun que les autres les obtiennent'.⁵ Hobbes indiquait ainsi que la vocation du savoir préserve le curieux de toutes les formes que revêt cette 'rapacité de bêtes farouches' qui conduit les hommes à la guerre civile.⁶ La curiosité que manifestent les deux interlocuteurs du *Behemoth* et qu'ils ne cessent d'éveiller mutuellement l'un en l'autre, n'est pas en elle-même raison, non plus qu'usage raisonné des signes. Mais elle les installe 'passionnellement' dans l'espace d'interlocution commun qui est celui même du calcul de la paix et des causes et conséquences de la guerre, autrement dit dans la quête renouvelée des raisons d'obéir à la parole souveraine.⁷

À ce désir d'ordonner les 'données' historiques pour les muer en autant de 'signes' qui 'fassent sens' en termes d'actes, de motifs et de conséquences au regard de l'obéissance ou de la désobéissance à l'autorité, le *Behemoth* oppose d'emblée, avant même que ne débute l'analyse circonstanciée des composantes de la rébellion, la manifestation concrète de la 'rapacité' à laquelle faisait allusion la lettre de 1646. À B qui s'étonne qu'il n'y ait pas eu 'assez d'hommes [...] pour empêcher le peuple de s'unir en corps capable de s'opposer au roi', A répond par la cupidité : le roi ne tenant pas les cordons de la bourse face à la City, il ne pouvait mobiliser 'les gens du commun' qui, ne s'engageant ni pour une cause ni pour une autre, 'eussent pris parti pour n'importe quel côté, pour une solde ou du butin'. Toutefois, une autre sorte de cupidité, intellectuelle et solidaire de l'ignorance, constitue la trame du *Behemoth*

---

3   *L* I. vi. 124.
4   *EW* VII. 467.
5   *L* I.. vi. 123.
6   *DC*, Epistle Dedicatory.
7   Cf. *B* I. 213-14.

C'est sur ces deux formes de corruption du peuple: désobéissance active et indifférence au devoir d'obéissance, que s'ouvre l'analyse historique-politique proprement dite, où l'abus des mots et le mésusage du discours tiennent une place centrale. Ignorance (des principes de l'obéissance à l'autorité souverain) et rhétorique perverse (religieuse et politique) ne cessent d'être rapportées à leur arrière-plan passionnel. Ainsi construit sur son soubassement anthropologique, l'artifice discursif du *Behemoth*, polarisé par l'artifice de l'autorité souveraine, peut à la fois donner à contempler le spectacle ordonné de la guerre civile en tant que système d'actes-signes rapportés à leurs motifs et à leurs conséquences, rendre cet ordre coactivement évident et montrer, par la coopération dans le dialogue qui en constitue la forme d'exposition qu'il est à la fois obéissance et savoir du pourquoi et du comment de celle-ci.

L'on peut, sur de telles bases, aborder la liste initiale du premier dialogue. Elle répond à la question de B qui rattache la corruption du peuple à l'œuvre de 'séducteurs'. Elle s'achève sur un dernier item qui reprend cette thématique de la corruption en la rattachant à l'ignorance des devoirs des sujets. Prêtons bien attention à cette série: corruption—séduction—ignorance. Elle permet d'établir un faisceau de relations entre l'anthropologie, la théologie et l'éthique, dont le lien est à chercher dans la puissance exercée par certains types de discours et d'usage des signes.

La rhétorique captieuse des fauteurs de la rébellion corrompt les sujets en entretenant l'ignorance des raisons d'obéir aux lois civiles et en obscurcissant leur fondement.[8] Elle touche aux questions cruciales où s'entrecroisent l'exercice du pouvoir politique et les conditions de production et de circulation des discours et des interprétations. Question du gouvernement de l'Église (ministres presbytériens d'une part, papistes de l'autre, unis dans leur même lutte contre l'Église d'Angleterre) ; question de l'interprétation privée de l'Écriture (les sectes qui en détournent le principe, maintenu par Hobbes sous conditions[9]) ; à la question de la 'tyrannie' dont le *De Cive* s'emploie à montrer qu'elle n'est pas une catégorie politique mais un 'nom' expressif de haine et d'outrage[10] (les parlementaires humanistes nourris de textes antiques). Les intérêts économiques (marchands de la City et personnages cherchant qui promotion sociale qui accroissement de fortune en servant 'sous ceux qui avaient le plus d'argent'), ne reçoivent finalement leur sens politique dans le *Behemoth* que rapportés aux vicissitudes des discours.[11] La liste initiale

---

8   Cf. *B* I. 169.
9   *B* I. 191. Cf. Le problème posé en *B* I. 228 et la position affirmée 231.
10 *DC* VII. iii.
11 Sur leur ambiguïté, cf. *B* I. 231.

du *Behemoth* montre donc toute une procédure de mise en ordre des discours, des motifs, des conséquences déchiffrées comme des signes. Le rôle de la séduction, par opposition à la contrainte de cette évidence monstrative (plutôt que démonstrative) que Hobbes trouvait jadis chez Thucydide avec sa manière de mettre sous les yeux des hommes 'the ways and events of good and evil counsels',[12] témoigne de ce que le discours peut faire. Lorsqu'il est couplé aux passions 'rapaces', à l'opposé exact de la curiosité qui dévoile les ressorts de l'illusion, il y puise ses motifs, et participe de la corruption dont il provient et qu'il entretient, tout comme de l'ignorance dont il témoigne et qu'il perpétue. Ainsi s'explique la structure même du *Behemoth*, telle que la dédicace l'expose. Les deux derniers dialogues, 'court résumé de la guerre elle-même' n'ont de sens, ne sont proprement lisibles, que rapportés aux deux premiers, l'un qui 'contient le germe' de cette guerre dans 'certaines opinions de théologie et de politique', l'autre qui en rapporte la croissance 'dans ces déclarations, remontrances et [...] autres écrits publiés entre le Roi et le Parlement'.

Les papistes, les presbytériens, les sectaires et une partie au moins des évêques, partagent l'idée selon laquelle des 'autorités' spirituelles peuvent intervenir en politique dès lors qu'il est question de doctrine et que des sujets sont 'légitimés' à désobéir au pouvoir civil en vertu d'une clause de conscience. Le premier dialogue produit un long historique de cette opinion des premiers temps de l'Église jusqu'à la veille de la Guerre Civile. Le temps long révèle la continuité d'une prétention à 'déterminer des points de foi, et d'être juges, au tribunal intérieur de la conscience, des devoirs moraux'[13] que, lors de la Réforme anglaise, les évêques élèvent à l'encontre du pape pour être ensuite contestés à leur tout par les sectaires une fois la Bible officiellement diffusée en langue vulgaire et l'interprétation de l'Écriture confiée à chaque individu privé.[14] L'enjeu est tout à la fois de vérité et de pouvoir; la question est essentiellement celle de l'autorité au nom de laquelle opinions et prétentions sont avancées, donc de sa source supposée. Papistes, presbytériens, sectaires et évêques prétendent également être les dépositaires d'un discours autorisé, par le pape, par une inspiration divine ou par un droit divin investissant la fonction. On retrouve une structure similaire lorsque le texte aborde le volet parlementaire de l'analyse[15] Les Communes sont noyautées par 'un grand nombre de messieurs qui ne désiraient pas moins un gouvernement

---

12 *Hobbes's Thucydides*, ed. Richard Schlatter (Rutgers, 1975), p. 18.
13 *B* I. 171.
14 *B* I. 171 sqq.
15 *B* I. 192 sqq.

populaire dans l'État que [les] ministres dans l'Église'.[16] Ces 'gentlemen démocratiques' Hobbes sont nourris de culture humaniste gréco-latine, d'où ils tirent un certain emploi des mots 'tyrannie', 'liberté', 'gouvernement juste ou injuste', 'régime conforme ou contraire à la nature'.[17] Outre ces 'républicains' ou 'démocrates' radicaux, nous trouvons aussi dans la même série les juristes de la common law préconisant le partage de la souveraineté entre le Roi, les Lords et les Communes avec pour résultat de désarmer le Roi au cours de la Guerre Civile.[18] Ici encore, l'opinion de chacun se couvre de l'autorité, soit des Anciens qui eux-mêmes s'autorisaient de la 'nature', soit de la 'coutume' comprise comme une sorte d'essence des 'libertés des anglais'. Toutes ces opinions convergent ainsi dans la prétention à disposer d'une autorité soit divine, soit naturelle, pour se prononcer sur ce qui est 'réellement' juste et injuste, bon et mauvais, légitime et illégitime.

Dans tous ces cas, Hobbes s'emploie à montrer que l'autorité divine, naturelle ou coutumière est toujours 'enrôlée' dans le but de s'attribuer le pouvoir d'allocation des prédicats éthiques qui appartient au souverain. Cela passe par l'invention de nouveaux dogmes manifestant l'insolence des prêtres qui se moquent 'non seulement de la stupidité des gens du commun, mais aussi de celle des rois et de leurs conseillers'.[19] Ou encore par la prédication, qui ne vise pas 'à enseigner aux hommes *que* croire mais *qui* croire. Car le pouvoir des puissants n'a de fondement que dans l'opinion et la croyance du peuple'.[20] Les thèses des théologiens scolastiques sont également incompréhensibles 'à tout homme et à eux-mêmes'[21] mais cette incompréhension provoque l'admiration aussi bien des partisans de la doctrine romaine que des négligents qui préfèrent 'admirer avec les autres plutôt que de faire l'effort d'examiner'.[22] Pour résumer: (1) Le *Behemoth* rapporte systématiquement chaque opinion à une revendication d'autorité. (2) Cette revendication se réclame d'une instance telle que Dieu, la nature, la coutume, ou l'équité. (3) Elle est toujours de fait contestée. Il en résulte que. (4) la contestation intellectuelle débouche sur l'épreuve de force. Ainsi, l'hérésie, qui n'est *à proprement parler* qu'une 'opinion' devient-elle un crime aux yeux de 'celui qui veut conserver le pouvoir spirituel sur la conscience des hommes' et prétend

---

16 *B* I 192.
17 *B* I. 193-4 ; 218.
18 *B* III. 309-310.
19 *B* I. 183.
20 *B* I. 184.
21 *B* I. 185.
22 *B* I. 186.

que son opinion privée est vérité.²³ Ce processus obéit a un double ressort, psychologique et pragmatique. Le ressort psychologique est amplement développé dans le *Behemoth*. Le ressort pragmatique demande à être déchiffré à partir de la science politique hobbesienne de la parole souveraine, qui justifie le type d'enquête critique et 'curieuse' du *Behemoth*, témoigne de son caractère rationnellement obéint et montre, à l'inverse, la nécessité d'une science politique rigoureuse.

Les opinions qui s'affrontent ainsi pour s'assurer le concours du pouvoir civil et, à défaut s'en emparer, s'expriment dans des discours obscurs ou tout simplement privés de signification. Comme le montre R. Kraynak, l'usage du discours équivoque ou dépourvu de signification est sous-tendu par la *vaine-gloire intellectuelle*, ce désir qu'ont les hommes de montrer leur supériorité en sagesse et en savoir et qui suscite en eux à la fois un sentiment de supériorité tiré de la conviction d'être élu par Dieu ou d'accéder à la nature des choses et un sentiment d'insécurité issu de la nécessité de voir confirmer cette supériorité par la reconnaissance d'autrui.²⁴ Ainsi, Hobbes relève-t-il que les auteurs de la *Petition of Right* ou ceux des *Nineteen Propositions* 'étaient tous des hommes ayant une haute opinion de leur compétence en politique, laquelle n'était pas, selon eux, suffisamment prise en compte par le roi'.²⁵ Ainsi encore, les ministres veulent-ils '[attirer] à eux toute la gloire' de la lutte contre le papisme en s'en éloignant plus loin que les évêques dont ils jalousent l'autorité parce qu'ils les estiment 'moins instruits qu'eux', tandis que les gens de qualité sont jaloux 'du *Privy Council* et des principaux courtisans, qu'ils [estiment] moins avisés qu'eux'.²⁶ Chacun, persuadé de son 'élection', conteste à la loi sa force de *commandement qui dit le vrai en matière d'éthique*. La détermination passionnelle est donc aussitôt associée par Hobbes à la structure institutionnelle qui l'entretient, tant il est vrai qu'il est 'difficile pour des hommes qui ont tous une haute idée de leur intellect' et qui sortent des universités 'de se laisser convaincre qu'ils manquent des dispositions nécessaires au gouvernement d'une république'.²⁷ À l'inverse, la curiosité qui anime les interlocuteurs du *Behemoth* conjugue obéissance et usage réglé des dénomination. Ainsi la science politique est-elle à la fois la projection d'une résolution possible de la crise que décrit le *Behemoth* et le fondement de l'analyse qu'il en fournit, la juste compréhension de ce

---

23 B I. 175.
24 Cf. Richard P. Kraynak, 'Hobbes's *Behemoth* and the Argument for Absolutism', *The American Political Science Review* 76, n°4 (1982), 837–47.
25 B I. 198.
26 B I. 195.
27 B I. 192. Cf. *DC* X. 9.

qu'est une parole souveraine se situant au point de jonction de l'analyse historique et de la construction scientifique.

L'armature du *Behemoth*, sa manière d'ordonner les enjeux de l'autorité politique et religieuse, réside donc dans la mise en rapport du discours rebelle et d'une cupidité intellectuelle qui importe, pour ainsi dire, dans le domaine du savoir l'appétit qui se porte sur les objets sensibles via le désir de faire prévaloir, dans le but d'acquérir la puissance, ses opinions sur le juste et l'injuste, le bon et le mauvais. Les hommes restent dans l'état nature ou sous la menace de la guerre civile tant que 'l'appétit personnel est la mesure du bien et du mal'.[28] Parallèlement, la 'perversité' d'une réification des prédicats éthiques à des fins doctrinales et politiques est constamment associée par Hobbes, d'une part à l'ontologie traditionnelle, d'autre part à la tendance des sujets (ou de *groupes* de sujets) à procéder eux-mêmes à leur allocation.[29] La lecture combinée de *Leviathan* et de *Behemoth* montre que l'enjeu est de *vérité politique*.

Les prédicats éthiques doivent toujours s'entendre 'par rapport à la personne qui les emploie' car

> il n'existe rien qui soit tel, simplement et absolument ; ni aucune règle commune du bon et du mauvais qui puisse être empruntée à la nature des objets eux-mêmes : cette règle vient de la personne de chacun, là où il n'existe pas de république, et, dans une république, de la personne qui représente celle-ci[30]

autrement dit du souverain.[31] Hobbes tient pour *pervers*, dans l'état civil, le fait de s'*arroger*, en tant que particulier ou que groupe, la *connaissance* de ce qui est bon ou mauvais, juste ou injuste puisque la loi-commandement est la condition nécessaire et suffisante de *l'application correcte* du prédicat éthique. C'est pourquoi le *Behemoth* rappelle que le 'pouvoir [...] d'être

---

28 *L* I. xv. 216.
29 Cf. *L* IV. xlvi, éd. latine, trad. française de François Tricaud (Sirey, 1971), pp. 699-700 qui reproduit le passage en note.
30 *L* I. vi. 120. Le *De Cive* étend ce propos aux autres prédicats éthiques, *DC* II. vi. 9, 16.
31 '[...] ce que le législateur commande doit être tenu pour *bon*, et ce qu'il interdit pour *mauvais*. Et le législateur est toujours cette personne qui dispose du pouvoir suprême dans la république [...]. Puisque donc il appartient aux rois de discerner entre le *bien* et le *mal*, il est scélérat de dire comme on le fait habituellement *que celui-là seulement est roi qui agit droitement*, et qu'*il ne faut pas obéir aux rois à moins qu'ils ne nous commandent des choses justes* [...]. Avant qu'il y eût des gouvernement, *juste* et *injuste* n'avaient pas d'existence, leur nature étant seulement relative à quelque commandement et chaque action étant de par sa nature propre indifférente ; qu'une action devienne juste ou injuste procède du droit du magistrat. Les rois légitimes, par conséquent, rendent justes les choses qu'ils commandent en les commandant et injustes celles qu'ils interdisent en les interdisant. Or, les homes privés, pour autant qu'ils s'attribuent la connaissance de ce qui est bon et mauvais désirent être comme les rois ; ce qui ne se peut sans que la république soit mise en péril.' *Philosophical Rudiments concerning Government and Society*, *EW* II. 150-1.

juge des mœurs et de la doctrine' que revendiquent aussi bien les ministres que les papistes 'est une souveraineté aussi absolue que possible'.[32] Reste que commander semble un acte radicalement différent de dire le vrai. Il nous faut donc comprendre comment l'allocation des prédicats éthique par le souverain peut relever d'une opération 'performative' qui ne fasse pas sortir du champ d'application de la valeur de *vérité*. Car seule cette opération rend concevable d'enseigner 'aux hommes leur devoir, c'est-à-dire la science du juste et de l'injuste, comme on a coutume d'enseigner d'autres sciences, à partir de principes véritables et de démonstrations évidentes'.[33]

Rappelons que pour Hobbes : (1) La vérité est *in dicto*. (2) Une vérité démontrable est solidaire de la validité d'une inférence dont la conclusion comporte un terme sujet dénotant une chose *supposée*. (3) 'Les premières de toutes les vérités ont été faites par le libre-arbitre de ceux qui les premiers imposèrent des noms aux choses, ou les reçurent tout faits des autres'.[34] Si donc une proposition est vraie, cela tient à 'ce qu'il a plu aux hommes d'imposer [...] deux noms à la même chose'.[35] Tout énoncé vrai est indexé à une énonciation antérieure.

Les jugements éthiques des hommes dans l'usage privé ne sont que des 'projections' de leurs désirs et de leurs appétits. Or, ils sont bien plutôt formulés comme des revendications de la forme 'X est légitimement mien' d'où sont tirés des prétentions et des commandements immanquablement voués à l'échec. Il s'ensuit une discorde qui est moins la conséquence d'une erreur de jugement que de la prétention à faire reposer les jugements éthiques sur autre chose que sur la parole souveraine. Cette prétention fait de l'état de nature, dans le *Leviathan*, et des sociétés civiles historiquement existantes, dans le *Behemoth*, le terrain de la coexistence belliqueuse d'une multitude de petits maîtres potentiels et vains du langage moral. Pour que les prédicats éthiques aient une *signification* commune, il est requis que pour un groupe d'hommes donné, il existe un maître commun qui en détermine la dénotation en les allouant à des classes d'actions déterminées, tout effort pour contester ou modifier ces allocations menaçant du retour à l'état de guerre.[36] Ce 'qui rend vicieuse une action, [c'est] le fait de ne pas se conformer aux lois'.[37] En effet, le souverain ne tranche pas entre des possibilités préalables. Ceux qui font les lois civiles 'ne se bornent pas à dire la justice ou l'injustice des

---

32 *B* I. 173.
33 *B* I. 212-13. Cf. DC XIII. ix.
34 *De Corp.* I. iii. 8.
35 *De Corp.* I. iii. 8.
36 Cf. *L* II. xxix. 365.
37 *B* I. 219.

actions: ils la font'.[38] La prérogative dont jouit le souverain de 'faire des règles communes à tous les hommes, et de les déclarer publiquement, par quoi chacun peut savoir ce qui peut être [...] appelé juste, et ce qui peut être [...] appelé injuste, bon ou mauvais'[39] fait qu'un sujet, qui prétendrait qu'un acte est injustement prescrit ou prohibé par la loi tomberait dans une *contradiction*. Pour ne pas rompre le lien *politique* qui lie la théorie politique de Hobbes à son épistémologie, force est d'admettre que la pragmatique de Hobbes associe performativité et vérité:[40] si Hobbes distingue bien l'énonciation qui est un simple dire de celle qui est *aussi* un *faire* ou qui *vaut comme* tel, il ne dit pas que les 'performatifs' du souverain ne sont ni vrais ni faux. Il soutient seulement qu'ils *ne peuvent pas être faux*.

Pour rendre raisons des analyses du *Behemoth* qui portent sur une guerre civile, pour ainsi dire sur une société civile menacée du retour à l'état de nature, il faut distinguer deux types de considérations concernant l'usage des prédicats éthiques: celles qui se situent au *terminus a quo* de la reconstruction de l'usage de ces dénominations[41] et en fournissent une définition capable d'expliquer leur emploi hors de la société civile; celles qui concernent leur maniement au sein d'une république.[42] Les premières concernent essentiellement la manière dont les hommes *appellent* les objets de leur désir ou de leur aversion. Les secondes concernent les *jugements*, les *opinions* et les *prétentions* qui leurs sont attachées. Hobbes établit une distinction cruciale entre l'acte consistant pour un locuteur à *signifier* quelque chose et la corrélation arbitraire et/ou conventionnelle entre les mots et les choses. La distinction est aussi génétique. Un *nom* ou une *appellation* n'est d'abord rien d'autre qu'une marque arbitraire destinée à amener à l'esprit d'un homme 'quelque conception concernant la chose à laquelle elle est imposée'.[43] Utilisé comme *marque*, le mot permet à l'individu une certaine maîtrise sur le flux de ses representations.[44] Utilisé comme *signe*, le mot permet de déclarer à autrui les pensées notées au moyen des marques.[45] L'*acte de signifier pour autrui* suppose en outre que le locuteur ait *l'intention* de communiquer à un auditoire ses passions, désirs ou pensées et que cette intention lui soit attribuée par inférence. L'intention peut être remplie

---

38   *L* III. xlii, t. f. 586.
39   *DC* I. vi. 9.
40   Comme le suggérait Martin Bertman, 'Hobbes and Performatives', *Critica* 10 (1978), 41–53.
41   Cf. *L* I. vi. 120 ou *EL* I. vii. 3.
42   Cf. *L* II. xxix, t. f. 365, III. xlii, *DC* II. xii. 1.
43   *EL* I. v. 2; *Critique du De Mundo*, xxx. 14; *L* I. iv. 100 ; *DCorp*. I. ii. 1 ; *De Homine* x. 1.
44   *DCorp*. I. ii. 1; *L* I. iv. 101.
45   *L* I. iv. 101.

inadéquatement (équivocité ou ambiguïté)⁴⁶ ou bien adéquatement si la communication suscite une certaine 'évidence' du discours.⁴⁷ Mais le remplissement repose toujours sur l'interprétation du destinataire. C'est pourquoi Hobbes affirme que seul le souverain peut fixer l'interprétation de la loi et de l'Écriture. Les deux sont liées puisque le souverain étant 'juge suprême de la rectitude de toutes les interprétations de l'Écriture, obéir aux lois du roi et aux édits publics n'est pas désobéir à Dieu mais lui obéir'.⁴⁸ Ici encore, la vaine gloire combinée à l'ignorance politique peut faire croire à un ministre, par exemple 'que sa compétence dans les langues latine, grecque et hébraïque', ou une inspiration divine, 'lui donne le privilège d'imposer à tous ceux qui sont sujets d'un même souverain, le sens […] qu'il prétend trouver' dans l'Écriture.⁴⁹ Il en va semblablement, et avec les mêmes effets destructeurs du recours des juristes aux 'lois fondamentales' comme critère d'interprétation de la parole souveraine. Il devrait être tenu, dit Hobbes, pour incompréhensible 'qu'une loi puisse être tenue pour plus fondamentale qu'une autre, hormis cette loi de nature qui nous oblige tous à obéir' au souverain. Aussi bien, l'appel aux 'lois fondamentales' au cours de l'*indictment* de Strafford relève-t-il d'une rupture du pacte de parole, puisque le Parlement 'dans sa façon de se servir des mots, ne regardait jamais leur signification, mais le poids qu'ils auraient […] aux yeux de l'ignorante multitude'⁵⁰

Pour que l'intention du locuteur de communiquer puisse être reconnue, il faut que son acte de parole puisse signifier à l'auditeur que ses idées sont semblables à celle que l'institution commune des dénominations attache à celles que le discours proféré met en connexion.

> Quand un homme, en entendant parler, a les pensées que les paroles prononcées et leur mise en relation avaient comme destination, comme tâche assignée de signifier, on dit alors qu'il comprend ces paroles. La *compréhension* n'est en effet rien d'autre que la conception causée par la parole.⁵¹

L'intention de communiquer ne peut être vraiment remplie que si l'auditeur infère du discours du locuteur (et du contexte) les raisons de l'imposition des dénominations qui constituent ce discours et qu'il puisse ainsi supposer que le locuteur, par l'accomplissement de son acte de parole, réitère en quelque sorte ces raisons. Cela est possible parce qu'en vertu 'de la similitude qui existe entre les pensées et les passions d'un

---

46 Cf. *EL* I. v. 14, *L* I. iv. 102.
47 Cf. *EL* I. vi. 3.
48 *B* I. 230.
49 *B* I. 230-1.
50 *B* I. 249.
51 *L* I. iv. 108-9.

homme et les pensées et les passions d'un autre', on peut, 'se lisant soi-même', connaître 'les pensées et les passions de tous les autres hommes en des occasions semblables'.[52] Quant à 'la remémoration des noms' elle est, 'une remémoration des pactes et des *covenants* que les hommes ont fait entre eux, concernant la manière de se comprendre les uns les autres'.[53] L'exercice de la curiosité scientifique peut devenir une norme des relations sociales parce qu'elle est cet usage des signes qui répond très exactement à la nature computatrice de la raison et que 'par nature tous les hommes raisonnent de même, et bien, s'ils ont de bons principes'.[54] Toutefois, la raison s'atteint 'par l'industrie' et, de fait, les hommes se gouvernent (plutôt mal) 'selon la différence de leurs expériences, la promptitude de leur mémoire, et la façon dont ils sont inclinés vers des buts différents'.[55] De plus, le discours adressé à autrui peut avoir pour but la tromperie ou que l'auditeur ne comprenne pas les paroles prononcées mais *croie* les comprendre alors qu'il ne peut que les répéter 'à voix basse' ou les 'repasser dans [son] esprit',[56] ou encore l'éveil des passions comme dans la rhétorique des ministres et des parlementaires. C'est pourquoi 'faire connaître à autrui' mes conceptions au sens de 'lui communiquer celles-ci' exige comme condition nécessaire (mais non suffisante) l'intention d'employer le langage à cette fin et celle que cette intention puisse m'être attribuée.

Revenons aux prédicats éthiques. Hobbes explique, *négativement*, que l'emploi de la dénomination 'bon' renvoie à l'usager pour deux raisons: (1) rien n'est bon *absolute* ou *simpliciter* ; (2) la nature des objets eux-mêmes ne fournit pas de règle commune du bon et du mauvais. (1a) À l'encontre de la supposition d'un bien en soi vers lequel tous les hommes tendraient, rien ne sera jamais bon ou mauvais que pour une *personne* singulière. (1b) 'Bon' ou 'mauvais' se donnent comme des dénominations *relatives*, imposées 'aux fins de quelque comparaison':[57] la sensation enveloppe une mémoire car elle implique comparaison, sélection, association, discursivité minimale.[58] Elle est informée par un fonds d'expériences indexées de valeurs vitales négatives et positives.[59] (2) Qu'entendre par 'règle du bon et du mauvais'? Règles d'action ou règles d'usage des dénominations ? Fausse alternative. La règle d'usage est en même temps

52 *L* Introduction, 82.
53 *EL* II. viii. 13.
54 *L* I .v.115.
55 *L* I. v., t. f. 43.
56 *L* I. iv., t. f. 35.
57 Cf. *DCorp*. I. ii. 13.
58 Cf. *DCorp*. IV. xxv. 5.
59 Cf. *DCorp*. IV. xxv. 5.

une règle d'action car l'acte de langage est solidaire d'une certaine intention et d'un certain *purpose*. C'est ainsi qu'il convient, semble-t-il, de comprendre l'évocation (négative) d'une règle *commune*, y compris dans le cas où, à l'état de nature, seule 'la *personne* de l'homme' qui fait usage du terme fournit la règle.

'Bon' est donc un terme indexical, mais la *distinction* entre 'bon' et 'mauvais' est *commune*[60] car expressive d'une polarité vitale qui fait partie de leur signification, c'est-à-dire des conceptions qu'ils évoquent. L'indexicalité essentielle[61] des prédicats éthiques n'interdit pas d'attribuer une valeur de vérité aux énoncés dans lesquels ils figurent mais cette valeur de vérité est fonction de la personne. Le recours à la notion de 'personne' est crucial. Hobbes la construit sur l'inclusion mutuelle de l'appartenance et de la représentation des paroles et des actions. L'espace d'interlocution et d'interaction, dans la 'situation naturelle' comme dans la 'situation civile', est un espace de représentation des individus et de leurs actes par eux-mêmes ou par autrui: (1) Dans l'état de nature ou dans les situations privées, les individus sont à eux-mêmes leur propre personnification. Qu'un même x soit bon pour A et pour B conduit à une simple *convergence* et non à une *communauté* des usages. La *distinction* des vocables bon/mauvais est, elle, *commune* au sens strict, car conventionnelle. De même, dans un 'langage bien fait', 'bon' désigne toujours 'l'objet du désir de la personne qui parle'. (2) Il n'y a pas lieu de modifier l'analyse des prédicats éthiques dans le cadre des lois de nature mais simplement de spécifier quel type de règles ces théorèmes introduisent. (3) Les prédicats éthiques peuvent ne pas être indexés aux temps. Les phrases exprimant ce qui est jugé bon en fonction des lois de nature sont 'éternelles' (au sens *logique*) mais demeurent relatives aux personnes (à toutes les personnes, distributivement). (4) Que la signification et les dénotations de 'bon' et 'mauvais' puissent devenir communes dans l'énoncé des lois civiles tient à ce que la personne-index est le résultat du mécanisme civil de personnification et d'autorisation.

Passons aux lois de nature, que Hobbes, dans le Behemoth, objecte aux Parlementaires qui se réclament des 'lois fondamentales'. La loi est dite *de nature* au sens où le droit *de nature* est ainsi dénommé parce qu'il est 'la liberté qu'a chacun d'user comme il le veut de son pouvoir propre, pour la préservation de sa propre nature, autrement dit de sa propre vie'.[62] Le vivant humain est immédiatement confronté à la polarisation des

---

60 *EL* I. vii. 3.
61 Selon l'expression de John Perry ('The Problem of the Essential Indexical', *Noûs* 13 (1979), 3–21).
62 *L* I. xiv. 189.

sensibles selon les valeurs vitales de la conservation. Il n'est donc aucun de nous qui ne soit porté à désirer ce qui lui *semble* bon et à éviter ce qui lui *semble* mauvais'.[63] Hobbes note que nombreux sont ceux qui, dans les conditions 'culturelles' et passionnelles qui sont les leurs, 'aimeraient mieux perdre la vie' et *a fortiori* renoncer à la paix 'qu'endurer un outrage', qui, 'prenant plaisir à contempler leur propre puissance à l'œuvre dans les conquêtes, poursuivent celles-ci plus loin que leur sécurité ne le requiert'[64] et rendent par la même dangereuse pour leur semblables plus paisibles la limitation de leurs ambitions. Le *Behemoth* applique un raisonnement semblable aux manifestations de la vaine gloire intellectuelle. Si donc le contenu spécifique des comportements varie aussi drastiquement selon les situations créées par des interactions individuelles au sein desquelles tous les hommes ne se conduisent pas raisonnablement, seule la science peut déduire la rationalité de la naturalité en posant que s'il est naturel de fuir la mort, alors 'il n'est ni absurde ni répréhensible ni contraire aux décrets de la raison véritable'[65] de se protéger. Une nature, c'est ce que la raison recompose : la même chose que la vie, mais après tout le parcours de la connaissance des causes et des effets, qui est à son service. Est naturel à l'homme ce qui rentre dans la composition de sa nature mais cela n'est pas seulement raison bien que seule la raison, qui est elle-même un composant,[66] y ait accès. Sa capacité opératoire et synthétique contribue à établir des contextes favorables à la préservation de la vie. Or, l'état de nature et la guerre civile sont ces contextes-limites où toute manifestation spécifique du désir originaire de préservation est susceptible de se mettre elle-même en échec. Dire que le désir rationnel de se conserver est naturel, permet de le poser comme désir de tous en dépit des exceptions, car celles-ci relèvent de situations sociales, culturelles, contextuelles, que l'on peut expliquer et où se déploie une nature connaissable rigoureusement comme telle. Tel est le lien entre l'anthropologie du *Leviathan* et l'histoire politique du *Behemoth*. Il y a du rationnel 'hors-contexte' mais l'irrationnel est toujours contextualisé, ce pourquoi contempler la folie humaine depuis la montagne du diable, revient à en ordonner l'histoire.

La loi de nature est donc dite telle en tant qu'elle développe, en un calcul rationnel, la représentation de ce qui est propre à la conservation de la vie et que le droit naturel définit comme liberté de faire. Dans le contexte des lois de nature, tant la signification que la référence des

---

63   *DC* I. i. 7. Nous soulignons.
64   *L* I. xiii. 184-5.
65   *DC* I. i. 7.
66   *DCorp.* I. vi. 2.

dénominations éthiques sont en mesure d'acquérir une valeur pragmatique universelle, la même pour chacun puisqu'elle est indexée à la *nature* de l'homme (du point de vue des agents à leur vie) et à une 'droite raison' capable de délivrer des définitions nominales de ce qui est bon et mauvais dans le commerce des hommes. De telles définitions fournissent un corpus cohérent de règles de premier ordre, de type 'régulatif' : (1) Les actes soumis à ces règles en sont logiquement indépendants. Les descriptions et qualifications qu'on peut en donner dépendent essentiellement de leurs relations causales. (2) La règle fournit une spécification supplémentaire ou un moyen permettant à l'acte de réussir ou d'avoir les conséquences souhaitées mais elle ne définit pas l'acte et ne permet pas de signifier quel il est. (3) La relation entre les conditions d'effectuation de l'acte et l'entrée en vigueur de la règle n'est pas logique mais *empirique*. Dans le cadre des lois civiles, il existe au contraire une relation de nécessité logique entre la réalisation des conditions d'application des lois de nature et leur entrée en vigueur, relation s'exprimant sous forme de règles de second ordre, de type 'constitutif', qui frappe d'inconséquence tout recours à une 'loi fondamentale' contre la loi positive. Le problème est donc de comprendre comment la force impérative hypothétique des lois de nature se combine avec une interprétation *commune* d'énoncés du type 'x est bon' ou 'x est mauvais' en l'absence de toute institution civile.

Rappelons que tout ce qui est actuellement désiré ('bon'), suppose une sensation ou une conception actuelle supposant une mémoire et impliquant compréhension, sélection, association.[67] La sensation ainsi adossée à un fonds d'expérience est un 'jugement que nous faisons des objets par leurs phantasmes'.[68] Processus intéressant la conservation, toute sensation est en même temps appétit et aversion,[69] si bien que la relation causale entre l'objet et le sentant présente une signification pratique pour ce dernier. La succession des phantasmes requise pour qu'il y ait sensation 'n'est pas sans cause' et ce n'est pas non plus sans cause 'que les mêmes phantasmes amènent dans l'esprit d'autres phantasmes qui parfois leur sont semblables et qui parfois leur sont extrêmement dissemblables'.[70] De fait, à peu près n'importe quelle pensée est susceptible d'en susciter à peu près n'importe quelle autre. Pour rendre raison de l'ordre des associations, il faut faire intervenir la dimension du 'but', du désir : 'la pensée ou phantasme de la fin désirée ramène tous les

---

67 Cf. *DCorp.* IV. xxv. 5.
68 *DCorp.* IV. xxv. 5.
69 *De Homine* xi. 15.
70 *DCorp.* IV. xxv. 8.

phantasmes qui sont les moyens conduisant à cette fin'.⁷¹ Dans ce que Hobbes nomme l'enchaînement non réglé des pensées, 'aucune pensée marquée par la passion' ne peut 'gouverner et diriger vers soi les pensées qui la suivent, comme feraient la fin et le but d'un désir'.⁷² Le discours mental réglé qui tire au contraire sa constance de la *règle* imposée par 'quelque désir et quelque dessein' peut être de deux sortes. Soit il consiste en la recherche des causes ou des moyens produisant un effet imaginé et le discours mental est en cela commun à l'homme et aux bêtes; soit il consiste, une chose étant imaginée, à 'chercher tous les effets possibles qui peuvent être produits par celle-ci', c'est-à-dire à imaginer ce que l'on peut faire d'une chose que l'on possède.⁷³ Nous avons alors un discours mental proprement humain où nos pensées sont les 'éclaireurs' de nos désirs.⁷⁴ Toute délibération y trouve son soubassement s'il est vrai que dans le processus délibératif réglé, finalité, causalité efficiente et imprévisibilité se conjuguent dans la possibilité de créer artificiellement des contextes de prévisibilité optimale. C'est que le concours de toutes les causes d'un événement ou d'une action comprend 'un nombre *incalculable* de chaînes jointes ensemble' pour constituer la cause entière.⁷⁵ Si donc 'la dernière injonction du jugement, qui touche le bien ou le mal' pouvant résulter d'une action produit *nécessairement* son effet, ce n'est qu'à titre de dernière partie de la cause entière.⁷⁶ En outre, on peut délibérer sur l'impossible que l'on *pense* possible.⁷⁷ L'action délibérée tient donc à l'ignorance dans laquelle nous sommes du maillage des chaînes causales multiples et l'incertitude dans la prévision des actions et réactions d'autrui est facteur de conflit et de guerre.⁷⁸ La contrainte ou la violence exercées sur autrui sont en partie des tentatives de modification du contexte par imposition de régulations qui limitent la latitude de manœuvre de l'adversaire réel ou potentiel. D'une certaine manière, ce que l'agression cherche à obtenir est du même ordre que ce que parvient en principe à réaliser la loi en constituant le contexte propice à une coopération qui régule le réseau des

---

71 *DCorp*. IV. xxv. 8.
72 *L* I. iii. 95-6.
73 Ibid.
74 *L* I. viii. 139.
75 *De la liberté et de la nécessité*, *Oeuvres de Thomas Hobbes*, XI/1 (Paris: Vrin, 1993), 65 [nous soulignons].
76 Cf. par exemple Ibid., 66.
77 Cf. *L* I. vi., t. f. 55.
78 Dans la cause totale, les chaînes ne sont pas 'jointes ensemble' dans toutes leurs parties, 'mais seulement le premier maillon, le Dieu Tout Puissant'. *De la liberté et de la nécessité*, 65. La Toute Puissance, c'est la production d'un contexte de prévisibilité maximale. On pourrait dire de la puissance souveraine qu'elle est (ou devrait être) la production d'un contexte de prévisibilité *optimale*.

chaînes causales en tous les 'nœuds' où il est au pouvoir des hommes de produire quelque effet souhaité. Tout cela permet de comprendre d'une part, comment l'allocation des prédicats moraux peut s'accompagner de tentatives de réorganisation (éventuellement violentes) du contexte de discours et d'action et, d'autre part, pourquoi les hommes peuvent si aisément s'imaginer que ces prédicats désignent des propriétés objectives inscrites 'dans la nature des choses' ou issues d'une 'inspiration divine'. Le *Behemoth* montre historiquement comment les opinions erronées ou insensées concernant l'autorité politique et religieuse placent leurs tenants dans un contexte à la fois de prétention passionnelle (vaine gloire) à une forme ou une autre d'élection (divine ou naturelle) et d'incertitude maximale dans leurs interactions. D'où le recours fatal à la violence.

Par contre, 'la cause finale, le but, le dessein, que poursuivirent les hommes [...] lorsqu'ils se sont imposés ces restriction au sein desquelles on les voit vivre dans les républiques, c'est le souci de pourvoir à leur propre préservation et de vivre plus heureusement par ce moyen'.[79] Servante des passions, la raison les 'typifie' et les oriente. L'état de choses possible que les théorèmes de la raison représentent universellement doit imprimer une certaine force et une certaine direction aux désirs et aux passions. Déterminés causalement par notre expérience, les éléments de la délibération sont finalisés dans la représentation et par le langage, en un processus réglé. Du fait que la bonté d'un état de choses représenté comme possible s'étend aux moyens de le produire, on peut supposer que la paix, qui rend possible l'obtention et la conservation d'une quantité *optimale* de biens, s'impose universellement comme bonne, quelle que soit la chaîne délibérative de chacun, le désir dominant étant, par construction, celui de la conservation de la vie et de l'intégrité corporelle.

Les lois de nature relèvent d'une opération complexe dont seul un calcul rigoureux sur des dénominations conventionnelles peut rendre compte. L'impératif exprime la règle qui a guidé le calcul, l'important étant que la proposition 'la paix est bonne', convertible en 'chacun doit s'efforcer à la paix', soit *vraie* et que cette vérité puisse être atteinte *quelle que soit la série des biens synthétisés* et quel que soit l'individu qui opère cette synthèse sur la base de son expérience. Les règles d'usage et d'action liées à la dénotation des termes moraux ne cessent pas pour autant d'être indexées aux différents locuteurs de même que les référents ne cessent pas d'être différents d'une série à une autre. C'est pourquoi aucune situation n'est *constituée* au sein de laquelle des biens pourraient être effectivement communs. Reste à comprendre comment ces règles peuvent 'obliger' au for interne. Il n'est pour Hobbes d'obligation qui ne naisse de

---

[79] *L* II. xvii. 268.

l'acte propre de l'individu.⁸⁰ Au for interne, elle peut être conçue comme naissant d'un assentiment. Donner son assentiment à la première loi de nature (donc aux autres qui s'en déduisent), c'est instituer un rapport tel à ses propres actes de raisonnement qu'on se soumette volontairement aux règles du calcul rationnel et à ses résultats, et qu'on décide, dans la mesure du possible (mesure extérieurement donnée par un contexte qui demeure totalement incertain en l'absence d'autorité contraignante commune) d'abandonner la liberté que l'on avait de se comporter au gré de ses passions quelles qu'en soient les conséquences pour sa propre conservation. En ce sens, la règle est bien 'impérative' tout en exprimant une vérité, sans que pour autant la nature soit source d'obligation. Au contraire, l'obligation (au for interne et sous des conditions qui ne la rendent effective qu'au sein du 'jeu' constitué par les lois civiles) *découle* de l'assentiment à l'ordre du calcul rationnel.

Nous pouvons maintenant aborder l'examen de la performativité de la parole souveraine. Dans le *De Corpore*,⁸¹ Hobbes répartit les discours entre (1) ceux qui 'signifient les désirs et les affections', (2) ceux qui sont 'absurdes et dénués de signification' et (3) et ceux, propositions, qui 'affirment ou nient et expriment la vérité ou la fausseté'. Les discours absurdes de la métaphysique et les interprétations superstitieuses ou séditieuses des Écritures témoignent d'une 'grammaire' fautive et du *purpose* de son emploi. De ce qu'on parle pour ne rien dire ne s'ensuit pas qu'on le fasse pour rien, ni que les conséquences de l'incohérence soient incohérentes elles aussi. Il s'agit non seulement de ce que tel ou tel individu comprend ou croit comprendre mais encore de certains types de conventions sociales et discursives relevant de 'formes de vie' et de leur histoire. Ainsi le *Behemoth* présente-t-il le tableau de toute une société précipitée vers sa ruine par les modes de production et de circulation des discours qu'elle entretient: prédication, pamphlets et 'gazettes' parlementaires, *inns of court*, universités, etc. Le mot vide induit un discours qui met en échec l'interprétation en lui offrant un nombre indéfini de possibilités toutes indécidables.⁸² Il accroît ainsi l'incertitude, donc la crainte, avec pour issue la violence illégitime ou le recours à une autorité abusivement revendiquée, offerte à la contestation ou à l'obéissance fanatiques. Le propos de la vacuité métaphysique ou 'inspirée' peut ne pas être immédiatement de conquérir la souveraineté mais le devient tôt ou tard nécessairement et c'est ici l'ensemble des formes traditionnelles de production et de transmission des discours que

---

80 Cf. *L* II. xxi. 268. Voir aussi II. xxvi. 331-4.
81 *DCorp*. I. iii. 1.
82 Cf. *B* I. 228.

le *Behemoth* met en cause, 'car si les hommes ne connaissent pas leurs devoirs, qu'est-ce qui peut les forcer à obéir aux lois? Une armée, direz-vous. Mais qu'est-ce qui y forcera l'armée?'[83]

Les discours incohérents se distinguent des discours signifiant les désirs car ils ne sont pas énoncés dans le but de signifier les passions qui les motivent, bien qu'ils en soient les *symptômes*, déchiffrables, comme *Behemoth* le montre, à partir de leurs conséquences pratiques. Le *De Corpore* range les discours signifiant les désirs et les affections en trois grandes catégories: les interrogations qui 'signifient le désir de savoir', les requêtes qui 'signifient le désir d'avoir quelque chose' et toute une série d'autres actes (promesses, menaces, vœux, commandements etc.) dont Hobbes explique qu'ils sont les *indicia* d'autres affections.[84]

Ce qui caractérise le commandement c'est, les conditions de l'exercice réel ou présumé de l'autorité étant réunies, la volonté (ultime appétit d'une chaîne délibérative) qu'un acte A soit accompli (ou qu'un état de choses A ait lieu) et ce, dans une situation telle que, (1) le locuteur L ne puisse (pour une raison ou une autre) faire, en tant que simple locuteur, que A soit accompli; que (2) le destinataire D soit en mesure de faire qu'A soit le cas ; et que (3) D se trouve (réellement ou de manière présumée) dans une situation d'infériorité institutionnelle à l'égard de L. On peut dire que tout ce qui peut *d'une manière ou d'une autre* signifier la volonté de L en dénotant A 'compte pour' un ordre. Si maintenant l'on change certaines conditions portant sur le statut respectif des interlocuteurs, et/ou la relation entre L'intention de L et A, il se peut que l'expression signifiant la volonté vaille pour une requête ou un conseil. La distinction pertinente repose sur la condition imposée au commandement: 'l'interlocuteur est obligé de faire ou de s'abstenir'.[85] À suivre les *Elements*, le conseil devrait être rangé dans la catégorie des conditionnels.[86] Or le *Leviathan* préfère les ranger avec les impératifs. Il s'agit d'une diversité de points de vue. *Elements* II.x. opère un certain nombre de distinctions, importantes au regard de l'institution civile, entre loi et pacte, loi et conseil, loi divine, naturelle et civile, loi écrite et non écrite etc. *Leviathan* VI est antérieur à toute définition de la loi. Lorsque dans les *Elements* Hobbes dit que la loi est impérative, il veut simplement rappeler qu'elle est un commandement, la forme grammaticale jouant le rôle de glose. De même, l'expression conditionnelle du conseil permet de le distinguer plus nettement de l'acte législatif. La confusion de la loi et du conseil repose

---

83 *B* I. 237. Cf. Ibid., 213-14, 217.
84 *L* I. vi. 128-9.
85 *L* I. vi. 128.
86 Cf. *EL* II. x. 1.

sur une erreur que deux textes des *Elements* et du *De Cive*,[87] ainsi que divers passages du *Behemoth* rapportent à des intentions politiques perverses sous-tendues par la vaine gloire intellectuelle. Si, note Hobbes, 'les hommes donnent habituellement au conseil le nom de gouvernement', c'est surtout parce qu'ils 'envient souvent les hommes que l'on charge de donner des conseils et manifestent ainsi leur colère à l'encontre de ceux qu'ils conseillent'.[88] 'Ceux-là confondent la loi et le conseil qui estiment qu'il est du devoir d'un monarque, non seulement d'écouter ses conseillers, mais de leur obéir'.[89] D'un texte à l'autre nous passons de ceux qui ne sont pas au conseil mais souhaiteraient l'être à ceux qui y sont et souhaiteraient de cette place usurper le pouvoir législatif et la manière dont le *Behemoth* retrace l'histoire du Parlement anglais de manière à le réduire au rôle de simple conseil montre toute l'importance historique de ces analyses pragmatiques. Hobbes situe en fait son explication sur trois registres successifs. (1) Description de la manière dont les sujets, dans un contexte politique déterminé attribuent certains types d'actes à certains énoncés. On rencontre ici les formes d'équivocation qu'il s'agit d'élucider : entre loi et conseil, loi et pacte, loi et droit. (2) Déchiffrement des passions et intérêts motivant ces diverses interprétations : Qui entend faire des conseillers les véritables législateurs confond loi et conseil ; qui souhaite ôter toute force à la loi en la ramenant à des conventions vides et fragiles interprète l'énoncé législatif comme un pacte ; qui a intérêt à opposer aux prohibitions de la loi civile les permissions du droit divin interprète l'énoncé de la *lex* comme celui d'un *ius*.[90] (3) Norme d'interprétation des énoncés, norme du contexte politique susceptible de promouvoir le maintien de la paix civile. L'enjeu est toujours d'isoler la loi-commandement quelle qu'en soit la forme grammaticale.

L'axe de la 'nature' et celui de l'artifice définissent l'espace politique. D'un côté, le constructivisme politique hobbien s'adosse à l'invariant d'une nature humaine que l'état civil ne transforme jamais. C'est pourquoi il était catastrophique de la part de Charles de laisser le débat théologique sur l'arminianisme infecter la reprise en mains institutionnelle de l'Église d'Angleterre car si 'un État peut contraindre à l'obéissance', il ne peut 'changer l'opinion de ceux qui croient avoir raison'[91] puisqu'il ne s'agit pas de contenus mais de motivations passionnelles. De l'autre côté, la loi civile, parce qu'elle est langage 'en acte', est un artifice. Tout discours

---

87   *EL* II. x. 4 ; *DC* II. xiv. 1.
88   *EL* II. x. 4.
89   *DC* II. xiv. 1.
90   *DC* II. xiv. 2.
91   *B* II. 242.

concernant la puissance 'thétique' de la parole souveraine, et son éventuelle impuissance historique, dépend du point de croisement des deux coordonnées, cette 'origine' du 'jeu civil' qu'est le pacte. La parole souveraine n'a pas besoin d'une 'nature' ou d'une 'surnature' qui la légitimerait, illusion partagée par toutes les forces en présence dont le *Behemoth* fait une des causes principales de la guerre civile. Il n'y a pas lieu de chercher hors du pacte ce que l'on souhaiterait être un rapport de dépendance de l'obéissance à l'équité; et il n'y a pas lieu non plus de disjoindre l'une de l'autre au point de rattacher la première à la force et la seconde à quelque transcendance:

> c'est dans l'acte où nous faisons notre soumission que résident à la fois nos *obligations* et notre *liberté* [...], nul ne supporte en effet aucune obligation qui n'émane d'un acte qu'il a lui-même posé, puisque par nature tous les hommes sont également libres [...].[92]

Cela explique l'analyse du *Behemoth* selon laquelle l'appel au ban du Roi et le fait qu'il n'ait pas proclamé la dissolution du Parlement ne sont pas contradictoires, puisque, 'selon la loi de l'équité, qui est l'inaltérable loi de nature, un homme qui détient le pouvoir souverain ne peut pas, même s'il le désirait, céder son droit à quoi que ce soit de nécessaire à la préservation du bon gouvernement de ses sujets, à moins qu'il le fasse en termes exprès disant qu'il ne veut plus détenir le pouvoir souverain', l'abandon d'une partie de ce qui constitue la souveraineté n'étant qu'une 'erreur' politique 'qui ne provoque rien d'autre que l'invalidité de la concession elle-même'.[93] Il ne s'agit pas là d'une argutie mais d'une conséquence directe de la théorie politique hobbesienne. L'équité est intimement liée au pacte comme structure de réciprocité dans le consentement et comme artifice premier instituant le jeu civil à partir de sa motivation 'naturelle'. Elle s'avère inséparable de la loi civile en tant que cette dernière est une parole produite et 'recevable' par convention et consentement, parole présumée pouvoir se substituer à tous ces actes qu'elle engendre, qu'elle norme *mais qu'elle n'est pas*. Hobbes saisit pour ainsi dire 'à bras le corps' le problème posé par le caractère absolu de la souveraineté, une fois dépouillé de tout fondement transcendant. Légiférer est aussi peu que dire et dire *n'est pas matériellement agir*. Que doit-il en être de la parole souveraine pour que la fragilité du souverain, dieu *mortel*, se retourne (en principe) en la puissance du *dieu* mortel? Pour que ce que cette parole dise 'bon' ou 'mauvais', 'juste' ou 'injuste' *le soit* sans que pour autant 'bon' ou 'mauvais' perdent leur signification essentiellement indexicale? Bref, comment une parole peut-elle valoir un

---

92 *L* II. xxii. 268.
93 *B* III. 311.

acte? Les lois civiles, commandements et définitions tout ensemble, sont des liens forgés par convention qui sont 'attachés d'un bout aux lèvres de l'homme ou de l'assemblée à qui [les hommes] ont donné le pouvoir souverain, et de l'autre à leurs propres oreilles';[94] or ces liens, dit Hobbes, 'n'ont aucune force' par leur propre nature.

Un commandement, chez Hobbes, asserte un certain état de choses qu'il dénote, disons, pour simplifier, le fait que le destinataire accomplit ou n'accomplit pas un certain acte. Or, comme le commandement porte sur le futur, l'état de choses en question *n'est* en réalité *pas le cas*. En même temps, le commandement *signifie* le désir du locuteur, auquel s'attache toujours une évaluation qui l'exprime ('bon' ou 'mauvais', par exemple). Toutefois, en un certain sens, le commandement *dénote* bel et bien un désir, mais pas celui du locuteur: celui du *destinataire* et, plus exactement, le *dernier* désir du destinataire, le moment ultime d'une délibération. Bref, le commandement *dénote* l'acte du destinataire et le désir ultime qui le porte en *signifiant* le désir du locuteur. En ce sens, il revient au même d'asserter que l'état de choses en question est le cas et d'asserter que cet état de choses est 'bon' (dans le cas d'une prescription). Mais, dira-t-on, quelle est la valeur de vérité de cette assertion? Après tout, d'abord le locuteur, pour une raison ou pour une autre, ne *peut* pas ce qu'il *veut* (le souverain n'est rien si on ne lui obéit), ensuite l'acte dénoté n'a pas encore eu lieu et enfin le désir ultime du destinataire demeure impénétrable (tant du moins qu'il n'a pas agi, mais là est précisément tout le problème). En d'autres termes, 'dire' n'*est* pas 'faire' mais *équivaut* à 'faire', ou se 'substitue' à un faire sans jamais s'y identifier. L'acte auquel le dire se substitue est inféré, et le problème est de comprendre comment la description d'un acte ou du résultat d'un acte inexistants est tenue pour vraie. C'est précisément l'écart entre la parole et l'acte qui sert de base (avec le contexte approprié) à l'inférence de la première au second. La parole efficace est une parole garantie *institutionnellement* et l'institution n'offre une telle garantie que parce que, d'une manière ou d'une autre, elle *lie* les destinataires à un certain *type d'interprétation*. D'où l'insistance de Hobbes à faire valoir que l'efficace de la parole souveraine doit s'allier à une maîtrise sur l'interprétation de tout discours susceptible d'être constitué en autorité ou en garantie.

Qu'en est-il de la vérité ? Comme '*Veritas in dicto, non in re consistit*' et comme la proposition n'est rien en dehors de l'énoncé, la vérité doit être indexée à son énonciateur ou son locuteur.[95] 'Vrai' et 'faux' sont à concevoir comme des *relations* entre des instances énonciatives et des

---

[94] *L* II. xxi. 263–4.
[95] *DCorp*. III. 7.

énoncés.[96] Dire d'un énoncé qu'il est 'vrai' (faux), c'est dire qu'il peut (ne peut pas) être *validé* par ce qu'Alain Berrendonner appelle un 'agent vérificateur'.[97] Ce peut être le locuteur, bien sûr, mais aussi n'importe quel ensemble d'individus parlant, autrement dit le 'on' doxastique,[98] ou encore cette 'personne d'univers' ou ce 'déictique de l'ordre des choses' exprimé linguistiquement dans le 'il' de 'il pleut' ou de 'il faut', par exemple, et que l'on peut symbolises par l'ensemble vide. Les jugements de vérité comportent toujours, y compris dans le cas de la valeur classique '*p* est vrai (tout court)' (Vrai (Ø, *p*)), un argument référant à un 'participant' au procès d'énonciation. On peut considérer que l'univers de référence du discours, est un 'participant' actif de l'événement de communication en ce qu'il valide ou invalide des propositions.[99] Une propriété importante de l'agent doxastique ON, est de désigner s'importe quel ensemble d'êtres parlants, divisible d'autant de manières que l'on voudra. La 'ON-vérité' est *toujours* susceptible de voisiner avec une 'ON-fausseté'. L'opinion est fondamentalement possibilité du désaccord. Localement convergente, elle est globalement divergente. Ce constat forme l'armature des analyses de *Behemoth*, relayant historiquement, le discours du *Leviathan* sur la multitude. Et comme la 'vérité tout court' est le cas particulier de la validation par une instance tierce ultime, elle peut être le résultat de *l'enrôlement* de cet agent à la fois fantomatique et porteur d'universalité, enrôlement qui, dans le discours d'opinion, ne va jamais sans hypostase (en tant que 'nature', ou 'Dieu', par exemple). On doit en conclure que la question de la vérité est la question de la confrontation entre les discours. Une parole n'est validable que par une autre parole.[100] 'L'agent vérificateur Ø' est épistémologiquement solidaire de notre 'action d'organisation rationnelle du monde'.[101] Linguistiquement indéterminé, il est philosophiquement déterminé comme 'raison naturelle', arrimée à la conservation et à l'aménagement des conditions d'existence du vivant humain. La recherche de la paix peut donc être dite offrir une mesure naturelle de la bonté de l'artifice de la parole souveraine sans que, pour autant, celle-ci ne cesse de mesurer que ce qu'elle construit. Il est fondamental, chez Hobbes, que la puissance humaine d'artifice exercée par le langage et le raisonnement s'accompagne d'une faiblesse

---

96 Alain Berrendonner, *Éléments de pragmatique linguistique* (Paris: Minuit, 1982), 38 sqq.
97 Ibid., 58 sqq.
98 Ibid., 60.
99 Ibid., 61. Berrendonner y voit un fait de langue.
100 *DCorp*. III. 9.
101 Martin Bertman, 'Sémantique et philosophie politique', in Zarka, C.-Y. (ed.), *Hobbes, Philosophie Première, Théorie de la Science et Politique* (Paris: PUF, 1990), 171.

ontologique insurmontable sur laquelle s'appuie la curiosité obéissante mais qui inquiète la vaine gloire intellectuelle.

Les définitions-commandements de la loi civile enrôlent la raison naturelle, raison de tous distributivement, qui vient valider la 'vérité tout court' (dans l'univers de discours du *commonwealth*) de la définition souveraine du bon et du mauvais, du juste et de l'injuste par le pacte. Quand, donc, Hobbes écrit qu'il n'y a rien de plus dans l'expression de la loi civile, sinon la mention de la personne qui ordonne, qui est *persona civitatis*, la personne de la république, il livre la clef du procès de validation des énoncés du souverain. Or, les paroles de la personne publique sont celles de chacun (ont chacun pour *auteur*) et la validation de ces paroles 'autorisées' renvoie aux énoncés de la raison naturelle dont la validité est formellement universelle. Pour autant que l'univers de discours est la république elle-même, dans la loi l'univers 'parle'. Cette 'personne civile d'univers' est la preuve constructive des théorèmes de la loi de nature, la réalisation du désir de paix. C'est pourquoi il serait contradictoire de la part de chacun des sujets de refuser d'admettre la substitution de la parole souveraine aux actes non encore accomplis que 'constate' l'énoncé du commandement et de récuser ou contester l'allocation des prédicats convenant légalement à ces actes, parce que chacun des sujets se définit précisément comme *sujet* en tant qu'il est un énonciateur validant son propre énoncé. Les performatifs du souverain sont les performatifs de chaque sujet. Il revient bien aux destinataires d'inférer des énoncés qui leurs sont adressés et du contexte de leur énonciation, la 'force' qui doit leur être attribuée. La théorie politique définit les axiomes d'interprétation que des sujets rationnels doivent utiliser dans ces attributions mais ne prédit pas qu'ils les utiliseront (elle prédit, par contre, les conséquences du fait qu'ils ne les utilisent pas). Elle montre par contre où se situe la garantie que les énoncés du souverain ont bien la force de commandements. La même instance de validation, arrimée aux appétits vitaux, conduit à la recherche de la paix, puis au pacte, et se voit mise à l'œuvre dans les inférences qui, dans la situation d'interlocution, conduisent de l'explicite à l'implicite, de l'acte substituable aux paroles qui s'y substituent prenant alors force de 'performatifs'. La loi enveloppe l'artifice langagier parce que l'artifice civil qui est en grande partie langage et processus de légitimation symbolique, fournit la réponse rationnelle au problème que la nature humaine pose à la perpétuation de l'existence des individus. Le commonwealth, artifice par excellence, est le lieu où les coordonnées de la nature et de l'artifice s'ajointent dans l'artifice lui-même, inlassablement répété, de la loi. Et parce que ce 'calcul des pactes' qu'est la science politique construit la possibilité de cet objet, elle est elle-même le lieu où le langage n'est plus l'exil des choses. Si le spectacle qui s'offre depuis la Montagne du Diable est une folie, l'institution civile de la paix est ce en quoi et en vue de quoi le langage atteint le réel.

Tomaž Mastnak

Godly Democracy

Democracy is a central, if overlooked, question in *Behemoth*. Hobbes's attitude toward democracy was fairly consistent in all his writings. But in *Behemoth*, he shifts focus from the forms of governments, of which democracy is one, to democracy in practice. He also hones in on the close connection between democracy and religion. Hobbes's views clash with dominant historiographical interpretative models today and with political sensibilities of our era. But that does not mean that his views are irrelevant to our own times. Precisely in our era of democratic regime change and the encroachment of organized religion into the political sphere, *Behemoth* needs to be read and re-read carefully.

War for democracy and seduction

The English civil war, in Hobbes's view, was a war for democracy. That was a view from the Devil's Mountain. The Devil's Mountain was where, in the very beginning of *Behemoth*, the older and more experienced interlocutor *A* took on the younger interlocutor *B*, who wanted to understand the civil war:

> If in time, as in place, there were degrees of high and low, I verily believe that the highest time would be that which passed between the years of 1640 and 1660. For he that thence, as from the Devil's mountain, should have looked upon the world and observed the actions of men, especially in England,

would have seen what Hobbes in *Behemoth* told his readers. In retrospect, efforts of the forces opposing the king to establish democracy were a spectacle 'of all kinds of injustice, and of all kinds of folly, that the world could afford', produced by 'hypocrisy and self-conceit, whereof one is double iniquity, and the other double folly'.[1]

---

1   Thomas Hobbes, *Behemoth, or the Long Parliament*, with an Introduction by S. Holmes (Chicago: The University of Chicago Press, 1990), 1. This was an elegant inversion of the biblical *topos*. In the *Gospel of Luke*, the devil led Christ 'up into an high mountain, shewed

Civil war, in Hobbes's view, is the worst calamity that can befall human society. 'All calamities which human industry can avoid arise from war, especially from civil war, for from this come massacres, loneliness, and shortage of all things', Hobbes wrote in *De corpore*.

> But the cause of these things is not that humans want them; for there is no will except for the good, at least for what appears so; and it is not that they do not know that these things are evils; for who is there who does not realize that massacres and poverty are evil and harmful for themselves? Therefore, the cause of civil war is that people are ignorant of the cause of wars and peace and that there are very few who have learned their responsibilities, by which peace flourishes and is preserved.[2]

In *Behemoth*, Hobbes depicted that ignorance of the cause of wars and peace, which is itself a cause of war (of which he had written in *De corpore*), as enamorment with democracy. Usually, democracy is seen as a form of government. In *Behemoth*, Hobbes portrays democracy as a set of opinions and actions bent on unmaking government. Since actions originate in opinions, the 'seed' of the civil war was 'certain opinions in divinity and politics'.[3] Those who held those opinions endeavored to 'draw the people to their opinions'.[4] It was easy to draw the people to erroneous opinions because they were 'ignorant of their duty'.[5] Hobbes described the process through which the people were drawn to erroneous opinions as 'seduction'. Seducers were those who held 'certain opinions in divinity and politics'. The people were the seduced.

The language of seduction appears in the first work Hobbes published under his name, his translation of Thucydides's *The Peloponnesian War*. Hobbes translated the opening of Thucydides's 'Melian Dialogue' as follows: 'Since we may not speake to the multitude, for feare lest when they heare our perswasiue and vnanswerable Arguments, all at once in a continued Oration; they should chance to bee seduced, (for we know that this is the scope of your bringing vs to audience before the Few)'.[6] Here, the

---

    unto him all the kingdoms of the world in a moment of time./ And the devil said unto him, All this power will I give thee, and the glory of them' etc. Luke 4: 5–6 (I cite King James version). Hobbes took his readers to the Devil's mountain not in order to tempt them with glory and power but to denounce such temptations. In the period of his life when he felt threatened by the powerful ecclesiastics who accused him of atheism, Hobbes, with this move, posed as the anti-devil.

2 *De corpore* I. i. 7, in *OL* 1. 7; I cite English translation in Thomas Hobbes, *Computatio Sive Logica: Logic*, translation and commentary A. Martinich, eds I. C. Hungerland and G. R. Vick (New York: Abaris Books, 1981), 185.

3 *Behemoth*, Epistle Dedicatory.

4 Ibid., 23.

5 Ibid., 4.

6 *Eight Bookes of the Peloponnesian Warre Written by Thvcydides the sonne of Olorus. Interpreted with Faith and Diligence Immediately out of the Greeke by Thomas Hobbes Secretary to ye late Earle of*

Athenians were speaking to the Melians. The Athenians, the superpower of the day, came with their army to subjugate Melos. Because the Melians had responded to previous Athenian provocations, the Athens now alleged they had a *casus belli*, a pretext for war.

After encamping on Melos, the Athenians first wanted to deal with the Melians 'by way of conference'. That is, they wanted to persuade them to submit without a fight. The Melians had little choice but to do as the Athenians proposed. Their magistrates — 'the Few' — went to talk to the invaders. The Athenians scoffed at the Melians because their interlocutors were few. They saw their small number as an expression of Melian weakness. They thought the Melians were afraid of letting their people listen to, and be persuaded by, Athenian orators. In fact, the choice of 'the Few' as negotiators was but an expression of the aristocratic form of Melian government. The Athenians, on the other hand, were democrats. As democrats on an imperial mission, they could hardly be expected to respect the government they came to obliterate.[7] But they seemed to believe that their power lay in persuasion. The Melians saw things differently. 'The equity of a leasurely debate is not to be found fault withall', they responded to the Athenians,

> but this preparation for warre, not future, but already heere present, seemeth not to agree with the same. For we see that you are come to bee Iudges of the conference, and that the issue of it, if we bee superiour in argument, and therefore yeeld not, is likely to bring vs Warre; and if we yeeld, seruitude.[8]

The context in which 'seduction' appears here is highly significant.[9] It would reverberate in Hobbes's later writings, and in *Behemoth* in particular.[10] Hobbes firmly places rhetoric in the context of war, not of *studia humanitatis*. Democratic persuasion is not 'leasurely debate'. It aims at 'se-

---

Deuonshire (London, 1629), 341. See also *Thucydides, The Peloponnesian War: The Complete Hobbes Translation*, ed. D. Greene (Chicago: The University of Chicago Press, 1989), 364.

7   Jacqueline de Romilly, *Thucydides and Athenian imperialism*, trans. P. Thody (Oxford: Blackwell, 1963).

8   *Eight Bookes*, 341 (Greene, 364–5).

9   In Rex Warner's translation of Thucydides V. 85, 'the mass of the people' would 'be led astray'. Thucydides, *History of the Peloponnesian War*, trans. R. Warner and ed. M. I. Finley (Harmondsworth: Penguin, 1974), 400–1. A number of modern translations speak of seduction. The Athenians believed they would 'deceive the ears of the multitude by seductive arguments'. Thucydides, *History of the Peloponnesian War*, trans. R. Crawley (London: J. M. Dent, [1910]), 393; similarly *Thucydides*, trans. B. Jowett (Oxford: Clarendon, 1900), 2. 168. '[T]hen people won't be deceived after listening to a single long, seductive, and unrefuted speech.' *The Peloponnesian Wars*, trans. W. Blanco (New York: Norton, 1998), 227.

10 The importance of the Melian Dialogue for our understanding of Hobbes is emphasized in David Wootton, 'Thomas Hobbes's Machiavellian Moments,' in *The Historical Immagination in Early Modern Britain: History, Rhetoric, and Fiction, 1500–1800*, eds D. M. Kelley and D. H. Sacks (Cambridge: Cambridge University Press and Woodrow Wilson Center, 1997).

ducing' the 'multitude' to support a regime change. What ultimately counts is not argument but the army behind the arguer's back. Democratic persuasion is pregnant with violence. Athenian democratic orators, dismissive of their adversary's political constitution, worked toward destruction of the adversary's government. Justice is not at issue here. As the Athenians put it, both they and the Melians knew that 'in humane disputation, iustice is then only agreed on, when the necessity is equall'.[11] Justice is only respected among equally mighty. To put it bluntly, justice is dependent on might.

But might was dependent on opinion. Hobbes went beyond Thucydides and commented directly on his own times, when he famously wrote in *Behemoth* that 'the power of the mighty hath no foundation but in the opinion and belief of the people'.[12] This is why opinion played such a key role in Hobbes's understanding of the English civil war. This is why, in his analysis of and commentary on the English civil war, Hobbes paid such close attention to opinions: to 'certain opinions in divinity and politics' and to the efforts to seduce the people to accept them.

Hobbes first turned attention to the king's inability to prevent the seduction of the people. The king was unable to keep 'the people from uniting into a body able to oppose him'.[13] Since this is a Baconian definition of sedition—sedition, wrote Bacon, 'joyneth and knitteth' people 'in a Common Cause'—the king was unable to prevent sedition.[14] But since sedition is seduction beginning to bear fruit, Hobbes simply said that the king was unable to prevent the people from being seduced. The king's inability was due to his lack of soldiers. He lacked soliders because he did not have enough money. He lacked money because of the strength of 'his enemies, that pretended the people's ease from taxes, and other specious things', and had 'the command of the purses of the city of London, and of most cities and corporate towns in England, and of many particular persons besides'.[15] Even if Hobbes was right, this was a poor explanation. You cannot explain *imbecilitas regni* with *imbecilitas regni*: the king was weak because the king was weak. And Hobbes knew well that soldiers alone could not suppress dangerous opinions. He knew that 'men's dis-

---

11 *Eight Bookes*, 341 (Greene, 365). The Athenians refused to discuss 'either the justice of their demand or any substantive arguments the Melians may wish to offer'. M. Finley's note in Thucydides, *History of the Peloponnesian War* (Penguin), 614.
12 *Behemoth*, 16.
13 Ibid., 2.
14 Francis Bacon, 'Of Seditions and Troubles', in *The Essayes or Counsels, Civill and Morall*, ed. M. Kiernan (Cambridge, Mass.: Harvard University Press, 1985), 46.
15 *Behemoth*, 2.

agreements about opinions ... cannot be eliminated by arms'.[16] As he made abundantly clear later in *Behemoth*, one of the king's weaknesses was the weakness of opinions offered to him by his 'counsellors'.[17]

Hobbes quickly abandoned this analysis of royal weakness and set out instead to explain the strength of destructive opinions. The strength of those opinions was their seductive force. But the seduced were not innocent. Moreover, the people appear in *Behemoth* not only as the corrupt object of seduction; they are seducers as well. In setting the stage for his narration, Hobbes describes the people as generally indifferent to the cause of either side that was heading toward civil war. The people 'would have taken any side for pay or plunder'. Yet even while 'so corrupted', the people still needed to be seduced. This led to the question Hobbes wanted to ask: 'And what kind of people were they that could so seduce them?'[18]

They were, first, 'ministers, as they called themselves, of Christ' (the Presbyterians); second, those 'known by the name of Papists'; third, the Independents and other sectarians (Anabaptists, Fifth Monarchists, Quakers, Adamites and others 'whose names and peculiar doctrines' were not worth remembering); fourth, the admirers of 'the ancient Grecian and Roman commonwealths', enamored with popular government; fifth, the city of London and other great towns of trade; sixth, the would-be war profiteers; and seventh, 'the people in general' who were almost completely ignorant of their duty and had 'no rule of equity, but precedents and custom'.[19]

Of those who would seduce the people, the would-be war profiteers and the 'people in general' were 'the people' themselves. Aspiring profiteers who 'saw no means how honestly to get their bread' at least partially overlapped with the people who 'would have taken any side for pay or plunder'. To both categories applied the old adage that Bacon cited in his essay on seditions: 'multis utile Bellum'.[20] A further distinction of the 'people in general', besides being their own seducers, was that they chose members of Parliament from their midst and thereby created an elite that was to seduce them.

Democracy, clericalism, and forms of government

Having described a motley of advocates and disseminators of 'certain opinions in divinity and politics', and before he turned to discussing some

---

16 Thomas Hobbes, *Leviathan: with selected variants from the Latin edition of 1668*, ed. E. Curley (Indianapolis: Hackett, 1994), 488; OL 3. 509. See below, n. 60.
17 See especially *Behemoth*, 114, 116, 125.
18 Ibid., 2.
19 Ibid., 2-4.
20 Lucan I. 182; Bacon, 'Of Seditions and Troubles', 45.

of those seducers of the people in detail, Hobbes asked another question. 'I desire to know', the younger interlocutor B proclaimed, 'first, the several grounds of the pretences, both of the Pope and of the Presbyterians, by which they claim a right to govern us, as they do, in chief: and after that, from whence, and when, crept in the pretences of that Long Parliament, for a democracy'.[21] That double question interrupted the narration in order to spell out its organizing principles. The two leading questions that were to organize Hobbes's narration in *Behemoth* were the question of clerical power in secular affairs and the question of democracy. From the start, Hobbes interlinked those questions.

If the English civil war was war for democracy, then democracy was intimately connected with clericalism. Hobbes made this clear when, in his discussion of the Papists as 'one of the distempers of the state of England in the time of our late King Charles', he made a passing judgment on the English reformation. The reformation of Henry VIII and the Elizabethan settlement were for Hobbes a model solution to the centuries long struggle between spiritual and temporal power. All 'Kings and States of Christendom' should have done 'within their own respective dominions' what Henry VIII did. They should have made themselves heads of the Church to free themselves from clerical 'tyranny'.[22] The English civil war was a temporary disruption of the reformation settlement. Hobbes called it 'the interruption made in this late rebellion of the presbyterians and other democratical men'.[23] They undermined the proper relation between secular and spiritual power. As such, they subverted the power of the sovereign.

Hobbes linked democracy and clerical pretensions to power even more closely when he discussed 'that other distemper by Presbyterians'. Presbyterians strove for 'popular government in the Church' as eagerly as 'a great many gentlemen' desired 'popular government in the civil state'. Popular government, democracy, was their common denominator and shared goal. They both envied the existing authorities in church and state. So the 'democratical gentlemen' inveighed 'against tyranny' and the ministers 'preached frequently against oppression'. In that way, they drew 'the people to their opinions' and worked together to execute the 'design of changing the government from monarchical to popular'.[24]

When Hobbes wrote of the 'design of changing the government from monarchical to popular,' he was more interested in the process of bring-

---

21 *Behemoth*, 4–5.
22 Ibid., 21.
23 Ibid., 20.
24 Ibid., 23, 26.

ing about that change than in the changing forms of government. Democracy here means designing a process of change and implementing that design more than it refers to an outcome — a particular form of government. In his earlier works, Hobbes as a rule treated democracy as a form of government.[25] In *Behemoth*, he parts with that conventional discussion of democracy that prevailed in English political treatises and historiography from the early sixteenth century onward. That convention resulted from what some have called a 'domestication of the classical-humanist constitutional terminology'.[26] Hobbes said more than once in *Behemoth* that reading of 'the glorious histories and the sententious politics of the ancient popular governments of the Greeks and Romans' had made many gentlemen 'enamored' with democracy.[27] Hobbes energetically dismissed those ancient doctrines and their authors. Moreover, he joined to that dismissal an attack on the universities, which he saw as disseminating seditious doctrines.

In *Behemoth*, the doctrine of forms of government was of little importance. Here, Hobbes had said most of what he had to say about democracy before he even mentioned the three classical forms of government. The first substantial reference to those forms of government, to monarchy, oligarchy, and democracy, appeared only at the beginning of the Fourth Dialogue, in the last section of the book. At the close of the Third Dialogue, the narrative reached the establishment of the Rump Parliament. The Rump was the issue of the abolition of the House of Lords, which was considered the institution of democracy: 'And thus the kingdom is turned into a democracy,' commented Hobbes in the voice of the older interlocutor, only to immediately subvert the idea by adding: 'or rather an oligarchy'.[28] For, as Hobbes explained, the parliament was 'presently' purged of the dissenting members of the House of Commons. What was left was the Rump.

---

25   See *Elements of Law* II. xx. 3; xxi. 1–2; xxiv. 1; *De cive* vii. 1–2, 7–11; *Leviathan* (Tuck), 129–30, 133, see also. 378–9. I cite Thomas Hobbes, *Human Nature and De Corpore Politico*, ed. J. C. A. Gaskin (Oxford: Oxford University Press, 1994); Thomas Hobbes, *On the Citizen*, ed. and trans. R. Tuck and M. Silverthorne (Cambridge: Cambridge University Press, 1998); Thomas Hobbes, *Leviathan*, ed. R. Tuck (Cambridge: Cambridge University Press, 1991).

26   Michael Mendle, *Dangerous Positions: Mixed Government, the Estates of the Realm, and the Making of the* Answer to the xix propositions (University, Alabama: The University of Alabama Press, 1985), 59; for historiography, see also F. Smith Fussner, *The Historical Revolution: English Historical Writing and Thought, 1580–1640* (London: Routledge and Kegan Paul, 1962), 166–7, 169.

27   *Behemoth*, 23.

28   Ibid., 155. Paul Seaward in a note ad loc. in his forthcoming critical edition of *Behemoth* for Clarendon edition of Hobbes, called to attention that the second part of Heath's *Brief Chronicle*, beginning its narrative at this point in time, was entitled *The Democracy or, Pretended Free State*.

Hobbes continued this polemics, turning the language of the forms of government against the regicides, in the opening of the Fourth Dialogue. 'Tell me first, how this kind of government under the Rump or relic of a House of Commons is to be called,' asked the younger interlocutor B. The older interlocutor, A, was happy to oblige:

> It is doubtless an oligarchy. For the supreme authority must needs be in one man or in more. If in one, it is monarchy; the Rump therefore was no Monarch. If the authority were in more than one, it was in all, or in fewer than all. When in all, it is democracy; for every man may enter into the assembly which makes the Sovereign Court; which they could not do here. It is therefore manifest, that the authority was in a few, and consequently the state was an oligarchy.[29]

In the classical doctrine of the forms of government, oligarchy was the corrupt form of the rule of the few. By pointing out that a hardly established democracy had already turned into oligarchy, Hobbes was not giving a compliment. But his critique did not stop there. Since, by English definition, parliament was 'a meeting of the King, Lords, and Commons', the very use of 'parliament' for the assembly in power was questionable. To style the Rump—a regicide assembly in which the Lords were eliminated and the dissenting Commons purged—a 'Parliament', as 'some' did, was a pathology of language inseparable from war. 'Men may give to their assembly what name they please, what signification soever such name might formerly have had', wrote Hobbes.[30] There is an echo of Thucydides here: in war, the 'receiued value of names imposed for signification of things, was changed into arbitrary'.[31] Thucydides's words, translated by Hobbes, applied to the war for democracy. Democracy, 'set up ... with an army',[32] was eroding its own governmental form. Worse still, because language was becoming arbitrary, democracy was losing its meaning. Hobbes masterfully played that language game to undermine the faith in democracy.

When Hobbes first mentioned 'monarchy, aristocracy, or democracy' in *Behemoth* as forms of 'commonwealth', he let these formal distinctions immediately collapse. He used 'commonwealth' both as generic and spe-

---

29 *Behemoth*, 156.
30 Ibid., 157.
31 *Eight Bookes*, 198 (Greene, 204). For a modern translation and commentary, see Simon Hornblower, A *Commentary on Thucydides: Vol. I, Books I–III* (Oxford: Clarendon, 1991), 483; P. J. Rhodes, *Thucydides, History III* (Warminster: Aris & Phillips, 1994), 236–7. In relation to Hobbes, Thuc. III. 82 is refered to in Onofrio Nicastro, 'Le vocabulaire de la dissolution de l'État', in *Hobbes et son vocabulaire: Études de lexicographie philosophique*, ed. Y. Ch. Zarka (Paris: Vrin, 1992), 260; the Italian text, 'Il vocabulario della dissluzione dello Stato,' is printed in Onofrio Nicastro, *Politica e religione nel seicento inglese: Racolta di scritti* (Pisa: Edizioni ETS, 1995), here 198.
32 *Behemoth*, 155, alluding to the Pride's Purge.

cific term. As a specific term, 'commonwealth' was distinct from monarchy: 'The Greeks had for awhile their petty kings, and then by sedition came to be petty commonwealths; and then growing to be greater commonwealths, by sedition again became monarchies.'[33] Here, Hobbes let the multivalence of the term commonwealth assert itself. Was this due to his own inattentiveness or his wish to show how imprecise was the language of the forms of government itself? It does not really matter. Elsewhere, Hobbes made the forms of government an object of derision, as when he alluded to those 'men of the better sort' who, in their youth, read famous Greek and Roman authors and 'became thereby in love with their forms of government'.[34] He represented the distinctions between the forms of government as a matter of sentiment rather than thought.

Hobbes pointed out another aspect of the conceptual instability of the forms of government. Once those 'fine men', or 'men of the better sort', were enamored with the forms of government, they became averse not only to 'absolute monarchy' but 'also absolute democracy or aristocracy, all which governments they esteemed tyranny'. And aversion to tyranny, thus understood, gave birth to another love affair. They were 'in love with *mixarchy*'.[35] Since none of the simple forms of government was absolutely preferable to the other two, the notion had emerged to combine what were considered the good qualities of each of the forms. The idea goes back to the Greeks, who invented the simple forms of government. The notion of mixing was made famous by Polybius, who was the first to describe the Roman republic as a mixed regime.[36] Polybius credited Lycurgus, 'the first to draw up a constitution', with having figured out 'by a process of reasoning' the perfect combination of the strengths of the 'three forms of state', whereas the Romans arrived at the same final result—a beneficial mixture of kingship, aristocracy, and democracy—through experience. By the time that Polybius wrote, the Romans had 'the best of all existing constitutions'.[37] That was a *respublica mixta*. In Hobbes's England, those who believed in mixed government thought of modified monarchy. They 'used to praise' *mixarchy* 'by name of mixed monarchy, though it were indeed nothing else but pure anarchy'.[38]

---

33 Ibid., 70.
34 Ibid., 3.
35 Ibid., 116.
36 Paul Pedech, *La méthode historique de Polybe* (Paris: Les Belles Lettres, 1964), 319.
37 Polybius VI, iii–x. I cite Polybius, *The Histories*, trans. W. R. Paton (Cambridge, Mass.: Harvard University Press, 1960), 3. 271–93. See commentary ad loc. in F. W. Walbank, *A Historical Commentary on Polybius* (Oxford: Clarendon, 1957), 1. 643–63. For a very helpful brief discussion, see Fergus Millar, *The Roman Republic in Political Thought* (Hanover: University Press of New England, 2002), 23 ff.
38 *Behemoth*, 116–17.

What the king's counselors failed to understand, in Hobbes's account, was that mixed monarchy undermined royal authority. Mixed monarchy was a politically dangerous idea. It was also philosophically untenable since it implied division of sovereignty.[39] Sovereignty, for Hobbes, was indivisible. The advocates of *mixarchy* did not consider 'that the supreme power must always be absolute, whether it be in the King or in the Parliament'.[40] Hobbes did not say that the supreme power must be monarchical but that it had to be absolute, regardless of who held it. The forms of government were basically irrelevant for the formulation of the central concept of Hobbes's political theory. Sovereignty was as a matter of principle indifferent to forms of government. If Hobbes was 'not committed to any form of government', this was because he was, rather, 'committed to government, or to sovereignty itself'.[41]

In Hobbes's own presentation, his idea of sovereignty — and thus his civil science, the 'science of just and unjust' — was articulated against that ancient 'vain philosophy' of which the doctrine of forms of government was an essential element. He singled out Aristotle as particularly odious. As Hobbes put it in *Leviathan*, 'scarce any thing' could be 'more repugnant to Government' than the *Politics*.[42] Anti-Aristotelian declarations notwithstanding, the forms of government retained a honorable place in *Leviathan*. In *Behemoth*, their standing deteriorated. They are an object of criticism rather than a tool of analysis. Their practical value and relevance was in helping those who embraced the doctrine of the forms of government to subvert sovereignty.

I have said that Hobbes was interested more in the process of bringing about change in government than in the form of government *per se*. But democracy as a form of government was crucial for imagining and designing government change. As the design of democratic change began to produce results, however, democracy unmade the government more than it changed its form. In Hobbes's analysis of the English civil war, democracy was less an alternative to monarchy than a threat to government as such. When the 'democratical gentlemen' advocated mixed monarchy, they promoted 'pure anarchy'. Hobbes's charge against the Presbyterians was the same: they 'reduced this government into anarchy'. When the Presbyterians pulled down the existing government, they faced a problem they were unable to solve. They were incapable of establishing

---

39 Ibid., 33, 112, 114, 125.
40 Ibid., 112.
41 Geoffrey M. Vaughan, *'Behemoth' teaches 'Leviathan': Thomas Hobbes on Political Education* (Lanham, Md.: Lexington Books, 2002), vii.
42 *Leviathan* (Tuck), 461–2, 470.

government in *any* form.[43] Democracy was a set of ideas that legitimized and directed *undoing* of the government and civil order. Democracy was a practice of anti-governmentality.

Democracy in practice

Hobbes's focus in *Behemoth* was on democracy in practice. There are some precedents for such an approach in his earlier works. In the introduction to his translation of the *Peloponnesian War*, Hobbes pointed out that Thucydides characterized the Athenian democracy as 'the emulation and contention of the Demagogues, for reputation, and glory of wit'. Democratic demagogues crossed 'each others counsels to the dammage of the Publique'. Athenian democracy was also fickle. It was characterized by 'the inconstancy of Resolutions, caused by the diuersity of ends, and power of Rhetorique in the Orators; and the desperate actions vndertaken vpon the flattering aduice of such as desired to attaine, or to hold what they had attained of authority and sway amongst the common people.' Through the working of democracy 'it came to passe amongst the *Athenians*, who thought they were able to doe any thing, that wicked men and flatterers draue them headlong into those actions that were to ruin them'. Small wonder that, in Thuchydides's 'opinion touching the gouernment of the State, it is manifest that he least of all liked the *Democracy*'.[44]

However, in at least one aspect, aristocracy appeared to Thucydides as more unstable than democracy. He had reservations with regard to the 'authority of the *Few*', wrote Hobbes, 'amongst whom he saith euery one desireth to be chiefe, and they that are vnderualued, beare it with lesse patience then in *Democracy*; whereupon sedition followeth, and dissolution of the gouernement'. He even praised a 'mixarchy', to use Hobbes's term from *Behemoth*, that is, 'the gouernement of Athens, when it was mixt of the *Few* and the *Many*'. But most he commended the Athenian government when it was under the rule of one: under Pisistratus and 'when in the beginning of this Warre, it was *Democraticall* in name, but in effect *Monarchicall* vnder *Pericles*'. In conclusion, Thucydides seems to have 'best approued of *Regall Gouernment*'.[45]

Hobbes symapthized with Thucydides. He did not change his judgment of the Greek historian and the importance of his work. In his own biography, published fifty years after the appearance of the translation, Hobbes made it be known again that among the Greek historians he esteemed Thucydides more than the rest and that he had devoted his lei-

---

43 *Behemoth*, 109.
44 *Eight Bookes*, 'Of the Life and History of Thucydides' (Greene, 572).
45 Ibid. (Greene, 572-3).

surely hours to translating Thucydides's history into English 'in order to make clear to his fellow citizens the follies of the democratic Athenians'.[46] In his *Verse Life*, written between April 1672 and April 1673 and published in an anonymous English translation in 1679[/1680], Hobbes reasserted that he shared with Thucydides his aversion to democracy: 'There's none that pleas'd me like *Thucydides*./ He says Democracy's a Foolish Thing,/ Than a Republick wiser is one King.'[47] Modern historians have followed Hobbes's lead when they considered his 'distrust of democracy' to be influenced by 'the lessons of Thucydides', or when they described his translation of the *Peloponnesian War* as, for example, mounting 'a sustained argument against republican democracy'.[48]

In the *Elements of Law*, Hobbes characterized democracy as, 'in effect, no more than an aristocracy of orators, interrupted sometimes with the temporary monarchy of one orator'.[49] This is very close to Hobbes's description of Thucydides's view of the Athenian government as *'Democraticall* in name, but in effect *Monarchicall.'*[50] In *De cive*, a feature of democracy was that, under

> *popular control* [*dominatio*], there may be as many *Neros* as they are *Orators* who fawn on the *people*. For every Orator wields as much power as the *people* itself, and they have a kind of tacit agreement to turn a blind eye to each other's greed (*my turn today, yours tomorrow*), and to cover up for any of them who put innocent fellow citizens to death arbitrarily or because of private feuds.[51]

In *Leviathan*, Hobbes remembered how destructive of peace and safety were the factions of 'Aristocraticalls and Democraticalls of old time in Greece', and how seditions finally undermined the 'antient Roman Common-wealth'.[52]

---

46 T. *Hobbes Malmesburiensis Vita*, OL 1. xiv. Reproduced in English in Anthony Wood, *Athenae oxonienses: An Exact History of all the Writers and Bishops who have had their Education in the University of Oxford. To which are added the Fasti, or Annals of the said University*, ed. P. Bliss (London: Printed for F. C. and J. Rivington et al., 1813-20), 3: col. 1206.

47 *The Life of Mr. Thomas Hobbes of Malmesbury. Written by himself in Latine Poem. And now Translated into English* (London, 1680; reprint Exeter: The Rota, 1979), 4. See also T. *Hobbes Malmesburiensis Vita*, OL 1. lxxxviii: 'Sed mihi prae reliquis Thucydides placuit./ Is Democratia ostendit mihi quam sit inepta,/ Et quantum Coetu plus sapit unus Homo.' In ms., lines 82-3 are written as follows: 'Sed mihi prae reliquis Thucidides placuit./ Is Democratiam docuit me quam sit inepta.' See a critical edition in Jean Terrel, *Hobbes: vies d'un philosophe* (Rennes: Presses universitaires de Rennes, 2008), 140.

48 George Klosko and Daryl Rice, 'Thucydides and Hobbes's State of Nature', *History of Political Thought* 6 (1985), no. 3, 405; David Norbrook, *Writing the English Republic: Poetry, Rhetoric and Politics, 1627-1660* (Cambridge: Cambridge University Press, 1999), 62.

49 *Elements of Law* II. xxi. 5.

50 See n. 45.

51 *De cive* x. 7.

52 *Leviathan* (Tuck), 164, 222.

But the closest Hobbes comes to his *Behemoth*-like take on democracy was in the Latin version of *Leviathan*. That translation was published in 1668 and was probably written at least in part in the same period as *Behemoth*.[53] Here, Hobbes tackles democracy directly as an English problem. In the substantially rewritten last chapter of *Leviathan latinus*, Hobbes gives the following lapidary characterization of the English civil war: 'The democrats won, and they established a democracy; but they paid the price of their great crimes by losing it in no time at all.'[54] The downfall of democracy was first brought about by Cromwell, that 'single tyrant' who seized control of England, Scotland, and Ireland and 'confounded' the anti-royalists' 'democratic prudence (both that of the laity and that of the ecclesiastics)'. The collapse of democracy was completed by the restoration of the 'legitimate king', whom the people 'asked for pardon (i.e., acknowledged their foolishness)'.[55] In *Behemoth*, Hobbes named this sequence of events a 'revolution'.[56] That was, of course, not the 'democratic revolution', nor was it a 'revolution' in today's conventional meaning of the word.[57] It was a cyclical movement of political events, in which democracy was but a temporary disturbance.

The rise and fall of democracy in England of the mid-seventeenth century was part of a broader phenomenon 'of those civil wars concerning religion in Germany, France, and England'. The origin of those wars in general and the beginning of English troubles in particular were democratic 'principles', derived from 'the ethical and political philosophy of Aristotle and of those Romans who have followed Aristotle'. The opposite of those principles was Hobbes's own teaching.[58] *Leviathan* was both the expounding of the sound, and rejection of seditious, doctrine, written

> at the time when civil war, born in Scotland over the issue of ecclesiastical discipline, was raging in England also and in Ireland, when not

---

53 On the composition date see editor's note in *Leviathan* (Curley), lxxiii–iv. Hobbes's views of the English civil war play a role in the debate on the date of composition of *Leviathan latinus*. But the comparison has been made only between the English 1651 edition and the Latin translation, not between the Latin translation and *Behemoth*. See Z. Lubienski, *Die Grundlagen des ethisch-poilitischen Systems von Hobbes: Mit kurzem Literaturüberblick* (München: Ernst Reinhardt, 1932), 263 ff.; François Tricaud, 'Introduction du traducteur', in Thomas Hobbes, *Léviathan*, trans. F. Tricaud (Paris: Sirey, 1971), XXV–XXVI; G. A. J. Rogers and Karl Schuhmann, 'Introduction', in Thomas Hobbes, *Leviathan: A Critical Edition*, eds G. A. J. Rogers and K. Schuhmann (London: Continuum, 2005), 1. 231–4.

54 *Leviathan* (Curley), 488; *OL* 3. 509.

55 Ibid.

56 See also *Behemoth*, 204.

57 As suggested in Quentin Skinner, *Hobbes and Republican Liberty* (Cambridge: Cambridge University Press, 2008), 178. For a good brief discussion of this 'revolution', see Nicastro, 'Le vocabulaire de la dissolution de l'État', 269–73; 'Il vocabulario della dissluzione dello Stato,' 205–8.

58 *Leviathan* (Curley), 476, 488; *OL* 3. 502, 509.

only the bishops, but also the king, the law, religion and honesty had been abolished, and treachery, murder, and all the foulest crimes dominated (but masked as something else).[59]

But Hobbes's own efforts, as he noted in retrospect, were 'of little benefit then', when he intervened in the English civil war with the English *Leviathan*. He hoped that his work 'would be of more benefit after the war was over'. For this reason he translated *Leviathan* into Latin:

> Who will believe that those seditious principles are not now completely destroyed, or that there is anyone (except the democrats) who wishes the suppression of a doctrine whose tendency toward peace is as great as that of my teaching? So that this would not happen, I wanted it to be available in Latin. For I see that men's disagreements about opinions and intellectual excellence cannot be eliminated by arms. In whatever way evils of this kind arise, they must be destroyed in the same way.[60]

Democracy of the English civil war had collapsed but, in Hobbes's view, the democratic threat persisted. If the Latin translation of *Leviathan* was declared a contribution to the struggle against the democrats, I am tempted to regard *Behemoth* as well as part of the same permanent struggle: as a text whose aim it was to help wash away 'that democratic ink'.[61]

In *Behemoth*, Hobbes's treatment of democracy was not at all systematical. Hobbes did not start with a definition of democracy but rather, in the course of his *discorsi*, produced a number of equivalences and oppositions that determine our understanding of democracy. The democrats make their most memorable appearance as the 'democratical gentlemen'. Who were they? The first and easiest answer is that they were parliamentarians. The parliament was a specimen of 'democratical assemblies'[62] and was, from another perspective, an assembly intent on establishing a democracy,[63] in which it eventually succeeded.[64] As such, the democrats were to be met in the parliament, like those gentlemen who, by their 'harangues in the Parliament', made the people 'in love with democracy'.[65] But at times they also had to work for the parliament to meet, such as when they pressured the king to call the parliament. A case in point were those English 'democraticals' who, when the enforcement of the new

---

59 In the conclusion of this sentence, an observer 'brought here from a remote part of the world' fulfills the function of the view from the Devil's Mountain in *Behemoth*. *Leviathan* (Curley), 488; *OL* 3: 508–9; see also Appendix ad Leviathan III, *OL* 3: 559–60; *Leviathan* (Curley), 538–9.
60 *Leviathan* (Curley), 488; *OL* 3. 509.
61 'Itaque atramentum illud democraticum, praedicando, scribendo, disputando eluendum est.' *OL* 3. 509–10; cf. *Leviathan* (Curley), 488.
62 *Behemoth*, 68.
63 Ibid., 5, 89.
64 Ibid., 155–6.
65 Ibid., 23; see also 68, 89, 155.

Scottish Prayer Book in 1637 led to rebellion in Scotland, encouraged the Scottish Presbyterians to attack the Church establishment. They knew that the king could only hope to suppress the rebellion if he were able to raise an army, for which he lacked money. To collect the money, he needed the consent of the parliament, but he had dissolved it years ago. In Hobbes's own words, 'the thing which those democraticals chiefly then aimed at, was to force the king to call a Parliament, which he had not done for ten years before, as having found no help, but hindrance to his designs in the Parliaments he had formerly called'.[66]

The crucial defining element of the 'democraticals' is the Presbyterian connection. Hobbes generally has the 'democraticals' coupled with the Presbyterians. But he does not uniformly define that relationship. When Hobbes attributes 'this late rebellion' to 'the presbyterians and other democratical men',[67] the Presbyterians are a subset of the democrats. The democrats are also represented as an incorporating category when Hobbes comments on the 1628 Parliament. Then, the 'democratical gentlemen had received' the Presbyterians 'into their counsels for the design of changing the government from monarchical to popular, which they called liberty'.[68] Consequently, Hobbes portrayed the Presbyterians as the originators of the vices and crimes on which the majority of the members of the Long Parliament rested their democracy.[69]

Hobbes most often sees the relationship between the 'democraticals' and Presbyterians as one between equals. The Presbyterians, for example, 'had the concurrence of a great many gentlemen, that did no less desire a popular government in the civil state than these ministers did in the Church'.[70] There was a clear affinity and agreement between the aims of the two groups, and both 'those preachers and democratical gentlemen' were teaching 'rebellion and treason'.[71] They favored, animated, and assisted each other. Thus, in the prelude to the civil war, after the king had agreed that the Scots abolish episcopacy, 'the English Presbyterians and democraticals' together took steps to obtain 'the assistance of the Scotch for the pulling down of bishops in England'.[72] Both 'the democratical and Presbyterian English' had animated the Scottish Covenanters to escalate the pressure on the king.[73] To the degree they were distinct groups, the

---

66 Ibid., 28–9.
67 Ibid., 20.
68 Ibid., 26.
69 Ibid., 155.
70 Ibid., 23.
71 Ibid., 39.
72 Ibid., 30.
73 Ibid., 31.

'democratical gentlemen' and Presbyterians were allies, working together and exerting influence together.[74]

The 'democraticals' and Presbyterians were, on the one hand, either jointly opposed, or supported each other in their opposition, to the Elizabethan religious settlement, ecclesiastical government, and episcopacy.[75] On the other hand, they joined forces in their opposition to the civil government, the king, and the king's interests.[76] They jointly inveighed against tyranny and extolled liberty, which they equated with popular government.[77] In fact, they strove for their own absolute government. They were the cause of disturbance of the commonwealth.[78] They founded their democracy on vices, crime, and folly, established it with an army, and ultimately failed because they had no army to maintain it.[79]

Democracy was the outcome of the 'democraticals' action and it was indelibly marked by those who had produced it. While 'democratical' action was a 'disturbance of the commonwealth' and a cause of the dissolution of government, the government it might produce, or maintain, was unstable itself and often 'democratical' only in name. In effect, it was a reign of orators and 'Neros', of ambitious men seeking 'absolute power' for themselves. No nobler in its foundation than other governments, democracy was a spectacle 'of all kinds of injustice, and of all kinds of folly.'

Interpreting Hobbes's 'Democraticals'

Hobbes first made public his understanding of democracy in his translation of *The Peloponnesian Wars*. That understanding of democracy culminates in the pages of *Behemoth*. Hobbes's understanding of democracy was not unique in his times. It was likely to upset, but not to puzzle, his contemporaries. But it was certainly not the element of Hobbes's political thought that upset his contemporaries most. Today, his understanding of democracy jars our political sensibilities. It seems alien to much of our political thinking. Hobbes's preoccupation with religion, ecclesiastical power, and jurisdictional claims of the clergy have long been pushed to the margins of what the modern age has made of Hobbes. His views of democracy continue to be neglected, if not ignored. Small wonder that

---

74 See also, ibid., 193.
75 Ibid., 20, 22–3, 30, 88–9.
76 Ibid., 22–3, 28, 88–9.
77 Ibid., 23, 26.
78 Ibid., 22, 68.
79 Ibid., 155.

Behemoth — a work that focuses on both these issues — has been neglected, too.

If we do not want to push them aside, then how should we understand Hobbes's views of democracy in *Behemoth*? Most serious recent interpretations of Hobbes's 'democratical gentlemen' discuss these figures in the framework of 'republicanism'. But Hobbes's view of the English civil war fits badly into this interpretative model, which offers the current dominant interpretation of political thought in Hobbes's times. Within the consensus about the central importance of republicanism, the following question arises: If 'republican thought only came of age in England with the appearance of James Harrington's *The Commonwealth of Oceana* in 1656', how can 'Hobbes's claims about the headway made by republicanism before the war be reconciled with these findings of its belatedness?'[80]

This question assumes a lot. Its premise is that 'the group of malcontents later stigmatised by Hobbes in his *Behemoth* as the 'Democratical Gentlemen'[81] were republicans, or proto-republicans. But were they? Hobbes did claim that 'two groups above all' were to be blamed for 'the catastrophe of the 1640s': the Presbyterians and the 'democratical gentlemen'.[82] Presbyterians tend to be of no great interest for these historians. They identify 'democratical gentlemen' as members in the House of Commons or as the gentry.[83] But their focus is the ideas those 'democratical' members of the parliament advocated. Hobbes's treatment of those 'democratical gentlemen' was both wrong and right, in their view. On the one hand, Hobbes gave the misleading impression that 'the gentlemen in question were self-conscious exponents of a radical ideology designed to limit the powers of the crown'. In fact, the 'democratical gentlemen', according to this interpretation, were only concerned to uphold 'their traditional privileges'. But Hobbes was right to see 'that their reliance on classical arguments about freedom and servitude eventually pushed them into adopting a standpoint so radical as to be virtually republican in its constitutional allegiances'.[84]

---

[80] Martin Dzelzainis, 'Ideas in Conflict: Political and Religious Thought during the English Revolution', in *The Cambridge Companion to Writing of the English Revolution*, ed. N. H. Keeble (Cambridge: Cambridge University Press, 2001), 36.

[81] Quentin Skinner, 'Classical Liberty and the Coming of the English Civil War', in vol. 2 of *Republicanism: A Shared European Heritage*, ed. M. van Geldern and Q. Skinner (Cambridge: Cambridge University Press, 2002), 15.

[82] Quentin Skinner, *Reason and Rhetoric in the Philosophy of Hobbes* (Cambridge: Cambridge University Press, 1996), 431–2; see also Martin Dzelzainis, 'Milton's Classical Republicanism', in *Milton and Republicanism*, eds D. Armitage, A. Himy, and Q. Skinner (Cambridge: Cambridge University Press, 1995), 3–4.

[83] Skinner, *Reason and Rhetoric*, 432, 433; Dzelzainis, 'Milton's Classical Republicanism', 3.

[84] Skinner, 'Classical Liberty', 15.

This interpretation has the merit of drawing attention to *Behemoth* and Hobbes's critique of democracy. But is it defensible to translate Hobbes's 'democraticals' into republicans? What assumptions does such a translation bring into play? Republicanism, in the telling of Quentin Skinner and his colleagues, was the result of ideological radicalization. Royal power was challenged on the basis of the principles drawn (even 'entirely drawn') from the 'legal and moral philosophy of ancient Rome'.[85] Royalism is usually equated with monarchy. So republicanism becomes anti-monarchism and, as such, a constitutional position. Skinner's conclusion was that, from the 'Parliamentary perspective, the civil war began as a war of national liberation from servitude. If there was any one slogan under which the two Houses finally took up arms, it was that the people of England never, never, never shall be slaves'.[86]

Salutatory a notion as 'national liberation' might be, it is not the most convincing description of the English civil war. I wonder if Hobbes could even understand such a term. If he could not, then how could such a characterization help us understand Hobbes? Hobbes would surely like Skinner's emphasis on the importance of classical political sensibilities and ideas in England's troubles. But Hobbes spoke of 'democratical' — not republican — 'principles'.[87] Does this matter?

Before the republican turn in the history of political thought, historians from Eduard Bernstein and G. P. Gooch to Perez Zagorin would accept Hobbes's characterization of the ideas he criticized as democratic.[88] True, describing the English civil war, or its particular aspects and protagonists, in democratic terms has often been an act of appropriation. That has been the general pattern: 'Much modern historical discussion of the English revolution has been governed by attempts to appropriate it'. The 'historiography of English republicanism, despite its quality, is no exception'.[89]

Since the republican turn was an offspring of the linguistic turn in the history of political thought, speaking of republicanism where historical actors themselves did not, strikes me as inconsistent with the methodological guidelines of this historiography. What assumptions does the slogan, emblematic for the 'virtually republican' constitutional position, that 'the people of England never, never, never shall be slaves', import

85 Ibid., 14-18.
86 Ibid., 28.
87 *Behemoth*, 43 (naming Aristotle and Cicero).
88 Eduard Bernstein, *Sozialismus und Demokratie in der Grossen Englischen Revolution* (Berlin: Dietz, 1895); G. P. Gooch, *English Democratic Ideas in the Seventeenth Century* (New York: Harper & Row, 1959; first published 1898); Perez Zagorin, *A History of Political Thought in the English Revolution* (Bristol: Thoemmes Press, 1997; first published 1954), especially page 2.
89 Jonathan Scott, *England's troubles: Seventeenth-century English Political Instability in European Context* (Cambridge: Cambridge University Press, 2000), 290.

into the historical situation under discussion? What is assumed when one assumes that Hobbes's 'democraticals' were republicans?

One assumption is clearly that the civil war was fought for the people. But the anti-royalist parliamentarians, whether we choose to call them 'democratical' or 'republican', did not have much to do with 'the people'. They tended to disregard the people, just like their critic Hobbes did. But Hobbes was perhaps more respectful of the people. He saw them as helpers: With their help the Parliamentarians were to set up democracy.[90] When the people entered democratic politics, they did so as 'hands'. They 'understood not the reasons of either party'. But, paradoxically, those 'hands were to decide the controversy'.[91] That is why the people had to be seduced and, as an 'ignorant multitude', could be seduced.[92] Instrumentalized by the seducers, the (common) people appear on the scene and act as a 'tumultuous party', 'insolent rabble of the people', or 'great multitudes of clamorous people', characterized by their 'fury'.[93] Hobbes cited a declaration of the parliament that 'the people, under God, are the original of all just power'.[94] He happily denounced that statement as part of the game played by ambitious, glory-seeking men.[95]

Hobbes did not have the highest opinion of the people in politics but important 'democratical gentlemen' disdained them outright. Henry Parker was a key figure in emerging neo-classical/Roman denunciation of royal policy[96] who had 'an almost mystical sense of the identity of people and parliament'.[97] But he shuddered at the idea that 'Mechanicks, bred up illiterately to handy crafts', would be 'placed at the helm', that 'ignorance, and sordid birth ... be lifted up to the eminent offices, and places

---

90 *Behemoth*, 89.
91 Ibid., 115–16.
92 Ibid., 68, 116, 188.
93 Ibid., 64, 69, 71, 88, 97, 98.
94 Ibid., 152.
95 See Deborah Baumgold, *Hobbes's Political Theory* (Cambridge: Cambridge University Press, 1988), ch. 7; idem, 'Hobbes's Political Sensibility: The Menace of Political Ambition', in *Thomas Hobbes and Political Theory*, ed. M. G. Dietz (Lawrence, Kansas: University Press of Kansas, 1990); see also Mary Dietz, 'Hobbes's Subject as Citizen', ibid., 97; Gabriella Slomp, *Thomas Hobbes and the Political Philosophy of Glory* (New York: St. Martin's Press, 2000), especially ch. 5. For Hobbes's frequently used language of acting and gaming, see also *Behemoth*, 24, 38, 136–7, 159.
96 Skinner, 'Classical Liberty', 15–16, 21 ff. But see J. G. A. Pocock, *The Machiavellian Moment: Florentine Political Thought and the Atlantic Republican Tradition* (Princeton, N.J.: Princeton University Press, 1975), 369, who denies Parker the title of a classical republican and speaks, instead, of an 'Aristotelian populism'. Michael Mendle, 'Parliamentary Sovereignty: A very English Absolutism', in *Political discourse in Early Modern Britain*, eds N. Phillipson and Q. Skinner (Cambridge: Cambridge University Press, 1993), 118, also speaks of Parker's populism.
97 Mendle, *Dangerous Positions*, 132.

of power', that that 'which was the Foot' would be made 'the Head', 'and that the foot, which was the Head'.[98] Marchamont Nedham was another important propagandist during the civil war. From his perspective, liberation of the people would have been one of those notorious liberations against the will of the to-be-liberated, for 'the more ignorant sort of People' were declaimers against 'all alterations of Government'.[99] To have people in power (which Nedham associated with democracy, not with republicanism) was a nightmarish vision.

> Such a *Democratick*, or *Popular Forme*, that puts the whole multitude into an equall exercise of the *Supreme Authority*, under pretence of maintaining *Liberty*, is, in the Judgment of all *States-men*, the greatest enemy of *Liberty*; For, the Multitude is so Brutish, that (as the Empereur *Claudius* said) they are ever in the extreames of kindnesse or Cruelty; being void of Reason, and hurried on with unbridled violence in all their Actions, trampling down all respects of things Sacred and Civill, to make way for their *Liberty*, which *Clapmarius* calls a most dissolute *licentiousnesse*, or licence to doe even what they list.[100]

A pamphleteer shortly before the Pride's Purge best formulated the prevalent opposition to the liberty of the people for whom the alleged republicans supposedly fought: 'It is not *vox*, but *Salus populi* that is the supream law'.[101] This anonymous anti-royalist pamphleteer saw the people as dim-eyed and dull and knew that they were not to be trusted. Because the people, or the majority of them, were a 'giddy multitude', 'sensual, ignorant, and inconsiderate', foolish and 'mad men', expected to be 'bestial in their Votes' (because they supported the king), the reasonable, tyranny-hating and liberty-loving minority was not to submit to them: 'it is major reason ... and not the major voice' that was to rule.[102] *Vox populi* has a connection with *populus*, the people; but *salus populi*, the safety or well-being of the people, is decided by the voice of the sovereign, whether the sovereign is the people or not. Safety of the people, the pamphleteer declared, is 'the chiefest Lord, Rule, Reason, and Law'.[103] He did not say that the people were 'the chiefest Lord'.

---

98 [Henry Parker,] *A letter of due censure, and redargution to Lieut: Coll: John Lilburne* (London, 1650), 21, 22; see also W. K. Jordan, *Men of Substance: A Study of the Thought of Two English Revolutionaries, Henry Parker and Henry Robinson* (Chicago: The University of Chicago Press, 1942), 156.
99 Marchamont Nedham, *The case of the Common-VVealth of England, Stated: or, The Equity, Vtility, and Necessity, of a Submission to the present Government,* etc. (London, 1650), 92.
100 Nedham, *The case of the Common-VVealth of England, Stated,* 71.
101 *Salus populi solus rex: The peoples safety is the sole soveraignty, or The royalist out-reasoned* (London, 1648), 19; see David Underdown, *Pride's Purge: Politics in the Puritan Revolution* (Oxford: Clarendon, 1971), 266.
102 *Salus populi solus rex*, 1, 18, 19.
103 Ibid., 18.

There is nothing inherently republican—or radical or democratic—in the *salus populi* formula.[104] Hobbes used that formula without a problem. For him, *salus populi* was a guideline for specifically royal policy or for the policy of any supreme power. On the other hand, he condemned the Long Parliament's use of *salus populi* as a pretext for rebellion.[105] Neither is *salus populi suprema lex* a constitutional position. 'Lex' in the formula is 'the supreme principle' rather than 'law' in the literal sense of the word.[106] More importantly, *salus populi* is the language of emergency—and *necessitas* knows no law.[107] A historian of the early modern English political thought has characterized parliamentary sovereignty during the English civil war as absolutism based on permanent emergency.[108] For Hobbes, the idea of 'supreme law' was probably no more commendable than the idea of 'fundamental laws'. For Hobbes, 'the only fundamental law in every commonwealth is to obey the laws from time to time, which he shall make to whom the people have given the supreme power'. All other was nothing but an abuse of the people.[109]

One cannot accept without reservations, I hope to have shown by now, that English civil war was fought along republican principles for the liberation of the people from servitude. So why did Hobbes call the men who, in his view, challenged royal government on the basis of the principles drawn from the classical legal, moral, and political philosophy 'democraticals'?

In the pamphlet war of the early 1640s, calling the opponents of the king 'democratical gentlemen' would have been an effective polemical device. That was precisely the designation to which they objected. In his polemics with the royalists, Henry Parker, for example, 'did all he could to minimize the imputation of democracy to the House of Commons'. For him, democracy was 'the greatest irritant'.[110] Why did Hobbes use that name after the event?

---

104 Skinner, 'Classical Liberty', 12, cites first 'salus populi suprema lex esto' from Cic. *Leg.* III. iii. 8 as one of the golden rules of a 'free state,' and then (ibid., 18 ff.) frequent references to that rule in the parliamentary documents of the early 1640s to demonstrate the process of radicalization leading to republicanism. See Lorenz Winkler, *Salus: Vom Staatskult zur politischen Idee. Eine archäologische Untersuchung* (Heidelberg: Archäologie und Geschichte, 1995).
105 *Behemoth*, 68, 73, 108, 180, 198.
106 Andrew R. Dyck, *A Commentary on Cicero, De Legibus* (Ann Arbor: The University of Michigan Press, 2004), 459.
107 See also ibid., 458–9.
108 Mendle, 'Parliamentary Sovereignty', 118–19. Mende worked on the same material as Skinner in 'Classical Liberty' but came to a very different conclusion.
109 *Behemoth*, 158.
110 See Mendle, *Dangerous Positions*, 182; and [Henry Parker,] *Observations upon some of his Majesties late Answers and Expresses* (London, 1642), 22–3. See also Jordan, *Men of Substance*, 155, that Parker made it plain that the civil war was not to inaugurate the evil of an 'irresponsible democracy'.

One reason may lie in the greater precision of the language of democracy (as compared with the language of republicanism) when it comes to talking about public authority. Democracy is a form of government. Republic is not. Republic can mean, among other things, a kingless government. Such has been the common meaning of the term since the French revolution. But that was not the predominant meaning of 'republic' in England of the sixteenth and seventeen centuries.[111] A prominent historian has called the reign of Elizabeth I a 'Monarchical Republic'. In Renaissance England, the term *respublica* did not mean 'a type of constitution incompatible with monarchy' and was 'an acceptable term for a variety of political systems'.[112] The English subtitle of Thomas Smith's *Republica anglorum*, for example, was 'The maner of Gouernement or policie of the Realme of England'. *Republica* was the generic term for political or civil community, 'politique body' or 'Citie'. In this sense, wrote Smith echoing Cicero, 'common wealth is called a society or common doing of a multitude of free men collected together and vnited by common accord & couenauntes among themselues, for the conservation of themselues aswell in peace as in warre'.[113] The main species of the *republica* were monarchy, aristocracy, and democracy. Specifically, *republica anglorum*, English 'common wealth', was a *'Monarchia'*, that is, a *republica* 'where one alone doth gouerne', 'King or Queene'.[114]

Notable diversions from this usage were few. Thomas Elyot did not want *Respublica* to be understood as the rule of the multitude, the *plebs*, which 'in englisshe, is called the communaltie' and contained 'the base and vulgare inhabitantes, not auaunced to any honour or dignitie'. He wanted *Respublica* to be understood as the rule of the public, *publike*, which 'is diriuied of people', *populus*, meaning 'all the inhabitantes of a realme or citie'. He proposed a distinction between a *publike weale* and a *commune weale*, corresponding to the Latin *Res publica* and *Res plebeia* respectively.[115] Walter Ralegh named 'monarchy or kingdom', aristocracy, and 'a free state or popular state' the forms of the state. He reserved

---

111 Neither was that the case on the Continent during Hobbes's lifetime. See, for example, Herbert H. Rowen, *John de Witt, Grand Pensionary of Holland, 1625-1672* (Princeton, New Jersey: Princeton University Press, 1978), 380 ff.; James. D. Tracy, *The Founding of the Dutch Republic: War, Finance, and Politics in Holland, 1572-1588* (Oxford: Oxford University Press, 2008), Epilogue.
112 Patrick Collinson, 'The Monarchical Republic of Queen Elizabeth I', *Bulletin of the John Rylands Library of Manchester* 69 (1987), no. 2, 400–1. I was not able to consult *The monarchical republic of early modern England: Essays in Response to Patrick Collinson*, ed. J. F. McDiarmid (Aldershot: Ashgate, 2007) in time for print.
113 Thomas Smith, *De Republica Anglorum. The maner of Gouernement or policie of the Realme of England* (London, 1583), I. 10; see also Cic. *Rep.* I. xxv. 39.
114 Smith, *De Republica Anglorum*, I.1. 7; II. 3, 4.
115 *The boke named the Gouernour, deuysed by syr Thomas Elyot knight*, 1537, I. i.

the name commonwealth 'or government of all the common or baser sort' for the degenerated form of the popular state.[116] But in his *Cabinet-Council*, published by Milton in 1658, Ralegh went back to the more conventional usage: 'All commonwealths are either monarchies, aristocracies, democracies' (also called popular government).[117] That was the usage conforming to the classical Roman sources, even though they lacked uniformity, as Thomas Smith had observed.[118]

Since Cicero defined kingdom as the republic in which the supreme authority is in the king's hands,[119] and accepted the contemporary custom of calling the authority of the people *ciuitas popularis*,[120] Hobbes was truer to the neo-classical/Roman literary conventions than are some of our contemporary historians. The convention in the mid-seventeenth-century England was to use the 'republic' as a generic term, of which monarchy was a species, and not as a synonym for kingless government. One can get an intimation of how strong were these terminological conventions from a parliamentary document issued after the beheading of the king, in the period when historians today agree republicanism did exist in England. The Rump required 'engagement' by the members of the Council of State to 'a Republic, without King or House of Lords'.[121] The document did not refer to a 'Republic' without qualification but to a republic that had undergone 'unkinging' (as Baxter would say).[122] The language of the document does not depict a transition from monarchy to republic but rather a transformation of republic.

Admittedly, parliamentary language was vacillating in that period. Let me cite just a few examples: England was defined as a nation whose gov-

---

116 Walter Ralegh, *Maxims of State*, in vol. 8 of *The Works of Sir Walter Ralegh, kt, now first collected, to which are prefixed the lives of the author, by Oldys and Birch* (Oxford: The University Press, 1829), 1–2.
117 *The Cabinet-council: Containing the Chief Arts of Empire and Mysteries of State*, in vol. 8 of *The Works*, 37.
118 '[T]he rule of the multitude which the Greeks called Δημοκρατια: the Latines some *Respublica* by the generall name, some *populi potestas*, some *census potestas*, I cannot tell howe latinely.' *De Republica Anglorum* I. 14.
119 'Quare cum penes unum est omnium summa rerum, regem illum unum uocamus et regnum eius rei publicae statum.' Cic. *Rep.* I. xxvi. 42. I cite Cicéron, *La république*, ed. and trans. E. Bréguet, Collection des Universités de France (Paris: Les Belles Lettres, 1980), 1. 223.
120 'Illa autem est ciuitas popularis (sic enim appellant), in qua in populo sunt omnia.' Cic. *Rep.* I. xxvi. 42. See commentary ad loc. in Karl Büchner, *M. Tullius Cicero De re publica: Kommentar* (Heidelberg: Carl Winter, 1984), 126, that 'sic enim appellant' refers to discussions in Cicero's time, not to the Greek philosophers. *Ciuitas popularis* was thus not a translation for Δημοκρατια, which would have been a 'very awkward' translation.
121 *The Constitutional Documents of the Puritan Revolution, 1625–1660*, ed. S.R. Gardiner, 2nd ed. (Oxford: Clarendon, 1899), 384.
122 Baxter cited in William Lamont, *Richard Baxter and the Millenium: Protestant Imperialism and the English Revolution* (London: Croom Helm, 1979), 98.

ernment was 'now settled in the way of a Commonwealth'; it was famously declared to be 'a Commonwealth and Free State'; but the engagement to be taken by 'all men of the age of eighteen' spoke, again, of the 'Commonwealth of England, as it is now established, without a King or House of Lords'.[123]

Hobbes did not think much of the 'Commonwealth and Free State.' That phrase simply meant that 'neither this king, nor any king, nor any single person', but only the Rump themselves 'would be the people's masters'.[124] The adjective 'free' is easy to use. It does not need to mean much since it can mean so many different things. When King James I, for example, wrote about 'free monarchies', he was explaining his idea about the true monarchy: a *Common-wealth* in the 'trew paterne of Diuinitie' in which the king thinks himself 'onely ordained' for the *weal* of his people who, in turn, are his 'louing and obedient subiects'.[125] 'Free' is not a constitutional term in itself. But, meaning different things to different people, it can be emotionally charged and express strong political sentiments, just like the vocabulary, images, and models conveyed by the classical literature in general.

Hobbes, as must be clear by now, thought that classical learning had played a fateful role in the outbreak of the civil war. He did not give particular credit to the neo-Roman legitimation of parliament's claims. He regularly spoke of Grecian and Roman political literature and, in *Behemoth*, named Aristotle more often than any other classical author, Cicero included.[126] The point Hobbes repeatedly made was that reading the 'glorious histories and the sententious politics of the ancient popular governments of the Greeks and Romans, amongst whom kings were hated and branded with the name of tyrants, and popular government (although no

---

123 Gardiner, *The Constitutional Documents*, 387, 388; further instances of 'Commonwealth' at 390-9.
124 *Behemoth*, 164. See also ibid., 157, Hobbes's comment on the Rump's calling themselves *Custodes Libertatis Angliae*: 'B. I do not see how a subject that is tied to the laws, can have more liberty in one form of government than in another. A. Howsoever, to the people that understand by liberty nothing but leave to do what they list, it was a title not ingrateful.'
125 *The Trew Law of Free Monarchies: or the Reciprock and mvtvall Dvetie betwixt a Free King, and His Natural Subjects*, in *The Political Works of James I*, ed. C. H. McIlwain (Cambridge. Mass.: Harvard University Press, 1918).
126 See also Scott, *England's Troubles*, 293: 'Aristotle was the most ubiquitous renaissance classical source and there is a republican Aristotle. It is because Aristotle was a key source for English humanist moral philosophy that Hobbes aimed his criticism particularly in this direction.' Among today's historians of seventeenth-century English republicanism, Scott in particular insists on the importance of the Greek ingredient. See his *England's Troubles*, ch. 13; and 'Classical Republicanism in Seventeenth-century England and the Netherlands', in vol. 1 of *Republicanism: A Shared European Heritage*, 61-2, 66.

tyrant was ever so cruel as a popular assembly) passed by the name of liberty', had led to rebellion.[127]

The reading of the classical literature that, as Hobbes claimed, had led to rebellion was only one possible reading of that literature. The principles Hobbes's contemporaries drew from the classical literature were neither necessarily nor exclusively democratic or republican. Royalists, for example, used the classics to ridicule parliamentarian apologists and to argue the royal cause.[128] In the 1650s, the royalists came to praise no other than William Prynne as the 'Cato of his Age'.[129] The examples are multiple.[130] Hobbes himself in his younger years sought to 'enlist the intellectual tradition of Greece and Rome behind a monarchist philosophy' in order to 'counter enthusiasm for democracy'.[131]

In *Behemoth*, Hobbes no longer fought within that shared discursive field of classicism. He rejected the political language that in his view paved the way to the rebellion. One could not be 'a good subject to monarchy', Hobbes believed, if one derived his principles from 'the enemies of monarchy, such as were Cicero, Seneca, Cato, and other politicians of Rome, and Aristotle of Athens, who seldom speak of kings but as of wolves and other ravenous beasts'.[132] What the Englishmen drew 'out of the works of Aristotle, Plato, Cicero, Seneca, and out of the histories of Rome and Greece' were 'arguments for liberty'. Those arguments equipped them 'for their disputation against the necessary power of their sovereigns'.[133] But to undermine the 'necessary power' of the sovereign is to threat the dissolution of the government.

State democracy and church democracy

It is debatable to interpret Hobbes's 'democratical gentlemen' as republicans (or proto-republicans) in neo-Roman fashion. It is equally question-

---

127 *Behemoth*, 23; see also 3, 43, 56, 95, 158.
128 See also Nigel Smith, *Literature and Revolution in England, 1640–1660* (New Haven: Yale University Press, 1994), 103; Mendle, *Dangerous Positions*, 15, 18; idem, 'Parliamentary Sovereignty', 116.
129 William Lamont, *Puritanism and Hstorical Controversy* (London: UCL Press, 1996), 23.
130 See, e.g., Smith, *Literature and Revolution*, 102 ff., 207 ff.; Malcolm Smuts, 'Court-Centred Politics and the Uses of Roman Historians, c. 1590–1630', in *Culture and Politics in Early Stuart England*, eds K. Sharpe and P. Lake (Stanford, California: Stanford University Press, 1993), especially 39 ff.; David Norbrook, 'Lucan, Thomas May, and the Creation of a Republican Literary Culture', ibid., especially 56 ff.; see also idem, *Writing the English Republic*, ch. 1.
131 Smuts, 'Court-Centred Politics', 42; see also Norbrook, 'Lucan, Thomas May', 58; idem, 'The English Revolution and English Historiography', in Keeble, *The Cambridge Companion to Writing of the English Revolution*, 246–7; and, generally, Quentin Skinner, *Hobbes and Civil Science*, vol. 3 of *Visions of Politics* (Cambridge: Cambridge University Press, 2002).
132 *Behemoth*, 158.
133 Ibid., 56.

able to relegate to obscurity the religious component of the opposition to the king. The 'greatest shortcoming of the modern analysis of English classical republicanism' is precisely that it 'has failed adequately to explain that religious dimension', which was so central to the English civil war.[134] Hobbes was well aware of the key role religion played in the civil war and hardly ever lost it out of sight. The strength of his analysis in *Behemoth* lies in showing the close connection between those he called 'democratical gentlemen' and those he called 'Presbyterians', between 'democratical' principles and religious claims for power. The mixture of democratic principles and clerical power claims that were driven by ambition and folly (and propelling ambition and folly), created a potent destructive force that brought about the dissolution of the government and thus anarchy.

In his memoirs, Richard Baxter remembered that

> many honest Men of weak judgments and little acquaintance with such Matters, had been seduced into a disputing vein, and made it too much of their Religion, to talk for this Opinion and for that; sometimes for State Democracy, and sometime for Church Democracy.[135]

Baxter loathed Hobbes even though, ironically, their books would be publicly burnt together 'in the court of our Scholes' at Oxford.[136] But the passage I cited here could have been written by either man (or many others). The passage makes clear that the debate about democracy took place within 'Religion'. The debate moved easily from considering State Democracy to debating Church Democracy. This passage describes forcefully the embeddedness of democracy in religion.

Religious militants, whom Hobbes occasionally called irreligious, and 'democratical gentlemen' do not stand for distinct secular and religious spheres.[137] They are hardly distinguishable in their actions and ideas. At first sight, there is a parallelism between the endeavors of the religious militants, most often personified by the Presbyterians, and the 'democratical gentlemen'. 'Democratical gentlemen' did

> not less desire a popular government in the civil state than these ministers did in the Church. And as these did in the pulpit draw the people to their opinions, and to a dislike of the Church-government, Canons, and Common-prayer-book, so did the other make them in love with democracy by their harangues in the Parliament, and by

---

134 Scott, *England's Troubles*, 252.
135 *Reliquiae Baxterianae, or, Mr. Richard Baxters narrative of the most memorable passages of his life and times*, ed. M. Sylvester (London, 1696), 53.
136 Charles Ripley Gillett, *Burned Books: Neglected Chapters in British History and Literature* (New York: Columbia University Press, 1932; reprint Port Washington, N.Y.: Kennikat Press, 1964), 2: 517–19.
137 See *Behemoth*, 155.

their discourses and communication with people in the country, continually extolling liberty and inveighing against tyranny, leaving the people to collect themselves that this tyranny was the present government of the state.[138]

But that parallelism was only apparent. It collapsed when Hobbes apportioned most of the blame to one side. The *bête noire* of the English civil war was the group Hobbes called Presbyterians. He maintained that it was the design of the Presbyterian ministers,

> who taking themselves to be, by divine right, the only lawful governors of the Church, endeavoured to bring the same form of Government into the civil state. And as the spiritual laws were to be made by their synods, so the civil laws should be made by the House of Commons; who, as they thought, would no less be ruled by them afterwards, than they formerly had been.[139]

Or:

> To the end that the State becoming popular, the Church might be so too, and governed by an Assembly; and by consequence (as they thought) seeing politics are subservient to religion, they might govern, and thereby satisfy not only their covetous humour with riches, but also their malice with power to undo all men that admired not their wisdom.[140]

Hobbes's portrayed the two sets of rebels in very similar terms. They shared the same vices. Among the Presbyterians, 'every minister shall have the delight of sharing in the government, and consequently of being able to be revenged on those that do not admire their learning and help to fill their purses, and win to their service those that do'.[141] Similarly,

> those fine men, which out of their reading of Tully, Seneca, or other anti-monarchics, think themselves sufficient politics, and show their discontent when they are not called to the management of the state, and turn from one side to another upon every neglect they fancy from the King or his enemies.[142]

Actions of different rebel groups stemmed from the same intellectual source. All those rebels embraced the democratic principles that Hobbes identified at the root of European 'civil wars concerning religion'.[143] They also had the same institutional background. They were all bred at the universities. The 'democratical gentlemen' had learned their classics there,

---

138 Ibid., 23.
139 Ibid., 75.
140 Ibid., 159.
141 Ibid., 89.
142 Ibid., 155–6. Hobbes denounces Cicero himself as being moved in his actions 'out of love to himself.' Ibid., 72.
143 See n. 58. Aristotle, for example, was an 'ingredient in religion', and the clergy was versed in the babbling philosophy of Aristotle. *Behemoth*, 41, 95.

and '[f]rom the Universities also it was, that all preachers proceeded'. The 'curious questions in divinity' as well as 'all those politic questions concerning the rights of civil and ecclesiastic government' were 'first started at the Universities', the 'core of rebellion'.[144] Furthermore, the rebels' actions were mutually reinforcing. Presbyterianism was 'the very foundation of the Parliament's treacherous pretensions'. Both 'seditious Presbyterian ministers' and 'ambitious ignorant orators', making their harangues from the pulpits and in the Parliament, 'reduced this government into anarchy'.[145]

In a Protestant country where the king was 'head of the Church' and religion was one of the laws of the commonwealth, any challenge to or change in the religious establishment was an unsettling of the civil government as well.[146] Such had been noticed and feared long before the civil war started. When Hobbes was one year old, for example, Bishop Cooper, a defender of the Church of England, published an argument in response to a Puritan attack on episcopacy that is relevant to the point at hand. Puritan principles of ecclesiastical organization and authority, Cooper argued, may have been good 'where the church was in persecution vnder tyrants; but where the assistance may bee had of a Christian Prince or Magistrate, it is neither necessarie, nor so conuenient, as it may be otherwise'. Commenting on the idea of the common election of ministers, Cooper noted that 'their whole drift ... is to bring the Gouernment of the Church to a *Democracie* or *Aristocracie*'. If the common people were made familiar with such principles, he warned, '[i]t is greatly to bee feared, that they will very easily transferre the same to the Gouernment of the common weale'.[147] He disliked Presbyterian schemes because the convulsion they would cause in the state would be damaging to religion:

> The reason that mooueth vs not to like this platforme of gouernement, is, that when wee on the one part consider the things that are required to be redressed, and on the other, the state of our countrey, people, and commonweale: we see euidently, that to plant those things in this Church, wil drawe with it, so many, and so great alterations of the State of gouernment, and of the lawes, as the attempting thereof might bring rather the ouerthrowe of the Gospel among vs, then the end that is desired.[148]

---

144 Ibid., 41, 56, 58.
145 Ibid., 82, 109.
146 Ibid., 46, 53.
147 T[homas] C[ooper], [Bishop of Winchester], *An Admonition to the People of England, 1589*, ed. E. Arber (Birmingham: English Scholar's Library, 1883], 70. Partly cited in Mendle, *Dangerous Positions*, 82.
148 Cooper, *An Admonition*, 65.

Anti-episcopalians themselves reflected on the homology between the ecclesiastical and civil government, which made them vulnerable to the charge of subverting monarchy. Thomas Cartwright, one of the most learned sixteenth-century Puritans/Presbyterians denied that the church was 'popular' only in the first centuries of Christianity, before there had been Christian magistrates:

> For the churche is gouerned wyth that kinde of gouernment, whych the Philosophers, that wryte of the best common wealthes, affirme to be the best. For in respecte of Christe the head, it is a Monarchie, and in respecte of the auncientes and pastoures, that gouerne in common, and wyth like authoritie amongste them selues, it is an Aristocratie, or the rule of the best men, and, in respecte that the people are not secluded, but haue their interest in churche matters, it is a Democratie, or a populare estate. An image whereof appeareth also in the pollicye of thys Realme, for as in respecte of the Queene her majestie, it is a Monarchie, so in respecte of the moste honourable Counsell, it is an Aristocratie, and hauing regard to the Parliament, whych is assembled of al estates, it is a Democraty.[149]

This was dangerous thinking. It implied denial of the supreme power of the prince. John Whitgift, the future archbishop of Canterbury, did not hesitate to raise this point. 'I know that all these three kinds of government may be mixed together after divers sorts', he replied to Cartwright, his fellow at the Trinity College,

> yet still the state of government is named according to that which most ruleth, and beareth the greatest sway: as, when matters are most commonly governed by the consent of the more part of the people, the state is called popular; when by divers of the best and the wisest, it is called *optimorum status*; when by one, it is called monarchy.

The conclusion Whitgift wanted to make was that 'in this realm' 'the state is neither "aristocraty", nor "democraty", but a "monarchy"'.[150] Making 'the government of the church popular' would be an impediment to civil government. The people 'are commonly bent to novelties and to factions, and most ready to receive that doctrine that seemth to be contrary to the present state, and that inclineth to liberty'.[151] If those people would elect the ministers, they would 'usually elect such as would feed their humours,' and as a consequence 'the prince neither should have quiet

---

149 T. C., *A replye to an ansvvere made of M. Doctor VVhitgifte, Against the admonition to the Parliament*, [1573], 51. In his section by section refutation of Carthwright, Whitgift cited this locus in his *The Defense of the Aunsvvere to the Admonition, against the Replie of T.C.* (London, 1574), in *The Works of John Whitgift, D.D., Master of Trinity College, Dean of Lincoln, &c., Afterwards successively Bishop of Worcester and Archbishop of Canterbury*, ed. J. Ayre, The Parker Society (Cambridge: At the University Press, 1851), 1: 390; see also Mendle, *Dangerous Positions*, 64–8.
150 *The Works of John Whitgift*, 1. 393.
151 Ibid., 466.

government, neither could be able to preserve the peace of the church, nor yet plant that religion that he in conscience is persuaded to be sincere'.[152] In support of his view that the popular government is 'the worst kind of government that can be', Whitgift cited Calvin's point that 'the fall from a popular state into a sedition is of all other most easy'.[153]

Hobbes engaged seriously with church, theology, and religion. It is reasonable to assume that he was acquainted with this kind of literature and arguments. It may be pure coincidence that Elizabethan Bishop Edwin Sandys and Hobbes both discredited democracy as a fruit of emulation and contention, but it is a coincidence worth noting.

For Sandys, democracy sprung out of emulation and contention — two 'great and pestilent infections of the hart' — that are generated by pride: 'Pride causeth emulation, and of emulation cometh strife: so that the cursed generation of vice is fruitful', he preached before the Queen.

> Pride made the diuelish Angel enuie that his Lord and God should be aboue him: it made Adam desire to be as full of knowledge as his Creator; Absolon to emulate his father and to thirst after his kingdom. Caesar was so prowde that hee could not abide a superior: Pompey could not beare an equall.

After this characteristic mixture of Scriptural and Roman exempla illustrating pride and rebellion in general, Sandys turned to democracy:

> Corah, Dathan and Abiram in the pride of their hearts sought to displace Moses and Aaron, the chiefe magistrate and the chiefe minister. They set downe a handsome platforme of equalitie, and many of the multitude allowed of it as well pleased with a popular estate; where the worst of them might be as good as the best. But GOD brought their deuise and themselues to nought.[154]

Hobbes used the story of Korah, Dathan and Abiram in all his major political treatises to illustrate rebellion against the sovereign. Rebellion here means rebellion against the authority to interpret the Word of God

---

152 Ibid., 466–7.
153 Ibid., 467. See Calvin, *Institutes of the Chrtistian Religion* IV. xx. 8 (Allen's translation, Grand Rapids, Michigan: Eerdmans, 1949, 2: 778, has 'democracy' at this place). Whitgift's reference is misleading, for Calvin states that, of the 'forms of government, which are stated by philosophers', aristocracy or a mixture of aristocracy and democracy was the best to his mind, and that the 'vice and imperfection of men ... renders it safer and more tolerable for the government to be in the hands of many', since they can assist, admonish, censor, and restrain each other. (Ibid.) See also *The Decades of Henry Bullinger, minister of the Church of Zurich*, translated by H. I., ed. Th. Harding, The Parker Society (Cambridge: At the University Press, 1849 [originally published 1587]), 1. 311: 'none can deny, but that great perils and infinite incommodities are in the aristocracy, but far more many in the democracy'.
154 *Sermons Made by the most reuerende Father in God, Edwin, Archbishop of Yorke, Primate of England and Metropolitane* (London, 1585), 118–19. In another sermon, Sandys likened Korah, Dathan, and Abiram's episode with our muttering 'against our good and lawfull magistrates, against our iudges, and against Lordes ministers'. Ibid., 272.

and supreme civil authority, which were united in Moses.[155] In his commentary on Thucydides 'emulation and contention' were for Hobbes the wellspring of democracy.[156] Pride, which in Sandys's words caused emulation and contention, was what in Hobbes's view the civil government had to bring under control. Leviathan, to whom Hobbes compared the 'Governour,' was *'King of all the children of pride'*.[157]

In *Behemoth*, Hobbes represented democracy as the offspring of the children of pride who succeeded in destroying their king. What destroyed 'that great LEVIATHAN called a COMMON-WEALTH, or STATE',[158] was an explosive mixture of Greco-Roman political sentiments and ideas, and religious militancy. The intimate connection between 'democratical' principles and religious power claims subverted and collapsed the State on both fronts, 'civill and ecclesiasticall'. It gave the war for democracy a holy nimbus. In the eyes of the rebels, the destruction of the state was authorized by the Word of God to establish the reign of God. In the Presbyterians' self-image, 'where they reign, it is God that reigns'.[159] The sovereign was killed because 'there ought none to be sovereign but King Jesus, nor any govern under him but the saints', as believed the Fifth-monarchy-men, 'of whom there were many' in the Parliament.[160]

The rebellion against sovereignty was a democratic holy war. If we choose to call classicizing political sentiments and ideas republicanism, that was a republicanism covered with the cloak of godliness. But that cloak was not a disposable garment: it was the tunic of Nessus. If we, rather, stay with Hobbes's own choice of names, we have to read *Behemoth* as a critique of democracy. That democracy was not the laudable secularist political pursuit we fancy it to be today. That democracy was driven by a gallery of vices. It was inseparable from religious claims on secular power. It was godly democracy. What democratic regime change brought about was dissolution of government and civil disintegration.

---

155 *Elements of Law* II. xxvi. 2; *De cive* xvi. 13; *Leviathan* (Tuck), 325–6; see also Numbers 16.
156 See n. 44. On emulation, see also *Elements of Law* I. ix. 21; *Leviathan* VI. 48; on contention, Leviathan XI. 3; on pride, VIII. 19.
157 Hobbes, *Leviathan* (Tuck), 221, citing Job 41: 34: 'he is a king over all the children of pride' (King James version).
158 Hobbes, *Leviathan*, The Introduction.
159 *Behemoth*, 50, 167.
160 Ibid., 182.

Ingrid Creppell

The Democratic Element in Hobbes's 'Behemoth'

Hobbes states at the end of *Leviathan* that 'the disorders of the present time' (L 491) provoked him to write his famous work.[1] *Behemoth* is Hobbes's retrospective look at the disorders of the English civil war and is therefore inherently interesting in what it reveals to us about Hobbes's view of the context that shaped his fundamental political theory, and which features of that context he found most provoking.[2] In what follows, I consider *Behemoth* not only as a work meant to reinforce the cause of peace against agitators, but also as grappling with fundamental problems about the nature of modern democracy. By reinterpreting the factors Hobbes highlights as contributing conditions of civil war, I believe we come to understand that it is not just disorder per se that Hobbes seeks to address in his work. Rather, his writings are a response to a new social condition — a democratizing world and the demands from mobilized populations. *Behemoth* is an extended description of and reaction to that dynamism, both positive and negative, of new conditions (circumstances) of democracy. While the text is at one level an attack on democracy, it is simultaneously at another level a recognition of the necessity of constructing political principles as responsive to a politicized people. *Behemoth* thus exemplifies Hobbes's ambiguous approach to the democratic

---

1   I have used the following editions of Hobbes's works: *Leviathan*, ed. R. Tuck (Cambridge: Cambridge University Press, 1996); and *Behemoth or the Long Parliament*, ed. F. Tönnies (Chicago: University of Chicago Press, 1990). All quotations from *Leviathan* will be cited in parentheses as L with page numbers following. All citations from *Behemoth*, because they are so numerous, will simply refer to the page numbers of the University of Chicago Tönnies text.

2   In the spirit of Skinner's work, I take historical context to be significant in understanding the meaning of a philosophical text such as Hobbes's. Skinner's recent work on Hobbes situates him in the rich literary and linguistic context in which Hobbes worked (primarily the rhetorical tradition of Renaissance Europe). I will focus on a specifically political context to which Hobbes was responding and I will read *Behemoth* as showing us that Hobbes's context of work is also not fully categorizable in Hobbes's own terms, that is, not all the problems that Hobbes struggled with were perfectly transparent to him.

question raised by the English civil war. In particular, I emphasize that Hobbes presents a history of the civil war in which ideas are active forces in a public setting, with the implications this has for how his own positive political philosophy might be made a source of motivation for people. *Behemoth* is a text that shows Hobbes confronting questions about the public mind—its shaping, motivation and the collapse of agreement.

I shall focus on both elites and the people but will pay special attention to the latter since it has remained relatively unremarked upon in the secondary literature. The question of the people may seem to be only tangentially relevant to Hobbes's analysis, but I argue that it plays a central role and that it has implications for understanding his basic political principles. *Behemoth* is about political rebellion and breakdown. Hobbes consistently blames ambitious elites for having instigated the disorders. In the larger picture, however, the breakdown would not have occurred if the common people had not gone along with the seditious elite. One might contend that their seduction was a foregone conclusion, but if one holds this, there must be some explanation for treating the co-optation of the mass of humanity as an easy achievement. The question in *Behemoth* is— how were the minds of the common people seduced? This same question confronts Hobbes: how are the minds of the people to be seduced into upholding his ideas?

Hobbes believed his own work constituted a body of ideas that could be transformative and conducive to peace and order. He also considered belief and opinion to be the basis of stability and power: 'For the power of the mighty hath no foundation but in the opinion and belief of the people' (16), is one of the more striking statements in *Behemoth*. In the best of all worlds, people would read or become aware of Hobbes's political principles and their justification, and this set of beliefs would then transform what had been a contentious, irreconcilable clash of religious and political doctrines leading to political disorder into an agreement about the rights of sovereignty for the peace and good of the whole. But how would the transformative effect work and who was the audience for these principles?

One of the more active areas in present Hobbes scholarship focuses on the means by which Hobbes sought to convey his ideas given their purpose to change minds and action. As Sorell notes, Hobbes 'intended his treatises to have an effect on public opinion and behaviour'.[3] The contemporary answer to this has mainly come in two (not mutually exclusive)

---

[3] Tom Sorell, ' Hobbes's Persuasive Civil Science', *The Philosophical Quarterly* 40 (July 1990), 342.

forms: rhetoric[4] and education.[5] Skinner's comprehensive treatment of Hobbes's use of science and rhetoric concludes that while the conventional view had held Hobbes to reject humanist rhetoric upon his discovery of scientific reasoning, the truth is that Hobbes goes back to rhetoric: 'having initially abandoned rhetoric in favour of science, he eventually sought to found his civil science on combining them'.[6] The purpose of his civil science is not to argue deductively from an egoistic conception of human nature to the necessity of a Leviathan but rather to argue for a 'steady commitment to justice and the full range of the other social virtues ... [his] civil science centres on the claim that the avoidance of the vices and the maintenance of the social virtues are indispensable to the preservation of peace'.[7] These truths (proved by Hobbes scientifically) must be conveyed to as broad an audience as possible through rhetoric, since scientific reason alone will not bring about persuasion. Alternatively, Lloyd emphasizes education as the most important mechanism for the transference of Hobbes's ideas. Her argument is that obedience (hence order) is brought about in two steps: first through Hobbes's construction of a version of political obligation that warring parties could come to adopt on a redescription of their 'transcendent interests' (these are, notably, beliefs about one's duty to God but also include beliefs about justice or liberty) — this revised construction brings about agreement/consensus on conflicting judgments, and second, by maintaining and reproducing this consensus in judgment through education.[8] Lloyd contends that

---

[4] See, among others, on Hobbes's use of rhetoric and scientific reasoning: Quentin Skinner, *Reason and Rhetoric in the Philosophy of Hobbes* (Cambridge: Cambridge University Press, 1996); Tom Sorell, *Hobbes* (London: Routledge & Kegan Paul, 1986), and 'Hobbes's Persuasive Civil Science'; and David Johnston, *The Rhetoric of Leviathan* (Princeton: Princeton University Press, 1986).

[5] See, for example, the works on Hobbes and education by S. A. Lloyd, *Ideals as Interests in Hobbes's Leviathan* (Cambridge: Cambridge University Press, 1992), and Geoffrey M. Vaughan, *Behemoth Teaches Leviathan* (Lanham, MD: Lexington Books, 2002).

[6] Skinner, *Reason and Rhetoric*, 12.

[7] Ibid., 11.

[8] She writes: 'It is not enough that the people who pick up *Leviathan* be persuaded by Hobbes's argument; the insights it contains must be very widely disseminated, and reproduced perpetually, if Hobbes is to succeed in this practical political project. Part of this task will involve reproducing acceptance of Hobbes's argument for his principle — his "science of politics" and part will consist in reproducing those interests that, when properly conceived, provide people with reason for adhering to the principle ... How are these things to be done? They are to be done through an aggressive process of education ... Pursuing a process of socialization, or of moral education, will encourage the formation of properly conceived interests, and instill in people a desire to do what the satisfaction of these interests requires. A solid education of this sort will, Hobbes thinks, eliminate both the discontent and the "pretense of right" that are, in his view, necessary conditions of rebellion. This makes reeducation *necessary* to Hobbes's project of building a perpetually stable social order ... But not only is proper education *necessary* if social stability is to be maintained: Hobbes comes very close to suggesting that it may also be *sufficient*.' (Lloyd, *Ideals and Interests*, 158, 159, 161.)

> Education in subjects' moral and civil duty will be enough to ensure the maintenance of social order because human beings are, in Hobbes's view, quite malleable ... Education involves for Hobbes not the mere *presentation* of ideas, but also their *inculcation*, or what we might call more broadly a process of socialization ... Hobbes stresses the need to educate people in their moral and civil duty, and to *instill* in them a *disposition* to do what they ought to do.[9]

While their approaches to Hobbes are very different, both Skinner and Lloyd agree that Hobbes emphasizes civic virtue as a means to bring about a stable and peaceful commonwealth.[10] Clearly, Hobbes sought to create citizens who acted upon a duty to obey the sovereign. This refocusing on Hobbes as a theorist of civic virtue is convincing and a welcome shift.

In this reading of *Behemoth*, I will offer an additional way to understand what Hobbes sought to change and how he saw the transformative nature of his ideas. I want very briefly to consider the relationship between *Leviathan* and *Behemoth* before presenting my view of the latter's independent value. It is impossible to read *Behemoth* without the shadow of *Leviathan* in mind.[11] The aim of all Hobbes's political theory is to instill obedience to the sovereign, because only then can the peace and flourishing of a country be secured. How one instills obedience is however an open question. It appears that Hobbes uses one means to advance this in *Leviathan* and another in his historical work *Behemoth*. In *Leviathan* Hobbes presents the content of his ideas in abstract terms (humans are described as basically driven by fear of death, competition and pride/glory; the state of nature is a state of war; consent to an absolute sovereign is justified rationally; and a revised exegesis of key components of Christian theology is offered) and

---

9   Ibid., 161, 162.
10 See also Mary Dietz, ' Hobbes's Subject as Citizen', in *Thomas Hobbes and Political Theory*, ed. M. G. Dietz (Lawrence, KS: University Press of Kansas, 1990), for a discussion of *Leviathan* as a tract on civic virtue.
11 Most commentators on *Behemoth* see it as reinforcing or reflecting the analytic conclusions of Hobbes's *Leviathan* and insofar as it does that, it is taken to deepen our picture of Hobbes's political theory. Royce MacGillivray, in 'Thomas Hobbes's History of the English Civil War A Study of *Behemoth*', *Journal of the History of Ideas* 31 (1970), 179–98, notes: 'it is necessary to ask what connection exists between the political doctrines of *Behemoth*, with its fierce Royalist loyalties, and the political doctrines of Hobbes's previous writings ... In *Behemoth*, Hobbes has applied to actual political events the conclusions of his political philosophy' (183). Stephen Holmes, in his 'Introduction' to *Behemoth or the Long Parliament*, ed. F. Tönnies (Chicago: University of Chicago Press, 1990), vii, likewise comments that in the later text, Hobbes applied historically and concretely the analytical framework about sedition, rebellion, and the breakdown of authority that he had developed in his earlier positive political writings. Richard Ashcraft, in ' Ideology and Class in Hobbes' Political Theory', *Political Theory* 6 (February 1978), 27–62, sees it as closely tied to Hobbes's moral science laid out in *Leviathan*, making it a 'scientific history,' and not a 'history' yielding only prudential knowledge, as Hobbes's classification of Thucydides might lead one to expect. Lloyd also emphasizes *Behemoth*'s corroborative effect—the causes of disorder are religious conflict and diversity of judgment about one's transcendent interests, which, according to her, a reinterpretation of the whole of *Leviathan* would lead one to see.

through the telling and in their content these ideas are presumed to work their effect. *Behemoth* takes a different approach. In the dedication, Hobbes states 'There can be nothing more instructive towards loyalty and justice than will be the memory, while it lasts, of that war' (x). He later reiterated his purpose: to demonstrate to the people why 'calamities ever follow disobedience to their lawful sovereigns' (144). History is a vivid reminder of the chaos and destructiveness of war, and Hobbes in opening recent wounds is keeping memory alive to lead his readers to a sober realization of the necessity of obedience as the only way to avoid those consequences.[12] The book is clearly not a typical 'history' as a cool recounting of a sequence of events, but a highly charged, engaged polemic defending the king against rebellious elites. *Behemoth* is emotional while *Leviathan* is abstract as a means of approaching obedience. Thus one might be tempted to conclude that obedience is instilled through prudence in the first case[13] and through the idea of duty and moral and scientific reason in the second.

An important insight of *Behemoth*, however, is that views are always in contention with other sets of beliefs to persuade the people. Politics is about contention and gaining the strongest position. The role of the people is essential here because they are the great mass of public opinion that must be moved in one direction or another to stabilize or overthrow the sovereign. If one holds that the people are basically empty-headed and will necessarily follow the most flamboyant orators, they become essentially ballast for the most emotionally charged views. But Hobbes doesn't assume this, and his portrayal of them is not so one-dimensional. In *Leviathan*, Hobbes had written about the people in this way: 'the Commonpeoples minds, unlesse they be tainted with dependance on the Potent, or scribbled over with the opinions of their Doctors, are like clean paper, fit to receive whatsoever by Publique Authority shall be imprinted in them' (L 233). This remark, far from a criticism of the people, was a recognition of their potential capacity to learn the essentials of a science of virtue and vice. In reality, however, all peoples are embedded somewhere and necessarily come to politics dependent on their ruler; only infants have minds like clean paper. Yet, one condition of the civil war was its calling into

---

12 Hobbes explicitly stated his intent to have *Behemoth* published. He explains in 1679: 'I would fain have published my *Dialogue of the Civil Wars of England*, long ago; and to that end I presented it to his Majesty: and some days after, when I thought he had read it, I humbly besought him to let me print it; but his Majesty, though he heard me graciously, yet he flatly refused to have it published.' *EW* 4. 411.

13 As many commentators have noticed, *Behemoth* is an example of what Hobbes commended Thucydides for accomplishing: 'the principal and proper work of history being to instruct and enable men, by the knowledge of actions past, to bear themselves prudently in the present and providently towards the future'. *EW* 8. vi.

question the accepted justifications for authority. In Hobbes's telling of the story, the people are not automatically controlled like puppets from above. He explicitly acknowledges that ideas in public cannot be fully controlled: 'A state can constrain obedience, but convince no error, nor alter the minds of them that believe they have the better reason. Suppression of doctrine does but unite and exasperate, that is, increase both the malice and power of them that have already believed them' (62).

Why then might the mass public have ended up being more susceptible to the leaders who sought the king's overthrow? Was it features of these leaders, of the people, or of the king himself (or his position) that made the breakdown likely? To claim that the people and leaders were made 'disobedient' by seditious ideas, and therefore that the solution is to cultivate a virtuous, obedient citizenry who see the king's rule as absolute is highly inadequate. For the solution of 'civic virtue' to work, the stress must be not on encouraging duty (the devoutly religious are supremely dutiful), but rather on transforming the values by which people act. Civic virtue is conducive to peace because it ranks civic, public, political accommodation ahead of particular beliefs about religious truth, or other matters contending for predominance. Therefore, before practices of civic virtue can become effective, there must be a shift in perception about how the world works and about the goals of a collective life. Specifically, civic virtue that would predictably lead to peace and order depends upon the existence of a powerful, public belief in the value of the political sphere.

If this is true, the breakdown is also due to the failure of the king to present a powerful ideology or world-view to counter the demands of particular mobilized groups. Hobbes recognized that the sovereign had to have a 'fighting creed' of his own to do battle with other competing world-views in a public sphere. At the time of the civil war the king did not have an ideology that could assert the dominance of political reasoning. *Leviathan* was Hobbes's comprehensive and systematic attempt to provide this alternative world-view to challenge and compete with those religiously inspired views that claimed so much of the public airwaves. Thus, *Behemoth* retrospectively demonstrates why *Leviathan* cannot accomplish its goals unless it secures itself in the public mind. *Behemoth* shows why conditions of democratization demand that the king maintain hegemony of belief and why his incapacity to do so led to his destruction.

Early modern democracy

One might object that democracy is a premature issue for this period, and certainly if we presume ' democracy' to consist in demands for full participation with accompanying rights and institutional safeguards that would be true.[14] But we cannot ignore the proto-democratic features that characterized the agitation of seventeenth century England. It becomes clear in reading *Behemoth* that Hobbes was and had to be centrally concerned with issues that we would identify as democratic questions, even though Hobbes would not have named them as such himself.

If democracy is an important concern of Hobbes, we should clarify what democracy meant at the time. Since classical antiquity, philosophers had denounced democracy as dangerous, seeing it as the rule of the mob who were by definition incapable of governing a state with any degree of competence. The connotations of the word democracy during the civil war in England were negative, therefore, when I speak of groups or ideas defending, supporting or advancing the cause of democracy, I mean by this components of political systems and relationships that we now take to be essential to democracies. We might describe the English civil war as a democratic revolution in two senses. First, the demands put forward by the rebels against the established powers constituted the origination of core ideas of modern democracy — notions of inalienable rights and equality of legal and political rights; participation as popular involvement in political decision-making in some form; accountability; and restrictions on sovereign/executive power.[15] These ideas were only beginning to be shaped in modern terms. Second, the civil war carried forward democracy not only in its ideas but also in the mass mobilization of the citizenry surrounding the war. It was democratic as an historical reality. That is to say, the civil war was much more than a spontaneous popular revolt on the one hand or a constitutional conflict among elites on the other.[16] Secular political parties like the Levellers and Diggers were only the most dramatic examples of popular involvement.

The civil war was notable in the extent to which it challenged at a fundamental level the regime of social and political hierarchy and in its engagement of a broad swath of the population in political and ideologi-

---

14 The modern form of democracy to which we now nearly universally pay tribute — the right of every adult regardless of sex, property, or educational status to elect officials — was not adopted until the twentieth century. And the word 'democrat' was until the late nineteenth century a negative term.

15 See David Wootton, 'Introduction' to *Divine Right and Democracy*, ed. D. Wootton (Harmondsworth: Penguin Books, 1986), for a helpful synopsis of the democratic elements of the English civil war.

16 There is obviously a long and complex story to tell about the connection between an increase in popular revolts and elite conflict during the sixteenth and seventeenth centuries. Christopher Hill observes that 'In all countries of Western Europe the period of peasant revolts was the period of the formation of absolute monarchies', but if and when those monarchies became 'absolute' they had first to quell not only the peasants and common people, but the newly empowered propertied classes. Christopher Hill, *Change and Continuity in Seventeenth-Century England* (Cambridge, MA: Harvard University Press, 1975), 182. Indeed, it was fear of the radical headless mass that led the bourgeois into dependence on the monarchy. Elite differences could be buried to crush the destabilizing aspirations of the lower orders.

cal turmoil. Parliament continually appealed directly to the people in their resolutions challenging the king, thus stirring up popular emotion and reaction, if not reflection. The conflict created a roiling public sphere of argument and debate. Lawrence Stone notes that well over 22,000 sermons, speeches, pamphlets and newspapers were published between 1640 and 1661, making the engagement much more than a set of grievances lodged against a despised ruler.[17] Hobbes in *Behemoth* describes at length the 'paper war' preceding the military conflict in which the question of the rights of sovereignty are debated and challenged even by the common people, ultimately leading to the destruction of the monarchy.

As a constitutional upheaval, the war challenged the fundamental institutions of church and state, but its radical aspirations quickly failed, monarchy was restored, and a hierarchical social system retrenched. This failure of what was clearly a revolution pursued with democratic means and ends may lead us not to take those democratic aspects of the conflict seriously. Their explosion appears only to have characterized an 'era of collective insanity'[18] before everyone came to their senses and settled back into traditional roles. Hobbes did not make that mistake. After the Restoration, when he was nearly eighty, he writes a vehement polemical history against the war. Why might Hobbes have been compelled to do so? It was probably not backward-looking anger that motivated him to write but a forward-looking attempt to assert control over the description and explanation of the most significant and traumatic collective event of the century. The terms in which the civil war was understood were necessarily part of a general ideological debate that continued after the Restoration.[19]

---

17 Lawrence Stone, *The Causes of the English Revolution 1529–1642* (New York: Harper Torchbooks, 1972), 49. See also Tuck's discussion of the republican nature of the English Revolution in Richard Tuck, *Philosophy and Government, 1572–1651* (Cambridge: Cambridge University Press, 1993). Hill emphasizes the politicization of the general population as well, noting that the Commons began to appeal to the people in resolutions against popery, Arminianism, and tonnage and poundage, and extended this appeal to the ' lower orders' by encouraging them to sign the Root and Branch Petition in 1640. Hill, *Change and Continuity*, 192.
18 Skinner, *Reason and Rhetoric*, 432.
19 Ashcraft 'Ideology and Class', 29, emphasizes Hobbes's 'outrage' in *Behemoth*, but as Skinner notes 'to think of Hobbes's prose as a clear window through which we can gaze uninterruptedly at his thought is a serious mistake' (*Reason and Rhetoric*, 13). Vaughan has perhaps gone farther than any other commentator on *Behemoth* in reading between the lines, indeed as ignoring what Hobbes seems to be evidently arguing in his explanation and denunciation of the civil war. I think this sensitivity to Hobbes's ulterior ends and his sophisticated use of language is very important but can be overextended. For a discussion of the *Behemoth* as a work of Restoration history see Vaughan, *Behemoth Teaches Leviathan*, 92 ff. He claims that Hobbes had no interest in joining the ideological war fought by historians after the cessation of civil war violence. While it may be true that he did not want openly to side with the Royalist as opposed to Republican camp, this should not prevent us from seeing

I will use the distinction between democracy as a set of ideas about freedom and self-government and democracy as the circumstances of active political mobilization of the people as a way to address Hobbes's response to it. When reading *Behemoth*, we can decipher his divided approach.[20] Hobbes rejected the appeal to democratic ideas and he scathingly attacks university scholars who, through their studies, fall in love with ancient Greek and Roman politics. But he took seriously the mass politicization of the people and the theoretical implications of putting the king on trial in the name of the people of England: this he could not ridicule.

The role of democracy should not only be addressed because of the historical fact that a politicization of the general population had taken place.[21] It is important also because of the implications it holds for the essential theoretical tenets of Hobbes's work. In concluding *Leviathan*, Hobbes explains the purpose of his writing: 'to set before mens eyes the mutuall Relation between Protection and Obedience' (L 491). In that relation, one is obligated to obey because of the power of the sovereign to protect. Yet, *Behemoth* describes in detail the collapse of the power to protect. Democracy is responsible for this collapse because it instigated ideas that challenged the king's authority, and also because once the king has been weakened and the people mobilized to make a choice, they were led to non-obedience to the sovereign. If it were just a matter of the publicity of a few seditious ideas, the power to protect would not have been fundamen-

---

Hobbes's efforts as essentially ideological nonetheless. 'Ideology' is not reducible to the standard party positions.

20 Normally, readers see only one half Hobbes's approach and paint him as an arch anti-democrat. For example, MacGillivray, 'Thomas Hobbes's History', 197, observes: 'Hobbes has sometimes been recognized as one of the prophets of modern totalitarianism, and there are passages in *Behemoth* in which he seems to foreshadow some of its darker practices.'

21 An interesting question is whether Hobbes saw himself as writing during a time of unique historical significance. One might interpret Hobbes to regard his own analysis and solution as unique without his considering the problem he was solving to be unique to a changing world. In this sense, Hobbes would not have believed that historically significant and truly new changes were taking place. In Dialogue II of *Behemoth*, Hobbes presents the following exchange which would support the conclusion that Hobbes saw the nature of his solution as singular but not the historical problem itself: A: '[F]or the government of a commonwealth, neither wit, nor prudence, nor diligence, is enough, without infallible rules and the true science of equity and justice.' B: 'If this be true, it is impossible that any commonwealth in the world, whether monarchy, aristocracy, or democracy, should continue long without change, or sedition tending to change, either of the government or of the governors.' A: 'It is true; nor have any the greatest commonwealths in the world been long free from sedition. The Greeks had for awhile their petty kings, and then by sedition came to be petty commonwealths; and then growing to be greater commonwealths, by sedition again became monarchies; and all for want of rules of justice for the common people to take notice of; which if the people had known in the beginning of every of these seditions, the ambitious persons could never have had the hope to disturb their government after it had been once settled.' (70) Ultimately, I believe Hobbes saw the conditions he lived in as new.

tally challenged. The cause of the collapse is the choice by the mass of the common people to follow the agitators instead of remaining loyal to the king, hence taking away his base of power. As Hobbes emphasizes: 'It is not the right of the sovereign, though granted to him by every man's express consent, that can enable him to do his office; it is the obedience of the subject, which must do that.' (144) *Behemoth* documents the dissolution into thin air of the authority to rule and to claim obedience, leaving the sovereign with a transparent shell of a mere right to sovereignty. The question must be, how in this situation of extremity is the power reconstituted, such that obligation to obey again comes into effect?

In what follows, I shall try to reconstruct a plausible interpretation of Hobbes's reaction to democracy and a possible answer to how power might be reconstituted.

The critique of democracy

Hobbes rejection of democracy appears first of all in his explanation of the civil war. In one guise, we might take him to say that the war itself was the inevitable outcome of democratic activation and ideas. We should turn to that explanation in order to determine the sense in which Hobbes links democracy and the civil war. Hobbes cites both ambitious elites and seditious ideas as responsible. While some commentators have accentuated either elites[22] or ideas[23] as more important, Hobbes explains the war as brought about by both factors, which he ultimately cannot completely separate. A major theme clearly is the cynical use of power through political, ideological and military means. The 'seducers' are mainly Presbyterians and democracy-loving Parliamentarians, but Hobbes sin-

---

22 Much of the secondary literature on *Behemoth* sees it primarily as an indictment of elites exploiting doctrines for seditious purposes. Deborah Baumgold in particular makes this argument in *Hobbes's Political Theory* (Cambridge: Cambridge University Press, 1988), 81–4: 'The menace of ambitious elites is a principal theme of *Behemoth* ... The work identifies ambitious Presbyterian ministers and ambitious gentlemen—i.e., Puritan leaders and Parliamentarians—as the chief leaders in the Civil War.' And she goes on to claim that 'sedition requires legitimation. With respect to the role of ideas as causes of rebellion and civil war, it is important to distinguish the idea of a conflict over ideology from that of conflict legitimized by ideology. Hobbes held the latter view of rebellion, but not the former.' Skinner claims that '*Behemoth* lays the blame for the catastrophe of the 1640s on two groups above all ... the Presbyterians "and other Fanatick Ministers" ... [and] the democratical gentlemen in the House of Commons.' (*Reason and Rhetoric*, 431–2.) Robert P. Kraynak in 'Hobbes's *Behemoth* and the Argument for Absolutism', *The American Political Science Review* 76 (December 1982), 837–47, links the content of ideas and elites but then denies the inherent power of the content itself: 'Hobbes's history shows that the civil war was caused by opinions and doctrines of right, which were created and exploited by ambitious intellectuals solely for the purpose of displaying their wisdom and learning.' (838)

23 Lloyd writes: 'For Hobbes, the English Civil War is first and foremost a religious war.' (*Ideals as Interests*, 193.) It is however not exactly clear what it means to call a conflict a 'religious war'—for discussion see for instance Konrad Repgen, 'What is a "Religious War"?' in *Politics and Society in Reformation Europe*, eds E. I. Kouri and Tom Scott (London: MacMillan Press, 1987), 311–28.

gles out as well Papists, Independents, Anabaptists, Quakers, Fifth-monarchy-men, Londoners, and opportunists of all sorts. In this key passage, he notes the intentional agitation pursued by religious elite:

> The mischief proceeded wholly from the Presbyterian preachers, who, by a long practised histrionic faculty, preached up the rebellion powerfully ... To the end that the State becoming popular, the Church might be so too, and governed by an Assembly; and by consequences (as they thought) seeing politics are subservient to religion, they might govern, and thereby satisfy not only their covetous humour with riches, but also their malice with power to undo all men that admire not their wisdom. (159)

This description seems to support his observation in *Leviathan* that man sought 'power after power' and has added to a typical ' Hobbist' reading that sees all motivations as a ploy for power. While ambition is indisputably a factor, these actors all use ideas to gain their ends, and indeed their ends and identities are based upon ideas. Ideas and ambition in the civil war were inextricably connected. Hobbes may impugn the authenticity of the actors by describing them as hypocritical but his analysis squarely focuses on the nature and interplay of ideas as well. Moreover, Hobbes is purporting to explain the complete destruction of a commonwealth. This destruction could not have come about solely through the play of individual ambition, as if it were a palace coup he were concerned with. It is only because of a certain conjunction of democratic conditions and a structure of beliefs that contention over power could have progressed to such fatal society-wide effect.

The three seditious ideas Hobbes blames for the king's downfall are (1) that politics is subservient to religion; (2) popular government; and (3) mixed monarchy. The most damaging belief is that political authority is not supreme in the public realm and must be subordinated to religious truth.

> If it be lawful then for subjects to resist the King, when he commands anything that is against the Scripture, that is, contrary to the command of God, and to be judge of the meaning of the Scripture, it is impossible that the life of any King, or the peace of any Christian kingdom, can be long secure. It is this doctrine that divides a kingdom within itself, whatsoever the men be, loyal or rebels, that write or preach it publicly. (50)[24]

In the past, this principle was dangerous because it juxtaposed the power of the church against that of the secular sovereign. By the time of the Reformation, however, its danger had taken on a new form. If each individ-

---

24 This doctrine confuses the public about which authority should determine action for public purposes, leading to 'two kingdoms in one and the same nation, and no man ... able to know which of his masters he must obey' (8).

ual's relationship to God were more important than any other and each person had personal access to interpreting the Bible, then the result would be a proliferation of competing churches. 'I confess this licence of interpreting the Scripture was the cause of so many several sects, as having lain hid till the beginning of the late King's reign, did then appear to the disturbance of the commonwealth' (22).

There is an additional problem with the effect of religion in the political realm. Hobbes opens Dialogue I with an attack on papal authority. While he does not blame Catholics or Catholic theology for the civil war, the principle of religious superiority is criticized. Another important feature comes into view here, however. Religion maintains habits of mind in thinking about and acting in the public sphere that emphasize dependence on a human authority. 'I think that neither the preaching of friars nor monks, nor of parochial priests, tended to teach men what, but whom to believe' (16), he pointed out. This objection to paternalistic religion may seem much more applicable to Catholicism than to Presbyterianism, Hobbes's main nemesis in *Behemoth*. But in that case as well Hobbes pointed out the advantages that any clergy gain when religion succeeds in claiming ascendancy over politics. A comments: 'for religion has been for a long time, and is now by most people, taken for the same thing with divinity, to the great advantage of the clergy', and B replies: 'And especially now amongst the Presbyterians ... To believe in Christ is nothing with them, unless you believe as they bid you' (57).[25] In this way, religion is dangerous because it grounds authority in a person, whose personal interests and egoistic pride are advanced under the trappings of the public good.

Hobbes does not believe the civil war could have come about only on the basis of religious causes, and he goes on to link religious agitators with Parliamentarians who had adopted ideals of liberty, democracy and popular sovereignty. 'It was not their own art alone that did it, but they had the concurrence of a great many gentlemen, that did no less desire a popular government in the civil state than these ministers did in the Church' (23). In the view of democrats, monarchy is equivalent to tyranny

---

25 In presenting the remarks of 'A' and 'B' as signifying a face-value meaning, I do not assume that Hobbes wrote without rhetorical effect in mind or without layers of pedagogy embedded in his presentation of ideas. There is no doubt that Hobbes was not always straightforward in his meaning. Yet, I read the dialogue in *Behemoth* as for the most part representing alternatives that Hobbes countenanced and that his purpose was to manage the logic of their presentation, leading the reader to denounce fragmenting religious and democratic demagogues. While I find Vaughan's imaginative reading of *Behemoth* fruitful, I am not convinced that the substance of what the interlocutors say is only meaningful to the extent that it tells us how A is educating B – such that we as readers are only meant to witness B's reaction to A's arguments and not meant to react to the arguments and narrative of war themselves.

and inherently prone to destroy the people's liberty. This cluster of ideas emanated out of the universities: Hobbes observes that most of the House of Commons was made up of

> men of the better sort, that had been so educated, as that in their youth having read the books written by famous men of the ancient Grecian and Roman commonwealths concerning their polity and great actions, in which books the popular government was extolled by the glorious name of liberty, and monarchy disgraced by the name of tyranny; they became thereby in love with their forms of government. (3)

In fact, Hobbes equates clerical behavior with that of classical democratic agitators:

> I do not remember that I have read of any kingdom or state in the world, where liberty was given to any private man to call the people together, and make orations to them frequently, or at all, without first making the state acquainted, except only in Christendom. I believe the heathen Kings foresaw, that a few such orators would be able to make a great sedition. (16)

The universities are the seedbed for this mutual agitation:

> For such curious questions in divinity are first started in the Universities, and so are all those politic questions concerning the rights of civil and ecclesiastic government; and there they are furnished with arguments for liberty out of the works of Aristotle, Plato, Cicero, Seneca, and out of the histories of Rome and Greece, for their disputation against the necessary power of their sovereigns. (56)

The linking of democrats and religious clerics is a constant theme of the book (see also 40, 43, 95).

If the downfall of a ruler were insured by the enthusiasm of his enemies, then perhaps Charles I would have been doomed by the existence of Presbyterians and Parliamentarians. But the monarchy was far from a house of cards, and the dynamic of disintegration required additional elements of belief. Absolutely essential in Hobbes's estimation was the idea of mixed monarchy. This was the notion that absolute monarchy 'should be divided between the King, the House of Lords, and the House of Commons' (33). This idea served as a fatal linchpin in the collapse because it was held by the King's supporters as well as his enemies, thus weakening and confusing their resolve in responding to attacks by the enemy. In Dialogue 3, B asks A: 'But what fault do you find in the King's counselors, lords, and other persons of quality and experience?' and A answers:

> Only the fault, which was generally in the whole nation, which was, that they thought the government of England was not an absolute, but a mixed monarchy; and that if the king should clearly subdue this Parliament, that his power would be what he pleased, and theirs as little as he pleased: which they counted tyranny. This opinion, though it did not lessen their endeavour to gain the victory for the King in a bat-

tle, when a battle could not be avoided, yet it weakened their endeavour to procure him an absolute victory in the war. (114–15)

The effect of each one of the ideas — religion, popular sovereignty and mixed monarchy — is to dissolve the absoluteness of the sovereign, hence by definition, Hobbes rejects them. However, in *Behemoth*, Hobbes is concerned more with the consequences of these ideas than axioms. Taken together they have two notable consequences, which characterize democracy as we know it as well: they lead to elite competition and they encourage mass political involvement. I take up the first of these here and consider the second in the next section.

As stated earlier, Hobbes's primary focus in *Behemoth* appears to be elite struggles for power,[26] but perhaps a better way to conceptualize this problem is elite competition within democratic conditions. Self-government institutionally requires that persons come forward and compete to lead the people, who in turn choose which candidate ought to govern. We are naturally led to ask — under these circumstances, who comes forward and why, and who wins and why? Hobbes focuses on the motives of those seeking political leadership (pride and power) and the debasing of the presentation of the public good due to competition among the contenders for the people's approval. Democratic politics rewards capabilities of leaders to appeal to the lowest common denominator, a familiar complaint about democracies: 'impudence in democratical assemblies ... 'tis the goddess of rhetoric, and carries proof with it' (68–9). The most clever, the best demagogues, not the most wise or the most just, triumph, as he notes:

> those that by ambition were once set upon the enterprise of changing the government, they cared not much what was reason and justice in the cause, but what strength they might procure by seducing the multitude with remonstrances from the Parliament House, or by sermons in the churches. (115–16)

---

26 Again Baumgold, in *Hobbes's Political Theory*, and in 'Hobbes's Political Sensibility: The Menace of Political Ambition', in *Thomas Hobbes and Political Theory*, ed. Dietz, argues that Hobbes's political theory was constructed as a response to the ambitious and power-hungry. Hadn't Hobbes described Leviathan as King of the children of pride? She writes: 'In the world of politics as Hobbes conceives it, elite actors are the principal figures. Ordinary subjects are subordinate figures on the landscape, followers who 'receive their motion' from rulers and those who would be rulers.'(*Hobbes's Political Theory*, 121.) While she rightly emphasizes his concern with elite conflict, we need to keep in mind that Hobbes was concerned with a more systemic social collapse and not simply with sources of disturbance or disruption that all political regimes inevitably harbor. There is no political system in which elites do not struggle for power. Under what combination of factors would system dissolution occur? The mobilization of the masses must be an important part in answering this. While they may initially 'receive their motion' from instigators (given the fact that they are not generally political initiators) ordinary people are not unthinking, disinterested place-holders for the elite. They cannot be counted on to be completely predictable and hence of no theoretical importance.

Democracies compel leaders to appeal to crudely emotional, awe-inspiring, fear-inducing, and self-inflating ideas and arguments. This trait of democracies arises from a need to gain the approval of the multitude in competition with other contenders. It is not that the people are too simple to understand any other type of public rhetoric but that *in competing* to gain one's widest possible appeal, the democratic contender must project a language that trumps his competitor's—it's a race to the bottom. In remarking on Thucydides's dislike of democracy he writes:

> And upon divers occasions he noteth the emulation and contention of the demagogues for reputation and glory of wit; with their crossing of each other's counsels, to the damage of the public; the inconsistency of resolutions, caused by the diversity of ends and power of rhetoric in the orators; and the desperate actions undertaken upon the flattering advice of such as desired to attain, or to hold what they had attained, of authority and sway amongst the common people. (*EW* 8. xvii)

Hobbes remarks upon the ensnaring of the people by public rhetoric:

> It is easier to gull the multitude, than any one man amongst them. For what one man, that has not his natural judgment depraved by accident, could be so easily cozened in a matter that concerns his purse, had he not been passionately carried away by the rest to change of government, or rather to a liberty of every one to govern himself? (38)

Those who come forward are driven by glory and by power, and their incentives in presenting themselves and their policies to the people are to distort the real interests of the commonwealth and of the people in the race to win. Hence, elite competition does not insure that the best will triumph, rather that the common good is destroyed. So much of *Behemoth* is a bitter indictment of the agitators: from the opening lines, Hobbes takes the reader to a mountaintop from which to view men with 'a prospect of all kinds of injustice, and of all kinds of folly ... produced by their dams hypocrisy and self-conceit' (1). Hobbes sees the struggle for leadership by those clamoring for self-government as a stage-set for self-glorification and not as leaders and the people debating public policy for the good of the whole. In a rebuke of the religious contenders for ascendancy, he asks:

> What needs so much preaching of faith to us that are no heathens, and that believe already all that Christ and his apostles have told us is necessary to salvation, and more too? Why is there so little preaching of justice? I have indeed heard righteousness often recommended to the people, but I have seldom heard the word *justice* occur in their sermons; nay, though in the Latin and Greek Bible the word *justice* occur exceeding often, yet in the English, though it be a word that every man understands, the word righteousness (which few understand to signify the same, but take it rather for rightness of opinion, than of action or intention), is put in the place of it. (63)

This presentation of Hobbes's critique of democracy leaves us with a view of the people as highly passive and narrow-minded, even if not dumb and malevolent. How ought we to interpret Hobbes's assertion that 'the power of the mighty hath no foundation but in the opinion and belief of the people' (16)? Even if we were to dismiss this assertion as a rhetorical ploy on his part, we cannot, I believe ignore the more subtle version of events portrayed in his history. In that subtler version, while the people are not civic heroes, nor enlightened choosers, their actions might be seen as reasonable. I turn now to consider the important role the people played in Hobbes's history.

The role of the people

There are three dramatic structures in *Behemoth*. First, Hobbes traces long-term causes of rebellion through the interplay of certain key beliefs (as discussed previously), which structure a logic of argument and reasons for action. The second major drama is the progressive usurpation of power by parliament and the king's gradual descent into physical and juridical weakness. I attempted to portray some aspects of the interplay between these two parts of the story in the preceding section. Here I look at the third main drama: the seduction of the people, the necessity of which stands as the background condition for the civil war. A key dynamic of the revolution is the battle between the sides for the allegiance of the multitude.[27] It was 'the common people, whose hands were to decide the controversy' (115). The designation 'the people' occurs ubiquitously in *Behemoth*, an indication of the central role it (they) plays.[28]

Before presenting this third version of events, we should confront an obvious objection to seeing the people as historically important and theoretically relevant. Hobbes had described the people as corrupted and seduced,[29] therefore, was there any drama to their co-optation? Hobbes portrays the people as ignorant and gullible. He notes that the 'ignorant multitude' (68) are swayed by the parliament's use of words and that 'the

---

27 Hobbes distinguishes between 'the multitude' and 'the people' in order to mark the difference between, respectively, a random collection of persons with heterogeneous motives and objectives (a crowd), and a constituted collectivity with a unified will. See *De Cive: The English Version*, ed. H. Warrender (Oxford: Clarendon Press, 1983), ch. VI. 'The people' is the conceptualization of a multitude who have unified into a single entity obligated to the sovereign. The actions of a multitude have no moral consequences according to this definition, unlike the actions of a people. I have used the term 'the people' less formally, to refer to the multitude on the cusp of becoming a moral entity. I believe Hobbes does so as well in *Behemoth*. One point of the sovereign was to overcome the anarchic element of the multitude and to form an obligating 'person' based on the consent of all.

28 132 times to be exact. If we also count 'people' the total is 199. I thank Lee Sigelman for providing this word count based on computerized text analysis.

29 These words are not synonymous though Hobbes uses them interchangeably.

common people ... are terrified and amazed by preachers, with fruitless and dangerous doctrines' (70–1). He states that the people don't understand the issues, and many do not (or cannot) read the controversies in writing, so the persuasive power of the orators is magnetic. He describes how the House of Commons 'put the people into a tumult upon any occasion they desired' (69), and that the rabble were made insolent and egged on by the provocations of the leaders. This all makes the people appear as completely passive props in a morality play: the king is the innocent embattled victim and the people hopeless dupes, used as tools to bring him down. The fact that the people may serve in a dramatically pivotal role in a morality play does not indicate independence of mind. If we assume that the people are ignorant and gullible, then the mere presence of strong, seditious ideas in the pulpits is enough to insure and explain the downfall of the king.

Yet, Hobbes's treatment of the people is not so simple. One feature of the people is that they care for their own local lives and welfare first and on the whole are not drawn to an active public life on a larger scale. About them, Hobbes says at the beginning of the book: 'For there were very few of the common people that cared much for either of the causes' (2). One reason for this is their lack of leisure, which prevented them from becoming more deeply involved in political disputes. The people are 'ignorant' not in the sense of incapable of learning but in the sense of not having access to knowledge about the issues being debated in universities and elsewhere, issues Hobbes believed were absurd on many accounts and certainly dangerous to the commonwealth. 'The people have one day in seven the leisure to hear instruction' (159), a condition that would tend to make them vulnerable to the ideas of their ministers. Another reason is that the common people are not inherently driven to seek self-glorification — indeed this may be part of the very definition of what is 'common' in the common people, their satisfaction with a life not lived on a larger, ambitious stage.[30] Because of this, the people exhibit another characteristic: they are moved to action primarily by leaders.

> For people always have been, and always will be, ignorant of their
> duty to the public, as never meditating anything but their particular

---

[30] The people act in typical ways. While Hobbes portrayed human nature in universal terms in *Leviathan* — notably, humans are afraid of death, they are competitive and seek glory — he also constantly took note of differences among individual *types* as well as distinctive characteristics pertaining to the roles of groups in society. Not all persons are equally glory-seekers, some are more generous than others, and so forth. Similarly, specific features are associated with various roles of persons in society. *Behemoth* clearly exemplifies Hobbes's sociological observations: the clergy, London merchants, Lords, vainglorious intellectuals in the universities — each group displays characteristic types of interests and attitudes in acting in the public sphere.

interest; in other things following their immediate leaders; which are either the preachers, or the most potent of the gentlemen that dwell amongst them: as common soldiers for the most part follow their immediate captains, if they like them. (39)

Notably, this observation puts as much onus on the king as on the other leaders.[31]

Hobbes consistently credits the people with the capacity to reason about politics to the extent necessary for the stability and development of a regime. 'Why may not men be taught their duty, that is, the science of *just* and *unjust*, as divers other sciences have been taught, from true principles and evident demonstration; and much more easily than any of those preachers and democratical gentlemen could teach rebellion and treason?' (39), he asks. When B exclaims in Dialogue 4 of *Behemoth* 'What silly things are the common sort of people, to be cozened as they were so grossly!', A replies, 'What sort of people, as to this matter, are not of the common sort?' (158). On the whole, the picture we can draw up is that the people are working people, busy with their own existence, politicized when they have to be and when they are drawn into it, tending to trust their immediate leadership, and fully capable of enlightened leadership. These are the people whose choice decided the direction of the conflict.

The overthrowing of a monarchy that had 'by right of descent continued above six hundred years' (1), cannot be easily explained by insubordination and the 'ambition of a few discontented persons' (L 491). The people began on the side of the monarch. At the beginning of the contest, the king naturally holds the advantage, or at most the sides are evenly matched. The inclination of the people to lean toward the veneration of the king or to be neutral, the institutional weight of hundreds of years of traditional monarchical power, and the army of 60,000 men under the king's command would all seem to give the king the advantage. Hobbes declares the people's predisposition to support the king on a number of occasions:

> the English would never have taken well that the Parliament should make war upon the King, upon any provocation, unless it were in their own defence, in case the King should first make war upon them; and, therefore, it behoved them to provoke the King, that he might do something that might look like hostility. (28)

Clerical and parliamentary leaders purposely set out to trap the king in a premeditated and machiavellian manner, realizing they could not openly defy his supremacy until they set the stage to make it look as if the king

---

31 That Hobbes does not have a theory of leadership per se is indicative of his approach to politics, justice and democracy. But it may also be a theoretical weak spot in a political theory. Rousseau, who took over so much of Hobbes's work, recognized the essential foundational role of the ' lawgiver'.

himself has provoked war upon England. After recounting the king's military loss to the Scots in 1640 and his being forced to call parliament into session (hence the initiation of the Long Parliament itself), Hobbes concludes:

> And yet for all this they durst not presently make war upon the King: there was so much yet left of reverence to him in the hearts of the people ... They must have some colour or other to make it believed that the King made war first upon the Parliament ... Therefore they resolved to proceed with him like skilful hunters; first to single him out, by men disposed in all parts to drive him into the open field with their noise, and then in case he should but seem to turn head, to call that a making of war against the Parliament. (35, 36)

What needs explaining then is why the bonds of loyalty to the king became weak and the mass of people joined the opposition side. The regime did not crumble all at once and had to be systematically attacked. At a number of key junctures, Hobbes states that the course of events could have shifted away from the momentum built up by the elite attacks and back to the traditional support for the monarchy.

Another logic of ideological interaction thus appears in *Behemoth*. The people do not appear solely as a back-up serving the purposes of seditious elites, but also as exercising a form of political judgment on their own. The king and parliament themselves credit the people with the power to decide the conflict. Both sides are constantly writing petitions and publishing proclamations accusing their enemy, defending themselves, and attempting to corner the other in political and legal traps. The dynamic of performing for the people constitutes a consistent theme in Hobbes depiction of the conflict. B asks A: 'But now that the war was resolved on, on both sides, what needed any more dispute in writing?' A replies:

> I know not what need they had. But on both sides they thought it needful to hinder one another, as much as they could, from levying of soldiers; and, therefore, the King did set forth declarations in print, to make the people know that they ought not to obey the officers of the new *militia* set up by ordinance of Parliament, and also to let them see the legality of his own commissions of array. And the Parliament on their part did the like, to justify to the people the said ordinance, and to make the commission of array appear unlawful. (118)

There are other instances in which Hobbes himself observes the independence of the people. Reiterating the predisposition of the people, he claims that if the king himself had acted more commandingly and decisively he would have garnered the people's support: 'such his stoutness being known to the people, would have brought to his assistance many more hands than all the arguments of law, or force of eloquence, couched in declarations and other writings' (116).³² That the people must decide does not of course indicate that their decision will be what Hobbes thinks is the right one, or that their decision is wholly independent, uninfluenced by the persuasion of those competing to lead them. It does signify however that there was a judgment to be made and that their choice mattered to the fate of the nation and the king.

Hobbes's explicit answer to the monarchy's destruction does not focus on what the king did (his original mistake in attempting to impose the Book of Common Prayer on the Scots is noted at the beginning of the book (28) but not seen as fatal)³³ but on the success of the opposition in painting the king as not to be trusted because of tyrannical intentions. The situation was one in which the people had been stirred up, mobilized and forced to make a choice. In that situation, they could not remain neutral, and the fear and distrust of a king even suspected of tyrannical intentions led them to lean away from him. Once this dynamic had come into effect, a point was passed and a pervasive context of distrust made it more rational to take a stance against rather than of trust in the king. The confiscation of power by the parliament is a story of seducing the people to the parliament's side, to perceiving the king as the real threat. Parliament is able to maneuver the logic of the situation such that given the juridical language of fundamental right and treason, the king stands accused and the people and parliament have no choice but to engage in war to defeat him. This dynamic uncovers the sense in which the people are at the very core of the balance of obedience and protection, not only in principle but in historical reality, a point I discuss more fully in the next section.

One might concede that in a condition of dissolution the constitutive role of the people comes to the surface, but that this crisis situation is one purposely manufactured by the ambitions of a few men, and should not therefore be taken to indicate a more generalized democratic circumstance. Yet, the evidence of Hobbes's theoretical constructs—notably his core idea of the state of nature as a state of war—is an acknowledgment that the potential for this crisis situation to emerge is always present. In this way, we might see the idea of the state of nature as an elemental dem-

---

32   Again, on the independence of judging, in Dialogue 4, in discussing the Rump Parliament in 1648, he concludes 'By these their proceedings they had already lost the hearts of the generality of the people, and had nothing to trust to but the army; which was not in their power, but in Cromwell's.' (160)

33   The king, assuming his power to be secure embarked on 'that unlucky business of imposing upon the Scots, who were all Presbyterians, our book of common-prayer' (28). This provocative move triggered alarm and anger among Presbyterians and other religious dissenters within England, mobilizing them to join with democracy-minded Parliamentarians in the House of Commons to challenge the king about more fundamental constitutional issues of authority.

ocratic condition, one in which the people are called on to make a decision about their collective existence.[34]

But Hobbes also recognizes democratic circumstances as more than an artificial or sporadic creation of agitators, which a social contract is constructed to overcome. A number of passages in *Behemoth* testify to the fact that democratized conditions have become a pervasive cultural and structural fact about the world. That is, the people in general have become more permanently engaged in politics through changes in religious belief and economic development. Hobbes notes the political demands of the London merchants and population in general. More importantly, he is constantly referring to the politicization of a mass public under the banner of religious freedom. While I have already discussed his criticism of the use of religion by the clerical establishment, it is noteworthy that Hobbes is not critical of one of the more democratic features of the new religion — it's accessibility to the common person, a feature he believes can contribute to peace via the education in duty. He writes for example:

> whereas you think it needless, or perhaps hurtful, to have the Scriptures in English, I am of another mind. There are so many places of Scripture easy to be understood, that teach both true faith and good morality (and that as fully as is necessary to salvation), of which no seducer is able to dispossess the mind (of any ordinary readers), that the reading of them is so profitable as not to be forbidden without great damage to them and the commonwealth. (53)

In these democratized circumstances — ones due to destabilization and ones growing out of more long-run social-cultural changes — the sovereign's justification must change as well. A observes that 'the people, for them and their heirs, by consent and oaths, have long ago put the supreme power of the nation into the hands of their kings, for them and their heirs; and consequently into the hands of this King, their known and lawful sovereign' (152). But no doubt that was part of the problem: the settlement on the king had taken place 'long ago'. In a newly democratizing age, the situation was fundamentally altered, and the traditionalist acceptance of authority was no longer sufficient to secure allegiance. The problem was not only that an ambitious elite could mobilize a broad population through democratically inspired ideas, but also that the conditions for independent judgment, social power, and the political mobilization had become general, permanent social-cultural conditions, thereby also making 'destabilization' by elites a more chronic possibility. The 'seditious' ideas of self-government themselves no doubt reflected in some sense developing conditions and aspirations. Under these circumstances, there

---

34 I thank John Ferejohn for helping to clarify this point.

would always potentially arise democratic demands. I believe Hobbes recognized an inevitable, forward-marching energy in the mobilization of the multitude in the political upheavals of his time and that he must have recognized this as a new circumstance. His radically new defense of sovereign power was a response to the ideological failure of the king to present the foundations of his power in this transformed political and mental environment.

Thus, in addition to his explicit, blameful depiction of the king's loss to a malevolent elite, Hobbes also gives an implicit explanation of what may have led to the failure of the monarchy.[35] On this reading, again we go back to the structure of ideas available for justification and reasons for action. The problem was that the king did not have sufficient ideological constructs with which to take up the battle for the hearts and minds of the people.

Ideology and obedience: the continuing power of the people

Hobbes's history portrays the people as playing a decisive role politically. Of what theoretical consequence is this? The people have always been recognized to play an essential normative role in Hobbes's construction of the sovereign through their consent.[36] Wootton does link the democratizing nature of early modern English politics to Hobbes's ideas. He notes the influence of the Levellers on Hobbes's thought after 1651:

> the Levellers had denied that the people could be bound by past acts of submission, and insisted that government must be founded on the continuing consent of all citizens. They had denied that the people could be fully represented by any corporate body legally acting on their behalf, and insisted that they must give their consent as a multitude of individuals. It is this universal consent, this continuing sover-

---

35 Skinner notes at the end of his study of Hobbes's rhetoric that, '[I]n teaching philosophy to speak English, Hobbes at the same time taught it a particular tone of voice. As we have seen, the tone is very much that of the sane and moderate *savant* beset on all sides by fanaticism and stupidity. We cannot expect reason to triumph, the tone implies, since the foolish and ignorant will always be in a majority. But we can at least hope to dicomfit them by wielding the weapons of ridicule, deriding their excesses, sneering at their errors, drawing our readers into a scornful alliance against their general benightedness.' (*Reason and Rhetoric*, 436.)

36 In principle, Hobbes stated that sovereignty could be institutionalized as monarchy, aristocracy or democracy, but that the form most conducive to peace was monarchy. In principle, Hobbes had also argued that democracy was the origination of all forms of government (see *De Cive*, VII, 5) because in the initial coming together of a group of people, their agreement to found a body politic was a democratic one. This original democratic moment must inevitably lead to a decision about who would govern on an ongoing basis, and this latter decision established the permanent form of government—preferably for Hobbes a monarchy or aristocracy. See Tuck, *Philosophy and Government*, 310 ff., and Baumgold, *Hobbes's Political Theory*, 41 ff., for discussion of this issue. See also Murray Forsyth, 'Thomas Hobbes and the Constituent Power of the People', *Political Studies* 29 (1981), 191–203, for the argument that Hobbes was the originator of the doctrine of 'the people' as the constituent power of the body politic, the founding principle of the American and French Revolutions.

eignty of the multitude, that Hobbes seeks to lay claim to through his theory of authorization. It is from this continuing consent that Leviathan derives his authority and power.[37]

As a matter of right, however, the people can make no claims on the sovereign. Most have stressed that while the 'continuing sovereignty of the multitude' may exist in principle, it does not obligate the sovereign and the democratic potential of the idea is therefore curtailed.[38] Thus, while the principle of consent grounds the normative role of the people in the justification of political obligation, consent remains a singular act of authorization, which, in creating the sovereign, relinquishes the people's continuing judgment of the sovereign. The people give up independent judgment as a continuous political right, and the tie between the sovereign and the people is solely one of obedience.

Historically, the power of the people appeared in their siding with the rebels and their disobedience of the king. This historical fact may have had nothing to do with Hobbes's demand for nearly unconditional obedience to the sovereign.[39] Nevertheless, many writers have accentuated the seemingly blind obedience that Hobbes required of the people. Wolin for instance notes Hobbes's 'despotic mentality,' which sought to make 'subjects fit for despotic rule'.[40] If those agitating against the king—rebels and the common people—had seen it as their duty to adhere to the king unquestioningly, then the war would never have come about. As it stands, this is an uninteresting tautology—if men were angels government would not be necessary. Could it have been Hobbes's intent in writing his extended works of political philosophy to tell us that if we would all simply act as sheep we would prevent ourselves from turning into wolves?

There is, however, one indisputable sense in which the people's power continues to play a decisive role in 'constraining' or shaping the sover-

---

37 Wootton, 'Introduction', *Divine Right and Democracy*, 57.
38 In Sorell's words: 'the obligations of subjects to their sovereigns are entirely one-sided. By the covenant that institutes the commonwealth each of the many makes a free gift of his right of self-governance to whomever becomes the sovereign, but since this person transfers or lays down no right himself, he can enjoy the benefit of the transfer of right from the multitude without having to give up some right in return.' Sorell, *Hobbes*, 119.
39 Tuck argues in 'Hobbes's Moral Philosophy', *The Cambridge Companion to Hobbes*, ed. T. Sorell (Cambridge: Cambridge University Press, 1996), 186, that 'Hobbes regarded politics as the solution to the conflicts characteristic of *mores*.' He interprets Hobbes's political theory as a response to skepticism implying that the philosophical context is more important to understanding Hobbes's work than the political one (granting of course that some philosophical problems and solutions are themselves more salient in some periods than in others). The fact that politics is itself always and necessarily a realm of conflict would seem to be an important obstacle to its providing a solution to skepticism.
40 Sheldon Wolin, 'Hobbes and the Culture of Despotism', in *Thomas Hobbes and Political Theory*, ed. Dietz, 19. Vaughan insists as well that Hobbes aimed to create 'docile people'. Vaughan, *'Behemoth' Teaches 'Leviathan'*, 134.

eign, even though this role is not a 'right.' Hobbes concludes in the final paragraph of *Leviathan* that his aim was 'to set before mens eyes the mutuall Relation between Protection and Obedience; of which the condition of Humane Nature, and the laws Divine, (both Naturall and Positive) require an inviolable observation'. The sovereign protects and therefore one is obligated to obey. Hobbes does not make the argument that the people are *obligated to believe* the sovereign will protect them, just that they are obligated to obey the sovereign because he protects them. But belief is crucial here, and it is incumbent upon the sovereign to continuously produce belief in himself. As Hobbes wrote in *Leviathan*:

> I conclude therefore, that in the instruction of the people in the Essentiall Rights (which are the Naturall, and Fundamental Lawes) of Soveraignty, there is no difficulty, (whilest a Soveraign has his Power entire,) but what proceeds from his own fault, or the fault of those whom he trusteth in the administration of the Common-wealth; and consequently, it is his Duty, to cause them so to be instructed; and not onely his Duty, but his Benefit also, and Security, against the danger that may arrive to himselfe in his naturall Person, from Rebellion.
> (L 233)

How might the sovereign do this? Part of the answer must lie in the maintenance of legitimacy through what we might call ideological hegemony, that is, a public set of ideas that serve as a collective resource around which argument and discussion can take place. Unlike a Gramscian or Marxist use of these terms, I do not mean to imply a purely manipulative control of the minds of the people. The need for hegemony as the persuasive hold on peoples' beliefs is a sign of their power—they must be persuaded, they cannot be taken for granted or counted as mental ciphers. Hobbes's recognition of the power of the people to determine outcomes did not lead him to insist on stifling political engagement but to turn people's attention to ideas and reasons for acting in the political realm that were conducive to peace, order and social productivity. One point of my reading of *Behemoth* is to show that Hobbes recognized an ineliminable element of independent judgment, which if not based solely on reason is generated from balancing various beliefs, values and interests. Therefore, we should not read the phrase 'taught their duty' to mean that people must be made unthinking rule-followers indoctrinated in the correct litany of behavior. Hobbes did not think it possible (or desirable?) to constitute a nation of such a type of person. Rather, Hobbes seeks to take the politicized mentality and turn it to a 'love of obedience' (59).

Behemoth demonstrates that obedience must itself be an emotionally based *idea* to which the majority attaches value, not just propositional truth value, nor simply value as individual virtue. The idea of obedience must itself be a cause; the act of obedience cannot just be an effect of other ideas. But when would obedience make sense as a cause or the basis of an ideology? Obedience becomes a cause one can 'love' when it is attached to a fully elaborated and explained view of the value of the political realm. Hobbes's solution is to give the sovereign the ideological tools for the people to identify with him as the protector of that realm. The appeal to the *unity* of the commonwealth and to the sovereign's capacity to ensure *justice* are the focal points of the sovereign's ideology. But there must be an acceptance of those values in the first place. The content of the sovereign's ideology must provide a world-view that turns people's public emotions and minds toward justifying and explaining how to achieve those values. Absolute power on the part of the sovereign is not self-justifying. It is derivative of this larger world-view. Obedience to this sovereign therefore signifies the triumph of a political point of view. This solves for Hobbes a major problem.

In *Behemoth*, Hobbes depicts in stark terms the consequences of disobedience to lawful sovereigns. Disobedience creates a collective situation of lawlessness because one authoritative version of the law is no longer collectively observed. But this collectively irrational result may be one that the parties in conflict are not convinced they want to overcome. The logic of the situation is not like a prisoner's dilemma in which all parties see the collectively rational result but cannot reach it from within the logic of individually rational behavior. In this situation, there is no collectively rational result because persons and groups see themselves and their interests in fundamentally different ways and do not want to agree to an accommodation because this would dilute who they are and what they stand for. The parties in conflict are driven to define the situation in their own terms. Therefore, one of Hobbes's rhetorical objectives must be to create a collective point of view that all could accept as meaningfully representative of them. Hobbes's theory cannot therefore aim to create passive, unthinking subjects but active, consenting citizens who have come to recognize the supremacy of a political point of view embodied in the sovereign. People must come to see who they are differently such that the self they want to protect in public terms is best secured through the unity of the commonwealth rather than through fragmenting ideological positions (mainly religious).

Granted, Hobbes does not clearly demarcate the act of obedience from the idea of obedience, but I believe this distinction makes a fundamental difference in how we read his vision of citizenship. There are two modes of calling for or instilling obedience: one says 'You should understand and see the need to be obedient' while the other says 'Be obedient'. These are two quite distinct directives to being a political person: the first treats persons as citizens (with implicit democratic foundations); the second treats persons as subjects. If the person's engagement with the public power is through embracing an idea of obedience, he or she is recognized as active. If that person is involved through behaving obediently, he or she is passive. Hobbes puts political justification on a democratic track by conceiving of citizen involvement in active terms, while at the same time attempting to curtail that involvement by restricting the activity to a positive assention of the mind to the sovereign himself and sovereignty generally, and not to the actual ongoing acts of the concrete sovereign. Hobbes recognizes that the human mind is irrepressible—to which *Behemoth* vigorously testifies—and that it must be harnessed to the peace of the political nation.

Hobbes acknowledges the continual involvement of the people in the sovereign's power through the sovereign's need to maintain hegemony: he (it) must keep the allegiance of the people through convincing them of the importance of a unified political nation and in the cause of justice. Hobbes's recognition that the state cannot control the minds of the people does not contradict Hobbes's doctrine that the sovereign controls public judgment. Once a sovereign is established, he determines and controls the content of public rules. The acceptance of the supremacy of the sovereign is however based not on the rules the sovereign will make once established, but on consent given initially and continually to his legitimacy and hegemony. Hobbes shows that the power of the sovereign to control public judgment is surrounded by the penumbra of the people's continual acceptance of this.

While the conception of ideology may seem foreign to Hobbes's mind, he, in some not fully distinct sense, recognized the need for the idea of absolute sovereignty to be elaborated in ideological terms—that is, not simply as 'the truth' as opposed to all false ideas, but as a comprehensive fighting creed, an elaborated view of how the world works and the corresponding ideas and actions that should follow.[41] We might say that what *Leviathan* offers and *Behemoth* demonstrates to be necessary is an ideology of politics itself, ironic as this might seem given Hobbes's reputation. As a political theorist, Hobbes' objectives were two-fold—to develop a science of politics that demonstrated the obligation of citizens to obey an absolute sovereign, and then to convey the necessity of this view of political obliga-

---

41 Sorell, in 'Hobbes's Persuasive Civil Science', esp. 350–1, discusses the concept of 'counsel' as a way to understand what Hobbes may be grasping for in a new type of public speech. 'When Hobbes tries to make room for an alternative to passion-stirring speech that is still prescriptive but also rational, scientific, and material for deductive reasoning, it is not immediately clear that he has the resources to do so' (350). I would suggest that what Hobbes's own writing exemplifies is the beginnings of modern ideology insofar as it is prescriptive, explanatory, and attempts to provide a 'world-view'—that is, it is not just a series of discrete counsels or pieces of advice, but gives an integrated depiction of human nature and institutions.

tion to his readers in order to help establish a more peaceful, ordered English commonwealth. A question arises about the compatibility of these two sides of Hobbes' work. If Hobbes's political morality is meant to solve the tendency of political conflict to degenerate into civil war due to ideological differences, then how is it possible to appeal to such persons as Hobbes describes them to be, driven as they are by the negative logic he presents? *Leviathan* must first create 'a people' who seek laws of justice out of a fragmented multitude; hence his work, as well as the king's, is meant to appeal to the people and to the elite. Without a transformation in popular thinking and culture, political authority cannot be made secure in the long run, and in this way the people are as important as the elite in making Hobbes's political philosophy more than an exercise in philosophical argument.

Christopher Hill wonderfully describes the ubiquity of the fear and disdain of the common folk — as the 'rude multitude' or 'many-headed monster'[42] — which the vast majority of writers and activists, not to mention aristocrats and gentry, displayed in the early modern world. Notably, Hobbes did not share this arrogance toward the common person. 'I am one of the common people', he had said, 'of plebian descent'.[43] Keith Thomas, who contended that Hobbes remained attached to aristocratic values (against the views of Macpherson and Strauss who saw Hobbes as an ideologist for the bourgeois classes), concedes that Hobbes strikingly dissociated himself from the generally disparaging attitude toward the people. On the nature of politics, all people share the same confusions and all are cognitively capable of reasoning and acting in the public sphere.[44]

Hobbes's work is not the reaction of a timid man (all is fear) or a cynical man (all is self-interest) to his times. It is the work of a powerful mind searching for grounds to construct as broad an ideology as possible to justify the power of a unifying sovereign in the face of competing, splintering ideologies, which had taken hold of a mobilized public sphere. In a new world where ideas are the currency of power, to fail to provide convincing ideas to the people is to relinquish the capacity to rule. While Hobbes defends the king's right to rule and thus the theoretical obligation of the people to obey, the act of writing *Behemoth* is a recognition of the need for ideological power. In a sense *Behemoth* tells the story of the king's failure to convince the people as much as it was a denunciation of rebellious elites. But Hobbes did not blame the king, not because Charles I did

---

42 Hill, *Change and Continuity*, 181–204, passim.
43 Quoted in Keith Thomas, 'The Social Origins of Hobbes's Political Thought', in *Hobbes Studies*, ed. K. C. Brown (Cambridge, MA: Harvard University Press, 1965), 200.
44 That Hobbes rejected the Aristotelian conception of natural hierarchy in favor of human equality provides a foundation for the normative centrality of the non-elite person as well.

not have the benefit of Hobbes's science of virtue and vice (no one did), but because Hobbes sought to maintain the ideological dignity of the sovereign power, and he believed in the fine art of dramatic storytelling as a means toward that political end.

William Lund

Neither 'Behemoth' nor 'Leviathan'
Explaining Hobbes's Illiberal Politics

Introduction

Scholars have often found Hobbes's *Behemoth* somewhat puzzling and less worthy of close attention than his more philosophical works. After all, he describes the book as a history relating 'the actions' of English politics between 1640 and 1660 to 'their causes, pretensions, justice, order, artifice, and event'.[1] The problem stems from his general view that history was neither epistemologically nor morally sound when compared with philosophical deductions. After publishing his translation of Thucydides in 1629, he had rejected the humanist ideal of relying on using history to guide current behavior, and by 1640 was arguing that 'Experience concludeth nothing universally' and that knowledge of prior events cannot tell us whether 'anything is to be called just or unjust, true or false'. These doubts about history's utility are repeated in his later works, including even *Behemoth*, where he argues that historical records provide mere 'examples of fact' and that it is impossible 'to derive from them any argument of right'.[2]

On the other hand, Hobbes also suggests that his history might keep alive the 'memory' of the frightening events of the civil war and interregnum in a way that would be most 'instructive towards loyalty and justice'. He intends *Behemoth* to be an anti-Leviathan, and his history serves as a realistic analogue of the hypothetical state of nature and the

---

1 Thomas Hobbes, *Behemoth or the Long Parliament*, ed. F. Tonnies (Chicago: University of Chicago Press, 1990), 1.
2 Thomas Hobbes, *The Elements of Law: Natural and Politic*, ed. J. C. A. Gaskin (Oxford: Oxford University Press, 1994), 33–4, and Hobbes, *Behemoth*, 76; see also Thomas Hobbes, *Leviathan*, ed. C. B. Macpherson (Harmondsworth: Penguin, 1968), 261.

dangers entailed in the absence of clear authority.³ His story of the civil war is meant to provide a vivid and rhetorically powerful illustration of his earlier philosophical critiques of private judgment, divided or limited sovereignty, and legal limits on public authority. Thus we might ask if the 'memory' provided by the *Behemoth* is still useful in our very different world, and if we take Hobbes to be focusing on the power and authority of sovereign states, there is a prima facie case for thinking that his history must still be instructive. After all, it is widely argued that the nation-state is threatened both from above and below. Globalization and supra-national alignments threaten the ability of nations to manage their own economies and preserve their distinctive cultures, while simultaneously and more importantly from a Hobbesian perspective, sub-state tribalism and 'identity' politics lead to secessionist movements or calls for 'difference'-based exemptions from various laws.

Hobbes's philosophy and the history he narrates in *Behemoth* do provide good reasons for resisting the anarchic potential of the latter claims.⁴ On the other hand, his prescriptions for overcoming anarchy seem insufficient to our needs. Simply put, while neither a Tory nor a communitarian anti-liberal, he is still insufficiently liberal, the consequences of which include too much room for generally applicable laws and too few constraints on public authority. Hobbes's relationship to liberalism is, of course, an old and complicated question: conservative and radical critics of liberalism treat him as a classic example of all that is wrong with that tradition and liberals respond that it is foolish to treat a prototypical absolutist as a liberal.⁵ Others offer a more qualified view in which his focus on state authority is countered by philosophical commitments that emphasize the goodness of individual desire satisfaction so that, 'without being

---

3   Hobbes, *Behemoth*, 'Epistle Dedicatory'. See Stephen Holmes, 'Introduction' to Hobbes, *Behemoth*, ix, with n. 5, on the role of the Biblical Behemoth as a symbol of the 'rebellion and civil war' that could only be corrected by the creation of a Leviathan.
4   Recent critics of limiting public authority in the name of difference and private judgment include Stephen Macedo, *Diversity and Distrust: Civic Education in a Multicultural Society* (Cambridge: Harvard University Press, 2000) and Brian Barry, *Culture and Equality: An Egalitarian Critique of Multiculturalism* (Cambridge: Harvard University Press, 2001). Neither, of course, endorses Hobbes's suggested solutions.
5   Classic attempts to associate Hobbes with liberalism include Leo Strauss, *Natural Right and History* (Chicago: University of Chicago Press, 1953), and C. B. Macpherson, *The Political Theory of Possessive Individualism: Hobbes to Locke* (Oxford: Oxford University Press, 1977). Contemporary liberals reflect Thomas Nagel's view, cited in Peter Berkowitz, *Virtue and the Making of Modern Liberalism* (Princeton: Princeton University Press, 1999), 199, n. 3, that describing Hobbes as a liberal indicates 'a very poor grasp of the fundamentals of political theory'.

himself a liberal, he had in him more of the philosophy of liberalism than most of its professed defenders'.[6]

On the other hand, and as I want to emphasize, those philosophical commitments are Janus-faced and ultimately entail slamming the door on more liberal prescriptions. Specifically, I argue that his metaethical voluntarism, his deterministic and materialistic denials of free will and an incorporeal soul, and his conception of citizens as pure subjects all lead him to reject core tenets of liberalism. Without hoping for a necessary and sufficient definition of liberalism, we can stipulate a few ideals that are widely shared in that protean tradition. As Holmes argues, while Hobbes's 'psychological presuppositions' — namely that we are 'compulsive and impulsive' creatures in need of the taming prescriptions of rational self-interest — do foreshadow liberalism, he cannot be a liberal because he lacks 'an appreciation of human dignity, individual and cultural diversity, and political democracy'. Moreover, he rejects the typical liberal demand that public decisions should be 'transparent' so that citizens can evaluate 'the reasons for the basic distribution of wealth, power, authority, and freedom'.[7] Thus, Hobbes's *Behemoth* and the philosophical prescriptions it reflects are insufficient because they allow for opaque public rules. They also deny that such rules should accept, if not celebrate in Madisonian or Millian fashion, ethical and religious diversity, should protect the dignity of the individual, and should rely on democratic practices for achieving those ideals.

Voluntarism, opacity, and the fear of diversity

Hobbes's metaphysics and his metaethical voluntarism undermine the ideals of public transparency and the acceptance of diversity. He begins from the premise that the individual's opinions and beliefs are naturally diverse and opaque. Since there are no innate ideas, mental life is just the sensory experience of external matter that itself lacks any intelligible essence, and these sensory experiences will be quite various. Thus, while that which is perceived may be 'the same; yet the diversity of our reception of it, in respect of different constitutions of body, and prejudices of opinion, gives everything a tincture of our different passions'. Emphasizing the dangers posed by this diversity and assuming that actions stem

---

[6] Michael Oakeshott, *Rationalism in Politics and Other Essays* (Indianapolis: Liberty Press, 1991), 283; see also Richard Flathman, *Thomas Hobbes: Skepticism, Individuality and Chastened Politics* (Newbury Park, Ca: Sage Publications, 1993).

[7] Stephen Holmes, *Passions and Constraint: On the Theory of Liberal Democracy* (Chicago: University of Chicago Press, 1995), 3-4, and on the liberal ideal of 'transparency', see Jeremy Waldron, *Liberal Rights: Collected Papers 1981-1991* (Cambridge: Cambridge University Press, 1993), 58.

from 'Opinions; and in the well governing of Opinions, consisteth the well governing of mens Actions', he concludes that a proper sovereign must have arbitrary control over 'what Opinions and Doctrines are averse, and what conducing to Peace'.[8]

Prior theorists had relied on the capacity for reason and speech to point us beyond such opaqueness, but for Hobbes, the promise of *logos* had been dramatically oversold. Reason allows us to add and subtract names into causal propositions, which with proper definitions and deductions can yield some certainties, but it cannot completely transcend the arbitrary nature of its matter. The problem is especially acute when we consider the use of typical ethical concepts. In considering actions or policies that 'please and displease us', hopes for transparency vanish in the face of '*inconstant* signification' following from the 'nature, disposition, and interest of the speaker.' Famously then, Hobbes roots the 'Vertues, and Vices', and the use of terms like 'Good, Evill, and Contemptible' in the desires and will of individuals. Given this voluntarism, 'such names can never be true grounds of any ratiocination' because they are always relative 'to the person that useth them: There being nothing simply and absolutely so; nor any common Rule of Good and Evill' in the nature of sensed objects.[9]

In thus undermining ideals of an objective and teleological '*Summum Bonum*' that had justified pre-liberal perfectionisms,[10] Hobbes creates an opening to more modest views of the purpose of politics and the acceptance of pluralistic conceptions of the good. However, the radical nature of his skepticism bars him from following through on this liberal move. Since nature is a normative void and reason is merely instrumental, moral argument cannot be a search for transparency regarding things that are independent of the will. Instead, if 'Haeresie' is just an opinion thought to be obnoxious and '*Tyranny*' is simply monarchy 'misliked', then such prescriptive language is really aimed at manipulating others to accept and act on our evaluations. Tracking the truth of such evaluations is baseless, and 'PERSUASION' is typically less about helping those being criticized

---

8   Hobbes, *Leviathan*, 233, 109; see also Thomas Hobbes, *De Homine*, trans. Charles Wood, T. S. K. Scott-Craig and Bernard Gert, in *Man and Citizen*, ed. B. Gert (Garden City, N.Y.: Anchor Books, 1972), 63. Flathman, *Thomas Hobbes*, 5, emphasizes Hobbes's portrait of the 'abyss of self- and mutual unintelligibility'.
9   Hobbes, *Leviathan*, 109–10, 120; see also, Hobbes, *De Homine*, 47, and Hobbes, *Behemoth*, 45.
10 Hobbes, *Leviathan*, 160. For efforts to root Hobbes's skepticism in the contexts of, respectively, medieval nominalism and voluntarism, the 'rhetorical culture of Renaissance humanism', and sixteenth-century skepticism, see Oakeshott, *Rationalism in Politics*, esp. 237–8; Quentin Skinner, *Reason and Rhetoric in the Philosophy of Hobbes* (Cambridge: Cambridge University Press, 1996), 3; and Richard Tuck, 'Introduction' to Thomas Hobbes, *Leviathan* (Cambridge: Cambridge University Press, 1991).

than an effort 'at getting opinion from passion' in order to further the speaker's purposes.[11]

If widely understood, these facts might yield the conclusion that religious and ethical disputes are not real disagreements: if I truly report that X is good according to my desires and you truly report that you regard X as bad, then there is no real conflict or inconsistency. For Hobbes, however, most people cling to the mistaken belief that ethical terms do refer to an external world, allowing them to rationalize manipulations as efforts to uncover the truth. As Tuck argues, Hobbes thinks language 'takes on a false realism' because it reports the illusion that the 'wholly subjective experience' of 'vision' is of an independent reality.[12] Combining this illusion with the general inclination to pursue power, including especially the 'Honour' that Hobbes defines as 'to agree with in opinion',[13] ethical and religious differences must inevitably turn into interminable and desperate battles. While some might naturally be 'at ease within modest bounds' and simply agree to disagree, the empirical incidence of such persons is low, and even they must act to coerce and manipulate out of 'Anticipation' with regard to their material and normative interests.[14] Thus, while Milton might 'rejoyce at' diversity and hope that 'generous prudence, a little forebearance of one another, and som grain of charity' would allow 'brotherly' relations among disagreeing parties,[15] Hobbes sees no possibility of simply living with religious and ethical diversity.

Claims for liberty of 'conscience' and 'actions' regarding 'transcendent interests' in religion, justice, and legitimacy must founder because individuals will not stop there. Instead, they inevitably seek to impose their judgments, inevitably want not just liberty of action, but also 'a farther liberty of persuading others to their opinions; nor that only for every man desireth, that the sovereign authority should admit no other opinions to be maintained but such as he himself holdeth'.[16] In *Behemoth*, he argues that such desires were a central cause of the civil war and casts blame widely. However, whether Catholics, Independents, or those who hated monarchy, they all abandoned their interest self-preservation and peace-

---

11   Hobbes, *Leviathan*, 165, 240, and Hobbes, *Elements of Law*, 76. See Flathman, *Thomas Hobbes*, 68 n. 16, celebrating Hobbes's opposition to moralizing 'shame' cultures.
12   Richard Tuck, 'Hobbes's Moral Philosophy', in *The Cambridge Companion to Hobbes*, ed. T. Sorell (Cambridge: Cambridge University Press, 1996), 181.
13   Hobbes, *Leviathan*, 153.
14   Ibid., 184–5.
15   John Milton, *Areopagitica and Other Political Writings of John Milton* (Indianapolis: Liberty Fund, 1999), 41.
16   Hobbes, *Elements of Law*, 154; on the role of 'transcendent interests' in Hobbes's political philosophy, see S. A. Lloyd, *Ideals as Interests in Hobbes's 'Leviathan': The Power of Mind Over Matter* (Cambridge: Cambridge University Press, 1992), 40, 44, 271.

ful coexistence in the name of getting others to believe as they did. In this, they mirrored Hobbes's problem with Presbyterians: 'To believe in Christ is nothing with them, unless you believe as they bid you. Charity is nothing with them, unless it be charity and liberality to them, and partaking with them in faction'.[17]

Thus Hobbes's extreme voluntarism and his emphasis on the prideful character of moral argument lead him to conclude that a sound politics must annul normative diversity and its ruinous consequences. The solution requires giving an artificial sovereign the authority to settle prescriptive meanings. Since there must be 'a common measure', and since 'right reason is not existent, the reason of some man, or men, must supply the place thereof ... '.[18] In rejecting the ethical realism of Plato and Aristotle, Hobbes rejects the idea that normative conflict can be resolved by discoveries regarding an external world, but he mirrors their belief that practical reason and the correct means of calculation can yield monistic unity.[19] His own 'science' of ethics, understood as the study of man as a body in 'NATURAL PHILOSOPHY', seeks to *explain* opinions of right and wrong as deductions from external and internal motion. From this starting point, the synthetic method explains just why there is irresolvable normative diversity, just why in taking 'men insofar as they are men', there will naturally be 'Many men, many different rules for vice and virtue'. However, since we can act creatively on nature, there are also artificial bodies such as the state, the study of which is 'POLITIQUES, and CIVILL PHILOSOPHY'. With this, even those without metaphysical knowledge can work backwards by analyzing their experience with normative diversity to conclude with the need for a sovereign. Either way, ethical and political 'science' demonstrates that natural diversity can and ought to be transcended, that what is true of natural persons is not true of 'citizens' who are 'obliged' to follow a sovereign's 'common standard for virtues and vices'.[20]

Acting on this knowledge requires acknowledging the inherent dangers of pride and diversity and recognizing the non-relativistic goodness of the desire to stay alive. For Hobbes, every man 'shuns what is evil, but chiefly the chiefest of natural evils, which is death'.[21] As Holmes emphasizes, Hobbes is well aware that various beliefs have led men to ignore

17 Hobbes, *Behemoth*, 16, 57.
18 Hobbes, *Elements of Law*, 180–1.
19 Lloyd, *Ideals As Interests*, 278–9; see also David Johnston, 'Plato, Hobbes, and the Science of Practical Reasoning' and Sheldon Wolin, 'Hobbes and the Culture of Despotism', both in *Thomas Hobbes and Political Theory*, ed. M. Dietz (Lawrence, Kansas: University Press of Kansas, 1990).
20 Hobbes, *Leviathan*, 149, and Hobbes, *De Homine*, 68–9.
21 Thomas Hobbes, *De Cive*, in *Man and Citizen*, 115.

this in the name of religious martyrdom, the risks of duelling, and other imprudent behavior. However, even the imprudent recognize that others' desires to stay alive are blameless. Since 'necessity of nature' leads men to avoid death, 'it is not against reason that a man does all he can to preserve his own body and limbs ... And that which is not against reason, men call RIGHT, or *jus*'. This natural right to preserve oneself entails a correlative right to the means to that end and, thus, it is also right 'for a man, to ... do whatsoever action is necessary for the preservation of his body'.[22]

Since humans are free and equal, no one can legitimately claim any natural moral or political authority. Thus in 'meer Nature' self-preservation hangs on individual judgments and *'every private man is Judge of Good and Evil actions'*.[23] When desire-based judgments come into conflict, men can neither ignore them nor assume that there is some rational truth of the matter. Resolving such conflicts by violence and coercion is not by nature morally wrong, but fighting it out is risky. Thus, in both hypothetical states of nature and countries marred by excessive private judgment, the solution is to understand that peace and order are impossible unless this right is abandoned. When 'no one mans Reason, nor the Reason of any one number of men' can provide certainty and agreement, 'the parties must by their own accord, set up for right Reason the Reason of some Arbitrator, or Judge, to whose sentence they will both stand'. The problems of normative diversity can be solved, then, only if individuals prescind from such conflicts, a move which liberals have typically suggested requires public neutrality in order to let individuals resolve such questions for themselves. Hobbes, however, requires subjects to abandon totally the right of private judgment and act as if they had said with others, I *'give up my Right of Governing my selfe, to this Man, or to this Assembly of men'*, so a sovereign can 'reduce all their Wills, by plurality of voices, unto one Will'.[24]

Diversity can then only be overcome by annulling it and filling ethical space with 'one Will', that is, the sovereign's commands. While subjects covenant away their right of private judgment, the sovereign retains this natural right to judge and use all available powers to preserve its authority and subjects' lives. Sovereign power must be 'no less absolute ... than before commonwealth every man was absolute in himself to do, or not to do, what he thought good'. Famously then, Hobbes's sovereign is given authority that is irrevocable, indivisible, and (nearly) absolute regarding

---

22   Hobbes, *Elements of Law*, 78–9. Holmes, *Passions and Constraint*, ch. 3, emphasizes the extent to which Hobbes treats self-interest as a prescriptive fix for human irrationality rather than an empirical generalization regarding human motivation.
23   Hobbes, *Leviathan*, 365.
24   Ibid., 111, 227.

questions of '*Propriety*', 'Lawes of Honour', and 'what Opinions and Doctrines are averse, and what conducing to Peace', including the power to prescribe what can be expressed or published. This power extends to questions of faith: since 'both State, and Church are the same men', the sovereign's judgment must cover 'all causes, as well Ecclesiasticall, as Civill'.[25] Moreover, since average citizens get their political opinions from 'their immediate leaders', his sovereign also has the power to reform university curriculum so that 'lasting peace' may emerge as commoners are taught 'a love of obedience by preachers and gentlemen that imbibe good principles in their youth at the Universities'.[26]

In suggesting that we can overcome normative diversity by the creation of, and the creations of, an absolute and unitary will, Hobbes relies on a number of dubious mid-level arguments. There is slippery slope pessimism: 'diversity of opinion' must yield 'disputation, breach of charity, disobedience, and at last rebellion', and any efforts at limiting or dividing sovereign power must also end in war.[27] Alternatively, there are absurdly optimistic claims about the coincidence of interests between sovereigns and subjects and about the coincidence of truth and peace, in which 'Doctrine repugnant to Peace, can no more be True, than Peace and Concord can be against the Law of Nature'.[28] The latter view may be a rhetorical gambit since he acknowledges elsewhere that there are truths that are not 'fit to be preached',[29] but his most general truth is that peace and its requisite uniformity of belief are overriding goods.

Hobbes qualifies his absolutism in ways that others have emphasized in order to liberalize his doctrine. To begin with, no man can covenant away the right of self-defense or the right not to incriminate himself. Moreover, one's right of private judgment covers only issues touching 'the preservation of his own Nature', which may allow diversity on less fundamental questions.[30] Moreover, a prudent Hobbesian sovereign will require obedience only in limited areas, leaving subjects free in 'those

---

25 Hobbes, *Elements of Law*, 114, and Hobbes, *Leviathan*, 233–5, 575–6.
26 Hobbes, *Behemoth*, 39, 59.
27 Hobbes, *Behemoth*, 52, and Hobbes, *Leviathan*, 367–8.
28 Hobbes, *Leviathan*, 388, 233; see also Hobbes, *Behemoth*, 96.
29 *Hobbes and Bramhall on Liberty and Necessity*, ed. V. Chappell (Cambridge: Cambridge University Press, 1999), 24; see also Hobbes, *Leviathan*, 703, on the sovereign's authority to punish even those who teach 'true Philosophy'.
30 Hobbes, *Leviathan*, 268–9, 189. Richard Tuck, 'Hobbes and Locke on Toleration', in Dietz, *Thomas Hobbes and Political Theory*, 165, emphasizes the potential limits on sovereign authority in the limited scope of man's natural right; for a challenge to any such liberalizing interpretations, see Charles Tarlton, 'The Despotical Doctrine of Hobbes, Part I: The Liberalization of *Leviathan*', *History of Political Thought* 32 (2001), 587–618; idem, 'The Despotical Doctrine of Hobbes, Part II: Aspects of the Textual Substructure of Tyranny in *Leviathan*', *History of Political Thought* 33 (2002), 61–89.

things, which ... the Soveraign hath praetermitted', and the sovereign's laws can be evaluated in terms of whether they are *'Needfull*, for the *Good of the People*, and withall *Perspicuous'*.[31] Finally, he appears to qualify his absolutism by arguing that faith and beliefs are independent of 'Compulsion, or Commandement' so sovereigns may regulate external actions but 'cannot oblige men to beleeve'. This linkage of inner conviction and faith allows him at least once to suggest that religious toleration might be the best policy. In *Leviathan*, he argues that Englishmen in 1650 had been 'reduced to the Independency of the Primitive Christians'. If 'without contention', this independence is 'perhaps the best' because there should be 'no Power over the Consciences of men, but of the Word itselfe ...'.[32]

On the other hand, Hobbes dropped the praise of independence from the Latin translation of *Leviathan*, and its earlier inclusion may have had to do more with intra-royalist disputes than any principled opposition to public control of religion.[33] Moreover, except for the right to resist overt attempts on one's life, none of his other qualifications yields more than contingent room for diversity. Natural men may give up the right to judge only matters relating to peace, but the sovereign still decides what those matters are. Religious toleration may be 'best', but only if 'without contention', and who but the sovereign will make that judgment? Hobbes's skepticism and his denial that beliefs can be compelled do hint at liberal ideals by undermining more absolutist or perfectionist claims for uniformity,[34] but his overriding fear of diversity requires a sovereign who can arbitrarily regulate and censor. There are pragmatic limits to this: in general, suppressing ideas 'does but unite and exasperate' true believers, a problem he illustrates by tracing the civil war to efforts at 'imposing on the Scots ... our book of Common-prayer'.[35] However, the same skepticism that denies a principled case for perfectionist uniformity undermines any principled case for toleration, and Hobbes is simply incapable of accepting, let alone celebrating, the religious and ethical diversity that marks our contemporary scene.

---

32 Hobbes, *Leviathan*, 264, 388.
32 Ibid., 526, 591, 711.
33 See, e.g., Tuck, 'Hobbes and Locke on Toleration', 164, and Johann Sommerville, 'Lofty Science and Local Politics', in *The Cambridge Companion to Hobbes*.
34 See, e.g., Richard Tuck, 'Scepticism and Toleration in the Seventeenth Century', and Alan Ryan, 'A More Tolerant Hobbes?' both in *Justifying Toleration: Conceptual and Historical Perspectives*, ed. S. Mendus (Cambridge: Cambridge University Press, 1988).
35 Hobbes, *Behemoth*, 62, 28.

Hobbes and the denial of individual dignity

Hobbes's solution to the problems of diversity assumes that individuals are rational enough to transform their natural condition into a peaceful artifice. However, in jointly creating a sovereign and self-generated obligations to obey, they alienate their future freedom and creativity by becoming artificially bound subjects. A 'common Representer' requires 'Authority without stint', and since each individual 'is Author of all the Soveraigne doth,' none can complain about sovereigns doing injustice or injury without self-contradiction. Famously, the sovereign has no analogous obligation to stick to his own self-willed rules since he may arbitrarily 'free himselfe from that subjection, by repealing those Lawes that trouble him, and making of new'.[36] Thus, 'Authority without stint' rests on a fundamental inequality in which one and only one agent is free to judge her own case. Moreover, since subjects abandon their right of private judgment, the sovereign is free to prescribe or proscribe both other- and purely self-regarding preferences on topics of fundamental interest to the individual. These aspects of Hobbes's theory violate the inherent equal worth of each person and illustrate the denial of dignity involved in allowing some to 'so tamper and "get at" others that the others do their will without knowing what they are doing; and in this lose their status as free human beings'.[37]

In treating individuals as naturally free and equal, Hobbes hints at the ideal of dignity. He denies that we can rank human worth according to ascriptive bloodlines or the realization of a particular *telos*. Moreover, his appeal to self-interest as an appropriate counter to the dangers of passion is 'a profoundly egalitarian and democratic idea. Only a few have hereditary privileges, but everyone has interests'.[38] Ultimately, however, his descriptive psychology and rigid determinism circumscribe freedom and equality in ways that are inconsistent with human dignity and that deny any special costs to subordinating individual judgment to sovereign control. In fact, the real problem is the prideful failure to acknowledge that the capacity to judge is the source of problems, not an intrinsic value to be weighed against efforts to crush pride and achieve peace. Hobbesian equality thus reduces to the fact that humans are equally matter in motion, equally subject to desires, equally subject to violent death, and roughly equal in the ability to kill. Moreover, Hobbesian freedom refers only to whether, as '*Bodies*', individuals confront 'external Impediments'

---

36 Hobbes, *Leviathan*, 221, 232, 313.
37 Isaiah Berlin, 'On Human Dignity', *New Republic* 24 (28 January 2002). For a contemporary's concerns that absolutism undermined human dignity, see Milton, *Areopagitica*, 61.
38 Holmes, *Passions and Constraint*, 63, 287 n. 18.

to 'motion', a freedom that applies as well to 'Irrationall and Inanimate creatures'. Thus the claim that individuals deserve certain treatment because they are equally capable of free agency or 'dominion' over appetites rests on 'confused and empty words'.[39]

Efforts to root intrinsic human dignity in free will fail because they miss deterministic necessity. Hobbes's ontological materialism means that the knowable '*Universe*' is 'Corporeal, that is to say, Body', and 'that which is not Body, is no part of the Universe ... '[40] In this universe, there are no non-corporeal but intelligible essences and there are no spontaneous or self-generated movements. His rigorous determinism treats every bit of human behavior as the necessary result of a chain of prior causes and bodily motions. The '*entire cause*' of rocks falling, animals procreating, or human action is just the sum '*of all the accidents both of the agents ... and of the patient, put together; which when they are all supposed to be present, it cannot be understood but that the effect is produced*'. To exempt humans from these causal chains by appealing to a special power of contingent action for the sake of self-determined purposes is verbal nonsense. '*Contingents*' are simply events whose causes we do not yet 'perceive', and while Aristotle's '*final cause*', or acting for the sake of self-chosen ends, may play some role in explaining human behavior, that behavior is ultimately reducible to an 'efficient cause'.[41]

Deluded by appearances and ignorance, human beings had been led to claim a special status for themselves when compared to inanimate nature, animals, and other humans suffering various compulsions and mental disorders. This self-deception had been abetted by power-hungry clerics using notions of free will to relieve God of any guilt for damning those who acted from necessity and to induce the sort of individual guilt that could only be assuaged by consultations with the clergy.[42] In countering such views, Hobbes denies that the will is a separate mental faculty and that it, rather than the actions that follow from it, can be either free or unfree. Instead, the will is a determined 'Act', explicable as an effect of the motions of external objects that cause sensory impressions in the actor, which then cause internal motions called desires and inclinations. The appearance of inner reflection and free choice simply masks the necessity of what we finally do, and 'In *Deliberation*, the last Appetite, or Aversion, immediately adhaering to the action, or to the omission thereof, is that

---

39 Hobbes, *Leviathan*, 261–2, and *Hobbes and Bramhall*, 72–3.
40 Hobbes, *Leviathan*, 689.
41 *EW* 1. 121–2, 130–2.
42 Hobbes, *Behemoth*, 42; see also Holmes, 'Introduction', xii n. 13.

wee call the WILL'.⁴³ The will, then, is whatever desire for or against something is strongest at the time of final decision, and absent any special power to control those desires, it cannot yield any special status for those who experience them. Experience and desires 'are not effects of our Will, but our Will of them', and thus whether 'children, fools, brute beasts' or normally functioning adults, there is only the liberty to 'do if I will; but to say I can will if I will, I take to be an absurd speech'.⁴⁴

In reducing the will to necessary appetites or aversions, Hobbes opens himself to the charge that he impoverishes the nature of humanity and moral life. Bishop Bramhall was only among the first to argue that Hobbes's reduction of 'reasonable will' to 'sensitive appetite' dishonors humanity by treating the individual as 'a tennis-ball, to be tossed to and fro by the rackets of the second causes'.⁴⁵ Charged with undermining moral reflection and responsibility, Hobbes responds with a version of compatibilism in which, if defined correctly, '*Liberty* and *Necessity* are consistent'. As bodies, we can be free or unfree to act on desires, but those desires and reflection on them are simply part of the determined universe. Absent external impediments or the 'Artificial Chains' of the law, men's voluntary actions '(because they proceed from their will) proceed from *liberty*'. At the same time, all acts and inclinations are preceded by a cause, 'and that from another cause, which causes in a continuall chaine (whose first link in the hand of God the first of all causes) proceed from necessity'.⁴⁶

Hobbes claims that his determinism is consistent not only with liberty, but also with notions of individual responsibility. To complain that determinism renders counsel and persuasion useless assumes that 'secondary' causes are limited to external events, but for Hobbes internal reflection is also a fundamental part of the causal 'chaine'. When a particular choice is determined, it is also determined 'for what cause it shall be chosen, which cause, for the most part, is deliberation or consultation', and internal opinions about the goodness or badness of an action, are then, if not 'the whole cause', at least analogous to 'the last feather' that breaks 'a horse's back'.⁴⁷ Denying that the will can control choice does not then mean that individuals have no capacity or responsibility to work their way to better opinions and choices. This process cannot be cashed out in terms of the

---

43 Hobbes, *Leviathan*, 127. Jürgen Overhoff, *Hobbes's Theory of the Will: Ideological Reasons and Historical Circumstances* (Lanham, Md.: Rowman & Littlefield, 2000), 11, demonstrates the consistency of Hobbes's theory of volition throughout his various writings.
44 Hobbes, *Leviathan*, 410; *Hobbes and Bramhall*, 16–17.
45 *Hobbes and Bramhall*, 56–7.
46 Hobbes, *Leviathan*, 263.
47 *Hobbes and Bramhall*, 26, 20–1.

autonomous formation of 'second' order desires aimed at checking immediate desires. Nor can it be seen in terms of traditional notions of *akrasia* such as Ovid's portrait of Medea as saying 'I see and approve the better, but follow the worse '. For Hobbes, that saying, while 'pretty' enough, is 'not true', and despite reasons for not killing her children, 'the last dictate of her judgment was that the present revenge on her husband outweighed them all, and thereupon the wicked action necessarily followed'. However, while the will cannot be described as either free or unfree or strong or weak, as the last appetite it can still be good or 'wicked', prudent or imprudent, and 'Fools and madmen manifestly deliberate no less than the wisest men, though they make not so good a choice …'.[48]

Punishing a determined but poor choice poses no particular problems given Hobbes's pure deterrence theory of law. Since the 'intention' of the law is not to 'grieve the delinquent for' past acts, but rather to 'make him and others just that else would not be so', punishments are warranted by 'the good to come'. The justice of punishment does not depend on whether an illegal action was produced by necessity, *akrasia*, or full free will. Instead, it depends purely on whether the behavior is 'noxious', and that judgment depends on the act's effects on others' desires. Praiseworthy actions are just those that are praised, blameworthy actions are just those that are blamed, and 'Things may be therefore necessary and yet praiseworthy, as also necessary and yet dispraised'. To say a thing is good is just to say that it is 'as I would wish, or as another would have it, or according to the will of the state …'. Thus the law and its punishments, as well as other forms of 'consultation', are not 'vain' because they enter the causal 'chaine' to 'make and conform the will to good or evil'.[49]

Hobbes undermines appeals to dignity not only by denying free will, but also by denying the existence of an incorporeal and immortal soul. His contemporaries might treat the soul as a distinctive element of personhood and a moral barrier against authoritarianism. As the purely internal site for the clash of good and evil and the appearance of Christ's grace, the soul transcended civil authority, and for some antinomians, also served as a barrier to clerical authority.[50] Hobbes, however, consistently treats the soul as a corporal element of the determined universe: the fact that everything in the 'Universe' is 'Body' does not mean that 'Spirits

---

48 Ibid., 34–5, 19.
49 Ibid, 24–6; See also the necessarily strained case for Hobbesian autonomy in David Van Mill, *Liberty, Rationality, and Agency in Hobbes's 'Leviathan'* (Albany: State University of New York Press, 2001).
50 See, e.g., David Parnham, 'Politics Spun Out of Theology and Prophesy: Sir Henry Vane on the Spiritual Environment of Public Power', *History of Political Thought* 22 (2001), 53–83, esp. 69–77.

are *nothing*: for they have dimensions, and are therefore really *Bodies*; though that name in common Speech be given to such Bodies onely, as are visible, or palpable'.[51] With regard to questions about the soul's immortality, his early view was that Christian faith, rather than any 'natural evidence', requires the belief that 'the soul of man is ... immortal'. By 1650 though, he had moved to the 'mortalist' view that Biblical references to the soul signified either 'the breath of life' by which God gave 'vitall motion', or more generally 'a mans intention, mind, or disposition'.[52] Thus the claim that the soul was 'Eternal, and a living Creature independent [of] the body' is 'not apparent in Scripture', and the proper use of the term is limited to 'either the Life, or the living Creature; and the Body and Soule jointly, the *Body alive*'.[53]

As others have made clear, Hobbes's 'mortalism' was not entirely novel, but his views in the *Leviathan* were put forth in a tendentious style that was bound to offend. His mockery of deep Christian verities suggests that he was interested in more than the logical consistency of his materialism and his views on the soul and its afterlife. Earlier, he had finessed the problem by distinguishing what was philosophically demonstrable from what could be left to faith, but the civil war had shown the weaknesses in that strategy, and in *Leviathan* his worries about the 'two swords/two masters' problem had become more acute. Since acknowledging sovereign power to reward and punish is the only way citizens can avoid the state of nature, no one should be able to claim powers more important than control over corporeal life and death. All the sovereign's powers would be bootless if religious authorities could continue to claim 'a power of giving greater rewards than Life; and of inflicting greater punishments, than Death', and the success of Hobbes's prescriptions required him to cast doubt on traditional views of the soul's afterlife.[54]

In denying free will and the immortal, immaterial soul, Hobbes undermines appeals to individual dignity. Absent such notions, there is no room for subjects to challenge sovereign judgments on the grounds of the intrinsic value of the individual. In fact, there may be no such value since he defines 'DIGNITY' as simply the 'publique worth of a man, which is the Value set on him by the Common-wealth'. The '*Value* or WORTH of a

---

51 Hobbes, *Leviathan*, 689; see Hobbes, *Elements of Law*, 66, for a more tentative case in which Scripture 'seemeth' to favor those 'who hold angels and spirits for corporeal'.
52 Hobbes, *Elements of Law*, 66, and Hobbes, *Leviathan*, 440, 464. David Johnston, 'Hobbes's Mortalism', *History of Political Thought* 10 (1989), 647-63, emphasizes and tries to explain Hobbes's change of mind on this issue.
53 Hobbes, *Leviathan*, 484, 637-8.
54 Ibid., 478; see Johnston, 'Hobbes's Mortalism', and Overhoff, *Hobbes's Theory of the Will*, esp. 193-6, for discussions of the political motivation behind Hobbes's adoption of 'mortalism'.

man' is the 'Price' others would pay 'for the use of his Power: and therefore is not absolute' but relative to others' judgments.[55] Claims to the contrary had often been buttressed by linking free will or an immortal soul to a special capacity called 'conscience' that enabled human beings to grasp moral truths. This had led to the doctrine, 'repugnant to Civill society … that *whatsoever a man does against his Conscience, is Sinne*'. Etymologically, Hobbes argues, 'conscience' refers to what could be known together, but over time it had come to be used metaphorically to turn 'secret facts, and secret thoughts' into constraints on authority. Since 'Conscience' just means 'Judgement', the simple conclusion should be that by nature men might act on their conscientious judgments, but in civil society 'the Law is the publique Conscience'.[56]

Having denied the intrinsic dignity of persons, Hobbes too often verges on treating individuals as fungible means to the agent-neutral good of peace. Human beings are like stones, not only in shunning death 'no less than that whereby a stone moves downward', but also in being the building blocks of a civil 'Aedifice'. Those who shun the gravitational force of peace and the absolutist means to it are, like irregular stones which 'hindereth the building', to be 'cast away as unprofitable, and troublesome'. Thus dissenters from either an original covenant or a sitting sovereign's judgment have no standing and are 'left in the condition of warre' where they 'might without injustice be destroyed by any man whatsoever'.[57] Some of his scarier reasoning shows just how little standing the individual has. For example, in *Behemoth*, Hobbes considers the ancient Ethiopian practice of kings committing suicide when priests informed them that the gods had decreed their death. While noting that it was clearly 'cruel', he nonetheless praises King Ergamenes for ending this 'superstition' by killing '*all the priests*'. He follows this with the counterfactual suggestion that Charles I might have saved himself and England's peace if he had acted preemptively to kill all the 'seditious ministers' in England. It would have been a 'great massacre', but the killing of perhaps '1000' such ministers would have been offset by the good of saving the '100,000' lives ultimately lost in the civil war.[58]

Since a covenant 'not to defend my selfe from force, by force, is always voyd',the religious leaders in his examples could legitimately resist those who came to kill them.[59] But, alternatively, neither Ergamenes nor

---

55 Hobbes, *Leviathan*, 151–2; see also Hobbes, *De Cive*, 295, where the '*honour*'of a man is in the '*honourer*'.
56 Hobbes, *Leviathan*, 132, 365–6.
57 Hobbes, *De Cive*, 115, and Hobbes, *Leviathan*, 209, 232.
58 Hobbes, *Behemoth*, 94–5.
59 Hobbes, *Leviathan*, 192, 199.

Charles I would be wrong to engage in the actual or proposed murders. This is because Hobbes's 'RIGHT OF NATURE' establishes first-person liberties, but does so without any duties to (or limits on) second-parties. The individual's right to do 'any thing, which in his own Judgement, and Reason' will preserve his life entails a right to all possible means to that end, including a right 'even to one anothers body'. While subjects ought to yield this right until they are directly threatened, the sovereign retains it wholly and completely, and a sovereign judgment that peace requires the death of this or that person can not be countered by a natural duty not to use others as means. Just as there is no natural right to property, but only the power to 'getteth it, and keep it by force', there is no natural self-ownership or intrinsic individual dignity that might check such judgments.[60]

Hobbes extends this argument to the opinions that lie behind willed actions. Just as the individual can't appeal to bodily self-ownership to resist being used as a means to peace, neither does she own her mental life in any fashion that might morally constrain sovereign efforts to shape and control it. Pragmatically, 'inward *thought*, and *beleef*' are of a sort 'which humane Governours can take no notice of', and being 'invisible', faith and mental life are 'consequently exempted from all humane jurisdiction'. As even Ryan admits, however, this is a matter of 'technique not principle', and if techniques for mind control were discovered, Hobbes has no reason beyond 'expediency' for not using them. His psychology means that, while thoughts and beliefs can't be directly determined, if they could be it would be no great loss since the individual doesn't determine or control them anyway.[61]

Hobbes's sovereign, then, has the authority to use the subjects' bodies and minds. Since 'dignity' is just others' estimation of individual worth, and since sovereigns control public estimation, the only thing that matters is the sovereign's judgment regarding a subject's contribution to peace. Of course it will almost always be better to eschew Ergamenes's murderous means in favor of efforts to shape the subjects' sensory experience and mental lives, and a prudent sovereign will take the steps discussed in section II in order to control what subjects hear, read, and see in order to cause more irenic opinions and wills. Such efforts certainly verge on the manipulation of things rather than the persuasion of persons, but Hobbes's determinism collapses that distinction and allows him to treat

---

60 Ibid., 189–90, 296.
61 Ibid., 500–1, 550, and Alan Ryan, 'Hobbes, Toleration, and the Inner Life', in *The Nature of Political Theory*, eds D. Miller and L. Siedentop (Oxford: Clarendon Press, 1983), 217. Tarlton, 'The Despotical Docrtine, Part II', 70, argues that for Hobbes, men's 'inner thoughts were not within any liberty of their own to control in the first place'.

'manipulation' as just misliked efforts at causing particular wills. Moreover, while we may talk about being compelled out of fear, 'Feare and Liberty are consistent'. Throwing 'goods into the sea for *feare* the ship should sink' or obeying 'for *feare* of the law' are actions 'which the doers had *liberty* to omit' despite very unpalatable alternatives.[62] Thus, manipulation of subjects' opinions poses no real threat to liberty, and Hobbes seems indifferent regarding whether fear, manipulation, or persuasion frames the more irenic opinions. There is nothing in (or about) the subject that ought to restrain the choice among such methods, and as long as subjects contribute to peace, Hobbes's psychology precludes worries about whether such actions stem from individual judgments. If a subject comes to believe the opinions imposed by the sovereign, so much the better, but even if she conforms only from fear of punishment, her actions will still be free, correct, and virtuous.

In this, Hobbes undermines any worries about whether overt behavior is consistent with inner conviction and thus undermines concerns about the denial of individual integrity. His primary concern is to refute those like Milton, who held that religious practice or other actions were sinful and hypocritical 'if not voluntary'.[63] He acknowledges the problem of what we might call self-benefiting hypocrisy, and in fact blames much of the civil war on those whose public pronouncements masked secret and less noble motives. And at least once, he acknowledges the problem for those, such as Charles I's wife, who might be forced to the hypocrisy of subordinating authentic religious beliefs to satisfy others' desires.[64] However, his more typical approach draws on his conception of voluntary and involuntary actions in order to treat the latter as an empty cell. While freedom is consistent with the fear of force, behavior that results from actual external physical force is neither free nor voluntary. If 'a man by force, seizing on another man's limbs, moves them as himself, not as the other man pleases', then the resulting movement is the action and the responsibility 'of him that uses the force'. In the *Leviathan*, he pushes this argument past physical manipulation to include the fear of punishment. With regard to questions of faith (and individual integrity), sovereigns may impose a particular 'Doctrine' that obliges subjects to actions 'such as they would not otherwise do', but those actions 'done in obedience' and 'without the inward approbation, are the actions of the Sovereign, and not of the Subject'.[65]

---

62 Hobbes, *Leviathan*, 262–3; see also *Hobbes and Bramhall*, 30.
63 Milton, *Aeropagitica*, 84.
64 Hobbes, *Behemoth*, 1, 61.
65 *Hobbes and Bramhall*, 78–9, and Hobbes, *Leviathan*, 591; see also Hobbes, *De Cive*, 306.

While this properly mitigates moral blame of those who are coerced to act against their real beliefs, it does so at the cost of subjects' subjective concerns for their own integrity and salvation. In confining accusations of 'Hypocrisy' to instances where a subject's 'behaviour bee contrary to the law of his Soveraign', Hobbes rules out both Socratic claims that we should do no wrong and the more liberal view that there are at least some wrongs besides death that we ought not suffer. He can waive aside such concerns because he treats almost all matters of religious faith and practice as indifferent. Since salvation requires only 'two Vertues, *Faith in Christ*, and *Obedience to Laws*',[66] he can take other questions regarding faith (or a secular good life) off the table and treat them as of no great significance. From God's viewpoint, Hobbes may or may not be correct here, but from the individual's point of view, even such indifferent questions are of supreme importance. Given that, liberals have typically left such matters to the individual's judgment so that she can be responsible for the outcome. But Hobbes's denial of individual dignity means that such considerations pale in the face of threats to peace and self-preservation. Thus, even for Christians who are commanded to deny faith in Christ, his only recommendation is either martyrdom or a false swearing in which, if the subject believes internally, he will be forgiven by God if he obeys the law because 'that action is not his, but his Soveraigns'. Whatever the latter hypocrisy might cost the subject with regard to integrity or dignity, it does not threaten salvation or bodily death, and in such cases, Hobbes requires that we neither disobey nor forcibly depose even 'Infidell, or Haereticall Kings'.[67]

IV. Hobbes and democracy

Liberals typically argue that representative democracy is the appropriate procedure for settling public questions about diversity and equal dignity. For some, like Berlin, democracy is an essential, but ultimately instrumental, 'means for protecting' more 'ultimate' values. Others have argued for a more 'intimate' relationship in which democracy itself expresses and is constitutive of values such as liberty, equality, and justice.[68] Either way,

---

66 Hobbes, *Leviathan*, 541, 610.
67 Hobbes, *De Cive*, 384, and Hobbes, *Leviathan*, 528, 605–6. Flathman, *Thomas Hobbes*, 157 n. 11, notes that by the time Hobbes wrote *Leviathan*, he had limited acceptable martyrdom to those who actually knew Christ. Locke, who also regarded many sources of religious conflict as indifferent, nonetheless assumed that individuals ought to treat such matters as 'the highest Obligation that lies upon mankind', and regarded proposals for false swearing as monstrous: 'A sweet Religion indeed, that obliges men to dissemble, and tell Lies both to God and Man.' See John Locke, *A Letter Concerning Toleration*, ed. J. Tully (Indianapolis: Hacket, 1983), 46–7.
68 Isaiah Berlin, *Four Essays on Liberty* (Oxford: Oxford University Press, 1969), lvii–lviii, 165; for an argument that there is a more 'intimate' relationship between democracy and liberalism,

the assumption is that democracy will be better for such values than rule by aristocratic or plutocratic minorities or the whims of even a benevolent despot.

For Hobbes, however, the ultimate value is 'the Peace, and Security of the people', and he evaluates forms of government only in terms of their contingent 'Convenience, or Aptitude to produce' those values. He follows Aristotle in part by arguing that public authority can be held by one, a few, or the many, but rejects the idea that regimes can be further evaluated in terms of whether they pursue a common good. Thus *'Tyranny'*, *'Oligarchy'*, *and 'Anarchy'* are simply names used when rule by the one, the few, or the many is 'misliked'.[69] In principle, any of these regimes could promote 'Peace, and Security' if they were absolute and undivided. He notes early on that his preference for monarchy has not been 'demonstrated, but only probably stated', and as late as *Behemoth*, he argues that the real question is whether there is sufficient unity so that the sovereign speaks with 'one voice, though there be many men'. If so, then even the many might 'govern well enough, if they had honesty and wit enough'.[70] Just as obviously, however, and from an early date, he emphasizes the inferiority of democracy. In introducing his translation of Thucydides, he argues that the best reason for continuing to read that author's gloomy history is his portrait of the idiocies of Athenian democracy. For Hobbes, it was obvious that Thucydides 'least of all liked democracy' because of its 'inconsistency' and tendency to demagoguery, and that his real preference was for 'regal rule'.[71]

Some aspects of Hobbes's political philosophy do point toward democracy. His emphasis on natural freedom and equality means that consent of the ruled is the only legitimate source of political authority and obligation. Moreover, the purpose of his sovereign is in some sense to be responsive to the interests, albeit very narrowly conceived, of the subjects, and at least from a God's eye view, the sovereign has a duty to procure *'the safety'* and 'Contentments' of the subjects and should make sure that 'Justice be equally administered to all degrees of People'. Thus, while subjects have no right to judge the sovereign's performance, Ryan suggests that Hobbes's 'ideal sovereign' would be 'absolute in principle, but indistin-

---

see Amy Gutmann, 'Rawls on the Relationship Between Liberalism and Democracy', in *The Cambridge Companion to Rawls*, ed. S. Freeman (Cambridge: Cambridge University Press, 2003).

69 Hobbes, *Leviathan*, 239–41.
70 Hobbes, *De Cive*, 104, and Hobbes, *Behemoth*, 156.
71 *Hobbes's Thucydides*, ed. R. Schlatter (New Brunswick: Rutgers University Press, 1975), 13–14.

guishable from a constitutional sovereign in practice'.[72] However that may be, his sovereign *is* absolute and subjects have no real opportunity to hold it accountable. Moreover, while not demonstrated with geometric certainty, his personal preference is clear.

If we look to mere 'examples and testimonies', we see that monarchy accords with the fact that '*one* God' rules the universe, that the 'ancients' preferred the rule of one, and that the government of families is 'monarchical'. More importantly, reason concludes that monarchy is more likely to yield 'Peace, and Security'. In part this follows from Hobbes's claim that any sovereign will be a 'naturall Person' as well as a public authority, which leads inevitably to conflicts between the sovereign's public duty and private interest. Monarchs are less likely to be led to ill-rule by this fact since 'no King can be rich, nor glorious, nor secure' if his subjects are poor and weak, while this link between private and public good is attenuated in rule by the few or the many. Moreover, monarchy will also yield superior advice because a king need not listen to those who don't know anything and can recruit information from those who might be excluded from democratic assemblies. Kingship will also be superior since it will not suffer the 'Inconstancy from Number' that leads the few and the many to reverse yesterday's decisions and to suffer internal conflicts rooted in 'envy and interest'. Finally, while kings may impoverish some in order to enrich a 'favourite or a flatterer', the same is true of all forms of government, and monarchy will be better on this score simply because one man will have few friends while 'the Favorites of an Assembly, are many'.[73]

Democracy, on the other hand, cannot be expected to yield peace and security. Prior to the civil war, Hobbes does suggest a certain logical/temporal priority for democracy since the choice of a sovereign must rest on 'the consent of the major part', which makes rule by one, the few, or the many the result of what is 'actually a democracy'.[74] But he also argues that a democratic decision to implement the rule of the many would be a serious mistake. In the first place, a democracy must be based on deliberations in mass assemblies, and there, as with Pericles, either one or a few will be 'eminent above the rest' so that the sovereign will really be either an 'aristocracy' or a 'monarchy' of orators. Moreover, democratic 'deliberations' are incapable of delivering sound policy: the participants are by and large 'unskillful' regarding complicated questions, the nature of '*elo-*

---

72 Hobbes, *Leviathan*, 376, 385; Alan Ryan, 'Hobbes's Political Philosophy', in *Cambridge Companion to Hobbes*, 232.
73 Hobbes, *De Cive*, 224–5, and Hobbes, *Leviathan*, 241–3. Berkowitz, *Virtue*, 65–7, roots the failure of Hobbes's argument for the harmony of monarchical and citizen interests in his question-begging assumption of 'virtuous monarchs' and 'craven aristocrats and democrats'.
74 Hobbes, *Elements of Law*, 118–19; see also Hobbes, *De Cive*, 195.

quence' is to aim 'not at truth (except by chance), but victory', and factions will naturally emerge as 'equal orators do combat with contrary opinions and speeches' so that losers hate 'the conqueror and all those that were of his side'. The result then is bad policy, 'inconstant' and divisive legislation, and an inability to maintain necessary secrets.[75]

Events of the 1640s only served to confirm and heighten these early fears. Looking back after the Restoration, Hobbes argues that the mass of citizens were (and remain) either illiterate or too preoccupied with private affairs to understand politics. They 'always have been, and always will be, ignorant of their duty to the public', and having little real care for the opinions that caused the civil war, 'would have taken any side for pay or plunder'. This civic weakness puts average citizens under the sway of 'their immediate leaders; which are either the preachers or the most potent of the gentlemen that dwell amongst them'.[76] From at least the Elizabethan era, the 'immediate leaders' had filled up the commoners' heads with 'the love of democracy' and a desire for 'popular government' in both church and state. While some acted simply out of 'error', the 'chief leaders' here were moved by 'malice' and the frustrated ambition of men who found themselves ruled by those they thought 'less learned' and 'less wise' than themselves.[77]

Being 'corrupted generally', the people chose these ambitious and democratically inclined men for their representatives, and if 'not the greatest part' of the House of Commons, they were 'by advantage of their eloquence ... always able to sway the rest'. Led by such men, parliament pandered to economic interests by disputing Charles I's demands for 'subsidies or other public payments' and brought accusations of treason against the king's more hierarchically-minded advisors—for Hobbes, an example of the 'Impudence' that 'does almost all, that's done' in democratic assemblies. Beyond being impudent, they were also hypocritical in claiming to desire only the restoration of a traditional 'mixed' monarchy, while their real goal, revealed only after they had first 'slain the King', was to shift from 'monarchical to democratical' government.[78] These democrats had successfully rationalized their ambitions by covering them in concerns for the people's prosperity and liberty. Economically, those with ambitions that had been frustrated by monarchy could trot out the example of the Dutch republic's success and argue that 'there needed no more to grow rich, than to change ... the forme of their Government'.

---

75 Hobbes, *Elements of Law*, 120, and Hobbes, *De Cive*, 230–2.
76 Hobbes, *Behemoth*, 3, 39.
77 Ibid., 23.
78 Ibid., 2–3, 68–9, 26–7.

Moreover, the availability of books from 'the Antient Greeks, and Romans' strengthened democratic forces by spreading the idea that 'Subjects in a Popular Common-wealth enjoy Liberty; but that in a Monarchy they are all Slaves'.[79]

For Hobbes, both claims are deeply confused. The first spuriously treats the form of government as the cause of economic 'prosperity', when in fact, national wealth stems 'from the Obedience, and Concord of the Subjects' whether ruled by one, a few, or the many.[80] The second claim is, perhaps, more dangerous, and he tries to refute classical republican arguments that liberty inheres in citizens' rights to share in creating the laws that bind them. Aristotle, Cicero, and other republicans had naively over-generalized from 'the Practice of their own Common-wealths', and contemporary readers had been gulled into thinking that these participatory rights were somehow at the core of liberty. In reality, he argues, classical 'Libertie' referred only to the freedom of a particular community from external control and was not 'the Libertie of particular men; but the Libertie of the Common-wealth' to make its own decisions. The gates of *'Luca'* may be inscribed with the word 'LIBERTAS', but that is not to say that the individual 'has more Libertie, or Immunitie from the service of the Commonwealth there, than in *Constantinople'*. Whatever the form of sovereignty, 'the Freedome is still the same', and it consists simply in the ability to do 'those things, which in regulating their actions, the Soveraign hath praetermitted'.[81] Thus, when the Rump Parliament changed England to a *'Commonwealth and Free-State'*, it did not mean that the people were 'no longer subject to law', but only that parliament would now be setting the laws. Absent the supposed linkage between individual liberty and democratic participation, prudent subjects should know that a prudent monarch, and even an imprudent tyrant, will be better for liberty since 'no tyrant was ever so cruel as a popular assembly'.[82]

Thus it makes no difference to Hobbes whether democracy is justified by appeals to the 'positive' liberty of fulfilling the human *telos* or as a means of holding authorities accountable for the scope of the subjects' 'negative' liberties. The former view rests on bad metaphysics, and the latter claim is historically, if not logically, mistaken in ignoring evidence that mixed or fully democratic sovereigns must collapse into internal fac-

---

79 Hobbes, *Leviathan*, 368-9.
80 Ibid., 380. Hobbes surely underestimates the connection between economic growth and the presence of either particular beliefs favoring productive activity or political/legal rules conducive to property rights and lower transaction costs; see, e.g., Robert Skedelsky, 'The Mystery of Growth', *New York Review of Books* 50 (13 March 2003), 28-31.
81 Hobbes, *Leviathan*, 264-7.
82 Hobbes, *Behemoth*, 164, 23.

tion and civil war. If not inflamed by erroneous opinions based on old books and foreign examples, he argues, 'it is the desire of most men to bear rule'.[83] And if taught more correct, Hobbesian opinions, they would put aside foolish desires for a democratic voice in public authority. Doing so would not only promote 'Peace, and Security', but would also eliminate a significant source of personal discontent. That is, for Hobbes, while democracy seems to give more citizens a chance 'to show their wisdom, knowledge, and eloquence', its actual result is a higher probability of individual shame:

> to see his opinion, whom we scorn, preferred before ours; to have our wisdom undervalued before our own faces; by an uncertain trial of a little vain-glory, to undergo most certain enmities ... to hate and to be hated, by reason of the disagreement of opinions ... these I say are grievances.

Given the zero-sum nature of these public struggles for honor, 'there is no reason why every man should not naturally mind his *own private*, than the *public* business' unless driven by the perverse ambition to 'gain the reputation of being ingenious and wise'.[84]

Ultimately then, Hobbes sees nothing but imprudence and self-defeating vanity in claims that citizens should have both the opportunity for public action and the freedom to decide how much energy to devote to public and private business. Rightly rejecting classical republican claims that full human flourishing requires an active focus on public business, he goes too far in the other direction by making the role of subject fully constitutive of citizenship. For Hobbes, no Rawlsian arguments for a democratic space in which some might find their chief good in public action and others must participate in order to express or protect justice can be instantiated without falling into dispute and decay. Instead, his critique of democracy reflects the view that 'all actions and habits are to be esteemed good or evil by their causes and usefulness in reference to the commonwealth', and the well performance of Hobbesian citizenship is 'comprehended wholly in obedience to the laws of the commonwealth'. This is not just individual 'prudence', but is also 'the virtue of a subject', and 'To obey the laws, is justice and equity, which is the law of nature ...'.[85] This appeal to 'virtue' cuts against pure 'rational choice' nterpretations of Hobbes and indi-

---

83 Ibid., 193.
84 Hobbes, *De Cive*, 229–32; Tuck, 'Introduction', xiii, emphasizes the influence on Hobbes of Renaissance skeptics, who suggested 'a retreat into privacy and quiesence' for private citizens.
85 John Rawls, *Political Liberalism* (New York: Columbia University Press, 1996), 205–6; Hobbes, *Behemoth*, 44–5.

cates an awareness that his politics could not work if there were nothing but sovereign force and subjects' self-interest. Rejecting a universal 'Summum Bonum' does not mean that he rejects the need for internalized ethical restraints, and substituting self-preservation for the higher ends of classical theory allows him to preserve the traditional functional form of virtue talk by treating as virtues those traits and dispositions that are good means to self-preservation. With this, we can understand his otherwise startling claim that in a state of nature, 'the two Cardinall vertues' are 'Force, and Fraud', since in nature's ethical vacuum those ethically dubious qualities are good means to self-preservation. Of course, since human beings are roughly equal in their capacity to deal death, exercising those 'vertues' is very uncertain, and both natural men and citizens need to acknowledge the instrumental links between peace, preservation, and the conduct recommended by his laws of nature. Where others also abide by them, '*Justice, Gratitude, Modesty, Equity, Mercy,* & the rest of the Laws of Nature' are 'Moral Vertues', and recognizing that they are superior to 'Force, and Fraud' as means to 'peaceable, sociable, and comfortable living' constitutes a grasp of 'true Morall Philosophie'.[86]

Hobbes's own vanity leads him to conclude that his new and 'true Morall Philosophie' can be the basis for making a 'constitution (excepting by external violence) everlasting'. Since the 'Common-peoples minds ... are like clean paper', if a sovereign properly controls the sources of elite opinion, he can eliminate from public view erroneous opinions that support democracy.[87] A sovereign's physical force and subjects' self- interested calculations must then be supplemented by internalizing the Hobbesian virtues if we are to avoid the calamities Englishmen endured in the 1640s. These valuable traits and dispositions are clearly not the 'civic virtue' of classical republicanism.[88] But neither are they the virtues of liberal democracy in which citizens must balance support for the regime with criticisms of particular policies and leaders based on interests and beliefs that might compete with the value of self-preservation. Instead, the citizen must be a pure subject, and Hobbes's science of virtue recommends the passive and anti-democratic ideal of a citizen who accepts a 'duty to obey all laws whatsoever', and whose pursuit of moral or religious beliefs is limited to 'a quiet waiting for the coming again of our blessed Savior'.[89]

---

86 Hobbes, *Leviathan*, 188, 216; see Berkowitz, *Virtue*, 53.
87 Hobbes, *Leviathan*, 378-89.
88 Mary Dietz, 'Hobbes's Subject as Citizen', in Dietz (ed.), *Thomas Hobbes and Political Theory*, 113.
89 Hobbes, *Behemoth*, 58.

Conclusion

On balance then, we must ultimately reject Hobbes's political prescriptions. His *Behemoth* and his more philosophical work do highlight the dangers of granting too much room for claims of private judgment and exemptions from general laws. And he does effectively undermine arguments for classical republican and other perfectionist views of politics, a move which aids the cause of individuality and ethical pluralism and clears some necessary ground for liberalism. But his contemporaries appear to have ignored his constructive arguments both in 1660 and, more relevantly, later in 1688, and we should follow their lead. Hobbes's ethical voluntarism and his determinism are extremely limiting in terms of what we can hope for in ethical and religious debates and in how we are to regard the relationship between the state and the individual. In denying the possibility of relatively peaceful diversity and the hopes for transparency in limits on that diversity, he denies individuals the opportunity to work out their own judgments on matters of fundamental importance. And his denials of individual dignity mean both that this process can be seen as cost free and that it does not require room for citizens actively to participate in and judge by democratic means the behavior of those they have placed in authority. In his failure to move toward these more liberal views, he fails to articulate a plausible and morally defensible political ideal even if we rightly continue to be fascinated by the logical and rhetorical power of his history and his philosophy.[90]

---

[90] Others argue that, with some qualifications, Hobbes can provide helpful insights for less optimistic and less rationalistic liberals; see, e.g., Richard Flathman, *Willful Liberalism: Voluntarism and Individuality in Political Theory and Practice* (Ithaca: Cornell University Press, 1992), esp. chap. 1; Patrick Neal, 'Vulgar Liberalism', *Political Theory* 21 (1993), 623–42.

Tom Sorell

Schmitt, Hobbes and the Politics of Emergency

To what extent do Hobbes's political ideas lend themselves to a general theory of civil emergency? He wrote at a time of civil war in England. *Behemoth*, his history of that war, is particularly critical of parliament, and accuses it, the universities and various religious interests of being the main fomenters of rebellion. According to *Behemoth*, a badly advised Charles I had tried hard to avoid conflict with parliament and his subjects in carrying out his obligations to raise money for military defence. But eventually the king's rights ceased to be recognised, and started to be usurped by parliament. What followed was military action regarded by one side as a war on parliament and by the other (which included Hobbes) as something necessary for the sake of public safety.[1]

The war made its impact on Hobbes not only as historian but as a political theorist. He thought that it was the principal task of civil philosophy to specify means of avoiding civil war. Civil war might be thought to set the pattern for emergencies facing states. So Hobbes's account of the causes and remedies of civil war might go far toward being a theory of emergency. Carl Schmitt reads Hobbes as a philosopher who thinks that politics is a response to emergency, and Schmitt adapts what he takes to be Hobbesian ideas to give a politics of emergency of his own, one that was supposed to have particular relevance to the upheavals of the Weimar Republic.

Like Hobbes's own theory, Schmitt's was inspired by a particular period of civil disorder, and, again like Hobbes's, it was supposed to have application to civil war in general, or threats to civil order in general. Schmitt believed that an emergency was best confronted by an unconstrained sovereign. A leader exercising his judgement and implementing whatever measures seem appropriate in time of national peril seems

---

1   *Behemoth, EW* 6. 136.

better to him than rule by committee or constitution. I shall consider how Schmitt's theory might apply to at least one recent emergency. I shall claim that when applied it has considerable shortcomings, but that these are not always inherited from Hobbes. Schmitt exaggerates the experienced singularity of emergencies, and he exaggerates the way in which the singularity requires a response in the form of a distinctively personal decision—the decision of a sovereign. It may be true that a perfectly impersonal legal order is incoherent, as Schmitt claims, and that the legal order in liberal democracies operates according to a logic that incoherently tries to remove all traces of the personal. That does not mean that there ought to be as large a personal element in the legal order, especially in the handling of emergency, as Schmitt's theory requires. On the contrary, and as Hobbes's own theory implies, the personal — in the form of a partly passionate act of will—is at the root of war, and averting war is largely a matter of suppressing the purely personal.

I

Schmitt's attachment to the personal emerges in several theoretical connections. A good place to begin is with his criticism of Kelsen's jurisprudence. In *Political Theology* he writes,

> The objectivity that [Kelsen] claimed for himself amounted to no more than avoiding everything personalistic and tracing the legal order back to the impersonal validity of an impersonal norm.
>
> The multifarious theories of the concept of sovereignty—those of Krabbe, Preuss, Kelsen—demand such an objectivity. They agree that all personal elements must be eliminated from the concept of the state. For them, the personal and the command elements belong together. According to Kelsen, the conception of the personal right to command is the intrinsic error in the theory of state sovereignty; because the theory is premised on the subjectivity of command rather than on the objectively valid norm, he characterised the theory of the primacy of the state's legal order as 'subjectivistic' and as a negation of the legal idea.[2]

One cannot eliminate the personal from the legal, Schmitt claims, because, for one thing, the objectively valid norm has to be applied by someone competent to do so,[3] and because the circumstances of its application in a particular case are not always anticipated in the general and

---

2 *Political Theology: Four Chapters on the Concept of Sovereignty*, trans. G. Schwab (Cambridge, Mass: MIT Press, 1988), 29.
3 Ibid., 31.

impersonal formulation.[4] How and when the norm fits has to be left to the judgement of someone.

The ineliminability of the personal is all the more clear, according to Schmitt, if one takes seriously the reality of legally exceptional situations. As he puts it in *Political Theology*,

> Because a general norm, as represented by an ordinary legal prescription, can never encompass a total exception, the decision that a real exception exists cannot therefore be entirely derived from this norm ...
>
> The exception, which is not codified in the existing legal order, can at best be characterised as a case of extreme peril, a danger to the existence of the state, and the like. But it cannot be circumscribed factually and made to conform to a preformed law ...
>
> The precise details of an emergency cannot be anticipated, nor can one spell out what may take place in such a case, especially when it is truly a matter of extreme emergency and of how it is to be eliminated. The precondition as well as the content of jurisdictional competence in such a case must necessarily be unlimited ... The most guidance the constitution can provide is to indicate who can act in such a case. If such action is not subject to controls, ... then it is clear who the sovereign is. He decides whether there is an extreme emergency as well as what must be done to eliminate it. Although he stands outside the normally valid legal system, he nevertheless belongs to it, for it is he who must decide whether the constitution is to be suspended in its entirety.[5]

There is something in the nature of an emergency, Schmitt seems to be saying, that keeps it from becoming the subject of a detailed law. The more detail, the less something counts as unanticipated, as an emergency must be. Again, the more the detail, the more the latitude for action required to deal with an emergency would be circumscribed. In a case where the emergency consisted of extreme national peril, the narrowing of room for manoeuvre would presumably aggravate the peril, add to the threat to the state, and, indirectly, threaten the rule of law in general and the authority of the constitution itself. Since the purpose of emergency laws is to spell out measures that get the state out of peril and back to the rule of law, the detail might be self-defeating. So the law must be general, in which case personal discretion will inevitably be called for in implementing it.

Extreme emergency, then, introduces a personal element into the relevant legislation. Not only must personal judgement take up the slack between the generality of the norm and the specific situation it is applied to, as in the case of non-emergency law, but personal judgement may need

---

4 Ibid., 30.
5 Ibid., 6–7.

to find means of saving the state that a constitution fails to envisage or prohibits. It is as if the emergency is the case *par excellence* of the need for free adaptation to circumstance—just what the universality of law prohibits in the normal case. This room for manoeuvre is what defines the sphere of sovereignty, for Schmitt. Sovereignty is precisely the role of taking over where legal rules lapse or a constitution gives out, paradigmatically in cases where national survival is at stake.[6]

There is a correspondence between Schmitt's definition of sovereignty and his definition of the political. Just as Schmitt decried the depersonalisation of the legal, and the attempt to make the concept of sovereignty redundant, so he decried the depoliticisation of the state through the institutions and assumptions of parliamentary liberalism or parliamentarism. Parliamentary liberalism, according to Schmitt, overvalues discussion, and especially 'balanced' discussion, and undervalues decision.[7] It is geared to the idea of policy being corrected in the process of open argument and counterargument between different clearly identified and clearly acknowledged interests. Not everything is discussible in parliament. Matters of deep ideology, or of metaphysical conviction, are not.[8] What *can* be discussed is anything about which 'relative truth' can be reached, that is, as I understand Schmitt, truth in the form of a conclusion reached through testing debate.[9] Parliamentary liberalism is also geared to the division of powers. Parliaments openly deliberate, and legislate; heads of state and the executive branch of government in general see to it that the law is implemented, or take measures only after consulting parliament. Courts interpret the law and settle disputes according to these interpretations. The press informs the public about the activities of the separate powers and about the problems facing government. The openness of the process prevents those who are in charge from ignoring parliamentary decisions or from trying to manipulate those decisions.[10] A free press reports the facts to a citizenry that is thereby empowered to make demands of parliament and the executive.

The emphasis in parliamentarism on balanced discussion and a balance of powers produces, if Schmitt is right, an emasculated state. Certain measures become unthinkable or controversial even if necessary, because

---

6   What happens when a threat to national survival is successfully seen off? Presumably, the constitution comes back into force. How can its existence in the background be squared with Schmitt's claim that the norm is 'destroyed in the exception'? (*Political Theology*, 12). I think this claim is an exaggeration.
7   *The Crisis of Parliamentary Democracy*, trans. E. Kennedy (Cambridge, MA: MIT Press, 1992), 35ff.
8   Ibid., 46.
9   Ibid.
10 Ibid., 38.

they seem to encroach on the freedoms—of property owning, of free speech—that in liberalism politics is supposed to be there to protect. Parliamentarism thus seems to undercut, if not exclude, the most momentous decision a state can make: namely, a decision as to what citizens can be required to fight against, and, if necessary, fight to the death against.[11] The decision to go to war is the extreme case of the political decision, according to Schmitt. The sphere of politics is that in which one collectivity has a sense of another collectivity as alien or allies, as enemies or friends.[12] The sphere of the political thus corresponds, in its most extreme case—the case of war between one nation and another—to the sphere of decision making in which the state faces an extreme peril—the sphere of sovereignty. And these two spheres in turn coincide with the sphere of what Schmitt calls 'democracy'.

He emphatically denies that democracy and parliamentarism are the same:

> The belief in parliamentarism, in government by discussion, belongs to the intellectual world of liberalism. It does not belong to democracy. Both, liberalism and democracy, have to be distinguished from one another so that the patchwork picture that makes up modern mass democracy can be recognised.
>
> Every actual democracy rests on the principle that not only are equals equal but unequals will not be treated equally. Democracy requires, therefore, first homogeneity and second—if the need arises—elimination or eradication of heterogeneity ... A democracy demonstrates its political power by knowing how to refuse or keep at bay something foreign and unequal that threatens its homogeneity.[13]

It is not necessary to read these sinister-sounding passages as meaning racial or religious homogeneity. What may matter is not people looking the same or worshipping in the same way, but taking one another to have a stake in the same way of life. This would bring Schmitt's talk of 'equals' in a democracy into line with what he means by 'friends' in a political order. Democracy, but not political liberalism, according to Schmitt, is able to distinguish between them and us, and to give weight to being one of us that does not attach to being one among others.

In an illiberal democracy, a decision by the state would not always be constrained to be a decision in favour of the individual in a state. It might be a decision in favour of a people. At the same time, the greatest political threat would not necessarily be any threat to individual freedom or institutions protecting individual freedom. It might be a threat to the existence

---

11 *The Concept of the Political*, trans. G. Schwab (Chicago: University of Chicago Press, 1996), 70 ff.
12 Ibid., 28.
13 *The Crisis of Parliamentary Democracy*, Preface to the 2nd edn, 8-9.

of a nation, or its way of life. This is the threat that, according to Schmitt, requires a sovereign, and, within the sovereign, a capacity for discernment of national interest, and a willingness to go to war for it. National interest and the willingness to go to war are both things that liberalism, with its internationalist and humanitarian tendencies, officially denigrates, or allows to be subject to international negotiation.[14] Not that liberalism is above military action — in the form of humanitarian or peacekeeping operations.[15] But for liberals the resort to force is always a desperate measure. Schmitt thinks that the fear and contempt for military action is another weakness in parliamentarism. But this is not because he thinks that military action *can* readily be justified. Part of his attack on liberalism in general and parliamentarism in particular is an attack on the rationalism of liberalism and parliamentarism. In keeping with this attack, he denies that there can be a principled or rational justification for war.

> It is a manifest fraud to condemn war as homicide and then demand of men that they wage war, kill and be killed, so that there will never again be war. War, the readiness of combatants to die, the physical killing of human beings who belong to the side of the enemy — all this has no normative meaning, but an existential meaning only, particularly in a real combat situation with a real enemy. There exists no rational purpose, no norm, no matter how true, no program no matter how exemplary, no social ideal no matter how beautiful, no legitimacy nor legality which could justify men in killing each other for this reason. If such physical destruction of human life is not motivated by an existential threat to one's own way of life, then it cannot be justified. Just as little can war be justified by ethical and juristic norms. If there really are enemies in the existential sense as meant here, then it is justified, but only politically, to repel and fight them physically.[16]

Schmitt is saying that the experience of threat to one's way, the experience of the presence and activity of enemies, is by itself all that is necessary, even if it does not justify or give a reason, for fighting or going to war. Again and again he returns to the 'existential' character of the threat, by which I take him to mean the lived compellingness of the threat, as opposed to arguments that might underlie the enemy position. It is enough for going to war that a people or a group present itself with some intensity as alien, or as other. The relation of enmity is the 'utmost degree of intensity of a separation ... or dissociation'.[17]

Whether enmity exists, or, what amounts to the same, whether a threat to the very existence of the state exists, is not determined by a norm but by

---

14 See *The Concept of the Political*, 78–9.
15 Ibid., 79.
16 Ibid., 48–9.
17 Ibid., 26.

a personal decision—in a strong state by the personal decision of a sovereign or dictator. There is no organising the state so as to eliminate completely any need for a dictator, and a national democracy may not have much chance of survival if its head of state cannot in some circumstances take on the role of dictator—the role of someone who declares an emergency and then uses personal judgement to eliminate it. A state with no potential to be led by a dictator, with no potential for authoritative identifications of the enemy would be, in Schmitt's terms, radically depoliticised: it would not have a principle of association based on intense public identification or repulsion from others. Such a 'state' might be a kind of economic union, an ethical movement, a religion, but not a political association with the right kind of unity to keep reliably intact a way of life.

II

'The high points of politics', Schmitt writes in the *Concept of the Political*, are simultaneously 'the moments in which the enemy is, in concrete clarity, recognised as the enemy'.[18] Schmitt quotes from a speech Oliver Cromwell gave in September 1656, declaring the Spaniard to be the enemy of the Englishman. A speech made by President Bush to a joint session of the U.S. Congress soon after September 11 2001 also seems to mark a Schmittian high point of politics. Here is some of what Bush said:

> On September the 11th, enemies of freedom committed an act of war against our country. Americans have known wars, but for the past 136 years they have been wars on foreign soil, except for one Sunday in 1941. Americans have known the casualties of war, but not at the center of a great city on a peaceful morning.
>
> Americans have known surprise attacks, but never before on thousands of civilians. All of this was brought upon us in a single day, and night fell on a different world, a world where freedom itself is under attack.
>
> Americans have many questions tonight. Americans are asking, 'Who attacked our country?'
>
> The evidence we have gathered all points to a collection of loosely affiliated terrorist organizations known as al Qaeda. They are some of the murderers indicted for bombing American embassies in Tanzania and Kenya and responsible for bombing the USS Cole.
>
> Al Qaeda is to terror what the Mafia is to crime. But its goal is not making money; its goal is remaking the world and imposing its radical beliefs on people everywhere.

---

18 Ibid., 67.

The terrorists practice a fringe form of Islamic extremism that has been rejected by Muslim scholars and the vast majority of Muslim clerics, a fringe movement that perverts the peaceful teachings of Islam.

The terrorists' directive commands them to kill Christians and Jews, to kill all Americans and make no distinctions among military and civilians, including women and children.

This group and its leader, a person named Osama bin Laden, are linked to many other organizations in different countries, including the Egyptian Islamic Jihad [and] the Islamic Movement of Uzbekistan.

There are thousands of these terrorists in more than 60 countries.

They are recruited from their own nations and neighborhoods and brought to camps in places like Afghanistan, where they are trained in the tactics of terror. They are sent back to their homes or sent to hide in countries around the world to plot evil and destruction.

The leadership of al Qaeda has great influence in Afghanistan and supports the Taliban regime in controlling most of that country. In Afghanistan we see al Qaeda's vision for the world. Afghanistan's people have been brutalized, many are starving and many have fled.

Women are not allowed to attend school. You can be jailed for owning a television. Religion can be practiced only as their leaders dictate. A man can be jailed in Afghanistan if his beard is not long enough.

The United States respects the people of Afghanistan — after all, we are currently its largest source of humanitarian aid — but we condemn the Taliban regime.

It is not only repressing its own people, it is threatening people everywhere by sponsoring and sheltering and supplying terrorists.

This speech and its immediate context have all the marks of a Schmittian high point of politics. The leader of a strong state, having seized emergency powers, declares a certain group to be the enemy of his state, and accuses them of having perpetrated an act of war. This declaration is accompanied by a declaration of war. No squeamishness about the use of military force. And a clear, widely felt, intense alienation caused by the attacks on the Twin Towers and the Pentagon. A democracy shaken into illiberalism by exactly the right sort of thing: the experience of spectacularly violent attack.

Yet, questions widely asked by liberals after September 11 appear to make sense, and to tell against Schmitt's account. Why were the attacks to be regarded as acts of war, rather than criminal acts? Why was the use of war powers and a military response to be preferred to an especially well-co-ordinated use of police powers, perhaps under laws against murder and hijacking? These questions have a particular edge when pressed against Schmitt, because they raise the possibility that legal norms intended for normal times also apply in extraordinary ones, and that the declaration of an exception can be gratuitous, even in the face of groups as intensely alien in America as al Qaeda, and actions as repulsive as flying airplanes into the World Trade Centre.

President Bush's speech itself darts between claims concerning criminal acts and acts of war. To the extent that it declares Al Qaeda to be the enemy rather than an organised criminal gang, Al Qaeda is not supposed to be the enemy only of America. The perpetrators of the September 11 attacks are also supposed to be enemies of the people of Afghanistan, whose country they have taken over as a base for terrorist attacks. Besides being enemies of these two nations, al Qaeda are made into the enemies of freedom. This claim makes them enemies of a certain international political grouping, rather than of America alone. My point is not that Bush's speech is confused in its application of the rhetoric of war and enmity, though the speech may be that; rather, there is no obvious limit on how relations of enmity can be described, no confinement of relations of enmity to nations, no need for it to be the *sovereign* of a single nation that declares these relations to hold. Schmitt was himself aware of the possibility of appropriating the friend/enemy relation to a global struggle between the global proletariat and the global bourgeoisie, with specifically national groupings apparently transcended. And he was conscious of how a strong country adjoining weak ones could by default exercise the power of deciding on friends and enemies for the weaker countries. These possibilities, however, seem to detach the power of declaring friends and enemies from people playing the role of sovereign. An Osama bin Laden can play the role; and so can the head of a superpower.

Another difficulty, this time with Schmitt's existentialist understanding of enmity, is illustrated by the aftermath of September 11. Was the enemy Al Qaeda, or was it any militant Muslim grouping, or was it any terrorist organisation? If people of Middle Eastern appearance began to occasion intense fear and loathing among American airline passengers or among the general public, would *they* be an enemy or part of the enemy, even if they had nothing to do with al Qaeda, even if they were third generation Arab Americans who voted for George W Bush? Nothing in the Schmittian apparatus prevents the drift or spread of enmity from al Qaeda to the Arabs. Perception of a group as threatening to a way of life, not *justified* perception of a group as threatening to a way of life, seems sufficient for enmity.

Suppose President Bush was right to say that the attacks of September 11 were acts of war, requiring international military retaliation rather than a series of police actions in different countries. Then are Al Qaeda members taken prisoner to count as prisoners of war, and are they to benefit from the protections of the Geneva conventions? The Bush administration claimed that al Qaeda members could be treated worse than ordinary prisoners of war, and that they could be incarcerated in a military facility outside mainland U.S. civilian jurisdiction. But if the al Qaeda members were not real prisoners of war, were their acts real acts of war? Schmitt's theory supports wide discretion for the president in the action against al Qaeda, and presumably also allows laws protecting suspects to be waived for terrorist suspects after September 11. These laws were in fact suspended in the U.S. after September 11, allowing many suspects to be detained indefinitely without charge, if their names came up in searches tracing the activities of the airline hijackers on September 11. But are these suspensions of laws consistent with a war against the enemies of freedom? Liberals thought not. And Bush's speech, with its description of a war of retaliation by freedom-loving America against its enemies encourages this line of thought. Schmitt's illiberalism, too, is not impervious to complaints about the suspension of the normal laws limiting the time and grounds for detention. For it is no obligation of the sovereign to keep an exceptional situation going, or to take all possible powers against a threat even where the powers seem to no one to be useful in counteracting the threat.

These objections count against more than the detail of Schmitt's account; they call in question his claims about the significance of the exceptional, and the general relation between norm and exception. For Schmitt, the exception to law is a better key to law, the political order, and the preferred form of democracy, than the norm. Up to a point, Schmitt seems to be right. There is no such thing as a system of norms that applies itself to situations and in doing so bypasses personal will and judgement. But for a personal element to be ineliminable is not for it to deserve to be given free reign. Even in a situation of extreme national peril and an atmosphere of intense enmity, it does not seem to be true that anything the sovereign thinks goes. Still less does authority seem to attach to the intensity of the existential situation of hatred or the perception of threat, with all of its invitations to exaggeration and distortion. The sovereign, exercising emergency powers, is not incorrigible about relations of cause and effect. Sweeping powers of arrest may remove terrorists from the street, or they may be ineffective because there is so little intelligence about them. In the latter case, the act of seizing sweeping powers of arrest may be questionable. This is not to say that in an emergency someone or a small group shouldn't be in charge or be able to exercise discretion. It is to say that the bigger the departure from the norms of pre-emergency times, the bigger the burden on whomever is in charge to be sure that the departures will have results that bring the emergency to a conclusion. And this means appealing not to personal judgement but to claims about what measures will produce what effects, claims that have *no* great personal element to them. Again, the fact that it is departures from the norms of normal times that have to be justified, shows that the normal casts its shadow on the abnormal, just as much as the abnormal or exceptional tells us something about the normal.

III

I come now to the question of how Hobbesian Schmitt's theory of emergency is. Schmitt himself thinks of Hobbes as the decisionist or personalist *par excellence*, and he finds it striking that these tendencies should co-exist in a writer who is so rationalist and scientific in his general philosophy. The rationalist/scientific turn *after* Hobbes rejected the idea of a sovereign declaring the law. Schmitt thinks that the subsequent tradition tended to detach law from its maker in much the way it had detached natural law from a personal God who created the world.[19] In Hobbes this had not yet happened. Schmitt thinks that this is because Hobbes wanted to grasp the distinctive reality of legal and societal life, a reality that he thinks Hobbes traced to concrete decision emanating from a particular authority.[20]

This explanation betrays a misunderstanding of Hobbes. Schmitt makes it seem as if the sovereign's personal will makes the law, which provides a unity to the polity; Schmitt also thinks there is no system of norms to which this will is answerable. Neither of these claims is Hobbesian. It is not the sovereign but subjects who make a polity into a unitary thing. Each passes the right of ruling himself to someone else, and it is this act, performed simultaneously by everyone other than the sovereign in the state of nature that makes those individuals into a commonwealth (*Lev.* ch. 18, Tuck ed. p. 120).[21] The right of each to rule himself is passed to the sovereign in the expectation that, once transferred, it can be used by the sovereign to see to the security of each better than each can himself. The reason why the sovereign can do it better than each individual is complex. First, he stands apart from each individual and is free from the biasing self-love that often drives each into conflict with the other. Second, he can muster the combined resources of his subjects to generally beneficial purposes. Third, he has a great deal to lose if he directs the combined resources of his subjects to his own benefit, or to the benefit of some favourite, rather than theirs. Not to secure the safety and well-being of the

---

19   *Political Theology*, 34.
20   Ibid.
21   *Leviathan*, ed. R. Tuck (Cambridge: Cambridge University Press, 1991), ch. 18, 120.

many is to face the dissolution of the state, the return of each individual to the status of free agent, and the risk that each will turn on the former sovereign in vengeance for failure to keep the peace. The commonwealth thus becomes a balancing act in which the sovereign does well to decide from the point of view of the union of individuals he personifies, and his subjects do well to lend their obedience to the commonwealth by obedience to the sovereign's decrees. The balancing act is what constitutes the unity of the commonwealth in practice. This is the 'reality of societal life' that Hobbes's theory captures, and it is a reality based more on co-ordination of the many with the one, rather than on the personal decision of the one.[22]

Schmitt is of course right to think that the sovereign's decision counts for a lot.[23] Hobbesian subjects are not in any sense co-legislators with the sovereign, or people who have to be content with the laws that they live under in order for those laws to be just. Except when it comes to immediate mortal threats, or choices that the sovereign's laws permit them in their private lives, ordinary subjects delegate entirely their right to judge what is necessary for their well-being or security. They agree amongst themselves to write the sovereign a nearly blank cheque, and to do what they are told so long as by obeying they avoid war. Even when the sovereign's judgements as to what is necessary for the public safety turn out to be wrong, and a commonwealth gets into economic or military trouble, the sovereign is in no way answerable to his subjects. Nor can his subjects reasonably regard themselves as innocent bystanders who are damaged by the sovereign's choice of unsuccessful policies. For it is *their* signatures on the nearly blank cheque, *their* acts of submission, *their* choice, to give the sovereign whatever latitude he thinks he needs to keep the peace.

In *Leviathan*, Hobbes introduces the apparatus of authorization and of representative person to make these points.[24] The many authorise the sovereign to act on their behalf in matters of security, and they own the sovereign's actions. What is more, according to *Leviathan*, since they own the sovereign's actions, they cannot accuse him of injustice when those actions turn out damaging:

> But by this Institution of a Commonwealth, every particular man is Author of all the Soveraigne doth; and consequently, he that complaineth of injury from his Soveraigne, complaineth of that whereof he himself is Author; and therefore ought not to accuse any

---

22 See my 'The Burdensome Freedom of Sovereigns', in *Leviathan after 350 Years*, eds T. Sorell and L. Foisneau (Oxford: Clarendon Press, 2004).

23 In the rest of this section I draw upon my 'Autorité politique et science politique', in *Hobbes et la question de l'autorité dans le Leviathan*, ed. M. Pecharman (Paris: P.U.F. 2003).

24 *Leviathan*, ch. 16.

man but himselfe; no nor himselfe of injury; because to do injury to ones selfe, is impossible. It is true that they that have Soveraigne power may commit Iniquity; but not Injustice, or Injury in the proper signification.[25]

Subjects cannot complain of injury, for injury is to do with going back on what one has agreed, and the sovereign has agreed only to seek the public safety as he sees fit. It may be implausible for Hobbes to claim that subjects are authors of *all* the sovereign does, for there must be some acts that the sovereign carries out as a natural person that are his in two senses: they are not directed at the aim of public security, and they are not carried out by the sovereign acting as agent for the many. Again, it may be irrelevant that one cannot do injury to oneself if one can *damage* oneself. But these things are beside the present point, which is that Hobbes's way of connecting the will of the many with the actions of the sovereign does not limit the sovereign's freedom of action, or increase the subject's latitude for opposition or action: on the contrary, it reduces the subject's scope for legitimate complaint virtually to the point of disappearance.

It does not follow that the sovereign is answerable to no norms in fulfilling his role. Like any individual, he is subject to the laws of nature. And Hobbes recognises such a thing as duties of sovereigns. There are chapters devoted to the duties of sovereigns in all three of the political treatises: chapter 28 of the *Elements of Law*; chapter 13 of *De cive*; and chapter 30 of *Leviathan*. These are remarkable chapters in two respects. First, they all operate with a concept of *salus populi* that requires as much liberty for subjects as is compatible with security. Not as much liberty as the sovereign feels like giving; not as *little* as can be given without threatening the means of the commonwealth to secure itself, but as much as is compatible with security. This does seem to re-open the question of whether Hobbes is a liberal, and it certainly indicates the possibility that not everything the sovereign decides will be right. Second, the three chapters recommend quite specific policies that sovereigns should adopt or avoid, different policies in different political treatises. Why isn't this presumptuous or even unjust, on Hobbes's principles? It is one thing to say what the rights of sovereignty are, and to say they cannot be divided; it is another to indicate, even by implication, how these rights are to be exercised, or what would count as a misuse of office: for this is to pass judgement, albeit in general terms, on matters that all subjects, Hobbes included, are, according to Hobbes's theory, supposed to leave entirely to sovereigns.

The apparent inconsistency would probably not be very serious if Hobbes's duties for sovereigns amounted only to duties to exercise the

---

[25] *Leviathan*, ch. 18, 124.

rights of sovereigns exactly as sovereigns see fit. But this is not quite what they turn out to be. It appears that Hobbes cannot resist the temptation to descend to the detail of sovereign prescriptions and prohibitions. For example, in the *Elements of Law*, he insists that a sovereign must explicitly outlaw the 'promiscuous use of women', polygamy on the part of women, and copulation with blood relatives.[26] In *De cive*, he makes policy again, calling for the appointment by the sovereign of intelligence agents,[27] and specifying a duty to permit redress against corrupt judges and to appoint a court of enquiry into regular judges.[28] In *Leviathan*, he seems to say that it is the duty of the sovereign to use universities for instruction in civil duty,[29] and also that sovereigns should tax consumption rather than income.[30] Even if these are defensible proposals, they imply that a sovereign is in breech of his duty if he does not impose a consumption tax, or if he does not appoint intelligence agents, and Hobbes's own theory implies that the sovereign is the *sole* judge of what is required for peace. If the sovereign judges that intelligence agents are no use, or too unreliable, or occasion a damaging general mistrust, then, on Hobbes's principles, he is not to be gainsaid; yet the chapters on the duties of sovereigns the political treatises *do* gainsay — apparently — a sovereign who disagrees with Hobbes about tax or promiscuity or the uses of universities.

Is Hobbes going back on his decisionism when he works out of the concept of *salus populi*? At first sight the answer is 'Yes'. For it seems to make the purpose of forming the commonwealth more ambitious than it is where Hobbes is speaking about it mainly as the antidote to slaughter in the state of nature. In these passages, the commonwealth is said to deliver human beings from the worst of avoidable evils, namely war, and this is a great benefit however much people are inclined to magnify the accompanying inconveniences. Life in the commonwealth may not be all that pleasant, but it is greatly to be preferred to life in the absence of the commonwealth. When Hobbes speaks of the commonwealth as assuring *salus populi*, on the other hand, the commonwealth ceases to be a security device simply, and is supposed, in addition, to create conditions for at least a modicum of contentment or well being.

The *Elements of Law* connects *salus populi* to the procurement of eternal as well as temporal good. To the extent the commonwealth promotes the eternal good, it is by authorizing the teaching of appropriate doctrines

---

26 *The Elements of Law*, ed. J. C. A. Gaskin (Oxford: Oxford University Press, 1994), ch. 28, iii.
27 *On the Citizen*, ed. and trans. R. Tuck and M. Silverthorne (Cambridge: Cambridge University Press, 1998), 8. vii. 145.
28 *On the Citizen*, 8. xvii. 152.
29 *Leviathan*, ch. 30, 237.
30 *Leviathan*, ch. 30, 238–9.

about the means to salvation.[31] As for temporal good, an important component of it is what Hobbes calls 'the commodity of living':

> The commodity of living consisteth in liberty and wealth. By liberty I mean, that there be no prohibition without necessity of anything to a man, which was lawful to him in the state of nature; that is to say, that there be no restraint of natural liberty, but what is necessary for the good of the commonwealth; and that well-meaning men may not fall into the danger of laws, as into snares, before they be aware. It appertaineth to this liberty, that a man may have commodious passage from place to place, and not be imprisoned or confined with the difficulty of ways, and want of means for transportation of things necessary. And for the wealth of people, it consisteth of three things: the well-ordering of trade, procuring of labour, and forbidding the superfluous consuming of food or apparel ... [32]

The conception of liberty outlined here seems clearly to limit the prerogative of sovereigns. For restrictions on what subjects may do not only have to do no harm to peace or help it a little: they have to be essential or necessary to keeping the peace, and the burden of proof seems to be on the sovereign to think out why any liberty must be taken away, rather than why it should be allowed to be retained. The requirements for promoting wealth are far less exacting. It is not for the sovereign to make anyone rich, or to employ anyone, but only to allow people to do these things privately: and wealth is the possession of necessary goods, not luxuries.

In *Leviathan*, Hobbes comes up with the concept of good *law* to explain how the public safety is to be achieved. A good law in the relevant sense is definitely not a law that a sovereign merely *thinks* is good, Hobbes says.[33] For a law may seem good and not be needful. It may seem good, for example, because it seems to benefit the sovereign. But benefiting the sovereign is not sufficient for a law to be good.[34] Besides giving the impression that liberty is only to be taken away from individuals if there is a good reason, which seems to give a pretext for those who are under strict laws to think that their safety is not being promoted, and that they may rebel, Hobbes once again seems to be coming up with a ground for something counting as a good law that is detached from the judgement of the sovereign.

De cive offers fewer pretexts for rebellion. While it also operates with a concept of *salus populi* that is wider than bare preservation, it makes virtually nothing of liberty. In a passage significantly different from *Elements of Law* 28. iv, but parallel to it, Hobbes writes:

---

31 *The Elements of Law*, 28. ii.
32 *The Elements of Law*, 28. iv. 173–4.
33 *Leviathan*, 240.
34 Ibid.

> Regarding this life only, the good things citizens enjoy can be put into four categories: 1) defence from external enemies; 2) preservation of internal peace; 3) acquisition of wealth, so far as this is consistent with public security; 4) full enjoyment of innocent liberty. Sovereigns can do no more for citizens' happiness than to enable them to enjoy the possessions their industry has won them, safe from foreign and civil war.[35]

Hobbes does not say that citizens can expect to retain all freedoms of the state of nature that do not threaten security, and he makes a contentment with the possession of goods other than security depend on individual success in gainful employment. This conception of *salus populi* seems to me *not* to exclude significant inconveniences of government. It is also a conception that fits in better with the general argument of the *Elements of Law* and *Leviathan* than the conceptions one actually finds in those texts.

IV

Although there are elements in versions of Hobbes's civil philosophy that seem to undercut, or at least limit, the authority of sovereigns, these elements do not always cohere with the texts of Hobbes's political treatises taken as wholes. The *Elements of Law* and *Leviathan* would make perfectly good sense if they dropped the expansive conception of *salus populi*, while *De cive* seems to do without it in the first place. Perhaps it is the same with the chapters on the duties of the sovereigns in general. If these were subtracted from the political treatises, a coherent political philosophy would still come over from each of the books. It would be a theory of the duties and rights of a sovereign permanently presiding over a potential emergency, and of the rights and duties of subjects permanently threatened by a potential emergency.

In Schmitt, the belief that human beings are evil, or at least dangerous, means that, for him, political arrangements are permanently threatened just in so far as they are arrangements involving human beings. He goes so far as to say that

> all genuine political theories presuppose man to be evil, i.e. by no means an unproblematic but a dangerous and dynamic being. This can easily be documented in the works of every specific political thinker. Insofar as they reveal themselves as such, they all agree on the idea of a problematic human nature, no matter how distinct they are in rank and prominent in history. It suffices here to cite Machiavelli, Hobbes, Bossuet, Fichte ... [36]

---

35 *On the Citizen*, 13. vi. 144.
36 *The Concept of the Political*, 61.

It is unclear, however, that it is to an evil nature that Hobbes traces the ingredients of war and therefore emergency. For him, certainly by the time of *Leviathan*, the crucial element seems to be the division of decision-making power among the many — the retention of the right of nature — combined with any credible distribution of competition, vainglory and diffidence among the many. He does not assume that all human beings are alike, still less that all are greedy, vain and aggressive. A whole chapter of *Leviathan* chronicles the variety of active ingredients in men. The chapter is entitled 'The *difference* in manners' — my emphasis. Nor is it thought impossible by Hobbes for men to refrain from the slaughter that the distribution of unpleasant character traits makes likely. Part of the reason is that the passions that incline people to war can be counterbalanced by other passions — the fear of death and the desire for a 'commodious' life — that civil science channels into submission to a single decision-maker.

But countervailing passions are not the only helps to avoiding war. At one place in *Leviathan*, Hobbes says that it isn't enough for durable submission that people be terrified at the thought of breaking the sovereign's law.[37] They need to be taught the grounds for the sovereign's right of declaring the law. And this means engaging faculties of human beings that are not passions, and that are not dangerous. If the education takes, it is hard to see human beings being unchanged by their involvement in a commonwealth. Instead, involvement in the commonwealth becomes genuinely civilising, and human beings, if not made good, are at least tamed. The danger goes out of them, and with it, any necessary connection between humanity and danger.

By the same token, danger does not have to figure in the motivation for staying in the state. If the early history of a single people or of humanity consists of coming in from the state of nature largely out of fear of something worse, then their subsequent history may substitute for that fear, or add to it, some *understanding* (based of course on Hobbes's civil science) of why staying out of the state of nature is for the best. Why it is for the best *anyway*, independently of fear. And then one starts to see the rationale for the state detached from emergency. It may be, as Hobbes says, that the division of labour, prosperity, the arts and sciences, are all impossible without submission. Seeing as much can be as great an aid to the maintenance of government as terrible punishment for law-breaking, or hair-raising accounts of the bloodbath of civil war. So staying out of the state of nature makes sense *anyway*.

Again, it may be — and this is Kant's reading of the significance of the state of nature — that so long as one stays in the state of nature all under-

---

[37] *Leviathan*, ch. 30, 232.

standings of what one ought to do, even ought to do for the sake of well-being or prudence, are on a level. Everything is permitted, because there is no common standard of the permissible. Hobbes certainly thought it was an advance for a single decision-maker to control the actions of the many. But he did not think that the decisions of the single decision-maker were incorrigible or that there were no general rules that a sovereign could and should follow. His books of political philosophy state these rules. There is a sense in which the rules are supposed to have an authority even over sovereigns. Nor was the authority meant to be local and temporary. Rules of science hold for good, and across epochs. In this respect, Hobbes is very far from being the personalist, the decisionist, or the existentialist about power that Schmitt is.

Robert P. Kraynak

The Fragility of Civilization in Hobbes's Historical Writings

Most people do not think of Hobbes as an historian, but his political science rests on the sweeping historical claim that all past and present civil societies are radically defective because they have never been free of 'disorders of state and change of government by civil war'. The reason this historical premise is easily overlooked is that Hobbes makes no attempt to prove it in his scientific treatises on politics, such as *Leviathan* and *De Cive*. In these works, Hobbes begins by examining the faculties and passions of men in the state of nature, a condition in which all political authority is dissolved; he then constructs the Leviathan state — a new form of government that will establish a secure and lasting foundation for civil society. By proceeding in this fashion, Hobbes excludes from the outset an analysis of the traditional forms of political authority and the historical causes of civil war. His treatises, therefore, are incomplete statements of his political teaching: they present the solution to the past failures of civilization, but they take for granted an understanding of the problem.

For scholars who draw their interpretations from the political treatises, Hobbes's procedure creates difficulties because the original understanding of defective civil society has been reduced to a simple psychological teaching, according to which the passions for security, profit, and glory have rendered men 'apt to invade and destroy one another'. But this teaching does not explain why the civil societies of the past have been unable to control these passions; nor does it identify the immediate causes of war, such as class conflict, economic competition, political faction, religious sectarianism, dynastic struggles, racial strife, military rivalry, or any of the other historical causes of war. Because the historical record has been expunged from the state-of-nature teaching, scholars have tried to explain Hobbes's view of the fundamental political problem by referring to the intellectual context of Hobbes's life and times or by searching in other parts of the treatises for models of human conflict.

The Fragility of Civilization in Hobbes's Historical Writings 313

While illuminating in certain respects, such investigations overlook the fact that Hobbes himself analyzes the defects of previous civil societies in his extensive set of historical writings. These writings appear in separate books, most notably in *Behemoth*, Hobbes's history of the English civil war, and in *A Dialogue between a Philosopher and a Student of the Common Laws of England*, his analysis of England's political and legal institutions. In addition to these major works, Hobbes wrote short histories, such as 'An Historical Narrative on Heresy', a work on 'Ecclesiastical History' in Latin verse, an introduction to his translation of Thucydides, and a few short essays that have been identified recently as early discourses by Hobbes on Tacitus, Roman history, and law.[1] Despite their variety, all of these writings are part of the scholarly discipline that Hobbes calls 'civil history' and provide the best insight into his understanding of past and contemporary civilization.

In the argument that follows, I will attempt to piece together these writings into a coherent whole and to show that they constitute a Hobbesian philosophy of history—an account of the evolution of man from barbarism to civilization and an explanation of the inherent fragility or self-destructiveness of civilization. After presenting the account, I will bring Hobbes up-to-date by comparing his views on the fragility of civilization with Samuel Huntington's views in *The Clash of Civilizations*. I will suggest that Hobbes was more optimistic than Huntington about overcoming the anarchical tendencies of civilization but that Hobbes's optimism reflects some of the naïve illusions of the early Enlightenment about changing man's irrational behavior.

The history of barbarism and civilization

A survey of Hobbes's historical writings shows that Hobbes investigated the condition of civil society from the time of ancient Egypt to seventeenth-century England. His sources were the great historians, poets, and philosophers of antiquity and the lesser-known historians of contemporary Europe. From the works of Diodorus Siculus, Caesar, Josephus, and the Old Testament, Hobbes acquired a knowledge of the ancient kingdoms of the Near East, such as Egypt, Israel, Persia, Assyria, and India. From the works of Thucydides, Tacitus, Plutarch, Seneca, Lucan, Cicero, as well as from historical observations in Aristotle's *Politics* and *Metaphysics* (Bk. 1), Hobbes acquired an understanding of the republics of ancient Greece and Rome. And from the works of contemporary

---

1 See Noel B. Reynolds and Arlene Saxonhouse eds, *Thomas Hobbes: Three Discourses: A Critical Modern Edition of Newly Identified Work of the Young Hobbes* (Chicago: University of Chicago Press, 1995).

historians, such as Selden, Heath, and the common law historians, as well as from Tacitus, Hobbes developed his views on the origins of feudal Europe and the institutions of monarchy, gentry, and church. Judging from these sources, one can infer that for Hobbes the known civilized world consisted of three types of society: the ancient kingdoms of the Near East, the republics of ancient Greece and Rome, and the monarchies of Christian Europe.

In addition to studying the kingdoms and republics of the civilized world, Hobbes investigated the historical condition of those people he calls savages or barbarians. Drawing from many of the same sources, Hobbes describes at least three distinct peoples as savage or barbaric: 'the savage people of America' and 'those that live near the Poles' (that is, the Indians and Eskimos of North America); the Germanic tribes of prefeudal Europe and their descendents who became the Saxon tribes of early England; and the barbaric people who lived by plunder and rapine before the founding of the Greek city-states.[2]

As this overview suggests, the primary theme of Hobbes's writings on civil history is the distinction between barbarism and civilization—a distinction we can begin to understand by reflecting on his terminology. When speaking of the societies of the past, Hobbes sometimes uses terms that emphasize their political characteristics—'commonwealths', 'cities', or 'polities'—and at other times uses terms that emphasize their civilized characteristics—'civil society' or 'civil life'.[3] He uses both sets of terms interchangeably because he regards civilization as a condition that combines a certain level of political development with a certain manner of living. Whenever government became sufficiently strong and well-established to provide peace and leisure, men began to cultivate philosophy or the arts and sciences. Thus, Hobbes observes as a general rule that 'commonwealth is the mother of peace and leisure; and leisure, the mother of philosophy. Where first there were great and flourishing cities, there was the first study of philosophy'.[4] Civilization, in other words, has been a condition in which government provided the leisure for intellectual cultivation. In the savage or barbaric condition, by contrast, political authority has been so weak and underdeveloped that no one has the leisure to cultivate the arts and sciences or to practice philosophy.

---

2   *Leviathan*, ch. 10, 83; ch. 13, 114; ch. 30, 324; ch. 46, 655. And *De Cive*, V. 2; *De Corpore*, I. 7; *Dialogue on the Common Laws*, 162-63. References are to *EW*: *De Cive*, *EW* 2; *De Corpore*, *EW* 1; *Leviathan*, *EW* 3; *Behemoth*, *EW* 6; Joseph Cropsey ed., *A Dialogue between a Philosopher and a Student of the Common Laws of England* (Chicago: University of Chicago Press, 1971); and Bernard Gert ed., *Man and Citizen* ('De Homine' and 'De Cive') (Indianapolis: Hackett, 1991).
3   *Leviathan*, ch. 9, 71; *De Cive*, X. 1; *De Corpore*, I. 7; *De Homine*, X. 3.
4   *Leviathan*, ch. 46, 660.

Using this standard, Hobbes is able to trace the evolution of man from barbarism to civilization. In the most primitive condition, the only form of political authority was that of patriarchs or conquerors who ruled over families and tribes by 'natural force'. Hence, Hobbes says, 'the beginning of all dominion amongst men was in families; in which the father ... was absolute lord of his wife and children ... [and of those] enemies they took and saved, [who] were their servants'.[5] In this condition, a continuous struggle for survival occurred, as clans and tribes waged war for territory, scarce goods, and servants. Accordingly, plunder and piracy were not regarded as dishonorable; indeed, it was 'a manner of living, and as it were a certain economy, which they called *lestriken*, living by rapine'.[6] The harshness of life was mitigated only by a primitive code of military honor which required magnanimity in victory and by the economy of plunder which counselled victors to spare the people, animals, and instruments that were useful for production. As for the cultivation of the arts and science, only the 'arts necessary for a man's life' were developed in the condition of barbarism. Primitive men lived by immediate sense experience because they lacked the leisure to cultivate speech, to develop writing, or to acquire systematic knowledge.[7]

Of the several historical conditions from which this description is drawn, the one Hobbes discusses in greatest detail is that of the Germanic and Saxon tribes of prefeudal Europe. In the *Dialogue on the Common Laws*, he traces England's political institutions to a prehistoric era when the island was inhabited by Saxon tribes whose ancestors came from Germany. As a 'savage and heathen people,' they lived 'only by war and rapine ... written laws they had little, or none, and very few there were in [that] time ... that could write or read'. Among such savages, authority was either paternal or by conquest, and the 'succession of lands was determined by the pleasure of the master of the family ... [or by] natural descent, [which] was held for the law of nature, not only amongst the Germans, but also in most nations before they had written laws'.[8] The prehistoric era was followed by a period in which the Saxon tribes came under Roman domination and England developed written laws and customs. Although this marked the beginning of political consolidation, England remained divided into many petty kingdoms, each of which developed the custom of meeting with a council of advisors to design laws. The third era began with the conquest of Saxon kings by William the Conqueror

---

5 *Dialogue on the Common Laws*, 159; *Leviathan*, ch. 17, 159.
6 *De Cive*, V .2.
7 *Dialogue on the Common Laws*, 198; *Leviathan*, ch. 46, 665.
8 *Dialogue on the Common Laws*, 190, 198-9.

who established a great monarchy and brought England to the state of civil society.

In the *Dialogue* and in *Behemoth*, Hobbes indicates that this general pattern was followed in the origins of all civilized nations. He remarks that

> great monarchies have proceeded from small families ... [which were extended] by war, wherein the victor not only enlarged his territory, but also the number and riches of his subjects ... [And in this] manner, which is by war, grew up all the great kingdoms of the world, viz., the Egyptian, Assyrian, Persian, and the Macedonian monarchy; and so did the great kingdoms of England, France, and Spain.[9]

As for the republics of Greece and Rome, their development was a variation on this theme. In early Greece, men lived by plunder and piracy until city-states were formed; thereafter, 'the Greeks had for a while their petty kings, and then by sedition came to be petty commonwealths [that is, small republics]; and then growing to be greater commonwealths, by sedition again became monarchies'. Similarly, Rome began with primitive tribes consolidated into monarchy; then, 'in Rome, rebellion against Kings produced Democracy, upon which the Senate usurped under Sylla, and the People again upon the Senate under Marius, and the Emperor usurped upon the People under Caesar and his Successors'.[10]

As a general rule, then, the evolution from barbarism to civilization followed a typical pattern: families, tribes, and small kingdoms were consolidated by war or agreement into commonwealths, which were either great monarchies or small republics. This political development was accompanied by a measure of peace and leisure, which allowed for intellectual development in various spheres, from the cultivation of speech and writing to the development of arts and sciences and philosophy.

To this point, Hobbes's analysis seems to indicate that the evolution from barbarism to civilization is a kind of progress. But is this really the case? Which condition is superior with regard to human felicity and misery? According to Aristotle, civilization as such is superior to barbarism. As Aristotle says in *Politics*, Bk. 1, the growth from families to tribes to cities improves men by making them increasingly self-sufficient and civilized; in political societies, they rise above 'mere life' and attain the 'good life', understood as a life of leisure devoted to the exercise of the moral virtues in politics and the cultivation of the mind in philosophy. For Aristotle and other classical philosophers, the good life is the end of civilization and includes all of the elements of a happy or self-sufficient existence.

---

9   *Dialogue on the Common Laws*, 95-6.
10 *Behemoth*, 252; *Dialogue*, 196.

Now, Hobbes agrees with Aristotle to a certain extent. Political consolidation into small republics and great monarchies constitutes progress because it brings some relief from the wars among clans and tribes. In addition, the increase in leisure and the advancement of the practical arts bring increased freedom from necessity and scarcity, enabling civilized people to enjoy some of the 'commodities of mankind'. In these respects, civilization provides greater happiness or felicity than pre-civil life and is superior to it. But Hobbes stops here in his agreement with Aristotle about the superiority of civilization and warns his readers about those aspects of civilized life that make it more miserable than savagery.

Hobbes's crucial insight is that the founding of cities and commonwealths turned the human mind to higher things than immediate sense experience and practical arts; it led to the development of speculative and moral sciences as well as to the formulation of general principles in philosophy, theology, and jurisprudence. As a result, a new type of authority arose: the primitive rule of patriarchs and conquerors was replaced by the rule of philosophers, priests, lawyers, orators, and intellectuals of all types who sought to rule *not by natural force but by opinion*. However, the replacement of force by opinion has not made civilized life happier or better than barbarism. Rather, it has produced a new kind of warfare that primitive men were spared by their ignorance: in civilized societies, the wars among tribes for territory and plunder have been superseded by wars among learned intellectuals over opinions and doctrines.

A change in human passions also occurred as civilized people began to pursue intellectual activities. According to Hobbes, savages were motivated by appetites for necessary things and confined their passion for honor and glory to competition for goods, children, servants, or military command, leading to displays of self-sufficiency in sparing the vanquished and abstaining from cruelty. For primitive men, honor was magnanimity. By contrast, civilized men feel secure from want and seek honor and glory in unnecessary things — in titles, symbols, and above all in opinions and claims of knowledge. In civilized societies, magnanimity degenerates into vainglory, which is a false sense of sufficiency, measured not by possessions and command but by flattery and agreement. The most powerful form of vanity among civilized men is *intellectual vanity* — the desire to be esteemed wise and learned by having one's opinions and doctrines recognized as the authoritative wisdom of society. This desire for intellectual recognition is the cause of civilization's misery and degradation; for 'man is most troublesome, when he is most at ease; for then he loves to show his wisdom, and control the actions of them that govern the commonwealth'. Moreover, intellectual vanity causes men 'to hate and be hated by reason of the disagreement of opinions', creating malice and cruelty of a kind unknown to savages.[11] Hobbes's conclusion (later developed by Rousseau) is that the government, leisure, and intellectual cultivation that traditionally were thought to mark the superiority of civilization have made it as miserable as and in certain respects more cruel than savagery.

The stages of civilization

This critical insight provides the theme of Hobbes's history of civilization. While each of the civilized nations of the world has been independently founded, a general development of world civilization can be traced through three stages — from the ancient kingdoms of the Near East to the republics of Greece and Rome to the monarchies of Christian Europe. It is a development characterized by the ever-diminishing influence of coercive power and the ever-increasing influence of learned opinions and doctrines.

The first stage of civilization might be called the 'prophetic age' (this is my label) because intellectual cultivation took the form of prophecy and inspired poetry. In the preface to *De Cive*, Hobbes describes this historical period as a time when prophets, priests, and poets sought knowledge of the divine and natural order and used it to enhance the authority of rulers. As Hobbes remarks, 'the most ancient sages' delivered their opinions 'either curiously adorned with verse, or clouded in allegories, as a most beautiful and hallowed mystery of royal authority'. Hobbes even speculates that these sages deliberately 'chose to have the science of justice wrapped up in fables, [rather] than openly exposed to disputation' so that kings could keep

> their empires entire, not by arguments, but by punishing the wicked and protecting the good. Likewise, subjects ... were not kept in peace by disputations, but by power and authority ... [and] reverenced the supreme power as a certain visible divinity ... whereof it was peace and a golden age.[12]

Hobbes's point is that, during this early stage of civilization, political rulers were supported by religious and poetic authorities who created myths about the divinity of kings in order to promote obedience — an arrangement that Hobbes looks upon with nostalgia as a time when naïve belief in authority produced a 'golden age' of civil peace.

If we turn to other writings, we can see that the account in *De Cive* is somewhat idealized. In *Behemoth*, Hobbes includes a lengthy narrative on Diodorus Siculus, a Roman historian of the first century BC whom

---

11 *Leviathan*, ch. 17, 157; *De Homine*, X. 3; *De Cive*, X. 9.
12 *De Cive*, Preface.

Hobbes refers to as one of the greatest historians ('the greatest antiquary perhaps that ever was'). What Hobbes admires about Diodorus is his ambition to write a universal history of civilization from ancient Egypt to Roman times as well as his detailed lessons on 'how philosophy, together with divinity, have much conduced to the advancement of the professors thereof ... next to the authority of kings themselves, in the most ancient kingdoms of the world'.[13] Drawing upon Diodorus as well as the Old Testament, Hobbes describes the relations between civil and religious authorities in ancient Egypt and Israel.

The Egyptians, Hobbes remarks, are 'the most ancient kingdom in the world, and their priests had the greatest power in civil affairs, than any subjects ever had in any nation'. The power of the priesthood was derived in part from its status as a hereditary class in a hierarchical society. However, the real source of its power was its control over opinions and beliefs about the gods, natural events, and law. Quoting Diodorus, Hobbes says '"the priests had most credit with the people, both for their devotion to the gods, and for their understanding gotten by education"'. The Egyptian priests were also influential as counselors to the king, '"partly executing and partly informing and advising, fortelling him by their skill in astrology and art in the inspection of sacrifices, the things that are to come, and reading him out of their holy books, such actions ... as are profitable for him to know"'. The priestly caste also supplied the judges in Egypt because of their reputation for knowledge, as symbolized by the medallions worn by chief justices which were inscribed with the word 'truth'.[14] Although political authority was virtually usurped by the power that Egyptian priests had over the minds of kings and subjects, the result was a fairly stable civilization in which public disputation of laws and opinions was avoided.

By contrast, the kingdom of ancient Israel was disrupted frequently by conflicts of opinion among rival prophets. As Hobbes reveals in *Behemoth* and *De Cive*, civil-religious authority was unified in the early period of the Jewish commonwealth because Moses was the political leader and the foremost prophet. But the distinction between coercive power and the authority to interpret the word of God left Moses open to challenge by a number of rivals during his lifetime—by Korah and his accomplices, by Aaron the high-priest and his sister Miriam, and by other prophets. Each of these groups disputed Moses's exclusive claim to prophecy and raised the threat of sedition. However, as Hobbes also shows, Moses was able to repulse these challenges because he skillfully used a certain method of

---

13 *Behemoth*, 276.
14 *Behemoth*, 278–9.

punishing his rivals. Instead of disputing their doctrines, Moses exposed the ambition behind the doctrines, thereby discrediting the purity of their claim to speak for God and inciting the people's anger against them. After Moses, the Jewish nation became a 'priestly kingdom' in which the interpretation of divine law and the word of God belonged to the high-priest who was also the king. This, too, was a troubled period. The high priests were continually challenged by prophets for the right to interpret the law and word of God; but they lacked the political skill of Moses in punishing their rivals, leaving the nation in a continuous state of turmoil.[15]

In sum, life in the ancient kingdoms of Egypt and Israel was not quite the golden age described in *De Cive*. Authority was based on the coercive power of kings as well as the learned opinions of priests and prophets, creating a potential source of conflict. The problem was mitigated by the fact that the priesthood had a natural basis as a hereditary caste, which limited the scope of rival opinions. Hobbes also indicates that the most unstable nation, ancient Israel, was the exception rather than the rule: the Israelites were 'a people greedy of prophets', meaning the peculiar problem of the Jewish people was the appeal of independent prophets (although even this problem could be managed by skillful leadership).[16] With these qualifications, Hobbes's view of the prophetic age as a period of relative stability (if not a golden age) can be sustained.

Further support for this judgment is provided by Hobbes's account of the republics of Greece and Rome. They were more unstable than the kingdoms of the ancient world, even though the priestly class was weaker in Greece and Rome than in the ancient kingdoms ('In Greece, one man and one woman had the priesthood', rather than a hereditary caste). In fact, the poets were 'the principal priests' because they delivered tales about gods and spirits to the people and codified doctrine. Furthermore, as Hobbes observes in his commentary on Diodorus, the Greeks were the first to free philosophy from religion. Previously, philosophy was equated with the explanation of natural events by astrology, magic, and inspection of sacrifices (although Egyptian and Chaldean priests also practiced astronomy and mathematics). But it was 'philosophy after the manner of the Greeks' that finally separated the study of nature from prophetic arts and weakened the power of priests.[17] As a result, the ancient republics never suffered from a division between political rulers and priests: their 'civil laws were the rules whereby not only righteousness

---

15 *De Cive*, XVI. 13-15.
16 *De Cive*, XVI. 14.
17 *Behemoth*, 278-81; *Leviathan*, ch. 45, 638.

and virtue, but also religion and the external worship of God, were ordered and approved'.[18]

Although philosophy and politics took precedence over religion in Greece and Rome, the republics were inherently unstable because the authority of received opinions was subject to public dispute. In this case, the received opinions were not derived from divine law but from political notions of justice and prudence interpreted by legislators, orators, and philosophers. The peculiar problem of the classical republics was political factionalism caused by two new kinds of intellectual discourse: rhetoric and dialectic. In this period, Socrates compounded the instability by inventing political science or civil philosophy which began a new stage of civilization, the philosophical age of public disputation.

Hobbes's early thoughts on Greek civilization are expressed in the introduction to his translation of Thucydides. There, he refers to Thucydides as 'the most political historiographer that ever writ' because his subject is the political realm in the strict sense: the public life of the Greek city-states where government was exercised by citizens in the assembly and forum. In recording their history, Thucydides shows the inherent defect of Greek political life to be the instability of opinion caused by public deliberations about justice and policy. The deliberations were dominated by 'demagogues contending for reputation and glory of wit' who created factional strife in domestic affairs, while encouraging hazardous adventures in foreign and military affairs, all for the sake of intellectual honor and glory, that is, for the sake of seeing their opinions preferred before others. The only hope for stability, Hobbes observes, was for sober statesmen to oppose the demagogues; but this was an exercise in futility, and most honorable men, such as Thucydides himself, simply withdrew from politics with a sense of resignation about the self-destruction of Greek political life.[19]

During this era, new problems arose when Socrates invented civil philosophy, which Hobbes describes in the preface to *De Cive* as follows. Philosophy first appeared in the ancient world as natural philosophy when prophecy was superseded by rational investigations into 'the faces and motions of things' (physics) and 'their natures and causes' (metaphysics). Similarly, the study of justice was originally part of divinity science in which rational inquiry existed only in embryo, barely 'glimmering forth as through a cloud of fables and myths'. After natural philosophy arose, Socrates invented civil philosophy because he 'set so great a value on this, that utterly abandoning and despising all other parts of philosophy, he

---

18 *Elements of Law*, II. 2. 6. 2.
19 Introduction to Thucydides's *The Peloponnesian War*, Hobbes's translation, EW 8.

wholly embraced this [civil science].' While the beginning of natural philosophy was 'to the advantage of mankind', the invention of civil philosophy produced misery and civil strife. No longer could political sovereigns rely on protective myths or the skillful punishment of rivals to rule; they now needed rational doctrines of right upheld by argumentation. The golden age of naïve obedience was over, and the philosophical age of disputative politics had begun.

The precise reason for this historic development was the method of dialectic or disputation that Socrates and his followers introduced. Their method was to examine commonly received opinions in order to attain true knowledge, which meant that they questioned the conventional definitions of justice in order to discover a higher standard of natural justice. The Socratic revolution thereby challenged established laws and opinions and made the appeal to higher justice the accepted practice of philosophers and intellectuals. Thus, when Hobbes attacks the troublesome men of antiquity who loved 'to dispute', he does not simply mean that they happened to disagree with established opinions. He means they were practicing the dialectical art of disputation, whose very method was to dispute received opinions and thereby to unsettle society.[20]

The philosophical method begun by Socrates eventually transformed the civilized world. As Hobbes observes, 'men were so much taken by this custom that in time it spread itself over all Europe, and the best part of Africa; so as there were schools publicly erected and maintained, for lectures and disputations, almost in every commonwealth'.[21] With the advent of Christianity it became part of divinity science and was established in universities and churches. The result was a new stage of civilization characterized by the popularization of disputative philosophy. In this age, the most casually educated men, even the common people, became practitioners of disputative science and owners of a doctrine: 'Now at length, all men of all nations, not only the philosophers but even the vulgar, have and do still deal with this as a matter of ease, exposed and prostitute to every mother wit, and to be attained without any great care or study'.[22] In Hobbes's age, disputation in religion and politics has become the ideal of civilized living for common people as well as the philosophers. It is the most advanced stage of civilization in which everyone owns a doctrine and intellectual vanity is a universal passion.

The problems of this age appear in Hobbes's analysis of the monarchies of Christian Europe. His writings follow his usual pattern of describing

---

20 *De Cive*, Epistle Dedicatory.
21 *Leviathan*, ch. 46, 667.
22 *De Cive*, Preface.

the development of political institutions out of conquest and hereditary succession and the development of cultural institutions based on opinion and learning. The political institutions of Western Europe—its monarchies and gentry—arose from the pre-civil state when Germanic tribes roamed the continent and Saxon tribes inhabited England. These tribes were ruled by warlords and petty kings whose realms were eventually consolidated by conquest into great monarchies, forming the nations of Europe. In the process, the warlords became a civilized gentry—a class of aristocratic families distinguished by symbols of honor, such as heralds and hereditary titles. The heralds were originally coats of arms used by the German warlords to identify their soldiers; when they were forced to lay down their arms, the designs were kept by families as signs of honor or distributed by monarchs as honorific rewards for service. Similarly, titles such as duke, count, marquis, and baron were once designations of military offices in the German militia and other armies; later, in more peaceful times, they were made into mere titles of honor, without power or command. In the evolution from warlords to gentry, the code of honorable conduct was also transformed from one of military prowess and magnanimity, acquired on the battlefield, to one of gallantry and vanity, derived from reading romances.[23] In describing the origins of monarchy and gentry, Hobbes shows that political consolidation brought peace among warlords, followed by the redirection of honor from the recognition of possession and command to the vanity of titles, symbols, and gallantry.

Accompanying the growth of political institutions in Europe was the development of the Church and the universities. They were shaped by the philosophical tradition begun in ancient Greece and its disputative method of reasoning, which shaped Christian Europe in two important ways. First, it implied that knowledge was acquired by reasoning from authority, which among the classical philosophers meant the authority of common opinion and among Scholastics meant the authority of the Bible and the classical authors. Appealing to authority was virtually equated with knowledge. Second, the search for knowledge was focused on words or speech, on the assumption that speech provides access to the nature and causes of things. The Greeks first developed this view of knowledge because they invented rhetoric and dialectics, the original arts and sciences of speech. Indeed, Hobbes says, 'the Greeks had but one word, *logos*, for both reason and speech ... [because] they thought there was no reason without speech'. Surprisingly, Christianity did not alter this view, despite its appeal to revelation as the highest form of knowledge. For the study of

---

23   *Leviathan*, ch. 10, 81–4; ch. 6, 46.

scripture consisted of analyzing 'the Word of God ... [which in Latin is] *sermo*, in Greek *logos*, that is, some speech, discourse, or saying'.[24] The synthesis of classical philosophy and scriptural studies turned dialectics into academic disputation, in which Schoolmen reasoned from scripture and ancient texts to define the meaning of words. They also transformed classical rhetoric into a more stylized form of public preaching, involving dramatic gestures and indoctrination through repetition of words. University disputation and public preaching thereby became the most highly honored activities in the Christian world, creating a civilization of academic speech.

In Hobbes's view, this stage of civilization is the most unhappy period of history. For the scholars and preachers of the Western world cultivated the arts of speech and spread their disputes to all sectors of society. By endorsing the Protestant idea that everyone could interpret Scripture for himself, they made every individual an amateur practitioner of disputation and introduced a new phenomenon, religious sectarian warfare. In the ancient world, Hobbes says, civil sovereigns never allowed private men as much freedom to preach publicly as they are allowed in Christian Europe; as a result, 'there was no such [public preaching] permitted in all the world outside of Christendom, nor therefore any civil wars on account of religion'.[25] Such wars cause great misery because disputes over doctrines and words multiply the number of sects indefinitely and the disputes of sectarians call forth intense malice and cruelty.

Hobbes's conclusion, then, is that the long march from barbarism through the prophetic, philosophical, and Christian stages of civilization has followed a persistent pattern of replacing savage wars over territory and plunder with 'civilized' wars over doctrines and words.

Doctrinal warfare in *Behemoth*

This history of civilization provides the context for Hobbes's most important historical work, *Behemoth,* and points to his distinctive interpretation of the English civil war. For Hobbes, the civil war was not about the particular deeds of King Charles I nor about class warfare nor even about the struggle for power as such. It was a war over doctrines whose sources were deeply rooted in Western civilization and whose leaders were motivated by intellectual vanity — by the desire to be recognized as the wisest or most learned of men and to have their doctrines and opinions established as the authoritative wisdom of society. As Hobbes says in commenting on the folly of the civil war: 'It is a hard case, that there should be

---

24 *Leviathan*, ch. 4, 25; ch. 36, 407.
25 *Behemoth*, 243–4.

The Fragility of Civilization in Hobbes's Historical Writings 325

two factions to trouble the commonwealth ... and that their quarrels should be only about opinions, that is, about who has the most learning, as if learning should be the rule of governing all the world'.[26]

The structure of *Behemoth*, which Hobbes outlines in the Epistle Dedicatory, highlights this distinctive view of the English civil war. Part I uncovers the underlying causes of the rebellion, the seditious 'opinions in divinity and politics' that arose from the Western tradition and that were taught in the universities. Part II exposes the artifices of the rebels, namely, the techniques of rhetoric and indoctrination that they used to corrupt the minds of the people and to incite them against the king. Only in parts III and IV does Hobbes actually narrate the events of the civil war from 1640 to 1660; here, his aim is to show how legal opinions about taxation, the conscription of soldiers, and military strategy crippled the king and led to a circular movement of power—from the Stuart monarchy under King Charles I to the Long Parliament and its 'Rump', to Cromwell and his son, then back to the 'Rump' and the Long Parliament, and finally back to the Stuart monarchy under Charles II. The continuous message throughout the book is the devastating effect of doctrinal warfare and learned folly on the exercise of sovereign power.

Hobbes begins his account by identifying the leaders of the rebellion and uncovering the historical origins of their seditious doctrines. The foremost leaders were the Presbyterian ministers who maintained that spiritual authorities may intervene in politics to defend the faith and that subjects may disobey the law if it violates their conscience. Hobbes shows that this doctrine has ancient roots, going back to the beginning of Christianity when the Papacy created it in order to conquer the world by controlling the minds of princes and people. The strategy of the clergy was to transform Christianity from the ethical religion of Jesus, which stressed actions and intentions, to a dogmatic religion of priests that stressed doctrines and beliefs. By making 'rightness of opinion [rather] than of action and intention' the test of salvation, the clergy acquired control over the minds the people which surpassed the influence of the state.[27]

The key to their control was developing the notion of heresy, which Hobbes claims was borrowed by the Christian clergy from the Athenian schools of philosophy and transformed from a neutral term meaning 'a private opinion' to a term of condemnation meaning wrong or false opinion. Henceforth, the mission of Christian clergymen became the defense of orthodoxy and the punishment of heresy by the device of excommunication. Using the pretext of defending orthodoxy, they intervened in poli-

---

26 *Behemoth*, 275.
27 *Behemoth*, 243.

tics and subordinated emperors and princes. And by teaching the people that one is damned if 'he die in a false opinion concerning the Christian faith', they captured the minds of the common people.[28]

As the papacy grew, it developed other weapons besides excommunication to maintain its hold on the minds of people. In the twelfth century, it developed the universities and an order of travelling preachers as instruments of domination which Hobbes describes as the 'second polity of the Pope'—the medieval phase of the Church which surpassed the early phase by 'turning religion into an art'. It drew upon Aristotelian philosophy and scripture to define Christian orthodoxy and developed disputation and rhetoric to defend it. The papacy also trained travelling preachers to disseminate its academic doctrine to the people, directing their allegiance away from their political sovereigns and toward the Church.[29]

When the Reformation challenged Catholic orthodoxy, this strategy for intellectual domination did not change; it merely changed hands. As the power of popes was broken in England, the bishops arrogated to themselves the right to define orthodoxy and used the techniques of excommunication, disputation, and rhetoric to become the established Church of England. But the Reformation also undermined the traditional strategy of domination by doctrine. By translating the Bible into the vulgate and allowing everyone to interpret scripture for himself, it produced an explosion of sectarianism that was the immediate cause of the English civil war. For the right of the bishops of the Church of England to define orthodoxy was challenged by Presbyterians who in turn were challenged by a variety of independent sects who proclaimed direct inspiration in proclaiming the word of God. Meanwhile, the king was unable to settle the disputes because all the sectarians asserted the right of the clergy to stand above the state and to speak directly to the consciences of the people. As a result, no power was capable of preventing the theological disputes about Christian orthodoxy from degenerating into sectarian warfare.

After uncovering the seditious opinions in divinity, Hobbes turns to the political and legal opinions responsible for the civil war. For the rebellion was fomented by an alliance of Presbyterian ministers who rejected the orthodoxy of the established Church and a group of 'democratical gentlemen' who challenged the legitimacy of monarchy.[30] The gentlemen championed the cause of the Long Parliament by accusing King Charles of tyrannical behavior and declaring that democracy or republicanism was

---

28 *Leviathan*, ch. 46, 684.
29 *Behemoth*, 184.
30 *Behemoth*, 192.

the only just form of government. In uncovering the source of their doctrine, Hobbes shows that it did not arise spontaneously from the political arena but was created by ambitious intellectuals for the purpose of domination. Indeed, Hobbes claims that the very idea of distinguishing just and unjust regimes (like the distinction between orthodoxy and heresy) was an intellectual invention — the invention of Socrates and other Greek philosophers who sought to diminish the power of kings and to defend the republics of their times, while making themselves the arbiters of justice.

Not surprisingly, Hobbes thinks that the gentlemen who were educated in classical literature at the universities fancied themselves to be as wise and learned as the philosophers of old and to possess a title to rule by virtue of their wisdom. As party leaders, they attacked monarchy as an unjust regime and used rhetoric and eloquence to arouse the anger of the common people, who otherwise were politically indifferent and 'would take any side for pay or plunder'.[31] By accusing the king of treason for subverting the laws of the realm, the democratical gentlemen turned the people into democratic partisans and led them in rebellion.

Allied with the radical republicans was a more moderate group of educated gentlemen, the lawyers of the common law. While joining the opposition to Charles, they were less interested in overthrowing the king than in limiting royal prerogatives because their doctrines were derived, not from classical literature and its abstract principles of justice, but from English common law and its notions of customary procedure. Unlike the democratical gentlemen who sought absolute power for the Long Parliament, the lawyers were drawn primarily from the House of Lords and favored a sharing of power among king, Lords, and Commons. They believed that England was a 'mixed-monarchy' by ancient tradition and that all power should be limited by customary procedures.[32]

Despite the moderation of the lawyers, Hobbes condemns them as harshly as the radical republicans. For their opposition to royal prerogatives and their insistence on legal procedures destroyed the king's capacity for self-defense. They opposed the king's efforts to raise taxes and conscript soldiers without the consent of parliament; and as counsellors to the king, they continuously opposed his drive for total victory in the civil war by urging truces and treaties, which 'took off the courage of the best and forwardest of his soldiers'.[33] Their doctrines blinded them to the imperatives of sovereign power, which requires extraordinary action in

---

31 *Behemoth*, 166.
32 *Behemoth*, 303-20.
33 *Behemoth*, 307.

extreme situations. As a result, the lawyers, who merely sought to limit prerogative, were as devastating in their effects as the Presbyterian ministers who maintained the supremacy of Church over state and as the democratical gentlemen who challenged the legitimacy of monarchy.

From this overview of *Behemoth*, we can see the essential features of Hobbes's critique of seventeenth-century English society. The structure of authority was inherently unstable because it rested on claims of authoritative wisdom by clergymen, gentlemen philosophers, and lawyers who were trained in the universities. As educated intellectuals or scholars, they claimed to be wiser and more learned than the political sovereign and to be guided by laws above the will of the king. But they turned out to be ineffective rulers because they could not agree about which higher law—divine law, natural law, or common law—should be supreme, and they had no appreciation for coercive power. Moreover, they fought among themselves over whose interpretation of higher law was best. Driven by intellectual vanity, each self-appointed wiseman sought to acquire a following for his doctrine among the common people and to have it established by the state as orthodoxy or authoritative wisdom. At the same time, the king was fatally weakened by a division of sovereignty between state and church or, more generally, between his own coercive power and the doctrines of intellectual authorities. All of the sectarians, despite their disagreements, conspired to keep the political sovereign subordinated to higher laws. This division was an invitation to anarchy because the state remained dependent on scholars who conspired against its sovereignty but who failed to agree amongst themselves about which doctrine was supremely authoritative—the problem of doctrinal warfare. This problem explains why King Charles was incapable of defending himself and of preventing the intellectual disputes of the universities from erupting into the open violence of the English civil war.

Can the Enlightenment save civilization?

Hobbes's view of the inherent fragility and self-destructiveness of civilization expressed in *Behemoth* and other historical writings usually puts in him in the camp of 'realists' or 'pessimists' about the human condition. Such labels are inaccurate, however, because Hobbes thinks that the historic failures of civilization can be overcome through the process that later became known as the Enlightenment—bringing light to the kingdom of darkness by re-educating the intellectual leaders and the common people in a way that cures their irrational and self-destructive behavior. Even in *Behemoth*, Hobbes sometimes sounds surprisingly optimistic about a solution:

B: For aught I see, all the states of Christendom will be subject to these fits of rebellion, as long as the world lasteth.

A: Like enough; and yet the fault ... may be easily mended, by mending the Universities.[34]

The apparently simplicity of Hobbes's argument is that the civilizational problem of doctrinal warfare originating in the universities can be solved by a change in the universities—ridding them of the seditious doctrines and learned folly that has destabilized Western civilization and seventeenth-century England. Hobbes sometimes seems so optimistic about saving civilization through re-education that he speaks of an 'everlasting' commonwealth in *Leviathan* and even of 'immortal peace' in *De Cive*—a permanent solution to the fragility of civilization that anticipates later theories of 'perpetual peace' (by Kant and other modern philosophers).[35] This would constitute a new and final stage of civilization characterized by lasting civil peace, freedom from false doctrines, and the enjoyment of commodious living.

When described in this fashion, Hobbes sounds like a philosopher of history whose outline of world history from barbarism through the several stages of civilization (ancient Near Eastern, classical republican, Christian medieval, and finally, modern enlightenment) is an early version of 'progress'. Of course, Hobbes's vision lacks the crucial element of inevitability that the later theorists of progress (such as Condorcet or Hegel or Fukuyama) see in the movement of history toward the modern age. Hobbes admits an element of chance in finding a king who will purge and reform the universities. But once the universities are properly reformed, Hobbes shares with other philosophers of the Enlightenment the optimistic belief that modern civilization will be different from past ages because it is based on enlightened thinking and the promise of transforming human behavior. In other words, there is an 'end-of-history' argument in Hobbes's hope for immortal peace: modern civilization will be different from all previous stages because the Enlightenment will free the human mind from the irrational doctrines of the past.[36] How could Hobbes believe that such an historic change could occur? And, what is different about Hobbes's teaching that will prevent it from becoming one

---

34 *Behemoth*, 252.
35 *De Cive*, Epistle Dedicatory; *Leviathan*, ch. 30, 324–5.
36 Stephen Holmes misses this optimistic side of Hobbes in his reading of *Behemoth*; see for example his statement: 'the human mind will never be free of ... intoxicating doctrines'. Stephen Holmes, 'Introduction' to Thomas Hobbes, *Behemoth or The Long Parliament*, ed. F. Tönnies (Chicago: University of Chicago Press, 1990), l. In contrast, see David Johnston, *The Rhetoric of Leviathan: Thomas Hobbes and the Politics of Cultural Transformation* (Princeton: Princeton University Press, 1986).

more 'doctrine' in the endless doctrinal conflicts that have destabilized civilization in the past?

For Hobbes, the answer turns on the distinction between two mental habits: the old habit of trusting in authority vs. the new habit of self-reliant thinking. The traditional mental habit is to trust in authoritative wisdom—to trust in intellectual authorities (such as priests, prophets, scholars, and other wisemen) who claim privileged knowledge of higher powers and who impose on others in the name of orthodoxy. By contrast, the new and enlightened mode rejects authoritative wisdom as a form of dangerous pride—as the frightening illusion of self-righteous fanatics who believe that they alone are wise. In rejecting authoritative wisdom, enlightened thinking encourages a more democratic mode of reasoning that teaches people to think for themselves—to form their own judgments using the evidence before them rather than deferring to the wisdom of authority. This will enable people to see their civil sovereign as an artificial creation of their will rather than as a ruler sanctioned by higher powers.

In explaining Hobbes's hope for radical change, the great Hobbes scholar Leo Strauss has argued that it all turns on the distinction between two basic passions: vanity and fear. Vanity is the passion that inclines men to believe in authoritative wisdom—to believe that they alone are wise, that they are self-appointed spokesmen for God or higher powers, that they may impose their doctrines on others because of their superior wisdom. This is the passion that has endangered civilization with religious fanaticism, sectarian disputes, and doctrinal warfare throughout history. By contrast, the fear of violent death enlightens men about their mortality and vulnerability and teaches them to be wary of submitting to self-appointed intellectual authorities. Hobbes thinks that history can be changed if vanity is countered by fear—if men can be re-educated to feel a reasonable fear of death and its positive desire for self-preservation. Mankind will then arrive at a new stage of civilization—a stage characterized by security, prosperity, personal freedom, and enlightenment (a stage that is often referred to, both positively and negatively, as 'bourgeois' civilization).[37]

In attempting to come to terms with Hobbes's philosophy and to form a judgment about its overall truth claims, we need to ask if Hobbes's hope for changing the course of history toward an enlightened civilization of everlasting peace is a real possibility. If it is not a real possibility, then a more pessimistic view of history and human nature than Hobbes's view is

---

37   See Leo Strauss, *The Political Philosophy of Hobbes: Its Basis and Its Genesis* (Chicago: University of Chicago Press, 1936), especially chs 2, 7, 8.

The Fragility of Civilization in Hobbes's Historical Writings 331

warranted. Interestingly, this question is now at the center of an important debate between Francis Fukuyama and Samuel Huntington about 'the end of history' vs. 'the clash of civilizations'. Their debate is illuminated by our study because it shows that the decisive issue between Fukuyama and Huntington is the same issue raised by Hobbes: whether or not the modern Enlightenment can save civilization by transforming human behavior in a permanent or lasting fashion, especially by bringing an end to the great ideological or doctrinal conflicts of civilization.

In this debate, Fukuyama sides with Hobbes and the Enlightenment philosophers by arguing that the process of modernization — combining modern natural science, capitalism, and the demand for recognition of individual rights and human dignity — has created the conditions for the lasting triumph of modern liberal democracy over all other ideologies. The proponents of this view think that the Enlightenment is capable of changing the world by bringing about 'the end of history' in which all of the great ideological or doctrinal wars of the past are over.[38] They are 'optimists' about historical progress.

By contrast, Huntington sides with the 'pessimists' who question the power of the Enlightenment to change the world. Huntington agrees with such thinkers as Edmund Burke, Friedrich Nietzsche, Oswald Spengler, Fyodor Dostoevsky, and many religious conservatives who argue that man is basically irrational in the sense of being a religious animal who will always bow down to authoritative wisdom. They also see man as a creature driven by a need for nobility or heroic struggles who will never be content with a bourgeois life of security, personal freedom, and materialism. The shock of Huntington's *Clash of Civlizations* is precisely its challenge to the naïve assumptions of the modern Enlightenment about historical progress and human nature. Huntington reasserts the pessimistic view that history is not progressive — it has not really changed nor come to an end — because the possibility of doctrinal warfare over the highest religious and philosophical truths will always exist and, in fact, will be more likely to occur in the future as ancient civilizational claims are reasserted against modernity by Islam, Hinduism, Confucianism, Christianity, and other cultures (as well as by sectarians and fundamentalists within those cultures).[39]

This debate about the course of civilization is difficult to resolve because there is impressive evidence on both sides. On the one side, the Enlightenment has changed history in the West by helping to overcome

---

38 Francis Fukuyama, *The End of History and The Last Man* (New York: The Free Press, 1992), especially chs 5, 6, 19.
39 Samuel P. Huntington, *The Clash of Civilizations and The Remaking of World Order* (New York: Simon and Schuster, 1996), especially chs 2–4.

the terrible religious wars of the past and by giving Americans and Europeans some of the blessings of freedom and prosperity while spreading this promise to other parts of the world. Moreover, the Enlightenment's most powerful agent, modern natural science, is a universal force that challenges or subverts traditional notions of authoritative wisdom wherever it is permitted to go.

On the other side, the Enlightenment itself quickly became a new kind of secular religion that produced new doctrinal wars—such as the ideological wars of the French Revolution and the Russian Revolution which made the tyranny and slaughter of the religious wars look relatively mild by comparison to the totalitarian state and its systematic murder of millions in the name of abstract justice and utopian dreams. The Enlightenment has also produced reactions in the modern world by religious fundamentalists who reject bourgeois modernity for its secularism and materialism. As I see it, the experience of Jacobinism, communism, fascism, and religious fundamentalism indicates that the optimism of the modern Enlightenment about changing man's irrational behavior was naïve because men will continue to seek an ultimate faith through authoritative wisdom and will not be afraid to die for the sake of the future or the afterlife (as the twisted religiosity of the suicide bombers and religious terrorists so clearly demonstrates). Hobbes was therefore wrong to think that the desire for self-preservation based on the fear of violent death could become the ultimate concern of enlightened humanity. What fundamentalists prove (to the shock and awe of enlightened Western intellectuals) is that the ultimate fear is not the fear of violent death but the fear of the loss of meaning in a secularized world of soulless materialism or the fear of the degradation of life in a Hobbesian-bourgeois civilization where people have no higher purpose than material comfort and personal freedom.

Judging from these observations, I would draw the following conclusions about the course of world history. Of the two views of civilization—the traditional one based on authoritative wisdom vs the modern one based on enlightenment—the enlightened view has the upper hand at this moment in history. The modern West, led by America, is currently the dominant force in the world and will remain so for at least another generation. But it is naïve to think that the Enlightenment's version of skeptical rationalism and dogmatic materialism is more powerful than the appeal of authoritative wisdom in the long run. The triumphs of the modern Enlightenment have always been insecure (as I noted above in pointing to the rise of totalitarianism in the twentieth century and of religious fundamentalism in the twenty-first century and as is further indicated by the entrenchment of post-modern irrationalism in today's universities).

Moreover, even though the traditional view of history is more pessimistic about the stability of civilization, it possesses a more enduring and, in a way, more noble vision of man that will never die out. According to the traditional view, man is a religious animal who bows down to authoritative wisdom because the deepest longings of the human soul are for immortality and eternity and these longings will never be satisfied with skeptical reason or the one-dimensional reality of bourgeois happiness. Of course, the possibilities for perverting the traditional view by using it as a pretext for doctrinal warfare and terrorism are frightening (though not as frightening, as I noted above, as the perversions of secular political ideologies growing out of the Enlightenment).

I would conclude, therefore, that Huntington's 'clash of civilizations' thesis is more convincing and bracing than Hobbes's 'enlightenment' and Fukuyama's 'end-of-history' thesis. The fragility of civilization is a problem that will never be overcome by some new historical force. We will simply have to rely on our courage and prudence to defend civilization as best we can, while remembering that the pessimistic view of history actually upholds a higher and more noble view of man than the enlightenment view. This awareness will be no small comfort as we face the future and the perennial threats and challenges to civilization.

Index

Aaron 239, 319
Abiram 239
Absolon 239
Achan 122
Acoluthus, Andreas 47
Adam 239
Alexander the Great 56
Allestree, Richard 83-5
Ammirato, Scipione 66
Andrewes, Lancelot 98
Anglesey, Earl of 64
Apollo 58, 61
Apronius, Lucius 62
Apuleius 54
Aristotle 8, 34, 81-2, 148, 155, 157, 162, 164, 168, 219, 222, 233-4, 236, 253, 274, 279, 287, 290, 313, 316-7
Arlington, Lord *see* Bennet, Henry
Ashcraft, Richard 11, 244, 248
Attila the Hun 55, 61
Aubrey, John 4, 47, 52, 150
Augustus 69
Austin, John 156

Bacon, Francis 21, 50, 58, 65, 176, 213-4
Bancroft, Richard 100
Bartlet, Judge *see* Berkeley, Robert
Baumgold, Deborah 14, 18, 94, 250, 255, 262
Baxter, Richard 112, 120-1, 232, 235
Bayle, Pierre 42 -3
Beckmann, Johann Christoph 46, 50, 65-6
Bellarmine, Robert 95, 98-9
Bennet, Henry 76, 91, 149, 175
Bentham, Jeremy 156
Beonio-Brocchieri, Vittorio 12-3

Berkeley, Robert 40
Berkowitz, Peter 288
Berlin, Isaiah 286
Bernard, St 89
Bernstein, Eduard 227
Berrendonner, Alain 207
Bertman, Martin 194
Beza, Theodore 89
bin Laden, Osama 301-2
Blackburne, Richard 52
Bloch, Olivier 161
Boccalini, Traiano 46, 50, 55, 58, 60-6
Bochart, Samuel 27
Bodin, Jean 167, 169
Bolaffi, Angelo 13
Borot, Luc 9, 14-5, 20, 25, 28, 90, 172, 186
Bossuet, Jacques-Benigne 309
Bowle, John 3
Boxhorn, Marcus Zuerius 63-5
Boyle, Robert 180-1
Bramhall, John 28, 74, 87-9, 91, 150, 280
Brant, Clare 182
Brantôme, Pierre de Bourdeille, seigneur (and abbé) de 42
Bratutti, Vicko 43
Braun, Dietrich 28
Brokdorff, Baron Cay von 20
Brownley, Martine Watson 21
Brunnemann, Johann 50
Büchner, Karl 232
Bullinger, Henry 239
Bülow, Joachim Hinrich von 50
Burgess, Cornelius 121-2
Burke, Edmund 331
Burnet, Gilbert 176
Burton, Henry 123

Index

Bush, Douglas 171
Bush, George W. 300, 302-3
Butler, Todd 24-5

Cabrera de Cordova, Luis de 42, 44, 53
Caesar *see* Julius Caesar
Calvin, John 89, 239
Campanella, Tommaso 50, 55, 58,
Cardano, Girolamo 50, 58,
Carneades 165
Carrive, Paulette 14, 22-3
Cartwright, Thomas 238
Cary, Lucius 115
Catlin, George E. G. 19
Cato 234
Cavendish, Charles 161
Cavendish, William, 2nd Earl of Devonshire 66, 174
Cavendish, William, 3rd Earl of Devonshire 108, 116, 151
Cavendish, William, 4th Earl of Devonshire 52
Cavendish William, 1st Earl of Newcastle 78, 150, 152, 187
Cazzaniga, Gian Mario 12
Charles I 42, 66, 69, 94, 100-1, 103, 109, 122-3, 125, 155-6, 175-6, 179, 204, 215, 253, 267, 283-4, 289, 294, 324-8,
Charles II 4, 33, 51, 53, 91, 95, 108, 173, 325
Charles V 42, 45, 56,
Chicheley, Thomas 87
Childeric 98-9
Choule *see* Jole
Christ 113, 210, 238, 252, 255, 274, 281, 286, 325
Christian V 63
Christina of Sweden 56
Cicero 155, 230-4, 236, 253, 290, 313
Clapmarius, Arnold 59, 65, 229
Clarendon *see* Hyde, Edward
Claudius 229
Cleland, John 66
Cleveland, John 21
Cocceji, Samuel von 44, 48
Coke, Edward 79 , 162, 165
Colbert, Jean-Baptiste 52
Collins, Jeffrey 11, 19, 26,
Collinson, Patrick 231
Columbus, Christopher 42

Condorcet, Marie Jean Antoine Nicolas de Caritat 329
Condren, Conal 31
Constantine the Great 98
Cooper, Thomas 151, 237
Corah *see* Korah
Corfield, Penelope 18
Crashaw, William 98
Cristofolini, Paolo 12
Cromwell, Oliver 1, 19, 32-3, 40, 45, 51, 53-4, 63-5, 67-70, 72, 78, 94-5, 100-4, 109, 134, 138, 222, 260, 300, 325
Cromwell, Richard 53-4
Crooke, William 4-6, 10, 89, 173
Cropsey, Joseph 172
Culpepper, John 115
Curley, Edwin 149, 161-3, 165, 222

Dathan 239
David 59, 106
Democritus 159-60
Descartes, René 156
Dewey, John 25
Dido 87
Dietz, Mary G. 14, 20
Digby, Kenelm 43, 54, 116
Diodorus Siculus 94, 313, 318-20
Dir-Ching Kow, Simon 12
Dostoevsky, Fyodor 331
Dubos, Nicolas 12, 15, 31

Ebert, Adam 9, 32, 38-72
Ebert, Gottlieb, 49
Elizabeth I 20, 231, 239
Elyot, Thomas 231
Engels, Friedrich 17
Epicurus 158, 160-3
Ergamenes 94, 283-4
Essex, Earl of 76

Fagiani, Francesco 13
Fairclough, Samuel 122
Fairfax, Lord 77
Ferejohn, John 261
Fichte, Johann Gottlieb 309
Filmer, Robert 96, 109
Finch, Heneage 124
Finlayson, Michael G. 22, 31, 178
Finley, Moses 213
Finnis, John 162
Flathman, Richard 272-3, 286, 292

Fletcher, Henry 53, 64
Flinker, Noam 14, 182-3
Forsyth, Murray 262
Fortier, John C. 171
Francesconi, Daniele 26
Frederick III, King of Denmark 63
Friederich I, King of Prussia 38
Fritsch, Thomas 48
Frost, Samantha 24
Fukuyama, Francis 329, 331, 333

Galardi, Ferdinand de 64-5
Gassendi, Pierre 161-2
Geropoldi, Antonio 42
Gilmore, M. P. 168
Goldsmith, M. M. 9, 21-3, 129, 177
Gooch, George Peabody 16, 18, 227
Goodwin, Thomas 122
Goodwin, William 99,
Gracián, Baltasar 42, 44, 62
Greenleaf, W. H. 11
Gregory VII 99
Griffenfeld, Peder Schuhmacher 63
Grimston, Harbottle 115
Grosseteste, Robert 89
Grotius, Hugo 56, 65, 94, 160-3, 165, 167
Guicciardini, Francesco 176
Gussoni, Vincenzo 46
Gutmann, Amy 287

Haller, William 122
Hampden, John 125
Harley, Robert 125
Harrington, James 129, 226
Harris, Richard 98
Harsnett, Samuel 97
Hart, H. L. A. 156
Heath, James 76-80, 111-2, 149, 175-7, 217, 314
Hegel, Georg Wilhelm Friedrich 329
Henrietta Maria 42, 285
Henry III 89
Henry VIII 56, 85, 215
Herbelot, Barthelemy d' 42-3
Herbert, Edward 42, 44, 51, 53
Hercules 41
Heylyn, Peter 96, 100
Hill, Christopher 18, 247-8, 267
Hoekstra, Kinch 25

Holmes, Stephen 9, 14, 26, 68, 75, 129-30, 180, 244, 270-1, 274, 329
Hood, Francis Campbell 25
Horace 39
Hornblower, Simon 217
Hotham, John 79
Houssaie, Amelot de la 44, 62
Hughes, Ann 111
Huntington, Samuel 313, 331, 333
Husbands, Edward 79-80
Huygens, Lodewijck 52
Hyde, Edward 3, 20, 23, 63, 79, 91, 115, 123, 125, 152, 155, 174, 176

Iljen, Baron von 44

James I 65, 233
James, Thomas 98
Jena, Friedrich von 54
Jesus *see* Christ
Johnson, Laurie M. 32
Johnston, David 282, 329
Jole, Robert 51-2
Josephus, Flavius 313
Julius Caesar 56, 239, 313, 316
Justinus 61

Kant, Immanuel 310, 329
Kelly, Duncan 31
Kelsen, Hans 156, 295
Knights, Mark 87
Knollys, Hanserd 122
Korah 239, 319
Korsch, Karl 30
Koselleck, Reinhart 156
Krabbe, Hugo 295
Kraynak, Robert 12, 14, 24, 94, 178-83, 191, 250

Laird, John 28
Lambert, John 134
Lando, Girolamo 46
Laud, William 105, 115, 124
Leibniz, Gottfried Wilhelm 48
Lentulus, Cyriacus 60
Leopold I 50
Leti, Gregorio 64
Letwin, William 17
Levy, Fritz 15, 21, 176, 180
Lips, Eva 30
Lips, Julius 9, 30

Index

Lipsius, Justus 58, 62, 66, 180
Littleton, Thomas 79, 165
Livy 176
Lloyd, David 177
Lloyd, S. A. 243-4, 250, 273
Lobkowitz, Wenzel 50
Locke, John 172, 286
Louis XIV 53
Louvois, François Michel le Tellier, Marquis de 52
Lubienski, Zbigniew 222
Lucan 214, 313
Lucretius 39, 150
Ludlow, Edmund 176
Ludolf, Hiob 47
Lund, William R. 24
Lycurgus 218

MacGillivray, Royce 11, 13, 20, 175-7, 244, 249
Machiavelli, Niccolò 21, 50, 58-61, 62, 64-5, 143, 152, 164, 169, 180, 188, 309
Macpherson, C. B. 17, 267, 270
Mailly, Louis Chevalier de 43
Malcolm, Noel 20, 66, 150
Malvezzi, Virgilio 58, 60, 62
Mandelbrote, Scott 12
Manning, Henry 78
Marius 316
Marshall, Stephen 121-2, 125
Martinich, A. P. 11, 26, 105, 178, 180
Marx, Karl 17, 178
Mary I 120
Maseres, Francis 6, 15-6, 19, 27,
Mastnak, Tomaž 13
Matthew of Paris 89
May, Thomas 23, 31, 79
Maynwaring, Roger 96
Mazarin, Jules 56, 63
Medea 281
Mehmet II 56
Menander 181
Mendle, Michael 228, 230
Metzger, Hans-Dieter 19
Millar, Fergus 218
Milton, John 12, 101, 119, 232, 273, 278, 285
Milton, Philip 20, 74-5
Miriam 319
Molesworth, William 6, 171
Monck, George 69, 94-5, 134

Monk, George see Monck, George
Mornay, Philippe de 89
Moses 239-40, 319-20
Münkler, Herfried 9

Nagel, Thomas 270
Nalson, John 176
Naville, Pierre 22
Neal, Patrick 292
Nedham, Marchamont 229
Nero 60, 221, 225
Nessus 240
Neumann, Franz 30-1,
Nicastro, Onofrio 9, 12, 15, 28, 32, 172, 217, 222
Nicastro, Rina Perona 12
Nietzsche, Friedrich 331
Numa Pompilius 55

Oakeshott, Michael 271-2
Octavian 114
Okin, Susan Moller 19
Olivares, Gaspar de Guzmán y Acevedo 63
Olpe, S. C. 66
Overhoff, Jürgen 280, 282
Ovid 281
Oxenstierna, Axel 63

Pacchi, Arrigo 161
Paganini, Gianni 161
Paioli, Alfonso 64
Parker, Henry 79, 228, 230
Paul, St 55
Paulsen, Friedrich 6
Payne, Robert 108
Pell, John 161
Pérez, Antonio 63
Pericles 220, 288
Perry, John 197
Peters, Richard 21
Pett, Peter 10-11
Philip II 42 , 56, 63,
Pisistratus 220
Plato 34, 148, 162, 185, 234, 253, 274
Plutarch 313
Pocock, J. G. A. 11, 23, 31, 228
Polybius 218
Pompey 239
Preuss, Hugo 295
Prinzen, Marquard Ludwig von 44, 48

Protagoras 159
Prynne, William 234
Pufendorf, Samuel von 65
Pym, John 122, 125

Rahn, Johann Heinrich 47
Ralegh, Walter 231-2
Ranke, Leopold von 20
Ravius, Christian 47
Reik, Miriam M. 20
Repgen, Konrad 250
Reynolds, N. B. 171
Richardson, Ralph 22
Richelieu, Armand Jean du Plessis de 63
Rinck, E. G. 57
Ritterbusch, Paul 30
Robertson, G. Croom 7-8, 16, 27,
Rogers, G. A. J. 222
Rogow, Arnold A. 25
Rousseau, Jean-Jacques 258, 318
Ruschi, Filippo 13
Russell, Conrad 111
Rutherford, Samuel 103
Ryan, Alan 287
Ryck, Theodore 61

Salmasius *see* Saumaise, Claude de
Salter, James L. 10
Samson 78
Sanderson, Robert 126
Sandoval, Prudencio de 42, 44-5, 53
Sandys, Edwin 239-40
Saumaise, Claude de 101
Sauter, J. L. 62
Saxonhouse, Arlene W. 171
Scheffer, Simon 25
Schelsky, Helmut 24, 29,
Schmitt, Carl 13, 24, 29-31, 36-7, 156, 294-305, 309, 311
Schneider, Herbert W. 28
Schröder, Wilhelm von 66
Schuhmann, Karl 91, 159, 222
Schwerin, Otto von 43, 48, 50
Scott, Jonathan 233
Seaward, Paul 216
Sejanus 62-3
Selden, John 97, 127, 314
Seneca 234, 236, 253, 313
Shapin, Steven 25
Sigelman, Lee 256

Simon, Thomas 53
Skedelsky, Robert 290
Skinner, Quentin 16, 18, 52, 75, 175, 222, 227, 230, 241, 243-4, 248, 250, 262, 272
Slomp, Gabriella 14, 145-6
Smith, Nigel 21, 177
Smith, Thomas 231-2
Socrates 321-2, 327
Sommerville, Johann P. 97, 101, 109, 116, 118
Sorbière, Samuel 52, 161
Sorell, Tom 22, 242, 263, 266
Spengler, Oswald 331
Springborg, Patricia 89, 159, 166
Stephen, James Fitzjames 11, 19, 21, 25, 28,
Stephen, Leslie 16, 19, 21,
Stolle, Gottlieb 45, 48, 56-7
Stone, Lawrence 111, 248
Strafford, Earl of *see* Wentworth, Thomas
Strauss, Leo 171, 267, 270, 330
Strimesius, Samuel 57-8
Strong, Tracy B. 183
Stryk, Samuel 50, 55
Stubbe, Henry 29
Suárez, Francisco 98-9, 162
Süleiman the Magnificent 56
Sutherland, James 176
Sylla 316
Szczekalla, Michael 15

Tacitus 46, 51, 54-5, 57-66, 69, 176, 180, 313-4
Talaska, Richard 66
Tarlton, Charles 276, 284
Taylor, Jeremy 51, 55
Tenison, Thomas 97
Terrel, Jean 11, 12, 26, 221
Thales 55
Thomas, Keith 17, 267
Thornton, James 7-8,
Thucydides 136, 146, 154, 171, 174, 176, 211, 213, 217, 220-1, 240, 244-5, 255, 269, 287, 313, 321
Tiberius 62-3
Toland, John 47
Tönnies, Ferdinand 6-9, 16, 19-20, 24, 27-8, 30, 40, 159, 171-2, 175, 177
Trajan 60

Trevor-Roper, Hugh 125
Tricaud, François 157, 222
Tuck, Richard 11, 16, 20, 67, 69, 74, 174, 249, 262, 263, 272-3, 276
Tully *see* Cicero
Tyrell, James 10

Uriah 106

Valla, Lorenzo 159
Van Mill, David 281
Varillas, Antoine 52-3
Vaughan, Charles Edwin 29
Vaughan, Geoffrey 12, 20, 23, 26, 183, 248, 252, 263
Vaughan, John 151
Verdus, François du 4-6, 91
Virgil 54, 87
Vives, Juan Luis 159
Vlastos, Gregory 160
Voegelin, Eric 145-6
Voltaire, François-Marie Arouet 20, 150

Walbank, Frank William 218
Waldron, Jeremy 271
Wallis, John 29, 50-2, 102, 109, 180-1
Warburton, Bishop 15
Ward, Seth 74

Warner, Rex 212
Watkins, John 22-3,
Wentworth, Thomas 122, 124, 132, 195
Wheatly, Charles 171-2
Wheldon, James 76, 79, 89
White, Francis 99
Whitehall, John 1-3, 11, 15, 27, 172
Whitelocke, Bulstrode 176
Whitgift, John 100, 238-9
Whitney, K. William 29
William the Conqueror 315
Williamson, Joseph 88
Willms, Bernard 13, 23-4, 29,
Windebank, Francis 124
Wolf, Friedrich Otto 171
Wolin, Sheldon 263
Wolsey, Thomas 43-4
Wood, Anthony 11, 25, 221
Wootton, David 16, 21, 172, 176, 178-82, 188, 212, 247
Wormald, B. H. G. 23
Wright, George 149

Xerxes 56

Yerby, George 17

Zacharias 98
Zagorin, Perez 227

www.ingramcontent.com/pod-product-compliance
Lightning Source LLC
Chambersburg PA
CBHW021134230426
43667CB00005B/117